The Right to Suburbia

The Right to Suburbia

COMBATING GENTRIFICATION ON
THE URBAN EDGE

Willow S. Lung-Amam

UNIVERSITY OF CALIFORNIA PRESS

University of California Press
Oakland, California

© 2024 by Willow Lung-Amam

Library of Congress Cataloging-in-Publication Data

Names: Lung-Amam, Willow S., author.
Title: The right to suburbia : combating gentrification on the urban edge
   / Willow S. Lung-Amam.
Description: Oakland, California : University of California Press, [2024] |
   Includes bibliographical references and index.
Identifiers: LCCN 2024000284 (print) | LCCN 2024000285 (ebook) |
   ISBN 9780520338166 (cloth) | ISBN 9780520338173 (paperback) |
   ISBN 9780520974418 (ebook)
Subjects: LCSH: Gentrification—Washington (D.C.) | Suburbs—
   Washington (D.C.) | Community development, Urban—Washington
   (D.C.) | Urban minorities—Washington (D.C.)
Classification: LCC HT177.D6 L85 2024 (print) | LCC HT177.D6 (ebook) |
   DDC 307.1/41609753—dc23/eng/20240221
LC record available at https://lccn.loc.gov/2024000284
LC ebook record available at https://lccn.loc.gov/2024000285

33 32 31 30 29 28 27 26 25 24
10 9 8 7 6 5 4 3 2 1

For MaGee

We all essentially wanted the same thing, which was to feel that we had a stake in shaping and defining what little part of the world we could claim as our own.

—Sepha

Dinaw Mengestu, *The Beautiful Things That Heaven Bears*

Contents

Illustrations

MAPS

TABLES

Acknowledgments

Like the process of redevelopment in the places I profile, this book went through many fits and starts. And like the activists and organizers I spoke to, it forged ahead with a sense of purpose and unflappable hope. I began thinking about this book during my first year as an assistant professor at the University of Maryland. By the time of its completion, I was a tenured associate professor with three director titles to my name. I could not have finished it without a village that buoyed my spirits, shouldered the load, and helped me stay the course.

My closest advisers have been long-standing and steadfast. Carol Stack is not only one of the most gifted writers I know but also a close friend, confidant, and reader. She reminds me of the weight of my words, pushing me to become sharper with my thoughts and clearer on why and for whom I write. Our regular check-ins involved colorful stories, family photographs, and virtual hugs that filled my cup. Since I began my PhD program, Randy Hester has been a close mentor, cheerleader, and model scholar-activist. Shenglin Elijah Chang, Margaret Crawford, Louise Mozingo, and Becky Nicolaides have been insistent that my research has an important mark to make in and beyond the ivory tower. The lessons I learned from the late cultural geographer Paul Groth guided my steps through the communities in this book, as I recalled his probes to pay close attention to the processes and politics that go into the making of the built environment and my place within it.

Many scholars whose work I greatly admire supported me in big and small ways. I am particularly grateful for the DC urban scholars whose books I often referenced and whom I am honored to call colleagues as well as friends, including Tonya Boza-Bansal, Carolyn Gallagher, Kathryn Howell, Samir Meghelli, Derek Musgrove, Brandi Summers, and Sabiyha Prince, whose art graces the cover of this book. My path to publication was also forged by those who opened new doors and lent helpful guidance along the way, including Solomon Green, Bernadette Hanlon, Loretta Lees, Christopher Niedt, Mai Nguyen, Gerardo Sandoval, and Andrew Wiese. I am indebted to a host of remarkable suburban inequality scholars, many of whom I met at a workshop at Harvard University organized by Natasha Warikoo and L'Heureux Lewis-McCoy. Their work and wisdom have provided a rich intellectual community and fertile ground for my own.

I have benefited from being a part of groups that have supported my identity as a scholar-activist for years, including the Planners of Color Interest Group organized by the Association of Collegiate Schools of Planning and the ADVANCE Program at the University of Maryland. I have met countless colleagues and mentors through these networks whom I have leaned on for support and comfort in my scholarly journey. A special shout-out goes to Andrew Greenlee, Tonya Sanders, Darrel Ramsey-Musolf, and Marisa Zapata, who remind me that the journey is better when we do it together.

I have been incredibly fortunate to work with many talented graduate students whose research has strengthened my writing and thinking. Bi'Anncha Andrews, Jordyn Battle, Emily Benoit, Lindsey Bullen, Jeanne Choquehuanca, Joe Christo, Erin Gannon, Katie Gerbes, Upendra Sapoka, Lauren Stamm, and Brittney Wong, I hope you see your hard work reflected in this book. I am especially thankful to Nohely Alvarez, whose critical eye brought me through the final phases of research. I have previously published on issues addressed in this book with other scholars who pushed my thinking about the dynamics and processes at play. Thank you, Katrin Anacker, Casey Dawkins, Nicholas Finio, Elijah Knaap, Rolf Pendall, and Alex Schafran for being kind collaborators and thought partners.

Many foundations and organizations provided valuable funding and research support. During my early research, I was awarded a Ford Foundation postdoctoral fellowship. As many scholars of color know, the Ford family is among the most powerful scholarly networks one can be invited into. During my year as a postdoc, I was hosted by American University's School of Public Policy, where I got to know many generous scholars. Among them was Derek Hyra and faculty and students associated with the Metropolitan Policy Center. Derek has been a staunch supporter since, providing feedback on all the chapters of this book, even while completing his own. I am excited to celebrate our "book birthdays" together and grateful for the journey (and many beers) we shared along the way. The year after my Ford, I became a Nancy Weiss Malkiel Scholar, a program supported by the Andrew W. Mellon Foundation. My cohort of interdisciplinary scholars of color, largely women, awed me with their dopeness, creativity, and insights. During my final phase of research and writing, I spent a year at the Woodrow Wilson International Center for Scholars in Washington, DC, where I was graciously hosted by the Urban Sustainability Laboratory. Blair Ruble and Allison Garland gave me not only an office with an incredible view but incisive feedback and connections throughout the region. Georgia Eisenmann was the best assistant I could ask for—pointed, persistent, and curious. Our fellowship group met weekly until the onset of COVID-19 and were a wellspring of knowledge about doing policy-relevant research locally and globally.

My program, school, and university championed this work from the start. I received early research funding from various University of Maryland programs, including the School of Architecture, Planning, and Preservation (MAPP), the Graduate School, the ADVANCE program, and the Qualitative Interest Group within the Center for Race, Gender and Ethnicity. While completing this book, I built a community of comrades and coconspirators in my school whom I often turned to for support. Chief among them are Ariel Bierbaum, Marccus Hendricks, Michelle Magalong, and Georgeanne Matthews, who have made my workplace a joy to step into. My former chair, Jim Cohen, believed in this book from day one and was unwavering in his support to me as a junior faculty. Clara Irazábal filled Jim's big shoes with an unmatched ethic of care and compassion. Dean Dawn Jourdan is someone that all faculty members would want in their corner, and I am lucky to have in mine. At the National Center for Smart Growth Research and Education, former director Gerrit-Jan Knaap gave me the space and time I needed to finish this book, as well as an interview. Many MAPP staff members lent logistical support with a smile and a kind word.

I have presented portions of this work at various conferences, symposia, and invited talks. A hearty thanks to the faculty, staff, and students at the Brookings Institution, Columbia University, George Washington University, Hofstra University, Ohio State University, University of Oregon, and the Urban Institute for inviting me to present. Thank you to colleagues who asked thoughtful questions during my talks at the Association of Collegiate Schools of Planning, Latrobe Chapter of the Society of Architectural Historians, Society of American City and Regional Planning Historians, Urban Affairs Association, and the Urban History Association.

While writing this book, I took up the directorship of the Small Business Anti-Displacement Network (SBAN). Without my SBAN fam stepping up in innumerable ways, I would have never completed this book. Tatiana Nelson-Joseph and Katy June-Friesen were the ultimate team players, whose perpetually positive attitudes and attention to detail gave me the space I needed. In the months leading up to this publication, I also took on another directorship at the Urban Equity Collaborative. There I have the joy of working with Julia Marchetti, Nancy Mirabal, Devon Payne-Sturges, and other scholars who have been generous in understanding the many hats I wear.

It is a dream to have a second book under the imprint of the indomitable Naomi Schneider, executive editor at the University of California Press. Naomi is bighearted and believes in publishing books that matter—and has done so for decades without fail. Her keen eye for what she wants and likes made me feel seen in ways that made my writing better and bolder. Thanks also go to Aline Dolinh and Stephanie Summerhays for carefully shepherding this book through its many production phases and to the reviewers, whose exhaustive feedback made me think deeper about the story I wanted to tell.

This book reflects my long engagement in the communities profiled within it. I am thankful to the partnership of CASA de Maryland and the Purple Line Corridor Coalition, organizations that I not only write about but also collaborated with closely with over the years. There are many people in

Silver Spring, Wheaton, Langley Park, and the larger International Corridor who opened their homes, businesses, offices, hearts, and minds to this project in ways that I never expected. Thank you!

My family and friends are my biggest boosters. Friends in many places always seem to know when I need a distraction, a laugh, or a glass of wine. Aunties, uncles, cousins, and siblings spoil me with compliments and confidence. Without fail on our regular check-ins, my aunt Mimi asks me how the book is coming so she can brag to her friends and anyone else who will listen. My mother and father are behind everything I write. Every story I tell starts in the hollow in which I was raised and the refuge they created for me there. Their belief in creating a more just world was as steady as their support of me. My in-laws not only told their stories and allowed me to share them but always let me know I was one of their own. Several family members passed during the writing of this book who inspired my journey. My late uncle Dr. Proverb Jacobs Jr. and aunt Dr. Jeanne Claire Johnson are among those most responsible for the academic path I have chosen. This book is dedicated to the memory of Judith White Riggins, forever MaGee.

I could not write about Chocolate City or its suburbs without my husband's wisdom and care. Had he not made sure the kids were picked up, the laundry was done, and the oil was changed in my car, this book would have never seen the light of day. He fed my body, soul, and mind when I was deep in the throes of writing and forced me to close my computer when it was clear I needed to rest. My sons, Ashay and Temani, grew from children to young men as I wrote. I am unbelievably proud they carry a small piece of me into the world. Their grace and patience are unmatched. They cheered me on with hugs, kisses, and everyday acts of kindness and courage. They have a byline in everything I write.

Introduction

Every book has two stories—the one that is written and the one of how it came to be. The latter for me began not in the suburbs but in Washington, DC, the city where I first fell in love. Not just with my husband, a native Washingtonian, but with the city. It is where I found my inner flaneur, wandering the streets for hours with no destination in mind but simply for the pure joys of urban life—the sense of collective identity and togetherness one often finds among strangers.[1] It's where I grew into my own as a young adult, proudly learning to navigate endless catcalls, recognize local landmarks on a dime, and hop on the metro without even a glance at the map. It's where I realized I loved cities enough to spend a lifetime studying them and the people who built their lives, livelihoods, and dreams within them. But I didn't love just any city. I loved DC—*the* Chocolate City—the first and largest African American city in the nation. I loved its Blackness, the sense of pride that coursed through veins of native Washingtonians every time they claimed the title, the go-go music that was the heartbeat of the city, the soul food and carryout Chinese restaurants that, as my husband told it, was DC's version of fine cuisine.

But when I returned to Chocolate City in 2013, after six years away, *that DC* was quickly fading. Sunday dinners with my in-laws, who lived in the suburb of Wheaton, Maryland, were peppered with haunted tales of a DC that no longer existed. Their family marked time and space by the storied places that constituted their beloved community.[2] Like most Black folks I knew, myself included, they were deeply pained to watch Chocolate City become something altogether unfamiliar. And like many, it pained them even more to watch the city's changes from its suburban sidelines. They never wanted to leave DC. But as violence overwhelmed the city in the mid-1980s, the final straw came when Billy Jo was shot near the alley where my husband once rode his bike and hung out with neighborhood friends, including Billy Jo. In moving to a newly built single-family development surrounded by rolling hills and dairy farms, his parents sought protection from the many forces that threatened Black life in the city. This included not only those that led to physical violence but also those that quickly turned thriving Black communities into scenes of devastation and distress.

As I set out to write this book, I wanted to pay homage to the "city of my heart's desire" and wrestle with the emotional weight felt by my family, friends, and neighbors over the violent loss of Chocolate City.[3] I wanted to capture the psychic toll wrought by gentrification on long-term African American residents who held deep attachments to *that DC*. Whether they had been pushed out or remained, I wanted to reflect on what it meant for them to lose the city's Black majority, Black leaders, and Black cultural institutions.[4]

But as I began this research, as often happens, I found a related but different story that needed telling. As I sat in my in-laws' sprawling suburban home, another conversation began to animate our Sunday dinners. They often spoke about the changes happening right next door in their chosen neighborhood. They asked new questions about the future of the diverse community that had grown up around them and which they had slowly come to treasure as their own. Was it possible that they or their neighbors might be displaced by redevelopment? Where would they go? And why was it that gentrification seemed to follow Black folks wherever they went—whether in the city or the suburbs? They worried not just about the city that once was but also about the suburb that was to be—the one that held their fragile future in its hands. I could not turn a blind eye to this part of their story. While the urban pull was strong, what they were seeing and feared would become of their new suburban home was not all that different than what they had seen happen to their beloved DC neighborhood. But what scholars so clearly talked about in the language of gentrification in the city was often thought to be something else in the suburbs. Suburbs, they implied, could not gentrify.

The Right to Suburbia is an homage to Chocolate City, but of a different kind. It is a response to the urgent questions of Black and Brown families like my own who have fought to secure a stable place in Washington, DC, and its suburbs for generations.[5] It aims to illuminate the forces that have repeatedly devalued their neighborhoods and uprooted them for the desires and convenience of White residents, city officials, developers, banks, and others. In the DC suburbs, I illustrate how the forces of racialized development continue to displace some residents' claims to place while profitably reinvesting in others. I center the struggles of those who were once largely excluded from suburbs and have since fought to keep them aloft in good times and in bad. And as redevelopment has come to suburbia, these suburbanites have pressed for greater control over investments happening in their backyards, a larger slice of benefits, or simply the right to remain.

The beloved author and activist bell hooks wrote that "choosing the margin" can be an act of radical openness—a site from which to imagine new possibilities and liberatory frameworks. In this book I have chosen to write from suburbia, a space often marginalized in the urban imagination, to reimagine new possibilities for justice and equity in redeveloping communities. This is not to say that the suburbs have ever been marginal or peripheral to the processes that shape metropolitan landscapes and the futures of marginalized people. Rather, it is to suggest that in discourses about gentrification and redevelopment, suburbs are often pushed to the margins—out of sight and out of mind. As hooks notes, "Language is also a place of struggle. The oppressed struggle in language to recover ourselves, to reconcile, to reunite, to renew. Our words are not without meaning, they are action, a resistance." To center people, places, and discourses viewed as marginal is a form of resistance—one that can inspire creativity and new forms of power.[6] In redeveloping suburbs I located that power and creativity in many forms, but most urgently in the people fighting to stay in place.

·   ·   ·   ·   ·

This was not an easy story to write, not just because it intertwines with my family's story but also because it reflects my struggle to place suburbs at the center of my work. Urban studies scholars rarely study suburbs. To many Americans suburbs conjure up stereotypes of tidy, uniform landscapes devoid of culture—little boxes made out of "ticky tacky," where the people all look the same.[7] They are not where things are happening, where new ideas flourish, nor where radical futures are imagined. There is no *there* there.

When I started graduate school in the early 2000s, this was a popular mantra—one that, as a budding urban scholar, I was happy to accept. Even as I lived and worked in a suburb and shopped and hung out with friends in suburbs, I harbored these stereotypes. Like many of my generation, I grew up watching shows like *The Wonder Years* that depicted happy heteronormative White families living "normal lives" in desirable neighborhoods where everyone just happened to look, talk, and think alike. Week after week I watched Kevin, the central character, ride his bike along tree-lined streets, passing the quaint single-family homes of his White middle-class friends. They would gather on their well-manicured lawns to fret over teenage problems that hardly resembled my own.

Having grown up in neither city nor suburb, I believed that this was what suburbs were. Born into the hollows of West Virginia, I was more intimately familiar with the rolling wooded landscape surrounding our nineteenth-century farmhouse than with street names and landmarks that were the sign of a true urbanist. My glimpses into suburban life were stunted and fragmented and thus not to be believed. Most summers my parents would hit the road, loading my brother, sister, and me into our rusty Volkswagen van to see one family friend, relative, or another, nearly all of whom lived in suburbs. We'd visit my dad's family in the Houston suburbs and stay with his siblings, who lived in identical homes mirroring one another at the end of a long cul-de-sac. During those blistering summers—the heat nearly burning through my clear jelly slippers—we'd move from Chinese strip malls to my grandmother's retirement community and a string of late-night mahjong parties. These summers are when I felt most acutely what was to be the daughter of an immigrant, as I rarely saw a non-Chinese face or heard much English.

Other summers I'd visit my mom's family in the suburbs of Detroit, Oakland, or Los Angeles. Some lived in plush middle-class neighborhoods, others not so much; some were single mothers, others happily married for decades; some lived in garden-style apartments, others in compact single-family homes. All lived in racially diverse or predominantly Black neighborhoods. My mother was most at home during our ritual trip to see her best friend in Shaker Heights, Ohio, not far from the small, racially integrated town of Oberlin, where she was raised. In this iconic streetcar suburb, her friend's biracial family and the life they had built there mirrored my mother's familiar stomping grounds. Her friend's daughter Jackie and I spent countless hours jumping rope and riding bikes through the leafy neighborhood, sometimes running into her friends, who neither looked nor talked like the characters I had become intimately familiar with on *The Wonder Years*.[8] Yet none of these experiences registered as suburban to me. To my young self, suburbia was far away, a deeply unfamiliar place where people like me did not exist.

Maps changed my mind. As I was growing up, aunts and uncles usually introduced me to new places by showing me their "best" and "worst" parts, mainly pointing out areas to be avoided. During my early years as a PhD student at the University of California, Berkeley, I took my cues from these lessons to navigate the Bay Area. Armed with countless maps filled with indicators of race, class, and segregation, I took to the road, hoping to understand more about the nature of neighborhood inequality. The landscape before me belied much of what I thought I knew. Most poor neighborhoods were suburban. Most diverse communities were suburban. Most communities of color were suburban. Most immigrant enclaves were suburban. Suburbs were also vastly unequal. I traveled from plush gated subdivisions to neighborhoods that some scholars disparagingly referred to as suburban "ghettos."[9] My travels revealed how false yet powerful the dichotomy of the Black ghetto and White suburb had become. That illusive geography shaped an entire generation of urban scholarship.

In my first book, *Trespassers? Asian Americans and the Battle for Suburbia*, I joined a cadre of scholars working to reshape suburbia's image by centering on a different cast of characters and politics at play. I spent most of my time in the middle-class Silicon Valley suburb of Fremont, a place that defied all my suburban stereotypes. This majority Asian American community was teeming with life in the most unusual and yet mundane places—storefront temples, colorful street festivals, and parks where elders gathered for each morning for qigong exercises. The community was also unequal, in ways that were not obvious at first glance. In the book I explored the community's racialized politics of development, as neighbor fought neighbor over the look and feel of everyday places—homes, schools, and strip malls. I revealed the often hidden and subtle ways that racial inequalities were produced and upheld through the rules and norms that govern the built environment, even in the most well-to-do suburban neighborhoods and among immigrants often thought to have defied the odds.[10]

But I was also haunted by the faces I did not see in Fremont—the Black and Latinx communities that could scarcely afford its million-dollar homes and one of the state's most competitive school districts. The other suburbs right next door—across the tracks or just another highway exit away—were nearly invisible to those who did not live, shop, work, or pray in them. Spending so much time in one suburb, I saw how its problems were easily ignored or dismissed by others. Suburbs were segregated and fragmented and so were people's experiences and imaginations of them. If the struggles of immigrants in Fremont, the largest Asian American-majority suburb in Silicon Valley, had not been told, what stories were being lost in suburbs I knew well from my childhood? How can people care about places and problems they literally cannot see?

The power of this erasure became more evident to me as I began to write this story. It was then I learned that the setting for *The Wonder Years* was inspired by Silver Spring, a redeveloping suburb that figures prominently in this book.[11] This is the very place where I lived as a young adult, watching redevelopment unfold before my very eyes. It is the place where my oldest son and I now ride our bikes together and a favored destination for his diverse group of friends. It is my downtown, barely a mile up the street from my suburban-looking neighborhood, located within the bounds of the city of DC. But it is also a place where I did not see myself reflected in its story—not in the heroic images posted on historical placards and buildings marking the city's founding and not in cheery banners that once lined its streets announcing that Silver Spring had finally "sprung."[12]

Writing this book has been in part a process of writing myself back into the story and embracing my role as a reluctant suburban scholar. To not tell my story would further perpetuate the suburban and the urban myth—

lending power to the stereotypes by failing to challenge them. I have sought instead to claim space for those who live on and embrace the urban margins and who are fighting for their right to remain and for their suburban dreams to be recognized and realized.

．　　．　　．　　．　　．

The Right to Suburbia is divided into six chapters. Chapter 1, "The Fight to Stay in Place," introduces the book's focus, methods, and argument about what I term the *new suburban renewal*. In a review of discourses about gentrification, displacement, and community resistance, it demonstrates how scholars and policymakers often miss how these forces take shape in suburbia. Recent trends in increasing suburban racial diversity, poverty, and large-scale redevelopment, however, have set the stage for local battles over suburban displacement. The Washington, DC, region is an epicenter of surging gentrification trends nationally. The chapter introduces three Maryland suburbs that have shaped the region's growing equitable development movement to combat these trends: Silver Spring, Wheaton, and Langley Park. As sites of resistance, the communities and their struggles to respond to state-led, racialized forms of uneven development have brought needed attention to the new suburban renewal and new possibilities for redress.

Chapter 2, "DC Suburban Shuffle," explores the dynamics of growth that have shifted regional geographies of gentrification and their politics over the past century. It profiles gentrified neighborhoods in Washington, DC, and the redevelopment battles that helped to build the city's current anti-displacement toolkit and grassroots capacity. During key decades that defined redevelopment struggles in the city, the region's suburbs also faced similar pressures. This chapter demonstrates that marginalized communities across city and suburban lines have been subject to many of the same predatory development practices and have responded with their own forms of protest. It also exposes how the regional dynamics of inequality have shifted toward suburbs in recent decades, spurring the redevelopment conflicts explored in subsequent chapters.

Chapter 3, "Trouble on Main Street," considers the battles won and lost in over two decades of redevelopment in Silver Spring's long-standing suburban downtown. As early Black and Brown suburbanites moved out of DC, Silver Spring was a popular first stop. There the traditional White suburban power structure, whom I call old-school suburban activists, and their perceptions of decline directed county-led redevelopment. The process took a heavy toll on downtown's commercial and residential affordability, a load that fell most heavily on Black-owned businesses. Community activism and policy responses came too little and too late to stem the tide of displacement. Silver Spring lays out the roots of equitable development organizing in the Maryland suburbs and the hard lessons learned by early activists and county leaders about building effective grassroots campaigns, political support, and anti-displacement policies.

Chapter 4, "Resisting the Suburban Retrofit," traces the history of redevelopment battles from downtown Silver Spring to the county's next major focus of revitalization in Wheaton. It recounts the fights over the retention of largely Latinx-owned businesses with new tools and politics at hand. Community-based organizations were more established, county officials were more attentive, and strong protections were in place to address the concerns of marginalized businesses. Grassroots leadership from below allied with leadership at the top to make significant strides toward an equitable development agenda. But Wheaton advocates, whom I call new-school suburban activists, also struggled with persistent suburban organizing challenges, including the constrained capacity of community-based nonprofits, political underrepresentation, and a still limited policy toolkit.

Chapter 5, "Somos de Langley Park," examines one of the latest redevelopment battles in the Maryland suburbs. Langley Park is home to the region's largest Latinx and immigrant populations and the future home of its first intersuburban light-rail line. The chapter follows the efforts of neighborhood and regional organizers to combat what many fear will be widespread residential, commercial, and cultural displacement. On the one hand, it shows the maturation of more than two decades of organizing in the Maryland suburbs, including the emergence of coalitions with greater capacity, sophistication, political connections, and policy tools. On the other it illustrates the many challenges that lie ahead for these coalitions that underscore how suburbia's social, spatial, and political structures continue to threaten the stability of its most vulnerable occupants.

The book concludes with lessons for advancing scholarship and practice toward more equitable suburban redevelopment. Chapter 6, "Place Matters," consolidates the lessons from the three communities, puts them in comparative perspective, and illuminates the critical factors that contribute to their successes and challenges. It argues that neither redevelopment processes nor the responses of communities most affected by them can be understood without close attention to how place dynamics shape the possibilities of local organizing. Considering a suite of anti-displacement policies and protections that can help to bring visibility and voice to disaffected communities, it offers practical insights into how they can collectively recalibrate redevelopment's risks and rewards and forge ahead with dignity, resist being pushed further beyond the urban edge, and shape more just futures that summon the best in us.

1 The Fight to Stay in Place

And I remember finding Grandmother the house on Linden
Avenue and constantly reminding her it was every bit as
good if not better than the little old house. A bigger back
yard and no steps to climb. But I knew what Grandmother
knew, what we all knew. There was no familiar smell in that
house. . . . Linden Avenue was pretty but had no life. . . . She
died because she didn't know where she was and didn't like
it. And there was no one there to give a touch or smell or feel.

—Nikki Giovanni, *Gemini: An Extended Autobiographical*
Statement

The rebirth of cities comes at a cost—a grim cost that has accrued, as the racialized revaluation and reclamation of urban land for the interests of state and private capital has remade more and more cities across the globe. The blunt impact of this process in the United States has been an abiding conversation among urban scholars. From early debates about slum clearance and urban renewal to contemporary gentrification, much has been written about new office towers, sports stadiums, upscale condominiums, and trendy boutiques. These narratives speak to the processes of gentrification in its historical and present forms that escalate land values and push Black and Brown residents and businesses out of central city neighborhoods. They inform a history of shameful policies, intentional disinvestment, underinvestment, and forced removals that violently strip communities of their economic assets and political power. As the poet Nikki Giovanni wrote after witnessing how her grandmother's home was lost to urban renewal, the process strips residents of their social connections, sense of place, and even their lives.[1]

Communities have shown staggering strength and resilience in the face of such organized, state-sanctioned assault and abandonment. Anti-displacement movements in New York, San Francisco, and other large urban centers have been the subject of well-documented efforts to claim what the Marxist philosopher Henri Lefebvre called "a right to the city"—the right to remain in the city and benefit from new urban investments.[2] Much of the discourse about gentrification, however, emerged from studies of major cities.[3] Studies that helped to conceptually define gentrification—the factors that contribute to it, how communities are impacted, and how they organize in response—have focused largely on the central city. For some scholars gentrification's very definition relies on its urban location. Suburbs like those my in-laws called home, it might seem, add little new understandings of gentrification processes and politics. *The Right to Suburbia* argues otherwise.

Some also see gentrification as a relatively banal process of class-based neighborhood change by which low-income neighborhoods become more middle class. I view gentrification as a violent process of cultural and community displacement rooted in racial capitalism. This definition centers on the racialization of neighborhoods and the displacement of people as well as culture and community.[4] In theorizing gentrification as deeply invested in processes of suburban neighborhood change, *The Right to Suburbia* signals the structural violence at work in suburbia and the need for racially equitable forms of redress.

In recent decades historical patterns of Black and Brown suburban settlement have been met with rapidly rising immigration and spiking poverty rates. At the same time, a slate of forces calling for the remaking of sprawling suburbs into more dense urban landscapes have converged. While presumably marginalized groups might benefit from more compact suburban neighborhoods, they often rightfully fear the impact of large-scale redevelopment. Projects that many urban planners and policymakers see as needed investments in underdeveloped neighborhoods are often experienced by communities as a recipe for displacement that spurs heated backlash and debate.

The Right to Suburbia investigates battles primarily waged by Black and Latinx communities in the Washington, DC, suburbs over the uneven costs and benefits of redevelopment. In case studies of three neighborhoods that have recently undergone a suburban renaissance, I ask how those most likely to bear the weight of suburbia's transformation have tried to balance the scales. To what extent have the processes and products of suburban redevelopment disadvantaged marginalized groups? And how have these groups mobilized to assert a more equitable stake and place in their suburban futures?

These chapters make clear that new urban renewal, which references the latest period of gentrification in US cities, does not fit tightly within the narrow bounds of our urban imaginary.[5] Similar processes are also at work in suburbs, producing and reproducing patterns of uneven, racialized development. But the *new suburban renewal* has not simply added a prefix onto an old concept. With a new cast of characters and spatial dynamics at play, suburbia has reshaped urban redevelopment processes and politics. Suburbia's unique brand of redevelopment has added to, rather than alleviated, the challenges that marginalized communities, especially Black and Latinx Americans, face.

The Right to Suburbia illuminates the key role of the state in processes of suburban renewal. Suburban municipalities have been critical to plans, policies, and public investments that disinvested and neglected Black and Brown suburbs and that enabled and encouraged profitable reinvestment within them. To spur dense mixed-use development in former sprawling suburbs, state and county governments aided and directed new developments that catered to White middle-class residents and consumers. They assembled parcels, raised height limits, changed zoning, and otherwise used their public power and purse strings to entice private investment. The new suburban renewal is not a natural process of neighborhood change; it is racialized redevelopment in which the state plays a pivotal role.

It is also a highly disruptive process in which marginalized communities hold little power. Suburbia's consolidated and privatized land uses facilitate redevelopment processes that are often large in scale and deep in impact. Political fragmentation, increasing suburban segregation, and sprawl isolate communities and render the struggles of one neighborhood invisible to and unconnected to others. Struggling suburbs often lack high-capacity, established nonprofits and advocacy organizations that can readily engage residents in sustained redevelopment battles. Organizing and coalition building is further hampered by suburbia's changing composition. Compared to their urban counterparts, gentrifying suburbs tend to have more diverse residents dispersed across larger areas.

Black and Latinx suburbanites, particularly immigrants, often lack well-established organizing platforms. They often hold less political power and representation than what I term "old-school suburban activists," represented by suburbia's traditional civic and business elite, and less than that which has been built over decades of struggle in central cities. When redevelopment arrives, residents in neighborhoods originally designed to exclude them face an uphill battle to build the politics and policies to remain in place. They confront a dearth of anti-displacement policies, a lack of political will, and scant financial capital. But just as Black and Brown communities have always done, they are fighting not only for access *to* suburbia and its opportunities, but also for more just and equitable communities *in* suburbs.

The Right to Suburbia reveals the vigorous organizing efforts emerging in one of the most rapidly and intensely gentrifying metropolitan regions in the United States. It tells the tale of how grassroots activists, community groups, and political leaders mobilized across race, ethnic, and class lines to fight for communities' right to suburbia—their right to stay put and benefit from new neighborhood investments. This right, I argue, recognizes marginalized communities as important constituents in shaping suburbia's future. It advances a more equitable distribution of the risks and rewards of redevelopment and prevents vulnerable groups from being pushed farther beyond the urban edge.

These chapters display how new-school suburban activists came together to challenge the exclusions and hypocrisy of their old-school counterparts. Their movement not only fought displacement but argued for a more inclusive suburban way of life that centered on equity and an acceptance of difference. It strove for a more vibrant suburban community and culture that served the impoverished and newly arrived and shifted power to marginalized groups to plan for their own futures.

Communities who had fought long and hard to get to the suburbs, however, often lacked the organizing infrastructure to combat the latest wave of suburban displacement. Building on a legacy of suburban protest, their reanimated movement borrowed capacity and strategies from former battles in both the city and suburbs. They fought to create community and common cause across their differences and mobilize the interests of new groups. They grew from the grassroots and the grasstops—developing vital community organizing and institutional capacity as well as political will to push new anti-displacement policies. Their efforts brought visibility to suburban gentrification and built the bones of a powerful suburban equitable development movement. Their wins were critical but hard-fought and limited. Given their difficult starting points, these precarious coalitions struggled to mobilize on multiple fronts, leverage new tools, and empower diverse communities and voices. Taking shape over several decades and disparate communities, their fight makes clear that a right to suburbia requires acute attention to conditions that prevent marginalized groups from imagining, let alone realizing, a future for their beloved communities. And though processes of uneven metropolitan development may shift their locus, they rarely go away—at least not without a good fight.

GEOGRAPHIES OF GENTRIFICATION AND RESISTANCE

Since Ruth Glass first coined the term in 1964, "gentrification" has been a topic of interest and heated debate among scholars, policymakers, the media, and the public at large. As new capital, people, and public investment flood into urban areas, gentrification has become common parlance for processes that transform lower-income neighborhoods into higher-income residential or commercial areas.[6] More critically, it is a manifestation of uneven development rooted in capitalist, colonialized, and racialized forms of perpetual development. Under capitalism, developers, lenders, and real estate agents take advantage of rent gaps to profit from the resale of urban property. Local, state, and federal governments aid in restructuring property values through public subsidies and new investments, whether parks or public transit, that make private development more profitable and attractive to new residents.[7]

US urban history tells a recurring story: the revaluation of neighborhoods takes place within racist structures of capital accumulation that profit from the repeated exploitation and devaluation of Black and Brown communities and property. During the early and mid-twentieth century, state and local governments adopted racial zoning that put in place long-standing patterns of residential segregation. In the 1930s the federal government introduced the practice of redlining, which was actively taken up by private banks that denied loans to African Americans and neighborhoods of color, hardening the racial lines between cities and suburbs as never before. Real estate agents and developers promoted or required practices of block busting, steering, contract deeds, and private restrictive covenants that raised White property values in exclusive suburbs while inflating the cost of dilapidated housing for African Americans in inner-city neighborhoods they deemed undesirable.

Supported by federal funds, cities across the United States adopted policies of slum clearance and urban renewal in the 1950s and 1960s that serially and forcibly displaced communities of color from valuable urban land.[8] They then enacted segregated public housing policies and exclusionary zoning that concentrated poverty and disadvantage on marginal, isolated, and sometimes toxic land. These neighborhoods were subject to active and intentional neglect and disinvestment or abandonment by city agencies and White developers. Federal funds for new highways sped the flight of White residents, businesses, and capital out of central cities, while underwriting circumscribed downtown redevelopment that allowed their safe and speedy return to work or for a sanitized glimpse at urban life and culture.

Contemporary gentrification is a late twentieth-century imprint of these pernicious development practices and policies that emerged under a globalized, neoliberal economic order. At least two previous waves of gentrification took place in US cities in which the state played a central role. The latest wave that began in the mid-1990s followed the "lost decades" that left many cities, including Washington, DC, on the verge of bankruptcy.[9] Under free-market fiscal reforms led by President Ronald Reagan, cities began to peel back basic public services and safety net programs secured during the Progressive and New Deal periods. Conservative congressional and municipal leaders recast cities as profit-making, globally competitive ventures more efficiently run by private companies than public agencies. Urban citizens were no longer publics with common wants and needs. They were reimagined as atomized consumers, free to rise and fall of their own choices. Neoliberalism remains the dominant paradigm of urban redevelopment, reflected in the rise of public-private partnerships and programs such as Empowerment and Opportunity Zones, HOPE VI public housing reforms, and Choice Neighborhoods.[10] Gentrification processes and politics reflect this new neoliberal bent at an unprecedented scale. Gentrification has gone global, as more places engage in urban restructuring under neoliberal market logics. Suburban land is among the chief products of neoliberal capital's incessant redevelopment cycles, as cities more often grow out than up.[11]

Neoliberal cities are increasingly privatized, securitized, competitive centers of global capital. City leaders and boosters promote innovative designs, cultural institutions, and flagship developments. They build entertainment complexes, art districts, festival marketplaces, sports arenas, and convention centers to attract young "creative class" professionals, middle-class consumers, tourists, and others with disposable incomes that add to the municipal coffers.[12] In this frame marginalized residents— Black and Brown, immigrant and native-born, young and old—have little value. Yet their imagined presence and culture become products marketed by developers and real estate agents to new residents. Ethnic retail, cultural spaces, and the imprints of urban culture are called on to give neighborhoods a multicultural flavor or authentic, gritty appeal. They stand in for residents who are increasingly pushed out of these spaces.[13]

Young White newcomers generate demand for revitalized urban neighborhoods. Some seek out these neighborhoods for their nostalgic sense of place. Others simply take advantage of cheap rents and housing prices, reduced commute times and travel costs, and new amenities geared to their tastes. Though middle-class Black and Latinx residents also sometimes move into gentrifying neighborhoods, their presence does not generally generate the same level of public and private investment.[14]

As wealthier residents and investments rush in, established residents are often displaced. While scholars hotly debate the extent of displacement, case after case testifies to displacement as an overwhelming concern to established residents.[15] Displacement can be either direct or indirect. Direct displacement is a forced move caused by a property conversion, eviction, or condemnation or a lack of affordability due to rent or tax increases. Indirect or exclusionary displacement occurs when units are vacated and then made unaffordable or otherwise unavailable for households of similar economic means or household compositions.[16] Economic, physical, and ownership changes also result in indirect displacement, including the conversion of public housing to mixed-income housing, rental units to condominiums, or three-bedroom to one-bedroom units. Not surprisingly, low-income renters often suffer the worst of these violent neighborhood reorderings.

Businesses do not lag far behind. Commercial redlining and the underdevelopment of communities of color leave many neighborhoods with fewer retail establishments, more small businesses, and less diverse retailers. As neighborhoods gentrify, new retail establishments that cater to middle-class White consumers often move in. Some established businesses may initially benefit from additional and higher-income customers, and established residents may enjoy greater access to retail and professional services. But, in the long run, new chain retailers and boutique businesses frequently replace local businesses owned by immigrants and people of color as competition and rents rise.[17] Industrial spaces serving small manufacturers convert to residential uses, displacing blue-collar jobs often held by immigrants and people of color. This leaves gentrified neighborhoods with less diverse local economies and more workers employed as day laborers and sweatshop workers and in jobs that operate outside of the formal economy.[18]

Nikki Giovanni reminds us that, as residents' homes and livelihoods are upended, they often lose a sense of place, belonging, and neighborhood control. Those who remain in or return to gentrifying neighborhoods feel ever more alienated and out of place. Their treasured places and memories disappear alongside their neighbors and familiar corner stores, churches, barbershops, and other places of everyday life. New and old residents tend to live separate lives—passing along the same streets, but without a friendly or familiar greeting. They rarely live in the same buildings or frequent the same businesses.[19] Separated by age, class, race, and family structure, they tend to hold different ideas about community and acceptable uses of neighborhood space.

When worlds collide, tensions emerge: sometimes over mundane practices, such as listening to music or backyard barbeques and sometimes over larger neighborhood issues—new homeless shelters, the policing of public spaces, or the building of dog parks and bike lanes. But new residents tend to hold the upper hand. They not only benefit from their racial and economic privilege, but also gain political power and representation quickly, with public officials ever more attuned to their needs and desires.[20] As established residents' daily rhythms become contested and devalued, even those who vowed to stick it out leave their neighborhood that no longer feels like their community.

Not all neighborhoods suffer the same fate. Those with high-quality housing close to public transit tend to gentrify first and fastest. New investments in transit infrastructure or more compact, mixed-used developments attract residents that benefit from reduced transportation costs. While low-income residents are more transit dependent, transit-oriented development commonly contributes to their displacement. Construction of new light-rail lines, streetcars, bus rapid transit, and metro stations can directly displace residents and small businesses through public takings for new rights-of-ways. More often once construction finishes, property values, rents, and taxes rise, increasing the prospect of displacement.[21]

Community activists have long resisted the multiple forms of marginality that attend gentrification. In New York, San Francisco, and other large urban centers, new social movements have come together to combat displacement. Pulling on Lefebvre's notion of people's collective power to reshape processes of urbanization, activist groups like the Right to the City Alliance have mobilized to enact anti-displacement policies in cities across the United States and the world.[22] Black communities have employed defensive development and other tactics rooted in the civil rights and Black Power movement to protect their neighborhoods from control by White elites and developers. They have built their collective capacity and economic power by establishing Black business-improvement districts and commercial cooperatives. Cross-racial and cross-sector coalitions have coalesced to oppose transit-induced displacement and introduced community-led transit-oriented development plans that leverage residents' assets and prioritize their needs. Black and Indigenous activists have staged housing occupations that challenge notions of private property, vacancy, racial capital, and colonial dispossession.[23] Communities have created displacement watch groups, "displacement free zones," neighborhood asset maps, and spaces for community storytelling to spur advocacy and protect valued spaces. These movements to ensure the survivability of marginalized groups in gentrifying neighborhoods are being scaled up by coalitions increasingly working across national borders.[24]

In many communities anti-displacement organizing has legitimized established residents' claims to neighborhood space, increased their participation in and control over redevelopment processes, and enacted new policies and protections. Their efforts have produced a bounty of new policy toolkits, equity indices, and mapping platforms that aid communities in tracking relevant property data, gaining leverage in redevelopment processes, and identifying effective solutions.[25] Equitable development movements built from below—among residents and community-based organizations—have increasingly allied with grasstops leaders in government and other critical decision-making bodies to elevate discourses about "development without displacement" and the root causes of housing insecurity and differentiated displacement risk. Their efforts have pushed nonmarket and market-conscious approaches that center principles of community control, collective ownership, permanent affordability, and housing as a human right.[26]

Few of the studies that have defined gentrification and organizing efforts to combat its devastating impacts, however, have taken place in suburbs. Even those that have often fail to cite the suburbs as a specific geography or analyze the ways that place mediates gentrification's politics or outcomes. By suburbs I refer not just to places that lie on the outskirts of major urban centers or a built form and land-use pattern that has come to typify the US imagination of suburbs. I also refer to suburbs as a way of life—places that share social characteristics, everyday practices, ideologies, and histories. In the US context, the history of race and class exclusion marks suburbs as distinct geographies as much as their built form does.[27] Yet many suburbs have, in recent decades, welcomed fresh waves of Black and Brown migrants and been the subject of racialized disinvestment, neglect, and other predatory forms of inclusion. Many of these same suburbs are now experiencing reinvestment and renewed interest among younger, educated, wealthier, and Whiter residents. In other words, they are poised to, or perhaps have already, gentrified.

SUBURBAN DECLINE AND RENEWAL

Though often written out of the suburban story, Black and Brown people—working class and wealthy, immigrant and native-born—contributed to the United States' rise as a suburban nation. While often on inhospitable grounds and on wholly unequal terms, they enriched suburbia's culture and character. Countering claims associating suburban settlement with assimilation into the US mainstream, these groups have instead been harbingers of suburban change—investing in new landscapes, civic and cultural institutions, social practices, and progressive politics.[28]

Within the past couple of decades, the suburbs of major US metropolitan areas have become even more diverse and home to the majority of racial and ethnic minorities and immigrants.[29] In a profound departure from the central city White flight that shaped the twentieth-century metropolis, young White professionals and aging baby boomers are moving into urban neighborhoods at unprecedented rates—displacing the manufactured and racialized poverty once concentrated within them. Meanwhile, racially diverse suburbs are growing faster than either central cities or predominantly White suburbs.[30]

Suburbia's racial and ethnic diversity has risen nearly in lockstep with increasing poverty. Since the 1980s suburban poverty rates have steadily climbed in many US metropolitan regions. By the mid-2000s, most households living below the poverty line were suburbanites. Not only did impoverished people move from cities, but suburban incomes also declined. While poverty rates had already been growing faster in suburbs than in cities, they picked up pace after the Great Recession.[31] Black and Brown suburbanites looking to purchase new homes or refinance existing homes found themselves targeted by predatory loans likely to end in default. As suburban unemployment and foreclosure rates spiked, decades of economic gains for communities of color, particularly for African Americans, were lost. And for the first time, troubling trends in concentrated suburban poverty captured the headlines. Between 2000 and 2014, the population of impoverished residents living in suburban neighborhoods with poverty rates of 40 percent or higher nearly tripled.[32] Given historical and contemporary practices of racialized housing exclusion and what historian Keeanga-Yamahtta Taylor calls "predatory inclusion," immigrants, Latinx Americans, and especially African Americans are overrepresented in suburban neighborhoods with high poverty rates.[33]

As people of color have gained ground in communities previously closed to them, and sometimes built over and around them, they have not necessarily found the suburbs of their American dreams. They have encountered a politically fragmented landscape divided by race and class. While suburbanites of color and suburban immigrants tend to live in more integrated and higher-income neighborhoods than their urban counterparts, their neighborhoods are still often highly segregated and isolated. This is most especially true for Latinx and African Americans, as their metropolitan regions have restructured around them, repeating familiar patterns of underinvestment in their new neighborhoods.[34] Some Asian Americans have bucked the curve, with greater integration in White and multiethnic, middle-class suburbs that geographer Wei Li termed "ethnoburbs." But their status as suburbanites, let alone Americans, continues to be contingent and contested. Their migration into predominantly White suburbs has prompted intraneighborhood segregation and new tactics of spatial control and order.[35]

Poverty is most acute in inner suburbs. Built in the postwar era, many inner suburbs were home to middle- and working-class White residents who left as their neighborhoods became more racially integrated and new housing opportunities opened in outer suburbs.[36] In their place Black and Brown residents, immigrants and native-born, found a plentiful stock of affordable housing and commercial space. While reinvesting in and keeping these neighborhoods afloat, marginalized groups also consistently fought the forces of so-called decline produced through active forms of disinvestment and abandonment. Inner suburbs have older, poor-quality housing and aging infrastructure that have been subject to decades of neglect and underinvestment. Compared to other suburbs, they have higher tax rates but less revenue-generating development and more service costs.[37] Metropolitan poverty has been slower to reach outer suburbs but has picked up pace since the Great Recession, particularly in areas with growing Latinx populations.[38]

Suburbanization has, in many ways, exacerbated the vulnerabilities facing marginalized groups. Many low-income Black and Brown residents live in communities that lack the traditional assets and amenities of central cities, while still suffering their challenges. Compared to White suburbs, their neighborhoods tend to have high rates of crime, unemployment, and foreclosure; poor health outcomes; and low housing values and educational attainment. At the same time, they often lack the social and physical infrastructure that impoverished households rely on to survive and gain economic mobility. This includes strong community-based organizations, dense kin and social networks, job opportunities, health care facilities, public transit, and subsidized housing.[39] Suburbia's dearth of nonprofits and antipoverty organizations, particularly immigrant-serving institutions, leave capacity-strapped social service providers struggling to reach clients who are far more diverse and geographically dispersed. In many suburbs the social and economic capital on which White working- and middle-class neighborhoods once thrived has crumbled, leaving Black and Brown suburbanites with what Alexandra Murphy calls an "ecology of scarcity."[40]

Traditional public policies often fail to address the critical needs of struggling suburbs. Suburbs exist in a "policy blind spot" with federal poverty and community development funding tailored to central cities.[41] State revitalization policies often overlook suburbs, in part because of their lack of political visibility. Philanthropic organizations tend to ignore the needs of suburban service organizations. Many suburbs are too small or resource-strapped to fund revitalization efforts or even keep pace with basic infrastructure repairs. Yet political fragmentation blunts cooperation with more well-resourced suburbs, particularly across racial lines.[42] While scholars have long argued for cross-jurisdictional collaboration to address disparities between cities and suburbs as well as among suburbs, few efforts have been undertaken. With little incentive for wealthier municipalities to cooperate and weak regional governance structures that could require them to do so, struggling suburbs are left to fend for themselves.[43]

The consequences of suburban poverty and racialized disinvestment were made all too apparent in Ferguson, Missouri. There the 2014 murder of Michael Brown, an unarmed Black teen, by a White police officer rocked the nation. As confrontations between protesters and police turned violent and catapulted the Black Lives Matter movement onto an international stage, questions abound about the forces leading to such vicious, militarized policing and why they had landed in this inner suburb north of downtown Saint Louis. Observers pointed out that African Americans in Ferguson were subject to not only decades of racialized police brutality but also violence at the hands of city councils, the state and federal government, banks, real estate and insurance agents, and their White suburban neighbors.[44] State-led and sanctioned structural violence had shaped the Saint Louis metropolitan area into a segregated and unequal landscape that, by the time of Brown's killing, left Ferguson fighting rapid disinvestment.

Like so many US suburbs, Ferguson had been built in the postwar period as a protected haven for White property and residents fleeing Black migration into downtown Saint Louis. Yet as African Americans broke through restrictive suburban housing policies, their outmigration precipitated further White flight. In the few suburbs like Ferguson where African Americans were able to settle, residents faced increasing segregation, a shrinking tax base, rising unemployment and poverty rates, and struggling schools, like the one that Michael Brown had recently graduated from. The uprisings revealed a host of racialized policies and practices that had followed African Americans from the city and were reconstituted in new ways in suburbia.[45]

In Ferguson African Americans bore the brunt of municipal finance through predatory policing and court-related fees and fines. The overpolicing of Black residents was a common fiscal strategy used by many Missouri suburbs to make up for declining tax revenues, particularly given the state's conservative property tax policies. In Ferguson it also justified massive new public-private partnerships and economic-development incentives to try to attract new investment that could spur suburban gentrification.[46]

Ferguson is not alone. Suburban redevelopment has boomed in recent decades, reflecting shifts in public policy and private interests. While the late twentieth century was characterized by low-density single-family homes, strip malls, and parking lots, the twenty-first-century mantra for good suburban development calls for more walkable, dense, mixed-use communities near transit. Smart-growth advocates have supported strategies, such as urban growth boundaries, that reduce sprawl, preserve open space, and promote compact development in already urbanized areas.[47] New Urbanists likewise argue for well-designed, walkable, mixed-use suburban developments that support a strong sense of place and community. More recently, architects and urban designers have advanced strategies to retrofit suburbia's existing fabric, reiterating claims about the economic, environmental, and aesthetic benefits of compact suburban design.[48]

Suburbia's urban rise has been lauded by many urbanists. Few have, however, addressed the social consequences and disparate costs of the new suburban renewal. Smart-growth advocates' narrow focus on sprawl and land-use controls have often ignored their uneven consequences, leading to fractured relationships with urban equity advocates. Though a growing equitable regional growth movement has built a platform for their shared concerns, significant fractures exist.[49] New Urbanists often view design as a proxy for racial and economic inclusion, assuming that diverse housing types and styles will naturally lead to more integrated, equitable communities. But without a focus on affordability and racial justice, their developments often lack diversity and contribute to rising housing prices, gentrification, and displacement. In Atlanta, inner suburbs that adopted New Urbanist revitalization and retrofitting strategies demolished affordable apartment buildings and displaced many low-income Latinx residents.[50]

Suburban redevelopment takes many forms. Sometimes the focus is on rebuilding single-family homes. In this particularly contentious arena of local politics, low-income communities of color and immigrants often lack an equitable voice and are most at-risk of displacement. Some suburbs, particularly near Rust Belt cities with slow-growing or declining populations, have developed strategies to welcome or attract immigrants to aid revitalization. While sometimes successful, such efforts are often hampered by state and federal anti-immigrant policies and local nativist backlash.[51] Other suburbs have taken a more comprehensive approach. The postrecession period saw an upsurge of "revanchist suburbs," in which established White residents and local governments sought to take back prime land increasingly occupied by Black and Brown residents. In Baltimore, inner suburbs heavily affected by economic restructuring and foreclosure used a range of aggressive tactics to spur redevelopment, including eminent domain and urban renewal. This reduced the supply of affordable housing, increased racial tensions, and led to the displacement of low-income, primarily Black residents.[52] Suburbs' increasing neoliberal bent and economic gravity have led some scholars to project a postsuburban future in which suburbs are increasingly disconnected from their metropolitan centers.[53]

The scope and impacts of suburban redevelopment trends, however, are little known, as is the response of affected communities. Despite their many challenges, suburbs are rarely seen as sites of social and political struggle. While the dense and diverse suburbs of European cities like Paris and Britian, which have long been home to marginalized groups, are well-known centers of social uprising, US suburbs are not. Early suburban historians widely depicted US suburbs as placid, peaceful zones of community building for a growing White middle class that positioned struggles over racial justice outside of their bounds. These narratives failed to acknowledge state-sanctioned and community-led violence and the consistent challenges raised by Black and Brown residents within suburbs.

Recent work on topics such as suburban police violence, urban renewal, environmental justice, immigrant rights, and fair housing has shown that US suburbs have always been contested sites where marginalized groups have registered claims to equal rights, citizenship, and a more just distribution of metropolitan resources. Black and Brown suburbanites have marched down cul-de-sacs, organized in their churches and backyards, and rallied suburban city halls and planning boards to contest their treatment as second-class citizens. They have built communities of their own and pioneered White suburbs, withstanding bombings and other violent assaults on their homes and lives to challenge exclusion from within.[54] But even as the image of suburbia has been slowly reshaped by greater media and scholarly attention to its diversity, suburban politics remain stubbornly associated with social and fiscal conservatism. As Genevieve Carpio, Clara Irazábal, and Laura Pulido write, "Suburban struggles are often assumed to be conservative and as a result are undertheorized as sites of liberatory struggle."[55] It is as if Black and Brown people moved to the suburbs but did not take their politics with them.

Recent suburban uprisings have underscored the rise of progressive suburban social movements commonly thought to occur only in urban neighborhoods. In an era of rising suburban inequality, racial segregation, and poverty, suburban uprisings have become ever more frequent. Carpio, Irazábal, and Pulido note that recent demographic shifts have transformed suburbs into central sites where new identities are being formed, racial identities challenged, and community notions contested—where residents are debating "who has the right to determine who can and cannot live in the suburb and under what conditions."[56] Such battles are visible in the widespread suburban activism associated with the Black Lives Matter movement—from Ferguson to those sparked by the police murders of George Floyd, Breonna Taylor, and others. These uprisings reflect not only suburbia's growing demographic diversity, but also the frustrations felt by new suburbanites that the suburbs have not lived up to the promise they once held. As R. L'Heureux Lewis-McCoy describes, the barriers to opportunity that Black suburbanites face at nearly every turn contribute to a collective sense that they have received the "suburban spoils" rather than its promises.[57] Suburban rebellion, whether over police violence or the brutality of state-sanctioned gentrification, draws needed attention to suburbs as a critical nexus of struggle for racial and economic justice. Yet dissent does not always take such bold, collective forms. More often it is enacted through residents' quiet claims to space and everyday resistance to their given spatial order, in the close confidence of suburban backyards and city councils.[58]

US suburbs have particular histories, racial and spatial contexts, and politics but are not altogether unique. They share distinct histories from the dense and diverse suburbs of Paris and Britian that have long been home to marginalized populations, including many non-White immigrants. In form and function, they vary from the informal settlements that line the outskirts of megacities in the Global South, like Mumbai and São Paulo.[59] Yet across the globe most urban growth, development, and economic activity occur on the urban periphery rather than at its center and often in a low-density pattern familiar to many US suburbs. "We live on a suburban planet," argues environmental studies professor Roger Keil. "The urban century is really the suburban century."[60] Indeed, the distinction between cities and suburbs has always been elusive, and their false dichotomies have often obscured understandings of larger metropolitan-wide processes. Yet suburbs have also been ignored as integral to urban histories and processes. As suburban scholars have long argued, understanding suburban spatial, economic, and social politics and dynamics paints a fuller metropolitan portrait—and highlights the linked fates between cities and suburbs.[61]

The Right to Suburbia illustrates the ties that bind gentrification in the city to its suburbs. It also adds to the growing body of scholarship on social movements as a response to uneven processes of metropolitan restructuring. As suburbs have become more racially, ethnically, and economically diverse, state-led redevelopment has spurred debates about gentrification and anti-displacement organizing. Marginalized communities have stood up and stood together, to challenge popular planning mantras about the benefits of suburban redevelopment that ignore their violent impacts. A new school of suburban activists and organizers have disrupted notions about where and how gentrification is taking shape and who is most affected. Building bridges and solidarities across difference, they have defied narrow race and class divides and interests that defined earlier generations of development politics in both the city and suburbs. They have built stronger policy tools, organizational capacity, and political will to shift the burden and protect marginalized communities' right to stay put. Their passion and persistence have generated an enduring equitable development movement that, though it has sometimes stumbled and struggled, has expanded the possibilities for what the suburban promise may hold for a new, more diverse generation of suburbanites.[62] They have done so in heart of US political power, where many of the tools of racialized exclusion have been tested and perfected.

RETHINKING REDEVELOPMENT IN THE NATIONAL CAPITAL REGION

Suburban redevelopment in the Washington, DC, region is not new. In the 1940s, just a few miles south of the DC border, Clarendon was a bustling streetcar suburb and northern Virginia's premier downtown. With retail anchors like Woolworth, JCPenney, and Sears that followed the rush of White suburbanites out of downtown DC, the neighborhood emerged as a popular shopping destination surrounded by garden-style apartments and single-family homes. In the decades that followed, as the Capital Beltway and other interstates opened new opportunities for development in far-flung suburbs in Fairfax County, many Clarendon shops closed their doors, only to reopen in shiny new shopping centers a few miles south.[63]

The struggling suburban downtown offered Vietnamese refugees a fresh start. Arriving in the region in several waves after the Fall of Saigon in 1975, many found their way to Clarendon through refugee resettlement agencies that offered financial aid and logistical assistance for families to settle in nearby neighborhoods. With construction of a metro station underway, streets were torn up in Clarendon's downtown and landlords were offering short-term commercial leases in dilapidated buildings at rock-bottom prices.[64]

Borrowing money from family and friends, Vietnamese emigrants set up small stores, professional offices, and restaurants along a three-block stretch of Wilson Boulevard in what quickly but quietly became the heart of the region's Vietnamese community and that of the entire East Coast. Known to regulars as Little Saigon, by the 1980s Clarendon's streets were packed with families coming from nearby suburbs and faraway cities on the weekends to shop for groceries, grab lunch with friends, and search newspaper stands and community boards for word of their hometowns or lost loved ones.[65] They came for employment and health care services, for church and language schools, or simply for a fleeting sense of reprieve and comfort after having lost so much in such a short time. Few county leaders and established residents, however, saw Little Saigon as vibrant and resilient. Many instead described it as overcrowded and rundown—an "eyesore" and an "embarrassment."[66]

Clarendon's redevelopment was set off by its metro station opening in 1979. The county then adopted a new sector plan in 1984 and a redevelopment plan five years later. The Clarendon Alliance, a group of established White developers, residents, and businesses oversaw the redevelopment process. They envisioned an upscale, high-density district with the look of an urban village and the feel of a small-town American Main Street.[67] Vietnamese business owners complained to county leaders that they would be displaced by the redevelopment process and higher rents to follow. The Clarendon Vietnamese Retail Business Association, formed in response to the redevelopment plan, called for policies that would allow retailers to remain or return to the redevelopment area, including protections for affordable commercial space.[68] "We have been good for Arlington. We have struggled and made success," explained Emerson H. Lee, vice president of the business association.[69]

Figure 1. Clarendon, Virginia, in the 1980s, as Little Saigon before redevelopment. *Little Saigon* (https://flic.kr/p/7z5t2Y), by @chucka_nc. Licensed under Creative Commons 2.0.

County and civic leaders expressed sympathy, promising to try to accommodate Vietnamese businesses in the new development. These promises crumbled, plans failed to emerge, and justifications for sweeping displacement came quickly. "For 30 years the county has been talking about development of the area," explained William Hughes, director of Arlington County's Community Planning, Housing, and Development Department, "[Vietnamese residents] had an opportunity to move into the area, but there was no expectation that we would change the redevelopment schedule because of them." "We would like for the Vietnamese to stay," agreed Andrea Grenadier, the Clarendon Alliance's executive director. "We like the ethnic flavor. But keeping the right balance is a little tricky."[70] Redevelopment plans mentioned the goal of preserving existing businesses but provided few incentives or requirements to do so.

Developers began to buy out leases from local businesses at a feverish pace and evicted occupants to renovate or demolish buildings. Tenants

Figure 2. The same corner in Clarendon in the 2000s, after redevelopment. *CVS Pharmacy No. 2* (https://flic.kr/p/bjw845), by Ron Cogswell. Licensed under Creative Commons 2.0.

who had been paying less than five dollars per square foot in older buildings were met with rents more than five times higher in redeveloped or new buildings.[71] With little voice in the process and few affordable options, Vietnamese businesses closed their doors or moved farther west to other Virginia suburbs. Many set up shop in Eden Center, an old strip mall in Falls Church, which soon assumed the title of Little Saigon. By 2014 only one Vietnamese-owned business remained in Clarendon.[72]

Clarendon is a telling tale of the process of dispossession and erasure that has disrupted the lives and livelihoods of low-income communities of color time and again. But it is not the typical tale of the DC region. As the home of the US federal government, the focus of urban scholarship has long been the region's civic and monumental core. In recent years scholars have begun to reshape this narrative with detailed accounts of neighborhoods' everyday life and politics. Their work highlights how Black and Brown residents, whether born into the deep southern soil or arriving from elsewhere, have repeatedly borne witness to urban redevelopment's promise and perils.[73] These stories, however, focus largely on Washington, DC, scarcely stretching beyond its municipal bounds. The suburbs have served as a background, but rarely have they been in the foreground or received much attention in the region's tale of uneven growth and development.

The District of Columbia has served as the testing grounds for multiple national urban redevelopment experiments—from slum clearance and urban renewal to Model Cities. As in many US cities, municipal leaders, planners, real estate associations, developers, banks, and others enacted racialized practices and policies that serially displaced African Americans from their homes and neighborhoods. In both city and suburb, they enclosed, fractured, and constrained communities of color in ever more tightly bounded areas of concentrated, manufactured disadvantage. Unlike other cities, however, the district's redevelopment politics have been shaped by its unique relationship to the federal government. Congress's capricious denial of the district's right to self-governance and its aggressive policies of control have repeatedly stripped the city coffers and undermined residents' basic citizenship rights. As the first US city with a Black majority, Washingtonians contested the racist roots of congressional control and pulled on strategies of collective resistance—from civil rights to Black Power—to challenge policies that threatened their place and voice in the city. Their activism formed the foundation of some of the nation's earliest and most progressive anti-displacement policies.[74] Within this narrative scholars typically imagine the suburbs as an escape or refuge for those fleeing urban decay and Black residents often scapegoated as the cause.

More recently, the region's dominant growth narrative has become inverted, with the city again capturing center stage. Scholars have focused on the region's back-to-the-city movement, its skyrocketing land and property values, the loss of its iconic Chocolate City status, and its emergence as the "mostly intensely gentrified city" in the United States.[75] They have documented the fight of residents, particularly African Americans, to remain in and be a part of "the new DC." From cultural and political displacement, microsegregation, and the aesthetics of dispossession to the loss of affordable housing, rising homelessness, and the politics of public space, Black Washingtonians have repeatedly borne the burdens of redevelopment and been pushed to the city's margins. These narratives highlight how activists have pulled on the city's legacy of anti-displacement organizing to chart new possibilities for staying put.[76] They have, however, yet to take account of what was taking place in suburbs like Clarendon. These gaps overlook the metropolitan scale of racialized patterns of growth and how the ravages of redevelopment shift from place to place.

Like the city itself, the demographic and development histories of DC suburbs tell a tale of regional and national import. The Maryland and Virginia suburbs are home to long-standing Black communities, including the nation's wealthiest Black-majority county. They are sites of robust immigrant settlement, including large populations of Ethiopian, Nigerian, Salvadoran, Guatemalan, Chinese, Korean, Indian, and Vietnamese emigrants. In several inner suburbs like Clarendon, immigrant communities are well established. In outer suburbs like Herndon and Manassas, Virginia, immigration has only recently spiked. And like many metropolitan areas around the country, many DC suburbs have swelling poverty. While the district has traditionally sheltered the vast majority of the region's poor, its poverty rate has been dropping for decades. Meanwhile, suburban poverty rates have moved steadily upward. Still, racial and economic segregation remains high, not only between the city and its suburbs but also among suburbs. While the western and outer suburbs have higher populations of wealthy White and Asian residents, eastern and inner suburbs have lower incomes, more immigrants, and larger Black and Latinx populations. The latter bore the weight of the foreclosure crisis that followed the Great Recession.[77]

The region's suburbs are not just typical auto-oriented bedroom communities; many have dense downtowns. Joel Garreau's 1991 study that coined the term "edge cities" documented multiple areas of concentrated business, shopping, and entertainment in the Washington suburbs. This included sixteen mature and seven emerging edge cities in DC's inner suburbs, such as Alexandria, Virginia, and Bethesda, Maryland, and in outer suburban communities along Maryland's I-270 corridor and the I-66 corridor in Virginia.[78] Since the late 1990s, Maryland has been a national leader in smart growth, with policies that established targeted growth areas in established communities and prioritized them for infrastructure and housing upgrades. Legislation supported suburban revitalization projects, such as downtown Silver Spring, often regarded by planners and architects as a national model of suburban retrofitting.[79]

While planners and designers have praised DC's dense and diverse suburbs, few have accounted for how communities have been harmed in their making. Royce Hanson's 2017 book, *Suburb: Planning Politics and the Public Interest*, offers a deep analysis of the politics of planning in Montgomery County, Maryland, known for its progressive land-use policies, including the nation's first inclusionary zoning ordinance. The book accounts for decades of struggle among homeowners, environmentalists, and developers to align planning decisions, including those about redevelopment, with the public interest.[80] But it largely skirts issues of race and class that are a constitutive part of planning politics—politics that privilege some publics over others. It does not ask how marginalized publics have participated in—and too often strained under—redevelopment's weight.

The Right to Suburbia tells the tale of three redeveloping Maryland suburbs. Silver Spring and Langley Park are inner suburbs that sit on the Washington, DC, border. Wheaton is also an inner suburb but lies further out, just beyond the I-495 Beltway, a major economic and demographic dividing line in the DC region. Silver Spring and Wheaton lie in Montgomery County, which is among the most wealthy, educated, and diverse counties in the nation. While the county was largely White for most of its history, today no group holds a majority. It has a reputation as a politically and socially progressive county that is welcoming to immigrants. Langley Park lies in Prince George's County, which is well known as one of the most wealthy and educated majority-Black counties in the country. In one of the highest-income regions in the country, however, it is one of the most distressed counties. Compared to neighboring counties like Montgomery, Prince George's has a lower tax base, more working-class neighborhoods, fewer jobs, and less immigration.[81]

Only a few decades ago, all three of these neighborhoods were predominantly White. None remain so today. Silver Spring is a racially and economically diverse neighborhood with an established White and Black middle class and one of the largest Ethiopian immigrant communities in the country. Wheaton is a more working-class neighborhood, known for its rich ethnic diversity. Among its White, Black, and Asian American populations and rapidly growing Latinx community, no group holds the majority. Among the

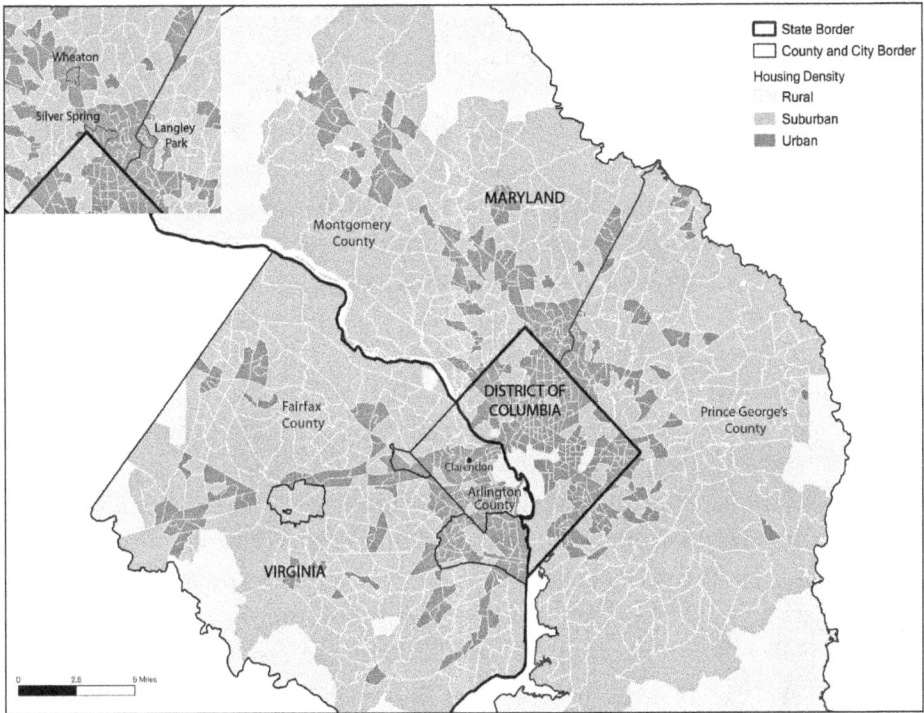

Map 1. Housing density by census tract in the DC region, showing the false lines often drawn between cities and suburbs. Areas classified as urban have more than 2,213 households per square mile; suburban have 102 to 2,212; and rural have fewer than 102. Map by Nohely Alvarez. Inspired by a similar map by Dan Reed. US Census Bureau, *2018 ACS 1-Year.*

suburbs, Langley Park is the lowest-income neighborhood. It is also one of the few popular immigrant gateways in Prince George's County. The neighborhood is home to the region's largest Latinx and immigrant populations, including many undocumented residents from Guatemala and El Salvador.

These suburbs differ in their redevelopment histories and politics. All have historical downtowns or commercial areas that were the focus of major county- or state-led redevelopment efforts. During my research, which began in 2013 and ended in late 2019, Silver Spring had already experienced decades of large-scale redevelopment that displaced low-income residents and small businesses from its downtown. In the face of these challenges, a new advocacy organization formed that pushed for a greater voice for marginalized communities in the process and policies to combat displacement. After several false starts, Wheaton's first major redevelopment plans took shape during my research. Organizing was led by a more established urban nonprofit that tried to advance a comprehensive fair redevelopment agenda, with many losses along the way. Redevelopment plans for Langley Park emerged a few years after Wheaton, sparked by the development of a new light-rail line. Robust grassroots and grasstops coalitions led a comprehensive campaign to address residential, commercial, and cultural displacement, with many successes. Anti-displacement activism remained ongoing across all three neighborhoods as my research came to a close.

These communities faced similar challenges, but at different times and to different degrees. Across the region they stand out as poignant examples of how activists doggedly built a promising movement for equitable suburban development during a period of intense regional growth and change. Collectively, the cases tell a tale of how community leaders and activists listened to and learned from one another, leveraged and honed new policy tools and resources, collaborated and connected, and built their capacities to mobilize across new geographic and demographic borders. They are what I call "connected case studies," in which activists slowly but surely built power that enabled them to combat displacement pressures that affected them all.

The Right to Suburbia documents redevelopment politics in these suburbs primarily from voices of those closet to them—neighborhood organizations, affected businesses, community leaders and activists, municipal planners, government agencies, local politicians, and developers—seventy-four in all. The people I came to know did not all share the same perspectives, positionality, or power. While some were fighting against displacement, others did not see the utility of using the term "gentrification" to describe what was happening in their communities. I sought out their different voices to understand the rich conflicts underlying redevelopment in each place. I also looked for people who had helped to ignite and inflame the fight, whether by constructing or opposing redevelopment plans. I supplemented their perspectives with other sources: transcripts from public hearing and community meetings, newspaper accounts, local development archives, planning documents, and census data.[82]

My ties to these communities are both personal and professional. I lived in Silver Spring as a young adult and witnessed the early phases of redevelopment. I currently live nearby and frequent the downtown area, nearly three decades later. I worked in Wheaton at an affordable housing nonprofit, regularly visited my in-laws there for over two decades, and mentored students on projects to help keep its small businesses in place. I have focused much of my research on redevelopment politics in Langley Park. For over a decade, I have attended protests and public meetings and worked closely with several research participants, particularly activists who are fighting for stronger tenant and small business protections. These relationships provided unique insights into the people and places I studied. But, as in many such studies, my ongoing relationships presented challenges. My goal as a researcher was to fairly represent the multiple points of view offered by participants, including those I disagreed with. The insights of other ethnographers guided my path toward seeing the value of my "long engagement," while also establishing the distance I needed to critically reflect on my positionality.[83]

I did not intend to write a comparative study. My initial interests and research guided me into the thick of these three communities. As I spoke to activists and leaders, their stories of redevelopment's wins and losses echoed and often referenced one another. The longer I lingered, the harder their resemblances became to ignore. What I at first saw as isolated circumstances and unique struggles became linked narratives. Had I only immersed myself in one place, I would not have grasped why their resemblances were so strong, nor why their differences mattered so deeply to their processes and outcomes. While doing a comparative case study, I experienced what other urban scholars—sociologists, anthropologists, and planners alike—have long understood about their value.[84]

My learning process in many ways resembled that of the community leaders and activists I came to know. Through their voices and actions, I learned how they learned and shared across the cases to build a bigger and stronger movement. In the face of daunting odds, they repeatedly renewed a sense of collective hope and built bolder visions for just community futures. As the prison abolitionist Mariame Kaba says, "Hope is a discipline" and "Organizing is both science and art." The activists featured in these pages did not look at past mistakes as failures; they learned from them to mobilize new people, raise awareness, build new solidarities, and challenge the status quo. They fought to maintain momentum for the next struggle, leverage the gains won by organizers before them, and bring the energies and wisdom of new and old into the fold. They collectively experimented, built power and trust, and strategized to advance not *the* solution but a constellation of solutions. As Kaba reminds us, "This is how we will win."[85]

2 DC Suburban Shuffle

During my first long, hot DC summer in the mid-1990s, I interned for a human rights organization in Capitol Hill. Like so many Capitol Hill interns, I entered the city completely unaware of its long history as a Black mecca, its local politics, and racial and class divides. A wrong turn on an otherwise normal commute brought these questions front and center. In the tangled freeways that hovered over the city's southeast side, I took an exit into the Anacostia neighborhood. With no clear way to get back on track, I found myself wandering into a city within the city. Boarded-up homes and liquor stores lined sidewalks teaming with Black life—families, children, and men blaring music and selling CDs from their car trunks and makeshift corner markets. The strong sense of community amid struggle had the air of the familiar for a young girl from Appalachia, while at the same time being completely foreign.

I stopped at a gas station to ask for directions. The attendant and stream of customers looked at me with blank stares, as if I were talking about a place light-years away rather than a mile or two down the road. Finally, a man gave me directions and a clearer sense of my place in the city. "You're not from around here," he said, more as a statement than a question. As I would later learn, I had crossed a deep divide in the city—the Anacostia

River. This line was drawn and reinforced by well over a century of development that separated, isolated, and disinvested in the East-of-the-River neighborhoods. In the early twentieth century, Anacostia was a largely White working-class neighborhood, upheld by legal and extralegal forms of racial violence. By the 1950s African Americans had broken down some of these barriers as Whites left en masse. Within a decade the neighborhood was majority Black. Anacostia welcomed African Americans displaced from other parts of the city and those seeking refuge from racial terror in the US South. Many found comfort and community in a Black-majority neighborhood cut off by the Anacostia River. To the city and private developers, however, Anacostia was ripe for exploitation. In the late twentieth century, it was targeted by multiple urban renewal projects and became the city's unofficial dumping ground for subsidized housing, environmental hazards, and other unwanted uses.

By the time I arrived, Anacostia was among the city's most disadvantaged neighborhoods. It had a poverty rate nearly twice that of the city. It was a food desert that lacked grocery stores and health care facilities. It was park poor with few green spaces or street trees. Rates of unemployment and chronic disease were among the highest in the city. Homeownership rates, home values, and educational attainment were among the lowest.[1] The Anacostia River was one of the most polluted urban waterways in the United States. Multiple freeways displaced, divided, and isolated residents from services and opportunities in nearby neighborhoods, including the wealthy and White Capitol Hill.[2]

Amid DC's latest wave of gentrification, the neighborhood became the symbolic heart of struggle for Black Washingtonians to remain in the city. Construction cranes and young White newcomers were spotted in the neighborhood for the first time in many residents' memories. White people were fixing up homes, riding down new bike lanes, and hanging out in trendy cafés. Major redevelopment projects were underway, such as the former St. Elizabeth's Hospital campus, which some long-term residents welcomed after being starved of investment for so long. But many also feared that development would push up already skyrocketing rents, eliminating some of the last vestiges of affordability in the city.

Anacostia is but one neighborhood through which to view the long arc of growth that shifted geographies of race, poverty, and redevelopment across the Washington region. This chapter traces a host of others both inside and outside the city, where residents struggled to remain in place. Through newspapers, municipal archives, and other secondary sources, I explore key moments of gentrification and anti-displacement organizing in the city over the past century and how these development pressures were experienced in the DC suburbs. This history reveals that in each decade that defined equitable development struggles in the district, similar patterns emerged in Maryland and Virginia suburbs, including Silver Spring, Wheaton, and Langley Park.

While marginalized communities across city and suburban lines were subject to many of the same vicious practices, equitable development battles have been most virulent and visible in the district. Decades of organizing built policies and grassroots organizations that activists in DC leveraged to fight for fair development—and sometimes win. In recent decades, however, the geography of regional inequality has shifted. Some suburbs now show signs of disadvantage that were once largely contained in DC neighborhoods like Anacostia. These dynamics laid the groundwork for contemporary suburban struggles that I explore in subsequent chapters. This chapter illustrates that, though less visible, these struggles were always present. During every phase of gentrification in the city, suburbs gentrified too.[3]

Suburban scholars have stressed the need to complicate histories of metropolitan growth and development by looking at the dynamic and symbiotic relationships between cities and suburbs as well as suburbs as sites of struggle.[4] Marginalized groups are not fixed in place, and neither are processes that produce marginalized spaces. Both are constantly reshuffled across metropolitan landscapes and reimagined through shifting spatial strategies—enclosure, containment, removal, isolation, and abandonment. As Black and Brown communities have moved or been forcibly relocated from city to suburbs, suburbs to city, or in between suburbs, so too have strategies to keep them "in their place."[5]

This chapter goes beyond the DC border to complicate the history of racialized redevelopment in the National Capital Region. It follows through lines of previous iterations of gentrification and their pushback in the city and suburbs that serve as prelude to recent battles, including earlier fights in Silver Spring, Wheaton, and Langley Park. Contests over gentrification did not just happen as communities of color moved from the

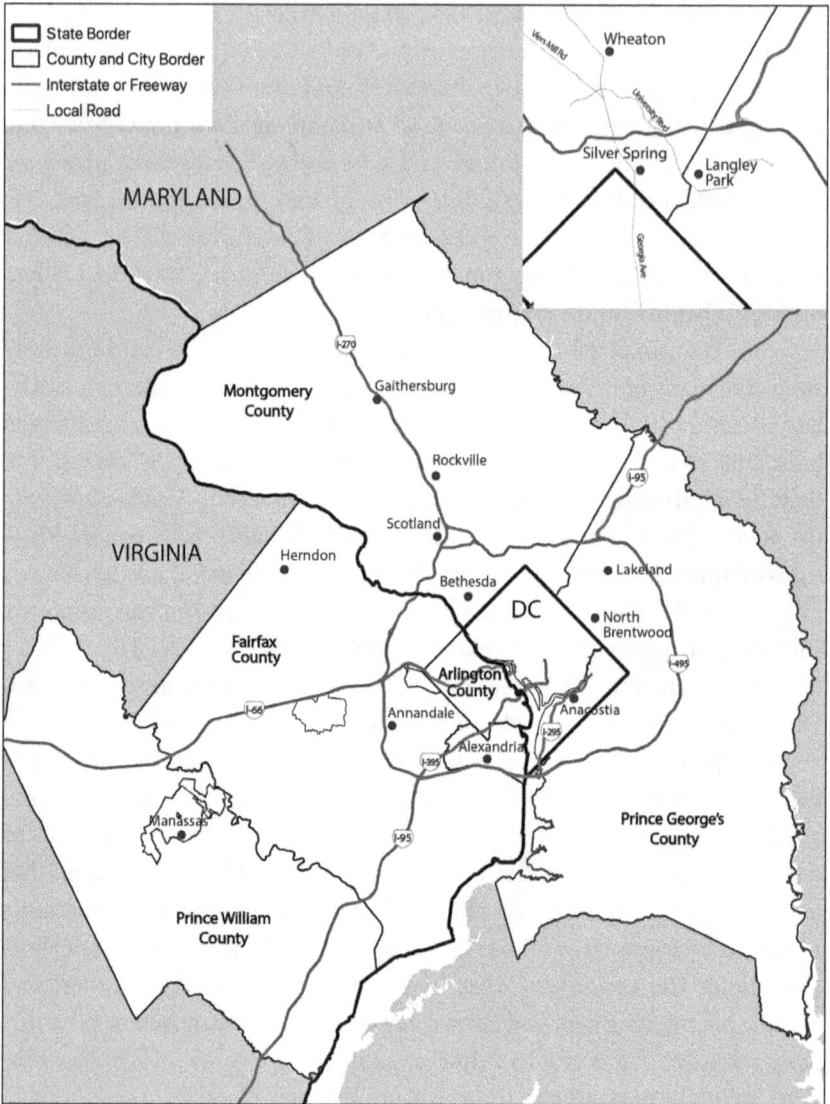

Map 2. Map of the DC region, highlighting city and suburban neighborhoods that struggled over multiple waves of disinvestment and reinvestment, which served as a prelude to contemporary suburban redevelopment battles. Map by Nohely Alvarez. Map data © OpenStreetmap contributors. Map design © Stamen Toner.

city; they occurred as suburban development enveloped Black and Brown communities already in suburbs. Repeatedly facing the threat of displacement, marginalized suburbanites have stood up over and over to claim their right to stay put.

FROM BLACK FREEDOM TO ENCLOSURE

In 1790 Maryland and Virginia gifted one hundred square miles of submerged swampland along the Potomac and Anacostia Rivers, the land of displaced Anacostan, Piscataway, and Pamunkey tribes, to serve as the nation's capital. A horse-and-buggy ride from George Washington's farm in Mount Vernon, it was a convenient location, but one that federal leaders felt needed to be fit for a capital worthy of the nation. Washington called on the French architect and engineer Pierre L'Enfant to tame its wooded hills and muddy swamps and lay out the city. After L'Enfant's assistant, Andrew Ellicott, surveyed the territory alongside Benjamin Banneker, a freed Black man and self-taught mathematician, the fledgling city began to grow. After the Civil War, the expansion of the federal government led to the region's first population boom.

Growth initially focused on a small band of communities near downtown. These were largely walkable neighborhoods, where Black and White residents lived close to one another, though on vastly unequal terms. But as African Americans pushed the bounds of Jim Crow that clearly demarcated the limits of Black economic and social mobility, White Washingtonians pushed back with new spatial strategies of control. Through public planning, slum clearance, and private racial covenants, White federal and city leaders, neighborhoods associations, and real estate groups sought to secure their property values and social power through legal and extralegal tools of segregation. They pushed Black Washingtonians out of their neighborhoods and into more bounded areas that could be controlled and exploited. These same processes were at work in the suburbs, both inside and outside the district. As the city expanded, Black rural townships in Maryland and Virginia found themselves in the way of White elites seeking to escape the unhealthy urban conditions, which included common diseases like malaria and typhoid as well as interracial mixing. Employing tools perfected in DC, suburbs grew segregated from the start.

Planning a Segregated Federal City

Most migrants arriving in the Washington region after the Civil War were Black. By 1890 it had the largest Black population of any city in the United States, a distinction it held until after World War I.[6] During the First Great Migration (1916–40), African Americans continued to flock to the region for well-paying federal civil service jobs. Congress took great pains to blunt this emerging center of Black political power. In the 1870s it stripped the growing city of the limited home-rule powers it held since 1802. The city became a federal fiefdom—"the voteless capital of democracy"—governed by a presidentially appointed three-member board of commissioners. As Alabama senator and former slaveholder John Tyler Morgan explained in 1890, Congress "found it necessary to disenfranchise every man in the District of Columbia . . . in order thereby to get rid of this load of negro suffrage that was flooded upon them."[7]

While stripped of the right of self-governance, Black life thrived in DC. With relatively high rates of Black property ownership and an established middle class, DC earned a reputation as the "colored man's paradise." It was home to prominent Black leaders, including orator and abolitionist Frederick Douglass and poet Paul Lawrence Dunbar; to Howard University, the nation's first and most esteemed university dedicated to Black education; and to Dunbar High School, the first and most prestigious public high school for African Americans. Lined by Black-owned restaurants, theaters, and banks, U Street was *the* center of Black life and culture. Known as Black Broadway, its crowded clubs hosted native talent, such as jazz superstars Duke Ellington, Count Basie, and Pearl Baily, along with many visiting Black luminaries.[8]

Even so, White supremacy structured the limits of Black life. While Black and White Washingtonians often lived nearby, they did so on very different terms. Before the electric streetcar arrived in the late 1800s, DC was a walking city, confined to a few downtown blocks. Most southern arrivals settled into crowded alley dwellings, hastily constructed behind the homes of more prosperous White and sometimes Black families.

Alleyways were thick with social capital but lacked plumbing, sunlight, and electricity, contributing to high rates of disease and infant mortality. In 1897 roughly 90 percent of alley residents were African American.[9]

Congressional and municipal leaders called for slum clearance to rid the district of unsightly alley dwellings and craft a city that would rival the European capitals of Rome and Paris. Drawing on L'Enfant's plan, the 1902 McMillan Plan crafted by Charles Moore, secretary of Senator James McMillan, envisioned DC as an orderly, grand city in the mode of City Beautiful. Following the 1893 World Columbia Exposition in Chicago, the McMillan Commission hired Daniel Burnham, the exposition's supervising architect, and renowned landscape designer Frederick Law Olmstead to lay out the vision for a "White City." The design focused on a monumental core filled with civic art, neoclassical buildings, and sweeping vistas. The city was to instill national pride, patriotism, and civic virtue. But this city of marble and monuments ignored those living in its shadows and removed unsightly slums that marred its gleaming image.[10]

In the Progressive Era, the logic of slum clearance pivoted from a need to project US power at home and abroad to the moral uplift of the nation. From Hull House director Jane Addams to tenement reformer Lawrence Veiller, leaders noted that DC's alleys were not only an eyesore but a public health hazard—one that if not contained could spread, bringing social deviance, crime, immorality, and corruption to the rest of the city. Testifying before Congress in 1902, acclaimed journalist Jacob Riis, author of the popular exposé on New York's slum conditions, *How the Other Half Lives*, remarked that the conditions in DC's alleys were "too dreadful to conceive."[11] Believing that order, beauty, and cleanliness could raise the poor to White middle-class standards of morality, progressive reformers sought to remake the so-called slums.

Powerful congressional and city leaders, including the Committee of 100 on the Federal City and the Washington Board of Trade, which represented the interests of White citizen associations, went further, calling for the complete elimination of alley dwellings. In 1918 and 1934, Congress passed the Alley Dwelling Acts, which translated their goal into public policy. The 1934 act established the DC Alley Dwelling Authority (ADA), the United States' first public housing authority, with the power to condemn and raze blighted property. Rather than eliminating poor housing conditions for African Americans, the ADA proved most effective in creating bulwarks to Black migration into White neighborhoods and segregating formerly integrated neighborhoods.

Municipal planners were even more effective than the ADA in segregating the city. The National Capital Parks and Planning Commission (NCPPC) was established in 1926 as DC's first permanent planning agency. Like many municipal planning agencies, it adopted the US Department of Commerce's zoning guidelines that cautioned against incompatible uses, including interracial mixing. With its newfound power of eminent domain, the commission cleared and redeveloped Black neighborhoods, particularly those near or in the way of White development. With the extension of water and sewer lines and streetcars in the late 1800s, new suburban-style development emerged inside DC. Around the turn of the century, as much as 15 percent of DC's Black population lived in suburban areas inside the city, roughly the same percentage as for White Washingtonians.[12] But new suburban subdivisions also often replaced unplanned and self-built Black communities. At the behest of White citizen associations, the NCPPC demolished a Black suburb near DC's Fort Reno, established by post–Civil War migrants. They bulldozed homes and churches and closed a Black school for a new park and Whites-only school.[13]

To further quell fears about the threat of African Americans to their personhood and property, White homeowners and developers adopted racial deed restrictions on existing properties as well as land slated for new development. These private covenants restricted property sales or rentals to Black and other non-White people. The National Association of Real Estate Boards and local associations such as the Washington Real Estate Board supported their adoption, stating in their code of ethics that properties in White neighborhoods should not be offered to non-White buyers. The US Supreme Court (*Corrigan v. Buckley*, 1926) and local courts upheld their legality. Residents, citizens associations, and police enforced them, often by brute force. Although DC never adopted racial zoning, it accomplished virtually the same thing through planning and racial covenants. Across the city nearly half of all housing was restricted with racial covenants by 1948.[14]

The combined force of these tools was evidenced in Georgetown, a former slave port and mixed-race neighborhood that by 1910 was majority Black. Georgetown's riverside location within walking distance to downtown, with easy streetcar access and affordable homes, was attractive to White Washingtonians facing a severe housing shortage. In the 1920s its all-White citizen associations pushed the ADA to redevelop its "slums," largely alley dwellings and rooming houses occupied by African Americans. White developers restored properties and converted rooming houses into single-family homes, evicting tenants and raising rents. Racial covenants adopted on new and existing properties ensured that few displaced Black residents could return. By 1950 only a couple hundred Black families remained. The displacement of African Americans from Georgetown marked the city's first major wave of gentrification.[15]

Segregating the Suburbs

While many of the region's earliest suburbs were built in the district as walking, horsecar, and later streetcar suburbs, by the eve of World War I, many of these neighborhoods had lost their suburban character.[16] Meanwhile, a string of railroad and streetcar suburbs emerged in Maryland and Virginia, many of which by midcentury had turned to automobile suburbs. As in the city, restrictive covenants and racist planning practices segregated the suburbs—practices that displaced, enclosed, and isolated Black communities already there.

As DC grew rapidly in the late 1800s, many nearby Maryland and Virginia communities shrank. Prior to the Civil War, these areas were filled with tobacco, wheat, and grain farms, cultivated by enslaved African Americans. In Prince George's County, Maryland, African Americans made up 60 percent of the population before the war, 90 percent of whom were enslaved. In neighboring Montgomery County, African Americans made up over a third of the population at the end of the Civil War. During and immediately after the war, many African Americans left their rural roots for DC's emerging Black mecca.[17]

Those who remained leased and sometimes bought land from former White plantation owners. They became iron and domestic workers, teachers, and tenant farmers, helping to build the National Capital Region while establishing tight-knit communities of their own. Building on or near former free Black settlements, Black towns were often established far enough from White towns to protect them from racial violence but close enough for the many African Americans who worked as domestics and laborers in White households. Montgomery County had over forty Black towns by the early 1900s. Many were unplanned suburbs filled with self-built homes centered on a church and school. Less common were planned Black suburbs like Freedman's Village in Arlington, Virginia, a model community built by the US military in 1863 and run by the Freedmen's Bureau. Whether planned or unplanned, Black towns were often established on land deemed unwanted or undesirable by Whites, including low-lying areas prone to flooding or unsuitable for farming.[18]

In Silver Spring, one of Maryland's earliest and most popular early twentieth-century suburbs, exclusionary planning mixed with racial covenants to exclude African Americans. Like many early Maryland suburbs, Silver Spring was the popular pleasure grounds and country retreat of wealthy Washingtonians, including Francis Preston Blair, one of Montgomery County's largest enslavers, who served in President Andrew Jackson's cabinet. After the opening of the Baltimore and Ohio (B&O) Railroad station linking Baltimore to Washington in 1878 and the streetcar connecting Silver Spring to downtown DC two decades later, platting for suburban development began. The establishment of the Washington Sanitary and Sewer Commission (WSSC) in 1919 brought critical infrastructure to the area and acted as Maryland's de facto planner. In 1927 WSSC's planning functions were taken up by the newly established Maryland–National Capital Parks and Planning Commission (M-NCPPC), which gave Montgomery County zoning power. Silver Spring neighborhoods were almost exclusively zoned for large-lot, single-family homes. Wealthy landowners, who were often also county public officials like Blair, became prominent suburban boosters and developers. Edward Brooke Lee, the great grandson of Francis Preston Blair, founded the North Washington Realty Company and the Silver Spring Chamber of Commerce. Known as the boss of Montgomery County, he helped to establish the WSSC and the M-NCPPC and led Montgomery County's Democratic Party. As Royce Hanson wrote, "Sewers made suburban living possible. Automobiles made it feasible. E. Brooke Lee made it happen."[19]

Envisioning the county as a destination for upscale homes and garden communities, E. Brooke Lee and other Silver Spring developers widely applied racial covenants to new homes. This made them valuable to White families seeking refuge from the crowded, unsanitary conditions of the city, including its racial mixing. Along Sligo Creek, Silver Spring's Woodside Park development was advertised as a "healthful place away from the noise and crowded atmosphere of the city" with all the conveniences of urban life. It was built by the Woodside Development Corporation, whose president, Charles W. Hopkins, was among the early presidents of the Silver Spring Chamber of Commerce. All its homes were on large lots, typically more than an acre; had minimum cost requirements; and mandated racial deed restrictions. In language typical of neighboring communities, its deeds read, "For the purpose of sanitation and health neither the said party . . . nor their heirs or assigns shall or will sell or lease the said land to any one of a race whose death rate is at a higher percentage than the white race." In Silver Spring most subdivisions platted from the turn of the century to midcentury had racial covenants attached to them.[20]

Not only did suburban developers build homes; they built racially restricted communities. As streetcar suburbs turned to automobile suburbs, new commercial developments arrived. By the 1940s Silver Spring was known as the region's first automobile suburb and the downtown of the northern suburbs, a reputation that extended for several decades. The Silver Spring Shopping Center opened its doors in 1938, with the *Washington Post* hailing it "one of the most complete ever built in America" and "representative of the best ideas in modern business center development."[21] It was the largest drive-in, integrated retail development in the region and the county's first modern auto-oriented shopping center. In 1938 traffic along Georgia Avenue, Silver Spring's main thoroughfare, was among the heaviest in the state.[22]

Montgomery County boomed with this "white collar invasion" of middle- and upper-class families. One resident remembered Silver Spring in the early twentieth century as a "gay and wholesome" community dominated by women's clubs and churches. She recalled horseback-riding parties, literary-society gatherings, musicals, debates, and active social clubs that held dances and costume balls lasting well into the night. "No one in the neighborhood had to lock his doors for fear of unwanted guests, thugs or criminals. Silver Spring was a secure and happy area," she recalled.[23] But African Americans could not live in Silver Spring. They could not

Figure 3. Silver Spring in the 1950s, when it was widely considered "the downtown" of DC's northern suburbs. Reprinted with permission of the DC Public Library, Star Collection © *Washington Post.*

shop in its stores and had to pick up orders from popular restaurants like the Tastee Diner and Little Tavern from their back doors.[24] Instead, African Americans built self-sufficient communities, often without county services and with active hostility of White neighbors. Black suburbs were often overcrowded and zoned for undesirable uses, including multifamily development.[25]

Lyttonsville is located west of downtown Silver Spring on land formerly owned by Samuel Lytton, a free Black laborer who worked for the Blair family in the mid-1800s. Beginning in the late 1800s, African Americans began to build homes, churches, businesses, and a school in Lyttonsville. Many worked in nearby Silver Spring. While a thriving Black neighborhood, Lyttonsville was cut off by the B&O Railroad. To White Silver Spring residents, it was the "other side of the tracks," sometimes referred to as

Figure 4. Lyttonsville residents in 1967. The neighborhood
served as the county's dumping ground for unwanted land uses,
but residents held a strong sense of community and
neighborhood pride. Maryland State Archives, Lynn Kapiloff
Montgomery Sentinel Collection, MSA SC 6269.

"Monkey Hollow." White antipathy and neglect created the conditions
residents decried. It was the county's dumping grounds for unwanted land
uses, including industrial, military, and public facilities throughout the
twentieth century. The county denied the neighborhood basic services,
including paved roads and water and sewer, until the 1960s. A bridge
spanning the tracks connected residents to jobs, public transit, and other
amenities not available in the neighborhood. But, like the Anacostia River,
the bridge also provided residents protection and reprieve from the insult
of everyday Black life in the Jim Crow suburbs.[26]

White suburbs also forced the containment and decline of Black settlements. Unlike Silver Spring, many White suburbs incorporated to protect
their borders from Black encroachment. Violence, predatory building practices, and public takings often forced African Americans from their land. In
sundown suburbs, White mobs drove African Americans from their homes
and required those working or passing through to be out by dark. In
Arlington the Good Citizens' League, a group of the county's most

prominent White men, conducted an armed clean up of Rosslyn's working-class Black neighborhood in 1904. A posse of six deputized league members stormed the neighborhood with sledgehammers, axes, and sawed-off shotguns to reclaim valuable county land for commercial development. Arlington County's 1914 Suburban Control Ordinance, the first county-wide planning law, then imposed strict regulations on new development. It required the county engineer to approve all new developments, prevented self-built construction common to Black neighborhoods, and gave the county the power to condemn existing properties.[27]

Restrictive and violent practices on the urban edge and new opportunities in the district drove African Americans to leave the region's expanding suburbs. Once a predominantly Black county, by 1930 Prince George's County's White population was over three times that of African Americans. Montgomery County's Black population had dropped to only 3 percent by 1940. But the city that former rural residents encountered was not simply a landscape of opportunity; it was one in which segregation defined nearly every aspect of daily life. With dual housing markets for Black and White Americans now codified in law and practice and race deeply entangled in notions of property value and risk, interracial neighborhoods became virtually extinct by midcentury. Near DC's core, neighborhoods were overwhelmingly Black. Those farther out were largely White, closely resembling suburbs beyond the city's border. The administration of President Woodrow Wilson (1913–21) took a particularly heavy toll on the region, as it segregated federal workers, demoted many high-ranking African Americans, and segregated DC's public facilities.[28] His racist reign served as a harbinger of what was to come—a period in which the federal government played an unprecedented role in creating and hardening the lines of regional racial segregation.

SOLIDIFYING THE SUBURBAN WALL

Black communities in both the city and suburbs resisted racial enclosure. Black people frequently fought the designation of Black neighborhoods as slums and filed lawsuits challenging racial covenants, which ignited the postwar push ending their judicial enforcement nationally in 1948.[29] The victory was, however, short-lived. Even without legal backing, White home-owners and the real estate industry continued to enforce covenants through the 1970s. Early twentieth-century planning and real estate practices laid the foundation for housing segregation. Federal New Deal policies cemented them. By the end of World War II, segregation hardly needed private enforcement—it was public policy and institutionalized practice.

While securing White wealth in new suburbs, federal policy excluded people of color from the fruits of postwar prosperity. Meanwhile, federal urban renewal policies forcibly removed African Americans from valuable urban and suburban land. Interstate highways rammed through Black neighborhoods, coinciding with a second wave of gentrification in the city. Displaced residents were often relocated into segregated public housing, further concentrating and entrenching racialized disadvantage. While drained by serial displacement and relentless plunder, Black communities in DC and its suburbs continued to fight for an equitable stake in the region.

A New Deal for White America

Under President Franklin D. Roosevelt (1933–45), the government estab-lished an alphabet soup of new federal agencies to lift the country out of the Great Depression, hiring nearly ten thousand civil servants per year. This "pencil sharpener revolution" grew the DC region by 135 percent between 1930 and 1950.[30] Drained by the Depression, many Americans hoped that the New Deal would provide a fresh start. It did so for some, but not for others.

Housing was a New Deal priority. The 1933 National Industrial Recovery Act and 1937 Housing Act, often referred to as the Wagner-Steagall Act, provided vast federal funds to local housing authorities, including Washington's ADA, to clear dilapidated housing and construct public housing in its place. The establishment of the Home Owners' Loan Corporation in 1933 and a year later the Federal Housing Administration (FHA) guaranteed loans for millions of Americans, many of whom had lost their homes during the Depression. Banks previously required home-owners to put down at least 30 percent of the home value, charged high-interest rates, and extended first mortgages for around five to ten years.

FHA loan guarantees allowed banks to extend mortgages up to thirty years, substantially cut interest rates, and lower down payments to around 10 percent. Between 1934 and 1972, families living in owner-occupied homes rose nationally from 44 to 63 percent.[31]

New Deal policies lent unprecedented federal force to Black dispossession and neighborhood disinvestment. Home Owners' Loan Corporation and later FHA standards for insuring mortgages required lenders to designate non-White and racially mixed neighborhoods as "high risk." They discouraged lending in areas lacking racial covenants, Whites-only schools, or single-family homes. The DC region's 1934 FHA maps graded neighborhoods for "value" and "marketability." Green areas reflected the highest ranking. They included "new high-class subdivisions . . . occupied chiefly by persons in the highest income groups" and "well controlled and restricted by developers." Red areas were the lowest grade and contained "no homogeneity of property design or racial grouping," were "showing effects of negro occupancy," or were "developed especially for negroes or have been left open for negroes to build for themselves." The FHA manual concluded that the only possible future for red areas was that "structures may be razed and new planned subdivisions instituted in their place." A 1940 FHA report for DC clarified that "in communities where there is any possibility of negro infiltration, application for insurance should be rejected."[32] Across the United States, 98 percent of FHA-insured loans issued between 1934 and 1962 went to White buyers. In the DC region, two-thirds went to the region's suburbs.[33]

Redlined areas were more clearly drawn along racial than municipal lines. The FHA green-lined DC neighborhoods west of Rock Creek Park, which were largely White. And while many Silver Spring neighborhoods received similar rankings, a small section of East Silver Spring received the lowest grade, indicating an area of African American settlement. Similar areas could be found in Prince George's and Arlington Counties. More prevalent were suburban areas graded red because, though they were "designated for use of white persons," they were "composed of scattered uncontrolled developments . . . [with] few if any facilities, poor streets, and no homogeneity of property or racial grouping." The FHA noted that these areas were salvageable "if controlled building should ever develop on a sufficiently large scale to warrant rerating."[34]

The full weight of New Deal policies would be felt after World War II. During the war the region became the epicenter of international political and financial institutions, such as the World Bank and defense and security-related industries. Yet again the region's population exploded—nearly doubling between 1950 and 1970. With little housing built during the war, White and Black veterans returned to the most severe housing crises in US history. Many found themselves doubled up in overcrowded, dilapidated urban housing.

To help solve the crises and stimulate the postwar economy, the federal government expanded the FHA loan program. Congress also passed the Servicemen's Readjustment Act of 1944, known as the GI Bill, to assist returning veterans in obtaining jobs, education, and housing. This included low-cost, low-interest Veterans Administration loans that adopted FHA's risk criteria. Unsurprisingly, the loans were issued largely to White veterans who joined a flood of White Washingtonians leaving the city.[35] In a trend that would last until the turn of the twenty-first century, the district's population declined, leaving a majority-Black city by 1957.

The dismantling of Jim Crow protections stoked fear and flight among White Washingtonians. By the early 1950s, racial covenants were legally unenforceable and local municipalities were beginning to desegregate public facilities. A critical breaking point for many White Washingtonians was *Brown v. Board of Education,* the 1954 Supreme Court ruling that found segregated schools unconstitutional. After the ruling DC led the way as the nation's first racially integrated school system, prompting panic among White families. By 1966 African Americans made up 95 percent of DC public school students.[36]

Many suburban schools resisted desegregation for decades. In 1972 Prince George's County initiated bussing under a federal court order to desegregate its schools. Due to ongoing resistance, the order was not lifted until 1998. To avoid integration Prince Edward County, Virginia, closed its schools in 1959. Integration also led to the closure of Black schools, which were often underfunded and overcrowded but served as the cornerstone of many Black suburbs. Despite protests, Montgomery County became the first county in the state to desegregate. In the process they closed all the county's Black schools, dispersing students to previously Whites-only schools with the stipulation that no school could be more than one-third Black. With the process of desegregation declared complete in 1961, forty-six all-White schools in the county remained.[37] And, just as in the city, newly integrated schools led to White flight that resegregated many schools, especially in inner suburbs, where Black and Brown residents were beginning to make inroads.

As legal barriers waned, White communities galvanized around even more aggressive tactics of segregation. White real estate agents steered Black and White homebuyers into already segregated neighborhoods. Neighborhood associations sometimes purchased homes to prevent them from being sold to Black buyers. Real estate agents blockbusted neighborhoods by preying on racist fears of integration and declining property values. Segregation was profitable. By alarming White homeowners about the possibility of African Americans moving next door, they were able to purchase homes at bargain basement prices. They then resold them at higher prices to African Americans and sold new homes to White families. Lacking equitable access to FHA- and Veterans Administration–backed mortgages, African Americans were targeted for predatory real estate schemes, like contract deeds. These agreements charged homebuyers high-interest rates and other fees, had short repayment periods, and did not allow buyers to accumulate home equity. This led Black homeowners to pay thirty to forty percent more than Whites to live in older, overcrowded homes with high rates of foreclosure.[38]

Black and White communities in both the city and suburbs combated these exploitative practices. Chapters of the National Association for the Advancement of Colored People (NAACP) and Congress of Racial Equity (CORE) pushed civil rights and fair housing throughout the Maryland and Virginia suburbs. Groups such as Maryland Fair Housing, Prince George's County Fair Housing, and Northern Virginia Fair Housing partnered with DC-based groups to oppose racist real estate practices. The Action Coordinating Committee to End Segregation in the Suburbs (ACCESS) was founded in 1966 to challenge segregated housing throughout the region. Led by longtime Student Nonviolent Coordinating Committee (SNCC) organizer Rev. Joseph Charles Jones, the group organized protests at apartment complexes throughout Maryland and Virginia. They also staged a four-day, sixty-four-mile march around the Capital Beltway (I-495) to highlight the "noose of segregation" ringing the city.[39]

White flight, however, was not driven just by exploitative housing practices and fears of racial mixing. The suburbs were flush with opportunity.
New housing and automobile technologies made suburbs more accessible
and affordable. With federally backed mortgages taking on the risk of
default, capital for home building flowed freely, and the scale of development exploded. Mass-produced suburbs, like Levittown, New York,
became standard of the day—starter subdivisions filled with modest
single-family homes, tree-lined streets, and white picket fences. For White
working-class families, the suburbs offered a path to the middle class.
"White" no longer simply implied Anglo-Saxon Protestant. It included
those from different classes, religions, and ethnicities whose common suburban trajectories broke through previous divides, redefining whiteness in
the United States. It bound them together through shared values—the
protection of their racial privilege, private property, and growing wealth
secured through homeownership in exclusive suburbs. They incorporated
to control their land uses and tax dollars, hired their own police forces and
fire departments, and built their own schools and parks. This federally
subsidized project was the makings of an American Dream—one bound
up in myths of White meritocracy, community, and exceptionalism and
upheld by racial exclusion and profiteering.

In what writer James Baldwin famously termed "Negro removal," Black
communities across the United States were targeted for new highway construction, which sped the commute of suburban workers to downtown DC.
The 1944 and 1956 Federal Highway Acts contributed massive federal
funds to create a national interstate system. These acts prompted the
NCPPC, headed by planner and avid segregationist Harland Bartholomew,
along with powerful suburban stakeholders, including shopping center
developer James Rouse, to adopt a regional plan in 1950. The plan called
for a highway network radiating out from DC's core to promote decentrali-
zation. Between 1952 and 1972, thirteen major highways were constructed in the Baltimore-Washington area to serve its growing suburbs,
including the Capital Beltway, which allowed suburbanites to bypass the
city altogether. Many freeways displaced and divided long-standing Black
communities.[40]

Residents across the region revolted against "Negro removal." In the
1960s the Emergency Committee on the Transportation Crisis rallied to

oppose the North Central Freeway, proposed to run from northeast DC to Silver Spring. The freeway would raze as many as four thousand homes, occupied largely by African Americans. Among its leaders were Black Power activist Reginald H. Booker and Takoma Park, Maryland, resident Sammie A. Abbott. This city-suburban coalition pulled on Black Power ideologies and tactics, centering race in their popular slogan: "No White men's roads through Black men's homes." They disrupted public hearings to fight the freeway and advocate that a subway line be built in its place. Their battles were enjoined by the Committee of 100 on the Federal City, a powerful White citizen's group, and the DC Federation of Civic Associations, a coalition of Black neighborhood associations. Together these groups fought decades-long battles that defeated a planned inner-loop Beltway and six other expressways, which would have destroyed as many as two hundred thousand housing units, largely in Black neighborhoods. Regional and national freeway revolts gave rise to new requirements for municipal agencies to consider the social impacts of highways, increase citizen participation, and reallocate funds to public transit. When the Washington Metro began operation in 1976, it was made possible by $875 million in highway funds. The northeast section of the metro's new Red Line would follow the path of the defeated North Central Freeway.[41]

Highways grew the suburbs as regional hubs. White-collar office and industrial parks and sprawling shopping centers sprung up near major interchanges. During the Cold War, federal defense agencies, including the Central Intelligence Agency, Federal Bureau of Investigation Academy, and National Security Agency, relocated from DC to the suburbs because of the perceived nuclear threat of densely clustered downtown agencies.[42] By the end of World War II, Montgomery County was a hub of private defense contracting and federal employment, including the National Institutes of Health and National Naval Medical Center. In 1959 about a third of the county's workforce were employed by the federal government. Wooed by tax breaks and public infrastructure investments, private companies followed closely behind, including research and development companies like IBM and General Electric, that expanded rapidly in the postwar period.[43]

Vast public subsidies underwriting White urban residential and commercial flight boosted development in popular suburbs like Silver Spring, turning established developers like the Lees and Blairs into "community builders."[44] In 1947 Hecht's, one of two big downtown department stores, opened its first suburban store in the Silver Spring Shopping Center. It became one the largest branches of a major department store outside of an established retail district in the United States. It was not long before Sears, Roebuck and Company and JCPenney closed their DC stores and reopened in Silver Spring. The intersection of Georgia Avenue and Coleville Road, Silver Spring's central crossroads, was flush with new shopping and entertainment options—from upscale clothing stores like Jellef's to the grand Silver Theatre. By 1950 Silver Spring was the second-largest commercial center in the Washington region. "It was unbelievable," recalled former Montgomery County executive Doug Duncan, who visited downtown Silver Spring regularly as a child. "I mean it really was the economic center of the county."[45]

Just east of downtown Silver Spring, in Prince George's County, Langley Park emerged as a more working-class automobile suburb during a brief period of intense suburban multifamily development. In the interwar and immediate postwar years, many low-density apartment complexes were built near the district border to address the housing crisis. But as the FHA and Veterans Administration pivoted to prioritizing single-family homes, suburbanites pushed for more exclusive development. By the late 1950s, many municipalities stopped approving multifamily permits. Development in Langley Park began in the 1940s and by the late 1960s was largely complete. Before roadways and sewer lines arrived, the land was the 540-acre country estate of Frederick and Henrietta McCormick-Goodhart, named after the Goodharts' ancestral home in England. New public investment and skyrocketing postwar housing demand prompted the family to subdivide and sell the property to private developers. Stables and carriage houses turned to modest single-family homes. The lake was filled in, and the family's prized cricket field became low-rise, garden apartment complexes. The polo grounds were converted to a local elementary school.

Touted by developers as "the first completely planned community in Prince George's County" and an ideal setting for young couples and returning veterans, Langley Park blossomed in the postwar boom.[46] Jewish families, previously restricted from many suburbs by racial covenants, found favor in the area's affordability and accessibility to DC and synagogues that had sprung up between Montgomery and Prince George's County. The first families arrived in 1949, after the completion of the 1,542-unit Langley Park Apartments. The rush continued with the opening of six hundred single-story brick ranchers that sold for around $10,000 apiece. The last segment of the community was completed in the early 1960s, as the twenty-five-acre parcel surrounding the McCormick-Goodhart mansion became home to a 400-unit apartment complex. By then the neighborhood was already one of the county's densest and fastest growing, with over five thousand residents—nearly all of whom were White. Langley Park was more modest than many of its Montgomery County neighbors, but with spacious courtyards and curvilinear, tree-lined streets, it still had the air of progress. The $4 million Langley Park Shopping Center, built in the heart of the neighborhood, anchored the new community. At its opening in 1959, it was one of the largest strip malls in the state, with several high-end regional stores, such as Lansburg's Department Store.[47]

A few miles northwest of Langley Park, Wheaton developed as a working-class suburb, particularly popular among returning World War II veterans. At the center of the Montgomery County's postwar housing boom, the community saw farms and fields transform to new shopping centers and modest Cape Cod, ranch, and split-level homes. Viers Mill Village was among the first subdivisions in the United States built with veterans in mind. Starting in 1947, the New York–based Harris Construction Company began mass-producing 1,400 modest twenty-seven-by-twenty-four-foot identical white frame houses on a rolling 330-acre tract, completing as many as ten houses per day. Many took advantage of Veterans Administration loans with 4 percent interest rates to purchase homes that sold for about $8,000 apiece. The median age of new families was twenty-one, with most working in white-collar positions, such as clerks, government bureaucrats, accountants, and teachers. To some the subdivision was an embarrassment. County leaders complained of the homes' shoddy construction, calling them "shacks," "hovels," and "potential slums." But veterans with limited housing options stood in long lines to purchase a home. As in Levittown, these starter homes offered an important foothold. Tony and Dorothy Pasqual moved to Viers Mill Village in 1958 and gradually expanded their modest home to accommodate their family, which grew from five to eleven children, while the house stretched from two to six bed-

Figure 5. A 1978 car show at Wheaton Plaza, which, upon opening, was the largest shopping center in the DC region. Courtesy of Jonathan Orovitz.

rooms. While the neighborhood lacked sidewalks and was accessible only via Georgia Avenue's two-lane road, which residents traversed to commute to DC for work, young families often considered themselves lucky to be able to purchase a piece of the American Dream.[48]

Black veterans were not included in this dream. One resident who grew up in Wheaton in the 1950s recalled, "The only Black people I ever saw were the garbage men." Even then, he noted, some neighbors locked their doors on garbage pickup days, since it was well known that Black people were "natural thieves."[49] With the opening of Wheaton Plaza in 1960, Wheaton's small-town feel began to change, but not its racial exclusions. With five thousand parking spaces and sixty businesses, Wheaton Plaza opened as the sixth-largest shopping center in the nation and the largest in the region. During its first week, more than 411,000 visitors walked through the open-air mall. Outside the Montgomery County NAACP picketed the opening of the popular department store Woodward & Lothrop, noting that African Americans could not enter.[50]

White suburbs displaced and further isolated Black settlements. Denied opportunities to purchase homes in expanding suburbs, many African

Americans continued to migrate to DC. Others left by force. Landlords evicted Black tenants as property became profitable for new subdivisions. Speculators intimidated Black homeowners with threats of violence and cheated them from land claims. Municipal governments denied Black neighborhoods public services, condemned homes for substandard conditions, and acquired properties by eminent domain. Black suburbs that persisted were increasingly disconnected. Nearby White neighborhoods sometimes built walls or fences to delineate an already clear racial divide, qualify for FHA financing, and increase their market value. Such tactics proved profitable. In 1959 the median value of White-owned homes in Montgomery County was four times that of Black homes.[51]

In Bethesda the River Road community established by African Americans after the Civil War vanished by the early 1960s. Located on land unfit for farming and prone to flooding, several dozen families had eked out a living against poor odds. Many left during the Depression. By the 1950s those who held out were engulfed by White subdivisions. After desegregation Montgomery County closed the neighborhood school and dispersed River Road youth among predominantly White schools. County officials later obtained a right-of-way through the neighborhood's historical cemetery to build a new road. Developers acquired the remaining land for a new shopping center. Between 1940 and 1960, Montgomery County's African American population declined from 11 to 4 percent, while the county population grew by more than four times, with nearly all-White newcomers.[52]

Concentrating Racialized Disadvantage

In the 1950s slum clearance turned to urban renewal, and the destruction of Black communities took on a new force and scale. In the district the Redevelopment Act of 1945 shifted control over redevelopment from its public housing agency to the Redevelopment Land Agency (RLA). The Housing Acts of 1949 and 1954 gave RLA and other local redevelopment agencies greater authority and funding to purchase and clear land in areas they deemed "blighted." Redevelopment agencies targeted alley homes and prime downtown land, relocated residents, and assembled parcels they sold at heavily discounted prices to private developers. Unlike slum clearance's more surgical methods, urban renewal imagined a much broader remaking of the city and suburbs.[53]

Office towers, sports stadiums, shopping malls, and other amenities for white-collar suburbanites often replaced cleared land in downtown central business districts. In Foggy Bottom, federal urban renewal funds cleared the way for the John F. Kennedy Center for the Performing Arts, the Watergate Hotel, and expansion of Washington University Hospital. The project also displaced apartments and alley dwellings occupied by African Americans to build higher-end housing. It was among a handful of DC neighborhoods that gentrified in the 1940s and 1950s.[54]

Residents displaced by urban renewal were oftentimes rehoused in public housing. While Progressive Era reformers once imagined public housing as a tool of social uplift, in the postwar era it became a tool to inoculate White communities and facilitate urban renewal. During World War I and World War II, the federal government built segregated public housing for White and Black war workers. By the postwar, however, suburban homeownership was the predominant form of White housing subsidy, and public housing became a tool of Black enclosure. The Housing Act of 1949 revived dormant local public housing programs like that of the district, centralizing control under the National Housing Agency and contributing new federal funds to their construction. Vigorously opposed by White conservatives in Congress, real estate industry lobbyists like the National Association of Real Estate Boards lost the fight against public housing but won the war. Municipalities could use federal dollars to construct public housing but were given few funds for their maintenance. Chronically underfunded, public housing fell into steep decline.[55]

For some White residents, public housing served as pathway to opportunity. For Black Americans it often prompted a spiral of downward mobility. All the Black public housing projects built by the National Capital Housing Authority (NCHA) were located in majority-Black neighborhoods in DC, largely southwest and east of the Anacostia River.[56] Most White suburbs made limited use of federal funds, placing an all-but-official ban on public housing. Only a few White public housing complexes were built, largely on the city's outskirts or in its expanding suburbs. In Silver Spring NCHA administered Fairway Homes, a complex of 238 low-rent homes built for White families during World War II. Set among exclusive subdivisions originally developed by E. Brooke Lee, neighbors filed lawsuits against NCHA for violating the terms of their restrictive covenants. By 1954 the homes were sold off to former residents, veterans, and other White homebuyers who built more "acceptable" suburban homes in their place.[57]

Though rarely built, Black suburban public housing still served the interest of local governments and developers in housing Black families displaced by highway construction and urban renewal in segregated neighborhoods. In 1940 the federal government displaced 225 Black families in Virginia's East Arlington and Queen City neighborhoods to build the Pentagon and Navy Annex, on land desired by White developers for their scenic views and access to public transportation. Homeowners were given only a few weeks' notice and cursory payments. After protesting, families were temporarily housed in government-built trailer camps in the Black neighborhood of Green Valley. Many were later resettled in segregated public housing in the largely Black Nauck and Arlington View neighborhoods.[58]

Urban renewal and concentrated public housing policies took a devastating toll on Black communities in the city and suburbs. In Prince George's County, just a few miles east of Langley Park, African Americans built a thriving community in Lakeland by the 1950s. While initially envisioned by developers as a resort town for White Washingtonians near Lake Artemisia, the area's easy access to the B&O Railroad and the 82 streetcar, which led straight to the heart of Black DC, made Lakeland attractive to African Americans. Enduring attacks on their lives and property, African Americans persisted in purchasing homes from former White residents, who sometimes burned their homes as they fled.[59] Black life thrived in Lakeland with recreational centers, restaurants, social halls, churches, and the area's only African American public high school.

Like so many Black suburbs, however, Lakeland was in a flood zone and repeatedly inundated with water. Labeled a "slum" by many White College Park residents and city officials, Lakelanders challenged such perceptions but supported the city's effort to obtain urban renewal funds to upgrade the neighborhood and address flooding. Plans emerged in 1970 calling for the clearance of two-thirds of the neighborhood's housing and other buildings. The process destroyed local landmarks, shuttered all the

Figure 6. After the City of College Park designated the historically Black community of Lakeland an urban renewal area, plans shuttered all the businesses and displaced about 70 percent of residents. Courtesy of the Lakeland Community Heritage Project.

businesses, and displaced 104 of Lakeland's 150 households. City officials assured residents that they would be fairly compensated and able to return. Neither proved entirely true. Homes were systemically undervalued and city mismanagement, federal bureaucracy, and opposition from White College Park residents led to multiple project delays. As planning stretched on for nearly two decades, developers reduced the number of below-market units and single-family homes. When new housing finally emerged, the bulk of units were apartments for seniors and University of Maryland students. Few former residents returned.[60]

Community resistance sometimes defeated, hampered, or altered urban renewal projects. In Lakeland residents fought both for urban renewal and against displacement. Longtime Lakelander Dervey Lomax served on the College Park City Council and spearheaded its initial urban renewal plan. Flood control was a long overdue civil right, as Black residents were not given the same protections as their White neighbors, residents argued. Several Lakelanders served on the Project Area Committee

(PAC), a group of community leaders that advised the city on its urban renewal plans. While PAC approved the original plans, they protested changes to them, complaining that the council and developers repeatedly ignored their wishes. Protests forced local redevelopment agencies to establish citizen-advisory councils like PAC and, in some cases, stopped or changed urban renewal plans altogether.[61] By 1971 fierce community opposition helped to end the federal program altogether.

Urban renewal and concentrated public housing reinforced the distinction between DC and its suburbs. Black neighborhoods became more isolated and underdeveloped, with discourses of the "dark ghetto" framing DC and other Black-majority cities in apocalyptic terms—a "no man's land" or "urban wilderness" that was hostile and uninhabitable. White suburbs became more disconnected from the city, as they grew from commuter towns to self-sufficient communities and employment, shopping, and entertainment hubs. With few reasons to venture downtown, White suburbanites' antagonism and fear of the city grew. Catalyzed by the publication of *The Negro Family: The Case for National Action,* penned by assistant secretary of labor Patrick Moynihan in 1965, urban policy turned toward a focus on the "culture of poverty." Welfare and other policies codified the psychological and behavioral traits many policymakers associated with the "urban underclass," such as crime, laziness, and sexual promiscuity. Stereotypes like the "welfare queen" blamed the victims of racialized policies, especially Black women, deflecting attention from the mechanisms, institutions, and policies at the highest levels that produced and sustained Black disadvantage inside and outside the city.[62] Narratives of pathological inner-city residents, however, erased the realities of the many Black and Brown communities struggling against the same forces in suburbia.

CHOCOLATE CITY, MOCHA SUBURBS

On a balmy DC evening, news hit that Dr. Martin Luther King Jr. had been shot and killed in a Memphis hotel. Within hours angry protesters took to the streets, calling out the hypocrisy of the White establishment and conditions of Black America. Black leaders called for calm. But tensions had been building over several hot summers and were not easily contained. Frustrated residents set fire to the city and looted commercial corridors. Over thirteen thousand federal troops occupied DC streets, shooting tear gas and rubber bullets at crowds. After nearly two weeks, 13 people were dead, hundreds injured, and 7,600 arrested. More than 1,500 homes and businesses were damaged or destroyed in one of the nation's largest and most destructive uprisings.[63]

The rebellion was not only a reaction to the murder of the civil rights icon but a visceral response to the oppressive conditions of state-sponsored segregation. Likewise, its effects were felt not only in the smoldering ashes of the city but also in new policies that opened suburbs to the first major wave of Black suburbanites. In search of their own suburban dreams, African Americans left behind a troubled but prideful city that was weathering a third wave of gentrification. They were joined by a rush of new immigrants, who largely settled in the suburbs, reshaping the Black-White region.

Chocolate City's Rise and Fall

The National Advisory Commission on Civil Disorders, known as the Kerner Commission, which reported on the causes of the uprisings, famously explained that "white society is deeply implicated in the ghetto. White institutions created it, white institutions maintain it, and white society condones it." In one of the most widely circulated government reports in US history, the commission called for policies to open suburbs and a shift away from " the traditional publicly built slum-based, high-rise project."[64]

At the congressional hearing on the DC uprisings, Black leaders demanded greater political control over the city, investments in housing and economic development, and a greater voice in redevelopment decisions. The uprisings fueled President Lyndon B. Johnson's War on Poverty, including Model Cities, a neighborhood revitalization program established in response to urban renewal protests. It hastened the passage of the Fair Housing Act (FHA) days after King's death. The FHA banned discrimination by race, religion, national origin, and gender in housing sales and rentals. The Housing and Urban Development Act of 1968 extended homeownership opportunities to low-income families affected by redlining.

Civil rights protests also pushed Congress to act on DC home rule. In 1967 Congress appointed a Black-majority city council and the first Black mayor of a major US city, former Alley Dwelling Authority supervisor Walter Washington. Six years later Congress finally passed a home-rule charter that allowed the district to tax residents, have a nonvoting congressional delegate, and hold its first election in nearly a century. Home rule raised hopes for the Black-majority city. The district adopted the nickname Chocolate City after Parliament's tribute album to DC. In the minds of many, the name symbolized Black Power and excellence in a city with high rates of Black homeownership, Black-owned institutions, and Black leadership.[65]

As Chocolate City developed, forces conspired to undermine it. The state-led and sanctioned introduction of crack cocaine into US cities in the 1980s devastated DC even more so than the uprisings. While illegal guns and customers flooded in from the suburbs, the impact fell on the city. Open-air drug and prostitution markets could be found throughout DC. Violent crime spiked as street crews fought bloody turf wars. By 1990 DC had more homicides per capita than any city in the country, earning it infamous titles like "murder capital" and "Dodge City." Residents left, housing prices plummeted, vacancies soared, and schools declined.[66] DC became the political staging ground for President Ronald Reagan's War on Drugs and the epicenter of its hard-hitting policies that ushered in the era of mass incarceration. As DC experienced what Tanya Golash-Boza calls "carceral investment," federal cuts for social welfare, housing, and other urban programs also left the city. DC's Black-led government became a punching bag for Congress, which questioned the city's ability to govern itself and hamstrung leaders' ability to do so.[67]

These challenges stalled but did stop gentrification. In the late 1960s and 1970s, developers targeted investment in established middle-class neighborhoods near the central business district—DC's so-called fertile crescent, including Capitol Hill, DuPont Circle, and Adams Morgan. Enticed by record low prices, speculators flipped houses and converted old apartment buildings and rooming houses into condominiums, displacing low-income tenants. Evictions and homelessness spiked citywide. Seeking to salve the city's fiscal crises, Mayor Marion Barry aggressively courted downtown redevelopment, which boomed in the late 1970s and early 1980s.[68]

A new generation of activists rallied against displacement. The *Washington Post* declared 1978 the year of the "tenant's revolt," with a surge of protests opposing the "Georgetownization" of DC neighborhoods.[69] These efforts pressured the city council to pass some of the nation's strongest anti-displacement legislation that residents used to remain in place. Over the next decade, this included caps on annual residential rental increases, or rent control, and right of first refusal, which gave tenants the opportunity to purchase their units if the property was being sold or converted to another use. DC adopted new restrictions on condominium conversions, increased tenants' power to approve conversions, and required landlords to assist displaced tenants with relocation. They passed the country's first antiflipping law and created a program to help low-income tenants avoid eviction.[70] While the story of Chocolate City's rise and fall has been well documented, far less has been noted of similar forces taking shape in its suburbs.

Suburban Dream or Nightmare?

DC suburbs organized to combat displacement. Scotland, Maryland, is an African American community founded in 1880 that included residents displaced from the River Road neighborhood. Through the mid-1960s, residents lived in "ramshackle homes of tar paper and tin" that lacked electricity and indoor plumbing. Montgomery County denied Scotland basic services, including trash collection, then condemned homes and purchased the property to build Cabin John Regional Park. By 1964 only ten of its original forty-eight acres and 255 residents remained. When the county threatened to condemn the remaining homes and annex the land, residents fought back. They joined with other county residents to form Save Our Scotland (SOS), a community-led organization that convinced the county to stop purchasing land. They then established Scotland Development Corporation, with a mission to keep land under community control. The Department of Housing and Urban Development awarded the development corporation funds to build one hundred affordable rental and ownership units for existing residents.[71]

Other Black organizations fought segregation in suburbs. In the late 1950s, the Montgomery County chapter of the NAACP staged demonstrations, boycotts, and sit-ins in stores and public facilities that refused to serve African Americans, forcing passage of the county's Open Accommodations Act. The act banned racial discrimination in restaurants, stores, and recreational spaces, two years before the 1964 Civil Rights Act.[72] Demonstrations at an all-White apartment building in Silver Spring contributed to the passage of the county's 1967 Open Housing Act. White real estate groups staunchly resisted, delaying the act's implementation, and requiring county leaders to pass a new fair housing act the following year.[73] Nationally, the FHA was slow to take hold, with groups like the National Association of Real Estate Boards flouting its decree.

Yet African Americans persisted in making inroads into racially exclusive suburbs like Silver Spring. The neighborhood's location on the DC border where African Americans had been pushing for decades made it popular among early pioneers. Due to protests, the formerly exclusive Rosemary Village was purchased by a developer in 1964 who transformed it into the first "deliberately integrated" apartment complex south of the Mason-Dixon Line. By 1976 half of residents in the 415-unit complex were Black.[74] Across Montgomery County the Black population doubled between 1970 and 1980. Black-owned businesses were also moving up the Georgia Avenue corridor, still heavily damaged by the uprisings. Jim Dandy Cleaners, the oldest Black-owned business in Silver Spring, located to the neighborhood in 1972. Run by Samuel Myers, a notary and minister, the popular dry cleaner offered pastoral care as well as other business services for decades.[75]

In Wheaton the arrival of Black families in the late 1960s prompted White residents' fears of crime and drugs they associated with the inner city. Wheaton Woods residents protested a fundraiser for antipoverty projects in DC at a local church. According to the *Washington Post,* "Wheaton Woods was not designed to solve the social problems of the city. It was built to house white people of a certain median income, of a certain median family size. The suburb functions according to design." Still, some Wheaton Woods residents believed integration was going smoothly. "We're pretty much middle-of-the-road around here," remarked one resident. "We don't go to extremes. I guess we're not rich enough." The ability to avoid integration was seemingly a luxury reserved for wealthier suburbs.[76] With an abundance of small single-family homes and apartments, the greater Wheaton area became home to more than half of the Montgomery County's Black population by 1980.[77]

In other working- and middle-class suburbs, Black suburbanization was more heavily fought. In Prince George's County, several former sundown towns near the DC line were home to multiple White supremacist groups in the 1970s. The Ku Klux Klan had branches in Mount Rainier, Brentwood, and Hyattsville. Klan members sat on the Mount Rainier government, served on its police force, and were active in local schools. The paramilitary group, the Minutemen, also had a large presence. Its East Coast spokesperson, Jesse Stephens, lived in Brentwood and was known to sic dogs on Black people walking in the neighborhood and hand out "back to Africa" leaflets to Black kids in schools. He and other White vigilantes patrolled the dividing line between Brentwood and North Brentwood, the first Black incorporated town in Prince George's County, with guns and dogs. In other White suburbs, African Americans were met with mob violence, bombings, and arson well into the 1970s.[78]

Still, Prince George's County was popular among Black suburbanites. To many it was DC's "Ninth Ward"—an extension of Chocolate City in the suburbs, with ready access to the northeast and southeast DC neighborhoods from which many African Americans moved. Some were pushed to leave rough DC neighborhoods. Others were pulled by job opportunities, quality schools, larger and more affordable homes, safer neighborhoods, and Prince George's reputation as a Black middle-class haven. In the 1980s nearly fifty thousand African Americans left DC in what was the first decade of Black population loss in the city's history. A decade later Prince George's County was not only majority Black but also one of the most wealthy and highly educated majority-Black counties in the country.[79]

But much like DC's emergence as a Black mecca, Prince George's County's rise as a hub of Black life prompted rapid White flight and disinvestment. Between 1970 and 1990, the county's White population fell by 43 percent, with many moving to exurban counties in Virginia and Maryland.[80] In 1978 the White-dominated county council passed the Tax Reform Initiative by Marylanders (TRIM), restrictions that capped property tax collections and limited property taxes rates to less than 1 percent. The legislation was pushed by White voters who sought to limit funding for increasingly Black public schools and prevent outmigration from the county. The act left the county struggling to invest in public facilities and infrastructure for its growing Black population.[81] The period of so-called inner-ring suburban decline began as White residents hoarded their wealth in farther-out suburbs and disinvested in new areas of Black and Brown settlement.

In Langley Park the White population plummeted to less than half by 1980, and African Americans were in the majority by the end of the next decade. Newcomers included many Caribbean, African, Latinx, and Asian émigrés. Longtime residents balked at "foreigners" dominating the neighborhood and complained of Langley Park's lack of stability, declining sense of community, and increasing crime. "Barely any whites," one resident told the *Washington Post* in 1988. "Blacks, Asians, Spanish and Orientals are moving in. They are a very low grade and illiterate. It's just pitiful." Business owners at the Langley Park Shopping Center, once the pride of the community, complained of idle teens hanging out and break-dancing in front of stores.[82] Former Langley Park resident and scholar Alice Sandosharaj reflected that racist, xenophobic attitudes fueled White flight:

> Families who had been here for [their] whole lives discreetly snuck away; newer families stayed for just a year or two, until they noticed which way the proverbial wind was gusting. There was a family across the street with first graders and [an] inflatable wading pool who, after looking nervously from their porch as two Salvadorian kids approached shoeless and ready for water play, staked Century Twenty-One signs in their yards and got the hell out.[83]

Similar processes of racialized disinvestment and underdevelopment that had devastated DC fueled Langley Park's swiftly declining conditions. As African Americans and immigrants of color moved in, property owners stopped investing in basic maintenance. High-end stores and customers left. By the mid-1970s, county planners found that over a third of Langley Park apartments were poorly maintained, and over two-thirds had at least minor defects. A decade later the iconic Langley Park Shopping Center lost its grocery and department store anchors, which were replaced by a laundromat and stores selling soul and disco albums and liquor.[84]

After private and public disinvestment came crime and drugs. By the late 1980s, Langley Park crews battled over one of the county's busiest drug markets. Kindergarten children, most of whom lived within walking distance to their schools, were bussed to avoid contact with drug dealers. Racialized neighborhood tropes justified the deteriorating conditions as fueled by the people who lived there, not by racialized capital or structural inequality. The *Washington Post* described it as a neighborhood where "apartment dwellers seemed to view the drug trade and its accompanying violence as a given, and the drug dealers could feel that the turf was virtually theirs." Sandosharaj described it as the "ghetto burbs," emphasizing that the term "ghetto" followed poor Black people wherever they went, "since the point of emphasis in the word was more race and class, and less locale." Langley Park's divergence from the "suburban ideal" clearly signaled that she "did not live in an average suburb populated by average suburbanites." Yet similar conditions pervaded many Prince George's County inner suburbs by the 1980s.[85]

African Americans continued to move up and out in search of more stable neighborhoods. Upwardly mobile African Americans left inner suburbs like Langley Park and joined middle- and upper-income African Americans who sometimes leapfrogged to new communities beyond the Beltway. In Prince George's County, developers built planned communities that actively courted Black homebuyers. A string of upscale suburbs emerged from Bowie to Brandywine with large, new single-family homes and lush lawns. By 1990 more African Americans lived in the region's suburbs than in the city.[86]

Remaking the Black-White Region

Long known as a Black-White region, by the 1970s the Washington metropolitan area was more diverse. Compared to industrial cities like Chicago and Cleveland, the region historically had little immigration. During the New Deal and World War II, international organizations and universities drew students and white-collar workers from Central and South America, who alongside diplomats and domestic workers previously made up the bulk of Latinx immigrants. In the 1960s Cubans fleeing Castro's revolution and Dominicans joined Puerto Ricans, Peruvians, and Bolivians who had begun to settle in the region.[87] Chinese Americans were the earliest and largest Asian immigrant group, despite a series of anti-Chinese exclusion laws adopted between 1882 and 1924. Still, by 1970 immigrants accounted for less than 5 percent of the regional population.

The passage of the 1965 Hart-Celler Immigration Act changed the calculus for non-White immigrants by prioritizing family reunification and establishing more equitable quotas from non-European countries, reversing decades of nationally declining immigration rates. During the late 1970s and 1980s, Central Americans fleeing civil wars and deteriorating economic and political conditions in El Salvador, Guatemala, Bolivia, Nicaragua, and elsewhere arrived.[88] Refugees, asylum seekers, and economic migrants also arrived from Southeast Asia, the Middle East, and Africa, including large Vietnamese, Afghani, Iranian, and Ethiopian populations. The 1965 Immigration Act was the first in a series of laws that opened the door for more educated, skilled migrants, many of whom arrived from East and South Asia, particularly China, India, and Korea. By 1990 the DC region was the fifth-most popular immigrant destination in the United States, with nearly four times the foreign-born population it had two decades earlier.[89]

Hemmed in by redlining and other restrictive housing practices, the first waves of migrants typically settled in DC's ethnic enclaves, including Mount Pleasant and Chinatown. But by the 1980s these neighborhoods were hard-hit by gentrification, prompting widespread suburbanization. Many Chinatown residents and businesses suburbanized after the 1968 uprisings. The flow continued in the mid-1970s, as construction of the Gallery Place Metro Station tore up its main street for years and caused many businesses to close. Construction coincided with the building of the Washington Convention Center, which opened in 1983, sparking a wave of high-end development and skyrocketing rents. Within less than two years, nearly a fifth of Chinatown's residents of Asian descent and forty businesses left.[90] In Mount Pleasant, a formerly racially restricted streetcar suburb that transformed into the heart of DC's Latinx community, gentrification began in the late 1970s. As young White bohemians rediscovered stately Victorian homes, Latinx residents clustered in the neighborhood's eastside apartments and were pushed to emerging "edge gateways" in the suburbs.[91]

In 1970 immigrants were already disproportionately suburban, with nearly three-fourths residing in the Maryland and Virginia suburbs. Two decades later the region's suburban immigrant population was eight times larger than that of DC. Popular gateway suburbs had abundant affordable housing, employment, and public transportation. Many also had high-performing schools, robust social services, low crime rates, and established immigrant populations. The suburban counties bordering DC, including Fairfax, Prince George's, and Montgomery, received the bulk of immigration, collectively hosting 65 percent of the region's foreign-born population in 1980. Montgomery County led the way with the region's largest immigrant population, made up mostly of Chinese and Latinx émigrés. As new immigrants took advantage of places carved out by people of color before them and grew diverse ethnoburbs, they entered a divided region.[92] And, while breaking new barriers, they also reinforced long-standing divisions.

Working-class immigrants tended to settle in suburbs pioneered by African Americans—but less often lived alongside them, with many avoiding African American neighborhoods, especially in Prince George's County. African immigrants were those most likely to settle in established Black neighborhoods.[93] Other working-class immigrants, refugees, and asylum seekers from Central and South America, the Caribbean, and Southeast Asia tended to move into older, dense inner suburbs that were inexpensive in part because they were in poor condition.[94]

In contrast, many post-1965 immigrants arriving primarily from East Asia with more skills and education tended to settle in outer suburbs beyond the Beltway and more often in White neighborhoods. Montgomery County's I-270 and Fairfax County's I-66 corridors became popular hubs of high-tech firms and dense clusters of office parks and commercial development that gave rise to DC's "edge cities."[95] Middle-class suburbs such as Annandale, Gaithersburg, and Rockville emerged as employment centers that offered new housing and high-performing schools popular among white-collar Asian immigrants. But they were less residentially concentrated than their working-class counterparts and instead spread out among different communities, maintaining connections through ethnic organizations, institutions, and businesses.[96] Langley Park, Wheaton,

Figure 7. The Asian Town mall marked Asian Americans'
presence in the neighborhood, which is today largely Latinx.
Photo by William J. Hanna. Action Langley Park Archives,
University of Maryland, College Park.

and Silver Spring all emerged as popular destinations for different
working-class and middle-class immigrant groups.

An affordable, mixed-used neighborhood close to the DC line, Langley
Park was a popular first stop for diverse immigrants. It was an "arrival
city" that provided a launching pad to the middle-class.[97] Beginning in the
1970s, South and Southeast Asian immigrants, particularly émigrés from
Vietnam and India, settled in the neighborhood. Langley Park was a place
many worked hard to get to and to leave behind. The child of Indian
immigrants, Sandosharaj recalled that many of her friends and neighbors
"exited Langley Park as soon as their parents were able to wield their
native educations as avenues to second ring suburbs." "Being able to separate from economically undesirable neighborhoods and people is a crucial
aspect of the upward mobility," she reflected. When her father arrived in
the United States in 1974 on a work visa, he stayed with family in a
cramped Langley Park apartment occupied "not by whites as he had
expected but by Blacks, Latinos, Vietnamese and South Indians like himself." To move up and out quickly, he worked two low-wage jobs, often
sleeping standing up.[98] The Asian Town mall marked Asian American's

significant but relatively brief presence in Langley Park, as did the nearby "Indian row," a strip of Indian restaurants, spice shops, and stores selling saris and Bollywood movies.

By the 1980s Asian immigrants were joined by a rush of Caribbean, African, and Latinx migrants, including many from Guatemala and El Salvador who fled civil war and rural poverty—some with documentation, some without. Langley Park changed yet again to reflect this diverse mix. In 1980 Latinx developers completed Plaza Internationale in the heart of the neighborhood, with stores selling Spanish videos and travel services, West Indian records, and Caribbean and African American literature. Day laborers lined the streets alongside fruit vendors and pupusa trucks in what was, by the early 1990s, the only majority Latinx census tract in the region. Langley Park–McCormick Elementary School, once predominantly Black, was largely immigrant and Latinx.[99]

Immigrants in Silver Spring also came in several waves—first from Southeast Asia, then Central America, and later East Africa. By the mid-1980s, diverse clusters of working-class immigrants could be found in older apartment complexes and modest single-family homes in East Silver Spring, sometimes doubling up to afford the rent. Longtime resident Erin Ross told me that when she moved into the neighborhood in 1985, she was one of the few White residents. "There wasn't the same ethnic group anywhere on the block," she recalled. "This was like an incubator for immigrants."[100] In the following decades, the region came to host one of the one of the largest Ethiopian populations in the nation, many of whom settled in the suburbs—shifting the heart of Little Ethiopia from DC's Adams Morgan neighborhood to Alexandria, Virginia, and Silver Spring.[101] While fleeing political oppression, many arrived with high levels of education and English proficiency, attracted by regional employment and educational opportunities, particularly at Howard University. The rush continued due to strong family ties and the emergence of places like Silver Spring, with clusters of Ethiopian-owned restaurants, beauty salons, and grocers. But, like their middle-class peers, Ethiopians' patterns of settlement were heterolocal, focused less on residential proximity and more on hubs of ethnic businesses and immigrant-serving institutions, like Silver Spring's Ethiopian Social Services Center. While Silver Spring remained the heart of the Ethiopian community, Ethiopians made up less than 6 percent of its population in 2000.[102]

Beyond the Beltway Wheaton initially attracted working-class Asian immigrants, particularly Chinese Americans displaced from DC's Chinatown. While the neighborhood was largely White through the 1970s, Chinese American residents and businesses established a small strip of stores and restaurants, which patrons affectionately called "small Chinatown." Like Langley Park, Wheaton became a popular first stop for immigrants, but not often their last. Many first-generation migrants like Ms. Lee saw Wheaton as a launching pad. While she and her husband rented a small apartment in Wheaton, she scoped out locations to launch a hair salon, which she had previously run in Taiwan. Settling on Rockville, where a sizable Chinese community had formed, she opened her business near many friends and former neighbors. After it became established, Ms. Lee joined her friends in Rockville, which gained the reputation among immigrants as the "real Chinatown." There she took pride in being able to "spend a day in Taiwan," enjoying her favorite foods, reading the Chinese newspaper, and going to the Chinese nail salon. Those who stayed in Wheaton tended to be less upwardly mobile, like Mr. Chang, a second-generation immigrant from China's Guangdong Province and former resident of DC Chinatown. Though small, Wheaton's Chinese community thrived on strong connections and its proximity to Rockville. "Most of us are from Guangdong. We are like a big family here," Mr. Chang noted, "Plus we're close enough to Rockville."[103]

By the late 1980s, Latinx Americans also become a major presence in Wheaton, as it adopted another popular nickname, Little Adams Morgan, referencing one of DC's most ethnically diverse neighborhoods. As Latinx Americans left their humble beginnings in suburbs like Langley Park, Wheaton benefited from Montgomery County's reputation as a welcoming community for immigrants. In 2001 the county opened the Charles W. Gilchrist Center for Cultural Diversity in Wheaton to serve immigrants with free English and citizenship classes and housing and health services. By 2000 the neighborhood was over a quarter Latinx, while the county was home to the largest Latinx population in Maryland. Newcomers filled the pews at Wheaton's St. Catherine Laboure Catholic Church for their Spanish-language mass—over one thousand strong.[104]

By the turn of the twenty-first century, the region was no longer clearly divided between Chocolate City and its vanilla suburbs. Prince George's

County was majority African American, and the White population in Montgomery County was in steep decline. Dense and diverse communities had sprouted across the region's suburbs. And while many Black and Brown suburbanites took trips to popular ethnic neighborhoods in DC, they were less dependent on them for work and community. The suburbs started to feel like home. These communities were flush with cultural pride and cautious hope that their more spacious, quiet neighborhoods would be gateways to other opportunities. But many suburbanites of color, particularly the poorer and darker they were, found themselves in aging, isolated, and resource-strapped neighborhoods—what Ruth Wilson Gilmore called "landscapes of disaccumulation."[105] Despite all the progress in desegregating the DC suburbs, most Whites lived in neighborhoods that were more than 80 percent White, and nearly half of African Americans lived in neighborhoods that were at least 80 percent Black.[106] And it seemed that prosperity was not just shifting out; it was also shifting inward to the very places many left behind.

CHOCOLATE CITY MEMOIR

Decades of population loss, capital flight, and federal power plays devasted Chocolate City. By 1995 the city was nearly bankrupt. Congress placed the district under a presidentially appointed fiscal control board that severely restricted its governance powers and ushered in an era of neoliberal economic reforms. To many Black Washingtonians, the board's top-down austerity and control confirmed what they called "The Plan" to disenfranchise African Americans, curb their power, and displace them from the city. The next decades bore out what many feared, as DC went from being referred to as the "murder capital" of the United States to the city with the most "intense" gentrification.[107]

As young White, middle-class residents and investment poured in, DC lost its Chocolate City status. By 2011 African Americans were no longer in the majority. Faced with skyrocketing rents and housing prices, Black Washingtonians further concentrated east of the Anacostia River. Many left the district altogether. But they also leveraged tools built by previous generations of anti-displacement activists and rallied for new policies to stay in place. Meanwhile, the suburbs emerged as the epicenter of racial and ethnic diversity, while also experiencing unprecedented levels of poverty.

The Edge Becomes the Center

Prosperity was a defining feature of the DC suburbs for much of the late twentieth century, while poverty concentrated at its urban core. But, by the early 2000s, wealth flowed in the opposite direction. Termed the "back-to-the-city" movement by some and "urban inversion" or the "new urban renewal" by others, many cities across the United States that had lost populations for decades were growing—and fast. In a period that historians Chris Asch and George D. Musgrove defined as DC's fourth wave of gentrification, investment fell across a broader swath of neighborhoods as capital from around the globe flooded into major cities.[108]

By the early 2000s, the district's population trended upward for the first time since 1950. Compared to established residents, newcomers were Whiter, younger, and more educated, with a higher income. Between 2000 and 2019, DC gained about 134,000 new residents, nearly all between the ages of twenty-five and forty-four. Most were single or couples without children. Adults with a graduate degree rose, as did median family incomes. By the mid-2010s, DC was among the most highly educated and high-income cities in the nation. White Americans ballooned to more than a third of the population, while African Americans fell to less than half.[109] Chocolate City was no more.

Inequality sharpened. Poverty rates declined citywide, but concentrated poverty rose, particularly in neighborhoods east of the Anacostia. There the number of single-parent and female-headed households, families receiving food stamps, unemployment rates, and adults without a high school diploma increased.[110] The gap between high- and low-wage workers rose, and by 2010 the city had a greater income gap than any state in the country. White households' net worth was eighty-one times that of Black households—$284,000 compared to $3,500.[111]

Policymakers courted newcomers. Having weathered a fiscal crisis, district officials took an aggressive probusiness, progrowth stance. Mayor Anthony Williams, the former financial officer for the fiscal control board, balanced the city's budget with a tough-love approach that included pub-lic-private partnerships to reform the city's education and health care sys-tems. In 2003 he declared the goal of attracting one hundred thousand new residents to the city. To make it comfortable for middle-class resi-dents, his administration focused on improving schools, cutting crime, and attracting upscale housing, shops, and amenities.

The timing was good. The nation's housing market was booming and so was the regional economy. After 9/11 the federal government made major investments in defense, intelligence, and information technology. To cap-ture a slice of the new prosperity, district officials seized abandoned build-ings, sold them to developers, and auctioned city-owned properties. They instituted new tax credits for first-time homebuyers, spurred development around transit centers, revitalized commercial areas, assembled parcels for major redevelopment projects, and built a new stadium for the city's first major league baseball team since 1971. In Chinatown they supported the building of the MCI Center, a 20,356-seat sports and entertainment complex, for its basketball and hockey teams. Construction and subse-quent rent spikes forced many of the few remaining Chinese businesses to close, including its last full-service Chinese grocery store.[112]

Mayor Williams's successor, Adrian Fenty, aggressively shuttered underperforming schools, largely in Black and Brown neighborhoods, and replaced them with private charter schools popular among young White families. The city revived dilapidated recreational facilities and installed new bike lanes, dog parks, and a streetcar along H Street. The city's rebirth was not the invisible hand of the market. It was visible state policies and private capital that reaped profits from the urban crises they had helped to create.

Developers and public-private partnerships sold the new DC to young, middle-class residents. Real estate agents rebranded neighborhoods or created entirely new ones. Near Union Station developers built more than three million square feet of office, high-end retail, and luxury condomini-ums in an area formerly characterized by public housing and vacant com-mercial land. Bright banners advertised the new North of Massachusetts (NoMa) neighborhood, one of DC's fastest growing neighborhoods. City-sponsored tours reinforced sanitized, whitewashed narratives about the resilience and cultural contributions of Black Washingtonians but erased the state-sanctioned violence that destabilized and displaced them.[113] As Brandi Summers argues, Blackness was deployed in DC as an "aesthetic infrastructure of gentrification" to control, define, and name urban space for the benefit of White people that made Blackness, but not necessarily Black people, cool.[114]

Those who had witnessed the long arc of disinvestment in Chocolate City often found the pace and scale of change bewildering. Between 2000 and 2010, over twenty-seven thousand new housing units dotted the DC skyline, and another forty-two thousand were planned or under construction two years later. Between 2000 and 2004, over twenty-six thousand housing units converted to condominiums—nearly a fifth of the city's rental units.[115] Housing prices and rents skyrocketed. Between 1995 and 2016, the median sales price for single-family homes in DC grew more than five times, to around $660,000, as the region became one of the most expensive housing markets in the country. Landlords who previously accepted Section 8 housing vouchers stopped renewing leases and took their units out of the program. The waitlist for voucher recipients reached crisis levels. In 2010 the city had less than half the number of low-rent apartments it had a decade earlier, while high-cost units more than tripled. Homelessness more than doubled for families between 2007 and 2014.[116]

Small business and institutional displacement, particularly for long-standing social service and antipoverty organizations, coincided with housing displacement. The closure of many established businesses began as metro stations were built. The opening of the Shaw/U Street station in the early 1990s, following six years of construction, prompted rising taxes and rents that forced many Black-owned businesses to shut their doors. In 2018 Martha's Table, a forty-year-old staple for low-income family services, moved its headquarters from the heart of U Street, east of the Anacostia. Between 2000 and 2015, more than half of the city's low-income tracts gentrified.[117]

The culture and politics that defined Chocolate City was also fading. The city shut down iconic clubs that played hip-hop and go-go, a sound born in DC. Black barbershops, salons, bookstores, and other community-serving businesses were increasingly rare, while yoga studios and expensive gyms popped up in every ward of the city. H Street and U Street transformed from cultural hubs to high-end entertainment and food meccas with crowds of young White professionals gathering on rooftop decks for happy hours and late-night parties.[118] Black churches fought new neighbors over parking for congregants who for decades had streamed in from the suburbs and double-parked on city streets.[119] Dilapidated public spaces received new life, as outdoor music and art venues.

Everyday spaces of public and private life for Black and Brown Washingtonians were policed in new ways. Newcomers complained about residents doing what they had always done—hosting backyard barbeques, hanging out on their porches, and playing basketball and checkers in local parks. They called the police on neighbors and appealed to city leaders about noise, litter, loitering, and property upkeep. A new generation of more conservative, free-market elected officials were open to their calls. Long-term residents often felt disrespected, marginalized, and out of place. They fought for many of the improvements taking place that seemed to be happening at their expense. Even if they could stay, as their families, friends, and beloved businesses left the city, many followed—to Prince George's County or southern states in search of a sense of community and culture increasingly hard to find in the new DC.[120]

Washingtonians did not leave without a fight. Renewed gentrification also reignited anti-displacement activism. Their fights leveraged policy tools and a community organizing capacity built during previous waves of gentrification. Long-standing advocacy groups like Empower DC and One DC were on the frontlines of opposing displacement throughout the city. Organizers helped residents apply the city's right of first refusal, rent control, condo conversion, and antiflipping laws.

Organizers also secured new anti-displacement tools and investments. Though widely criticized for its ineffectiveness, Mayor Williams launched the New Communities Initiative to develop affordable housing with community input and staged development to minimize displacement. His administration also passed the DC Local Rent Supplement Program, allowing tax dollars to subsidize new affordable housing developments. Under Mayor Vincent Gray (2011–15), the city adopted inclusionary zoning, requiring new residential buildings to set aside up to 10 percent of units for low- and moderate-income households. Muriel Bowser, who succeeded Gray, made affordable housing central to her mayoral bid. Between 2016 and 2020, her budget included $100 million in investments for

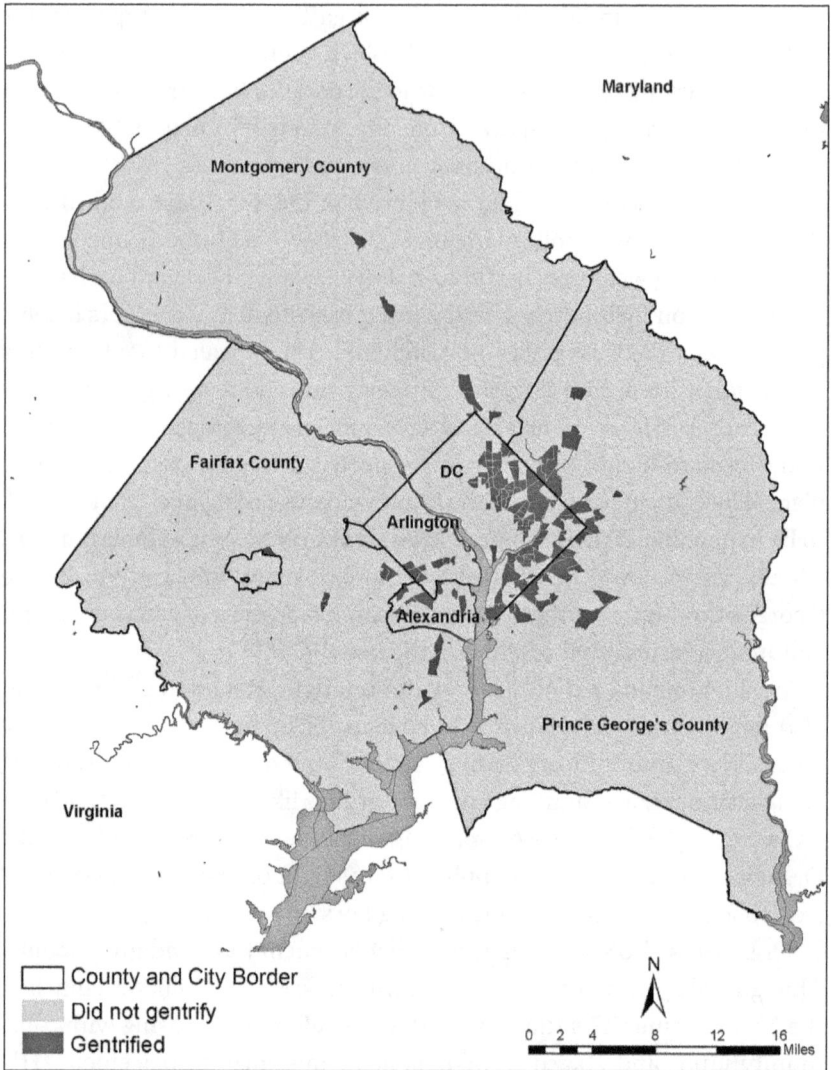

Map 3. Census tracts in DC and surrounding counties that gentrified between 2000 and 2014. Map by Nicholas Finio. US Census Bureau, *2006–2010 Summary File;* US Census Bureau, *2014 ACS 1-Year.*

new affordable housing. Activists argued these efforts fell short and rallied for more funding and to close loopholes in existing programs. In 2019 the National Community Reinvestment Coalition ranked DC as the city with the most intense gentrification in the nation, noting that displaced residents were almost exclusively African American. Less often noted was that the same study and others found that many DC suburbs were either "eligible to gentrify" or had already gentrified.[121]

Edged Out

As White millennials moved to the district, suburban poverty rates soared. By the late 1990s, more people living in households with incomes below the poverty line lived outside of the district than within it. In earlier periods suburban poverty was relatively isolated to a few inner suburbs. But by the start of twenty-first century, poverty was a fixture of many inner and outer suburbs and reached the exurban fringes of the metropolitan area.[122] By 2008 the population of impoverished residents in the DC suburbs was more than double that of DC. Neighborhoods with rates typically associated with concentrated poverty emerged in the region's suburbs for the first time. Struggling suburbs faced high rates of income and educational disparities, poor housing conditions, housing price declines, and major infrastructure needs. These neighborhoods clustered in and near established Black and Brown suburbs, especially Prince George's County. As banks targeted Black homebuyers for predatory loans, the county became the epicenter of the region's foreclosure crises during the Great Recession.[123]

Rising suburban poverty coincided with unprecedented suburban racial and ethnic diversity. Immigration continued to surge, with foreign-born residents accounting for nearly one in five regional residents by 2010. Nearly all newcomers settled in the suburbs.[124] Working-class immigrants were also moving farther out, making headway in outer suburbs that had not previously seen much immigration, though not without a struggle. As housing prices boomed in the district, exurban Prince William County became a haven of affordability. There the Latinx population tripled, making it one of the nation's top counties for Latinx growth between 2000 and 2006. Strong nativist backlash followed, with longtime residents complaining about housing code violations, overcrowded schools, and demands on public services, and county leaders launching aggressive police crackdowns on undocumented immigrants. In Herndon and Manassas, Virginia, residents passed restrictions on day-labor centers and housing ordinances that redefined "family" to address overcrowding.[125]

By the end of the first decade of the twenty-first century, the region was more deeply divided than ever. While the suburbs were more diverse, they were increasingly segregated between high-income White and Asian outer suburbs and lower-income Black and Latinx inner suburbs. The region's east-west divide was more starkly defined, not just among neighborhoods within DC but between eastern suburbs in Prince George's County and wealthy western suburbs in Montgomery and Fairfax Counties. Entrenched patterns of race and class had also shifted—with wealth and opportunity moving closer to the region's core and poverty and disadvantage moving toward its edges. The Washington, DC, metropolitan area had become one of the nation's hottest housing markets and most rapidly growing regions. And while DC had taken center stage in debates over gentrification and displacement, many suburban municipalities were busy setting the stage for what I call a *back-to-the-suburbs* movement. In some suburbs it had already begun.

.   .   .   .   .

In the mid-1990s the DC region was a bit of a mystery to me. But by the early 2000s, it was home. Having met and married a native Washingtonian, I was introduced to different sides of Chocolate City. Over the years I had come to enjoy go-go music and look forward to our late-night trips to the Chinese carryout and hole-in-the-wall Caribbean and soul food restaurants. Living just a few blocks from Howard University, I often strolled down Georgia Avenue to check in on my favorite independent Black-owned bookstores, herbal and medicine shops, and vegan restaurants.

After a few years spent outside the region, I returned with my family in the early 2010s to a city that was nearly unrecognizable. In our old neighborhood, the El Salvadoran couple next door had moved with their three children to Langley Park. The Black elder two doors down, who swept the block every morning and kept us abreast on the neighborhood happenings, had moved to North Carolina. The halfway house on the corner, where residents once greeted us every day, had converted into a single-family home. And while its new White residents still hung out on the back porch, they sat silent as we walked by. The plumbing shop across the street had transformed into million-dollar townhomes, blocking our views and the light while complicating an already difficult parking situation. I was pleased that the city finally installed stop signs that I had relentlessly requested and fixed our broken sidewalks and potholed street. It was refreshing to see the house on the corner that stood vacant for years occupied. But many of our favorite late-night eateries were gone, and the new ones were too expensive and, frankly, not as tasty. There were fewer places to listen to live reggae or DJs spinning old-school hip-hop. While we were intent on moving back inside the district and fortunate enough to be able to afford to do so, we also wanted to live as far as we could from downtown neighborhoods we once loved but no longer enjoyed. We settled into a long-standing Black neighborhood near the DC-Maryland border.

The DC metropolitan area changed not only in the short two decades since I first moved there but over the two centuries after it was claimed as the National Capital Region. The district transformed from first and most prominent Chocolate City to one in which African Americans were no longer the majority. The Black-White region became a popular immigrant destination, where diverse migrants broke through some old borders and reinforced others. Increasingly, residents seemed to live in separate worlds divided by race, class, and geography. Pockets of concentrated disadvantage and advantage characterized neighborhoods both in the city and its suburbs.

The long arc of regional redevelopment foreshadowed this new reality. It revealed how patterns of disinvestment followed Black and Brown communities inside and across city lines. It showed how public policymakers at all levels conspired with private developers to manufacture urban crises they later exploited. Time and time again, intentional neighborhood underdevelopment created the conditions that made for profitable reinvestment. Sometimes the scale of redevelopment was limited. At other times entire neighborhoods vanished and reemerged. But it was always orchestrated by those who stood to benefit from its creative destruction—real estate agents, neighborhoods associations, banks, city planners, council members, and congressional leaders. Repeatedly, they positioned Black and Brown neighborhoods as expendable, exploitable, and replaceable.

Just as dependable was opposition to racialized neighborhood plunder. In every period of gentrification across the region, marginalized communities in the city and suburbs fought back. They protested, filed lawsuits, and appealed to municipal leaders. They became mayors and county council members. They started civic associations, block groups, tenant associations, real estate firms, lending institutions, and community development corporations. They fought for a right to stay put, to return, and to control development decisions.

This history provides the critical context for understanding the forces at work in contemporary suburban redevelopment battles. Black and Brown communities fought long and hard to access the suburbs. As they moved in, their White peers and businesses dependably left—draining their tax base, amenities, and the promise these places once held. This all-too familiar pattern of disinvestment framed their understandings of what came next. Multiple waves of gentrification and displacement in the Washington region taught communities of color a lot about who benefited and who were harmed in such processes.

The redevelopment history that played out across cities and suburbs also taught communities how to resist. As the latest wave of gentrification swept over the region, communities reliably mobilized. In the Maryland suburbs, the initial spark was lit in Silver Spring. This popular site of early African American and immigrant suburbanization was by the 1990s engaged in large-scale redevelopment. But unlike equitable development battles in DC, Silver Spring advocates did not have sophisticated anti-displacement toolkits, long-standing grassroots groups, or progressive city leaders to rely on. Given their different starting places, their struggle for fair redevelopment was bound to look different. The subsequent chapters reveal the differences as well as striking parallels between city and suburbs and among suburbs in these fights—and what was lost and gained in the process.

3 Trouble on Main Street

In 2013 community elders gathered to honor the seventy-fifth anniversary of the Silver Theatre in downtown Silver Spring. Just outside about ten thousand people converged on the public plaza for an Ethiopian festival that was being broadcast live in Ethiopia. The date is important to Silver Spring's history, Reemberto Rodríguez, a longtime community and county leader explained to me, as we gathered in his office overlooking the plaza the following year. "That is the date when this community celebrated its past and celebrated its future at exactly the same time."[1]

This image of downtown Silver Spring hardly resonated with my mind's eye. When I first arrived in the DC region in the mid-1990s, Silver Spring was my home. Friends, family, and colleagues had warned me against moving into several DC neighborhoods they perceived as dangerous. Instead, I moved in with my cousin, a Howard University medical student, who lived in downtown Silver Spring. The apartment complex was affordable and convenient—a close walk to the metro, restaurants, and shopping. But the vibrant plaza that Rodríguez referenced was a large hole. Throughout the summer I skirted construction barrels to grab a meal at my favorite Chinese carryout and shop in one of several discount stores in City Place Mall—all the while wondering what could possibly fill the large

Figure 8. Downtown Silver Spring in 2016, with redevelopment still underway. Photo by the author.

crater at the center of this suburban downtown. To my surprise, over the next several decades, that hole transformed into the centerpiece of one of the most expansive examples of suburban redevelopment in the DC region.

Downtown Silver Spring is part of the vast unincorporated area of greater Silver Spring in Montgomery County that claims the title of one of Maryland's largest "cities." When most locals refer to Silver Spring, however, they picture downtown—a dense and diverse mixed-use area abutting DC's northeast border. Their mental map turns to the 265-acre Silver Spring Central Business District (CBD), which includes nearly two million square feet of retail stores, restaurants, offices, and entertainment complexes. They imagine not a suburb but a city with a vibrant daytime and nighttime economy—a packed plaza and pedestrian street, surrounded by civic buildings, a mix of upscale and discount retailers, a weekly farmers' market, and year-round cultural and community festivals. Silver Spring is a transportation hub, served by the MARC train, a metro line, and the B&O Railroad. Georgia Avenue, downtown's main street, extends north to the Pennsylvania border.

In many ways Silver Spring appears to be the model of a thriving suburban downtown. It includes one of the most diverse populations of any community in the nation, in which two-thirds of residents are non-White and more than one-third hail from outside of the United States. Residents are relatively prosperous and educated, with nearly one-third of adults holding advanced degrees and household median incomes well above the region (see Table 1).

County leaders often paint this rosy picture of Silver Spring to tout the success of county-led redevelopment. But the image belies the many struggles that went into its making and remaking. The previous chapter highlighted how downtown Silver Spring was built on racial exclusion—from its history as a retreat for wealthy White Washingtonians fleeing the city's unhealthy conditions to its development as a racially exclusive, middle-class haven. This chapter picks up where the last left off. As Silver Spring transformed from the downtown of DC's northern suburbs through what many associate with its decline and rebirth, it probes the battles won and lost in more than four decades of debates over its future.

By the late 1980s, Silver Spring had transformed from a vibrant suburban downtown for a growing population of middle-class Whites to what many long-term residents and county leaders characterized as its decline. The latter corresponded with the settlement of African Americans and new immigrants that fueled White flight and commercial disinvestment. Narratives of decline and decay prefaced the county's battle cry to clean up downtown and make it safe for new residents. The narratives justified massive public investments, new redevelopment policies, and the county's cursory but costly denial of their impacts on immigrants, residents of color, and small businesses.

Silver Spring's redevelopment story echoes a familiar tale of structured decline in US cities. Particularly after World War II, urban decline reflected how White Americans viewed Black and Brown neighborhoods and rendered reasonable development policies that shifted resources away from them—or wiped them away altogether. Discursive violence prefaced racialized violence. By labeling neighborhoods as "slums," "blighted," and "vacant," planners and other government officials applied seemingly race-neutral language to a host of policies that were racist in both their intent and impact. As evidenced in Chapter 2, such terms defended the state-led stripping of assets, economic abandonment, and forced removals. It justified the infusion of private and public capital on brutally cleared land.

Table 1 Demographic and housing data for Silver Spring Central Business District (CBD) and Census Designated Place (CDP), 1970–2019

	1970		1980		1990		2000		2010		2019	
	CBD	CDP	CBD	CDP	CBD	CDP	CBD	CDP	CBD	CDP	CBD	CDP
Population	15,550		13,783	72,893	13,506	76,046	16,042	76,540	16,958	70,049	22,979	81,773
Race, ethnicity, and immigration												
White (%)	92		54	72	34	60	33	39	41	36	41	33
Black (%)	7		32	17	34	22	42	27	36	27	35	28
Hispanic or Latinx (%)[1]	5		8	6	24	13	14	22	11	28	12	28
Asian (%)	—		4	4	7	5	7	8	8	7	6	7
Other (%)[2]	0		0	1	1	1	4	4	4	3	5	4
Foreign-born (%)	39		28	18	32	24	33	35	27	37	29	37
Income												
Adjusted median household income[3]	$88,302		$49,801	$73,496	$59,385	$84,557	$62,957	$79,507	$71,829	$79,810	$68,335	$83,782
Families in poverty (%)	6		9	7	7	4	6	6	12	8	4	7

Education											
High school or less (%)	62	50	42	35	30	25	32	19	32	17	29
College (%)[4]	37	49	58	44	46	50	44	46	41	45	40
Advanced degrees (%)	—	—	—	21	24	24	24	35	27	38	31
Housing											
Total housing units	7,745	7,901	31,968	7,961	33,494	8,477	31,208	9,753	29,729	12,767	33,396
Renter occupied (%)	67	94	48	83	47	86	56	81	59	84	64
Renters' cost burden (%)[5]	27	23	24	46	44	35	25	46	47	47	49

SOURCES: US Census Bureau, *Census 1970*; US Census Bureau, *Population and Housing, 1980*; US Census Bureau, *Population and Housing, 1990*; US Census Bureau, *2000 Census of Population*; US Census Bureau, *2006–2010 Summary File*; US Census Bureau, *2019 ACS 1-Year*.

NOTE: The Silver Spring Central Business District is defined as Census Tracts 7024.02, 7025.00, 7026.01, and 7026.02.

[1] The "Hispanic or Latinx" group was double-counted in 1970. All other groups are Non-Hispanic from 1980 onward.

[2] "Other" consists of American Indian, Alaska Native, Native Hawaiian, other Pacific Islander, some other race alone, and two or more races. The year 1970 includes Asian groups.

[3] All years have been indexed to 2019 values.

[4] The years 1970 to 1980 include advanced degrees.

[5] The cost burden from 1970 to 1980 is more than 35 percent of income spent on rent; from 1990 to 2019, it is more than 30 percent.

From office towers to securitized public spaces, revitalized downtown spaces prioritized the comfort, security, and convenience of White, middle-class consumers, residents, and workers.[2]

Silver Spring shows how recent suburban redevelopment and retrofit practices have adapted these narratives and their attendant strategies. It affirms the continued stronghold of White civic and business elites—its old-school suburban activists—over redevelopment processes, as suburbia's traditional power structure rallied to control downtown's future. In Silver Spring this group largely represented established White homeowners, neighborhood associations, and chambers of commerce that historically opposed racial and class integration. Many revamped into no- and slow-growth coalitions that opposed density and traffic in the name of preserving their suburban way of life, while also relentlessly expanding their tax base. This suburban double movement, which geographer Jamie Peck calls "urban subgovernance," represents a mode of suburban self-rule that imposes regimes of deregulated, decentralized, and privatist development. These regimes mark a turn away from, rather than toward, the urban and marginalized communities associated with it, he argues.[3]

In tracing the roots of the equitable development movement in the Maryland suburbs, this chapter also shows the emergence of a new group of community advocates who fought these narratives of decline and visions of redevelopment that happened at their expense. Their emergence marked the rise of a new school of suburban activists whose aims were more progressive. Rather than freeze Silver Spring in the past or protect elite economic interests, new-school activists fought for a more inclusive downtown. These activists, some of whom would come to sit on redevelopment committees and boards, worked to make downtown Silver Spring safe, comfortable, and welcoming for residents from different walks of life. This departure from the stereotypical suburban growth politics shows the rise of more progressive voices within the pseudoprivatized suburban governance apparatuses that dominate redevelopment discourses.[4]

At the same time, it exposed their limits. Still largely led by White middle-class homeowners, this new cadre of community leaders failed to connect to the diverse community of Silver Spring or achieve a level of political influence on par with their old-school counterparts. This was particularly evident in the case of IMPACT Silver Spring, a group founded to give voice to underrepresented groups in downtown redevelopment. IMPACT's lack of community connections and funding challenged the fledgling organization to slow or divert the process. While the county eventually provided some relief, its efforts were too little and too late to stem the tide of residential and commercial displacement. Silver Spring's redevelopment fight underscores the hard lessons learned by early advocates about the grassroots capacity, political support, and policy tools needed to achieve their aims. With little existing infrastructure to rely on, they built Silver Spring's equitable development ship as it was setting sail.

NARRATIVES OF SUBURBAN DECLINE

The steady movement of African Americans and diverse immigrants into downtown Silver Spring after 1968 led many established White residents to leave. Commercial businesses also left, leading to downtown's so-called period of decline. Clustered in working-class apartments in South Silver Spring, a diverse mix of new suburbanites kept downtown afloat. They started businesses, played on the vacant sidewalks, and built a strong sense of community. But this robust social life was hardly visible to Silver Spring's White civic and business elite. Instead, their presence provoked discomfort and fear among established community leaders that enflamed urgent calls to redevelop downtown and reestablish its rightful place in the county.

As communities of color moved in, Whites left or avoided downtown. Between 1970 and 1990, as the African American population rose from 7 to 34 percent, and Latinx Americans from 5 to 24 percent, the White population plummeted from 92 to 34 percent (see Table 1). Former White Silver Spring residents often purchased homes in Mid- and Up-County neighborhoods, like Damascus and Olney, that they considered more desirable. "That's where Olney came from," explained Gus Bauman, a land-use attorney and former Montgomery County Planning Board chair, "A lot of people in Olney fled Silver Spring." Mr. Bauman and I sat tucked in a quiet corner of Panera in the iconic Silver Spring Shopping Center. Just outside a glittering sign welcomed visitors to downtown. The restaurant was relatively new, but its history was not lost on Bauman, author of

"The Silver Spring War and Rebirth," a brief timeline that anchored me in Silver Spring's rich past, including White flight.[5]

While Bauman associated White flight with the deteriorating conditions of downtown, historian David Rotenstein was far more critical of its social causes. "It was a continual history of succession of folks fleeing Washington and ultimately folks fleeing Silver Spring because increasing numbers of African Americans and later new immigrants [they] perceived as unwanted neighbors," he argued. A native Floridian, David worked for nearly three decades in the public sector as an independent historian after getting his PhD. In the early 2000s, he settled near downtown Silver Spring and later served two terms on the Montgomery County Historic Preservation Commission. Having read his blog, *Historian for Hire*, in which he details the long and sordid history of Silver Spring's racial exclusion, I was excited to talk. When we met at my favorite coffee shop in downtown, one of several independent, Ethiopian-owned shops I spent time in during my research, I was surprised by his calm demeanor, which hardly matched the fierce tone of his writing.[6]

Both David and Mr. Bauman agreed that the most dramatic shifts were in the apartments clustered in South Silver Spring, while middle-class neighborhoods in North Silver Spring like Woodside experienced less churn. South Silver Spring remained among the most affordable neighborhoods in downtown, despites decades-old plans to restrict affordable housing and bring in higher-income residents. The same plans sought to combat White flight in the middle-class areas of North Silver Spring.[7]

The few White residents who moved to Silver Spring during the period, like Jerry McCoy, tended to be steered into North Silver Spring. Mr. McCoy recalled that when he and his wife moved from DC in 1991, they were immediately attracted to the eclectic homes in East Silver Spring on the city's south side, even though the neighborhood "had a bad reputation." His real estate agent, however, refuted his decision, arguing, *"You're more Woodside Park people."* Declining the agent's advice, they settled into a small, early twentieth-century bungalow in East Silver Spring that Mr. McCoy lovingly restored. A self-taught history buff, his house, where we met, was plastered with memorabilia of all kinds. It included old pictures of downtown Silver Spring he collected while writing a book with the Silver Spring Historical Society, for which he was founder and president.

Surprisingly, Mr. McCoy had chosen the house not for its architecture but largely for its urban conveniences. With the metro and grocery store just blocks away, it reminded him of the DC neighborhood that he had reluctantly left.[8]

Few White families followed the McCoys. They headed instead to farther-out suburbs, as did businesses. Following the success of the Silver Spring Shopping Center, other major suburban shopping centers opened in farther-out suburbs, including Wheaton Plaza in 1960.[9] New malls lured stores and customers away with affordable rents, new amenities, and parking, as the county's wealth continued to shift to new "favored quarters" west and north.[10] Throughout the 1970s many of downtown Silver Spring's established retailers, including JCPenney, People's Drugs, Sears, Hahn's Shoes, and Jellef's, closed their doors. Hecht's was among the last holdouts but moved to Wheaton Plaza in 1987. "Retailers were running from Silver Spring," recalled Robert Wulff, a developer who worked in downtown during the 1990s. By the time we met, Mr. Wulff had left his thirty-five-year tenure as an executive in some of the region's largest real estate firms, including the Peterson Companies, a major developer in downtown Silver Spring. He traded his fast-paced life for a quieter job as director for George Mason University's Center for Real Estate, which seemed to suit him. Like Gus Bauman, Wulff saw White commercial flight as a reasonable response to downtown's deteriorating conditions.[11]

Less obvious to county officials and developers was their role in the process. Under the tight control of developer-politicians like the Lees and the Blairs, machine growth politics promoting sprawl dominated the county's land-use and planning policies through the mid-twentieth century. After World War II, control shifted to merchant builders and land-use attorneys, who led a second-generation growth machine. It was not until the mid-1960s that a more progressive planning regime accountable to local constituents emerged, adopting many of the county's antisprawl policies, including its well-known 1969 "General Plan: On Wedges and Corridors." The plan directed growth to existing urban areas of the county and protected open space and farmland, becoming a touchstone for land-use decisions thereafter. But while it contained sprawl that enabled White flight, it also redirected growth into places like downtown Silver Spring.[12]

Signs of fiscal stress, evident in the 1970s and 1980s, reached their peak by 2000.[13] Exacerbated by recessions in the 1980s and 1990s, 220 businesses left downtown between 1988 and 1996, including major employers like Bell Atlantic and Citibank. Office-vacancy rates rose by nearly 40 percent, and nearly a fourth of storefronts were vacant.[14] Cycles of disinvestment followed. As vacancies increased, customers decreased, and business turnover rates went up. Major retailers refused to locate in downtown. While investors continued to purchase apartment buildings, few maintained or upgraded them. "It was disinvestment, vacancies, companies fleeing the downtown, stores fleeing the downtown. Was hardly a bank here. All the banks were gone, it was unbelievable," Gus Bauman recounted, pointing across the street at the Lee Building, named for the racist real estate scion E. Brooke Lee, which housed a bank. The only businesses that survived or opened during the period Bauman described as "just hanging on places."[15]

White residents' and county leaders' perceptions of decline and their discomfort with it contributed to downtown's disinvestment and instability. Even though Jerry McCoy was drawn to his East Silver Spring home for its amenities, he was unhappy with the downtown he encountered in the early 1990s: "There was nothing going on. On weekends you could be out on Georgia Avenue and . . . I always give the description that you could shoot a cannonball up and down Georgia Avenue and not hit anything. Completely dead. Because there was nothing down there to go to." Mr. McCoy's comments dismissed the nearly one hundred dry cleaners, tailors, ethnic markets, restaurants, convenience stores, beauty salons, barbershops, and other small businesses that remained in downtown during the period. After Hecht's departure an expanded Silver Spring Shopping Center reopened in 1992 as City Place Mall, filled with many discount retailers and small businesses I once frequented. When I asked Mr. McCoy if the loss of these businesses concerned him, he responded, "That wasn't on my radar of mourning the loss of these small, independent businesses because there really wasn't all that many of them I patronized."[16] For many White residents, small businesses were neither desirable nor entirely visible in their perception of downtown. "While my white friends complained that there was 'nothing' in downtown Silver Spring, few storefronts there were empty," Paul Boudreaux Jr., a longtime resident, reflected of the period, noting the particularly large number of restaurants and stores catering to new immigrants.[17]

Multiple county and community leaders repeated Mr. McCoy's cannonball metaphor to me or some version of it. "The streets were so empty that you had the feeling you could fire a cannon down there and no one and nobody would hear it, much less be hurt by it," suggested Melvin Tull Jr., former Silver Spring Enterprise Zone manager. Ever the salesperson for downtown, a title he readily embraced, Mr. Tull was quick to point out that the cannonball was a concept, not real. Still, sitting in a new popular chain restaurant in the town center, he beamed with pride at how far downtown had come.[18] Others described Silver Spring as a "ghost town," "a no-man's land" and "a graveyard." Blair Lee, grandson of E. Brooke Lee and president of Lee Development Group, a company started by his grandfather in 1930 that remained one of downtown's most prominent developers, called it "Beirut." Lee's epithet recalled names used to describe DC neighborhoods during the height of the crack epidemic.[19] Former chair of the county's planning board, Royce Hanson, referred to the 1980s and 1990s as downtown's "see through era." Former Montgomery County executive Doug Duncan described it as a "pit." "Silver Spring was a bunch of vacant, boarded-up store fronts and no good stores there. You didn't want to be there," he told me. "When you left work, you went to your car and got out of there as fast as you could." "Downtown was dead in the water," Robert Wulff stated conclusively.[20] As in other gentrifying neighborhoods, narratives of Silver Spring's vacancy and abandonment justified the adoption of aggressive policies to fill downtown and reinforced neocolonial frontier myths held by many newcomers that they somehow discovered a community that already existed.[21] "Things were not all that dire in Silver Spring in the 1990s—it just didn't look the way that the movers and shakers in Montgomery County thought that a suburban retail community should look," noted Boudreaux.[22]

Some who reinforced narratives of downtown's decline, vacancy, and blight recognized that the perception was far worse than the reality. Doug Duncan told me that the crime statistics in downtown hardly matched perceptions of crime. "It wasn't necessarily that it was less safe than any other place; it just felt less safe," he projected, "because of the decay." As county executive at the height of Silver Spring's redevelopment, Duncan's views carried great weight. I met Mr. Duncan in early 2015, nearly a decade after he left the post he had served in for three terms. But he had not lost his political ambitions, having recently been defeated by incumbent Ike Leggett in a race to regain his former title. Strident but personable, Duncan appeared ever the preeminent political figure, recalling his time in office while throwing occasional jabs at his rival candidate.[23]

Vacancies were not the only points of reference in the refrain of Silver Spring's decay and disorder—so too was downtown's reputation as an affordable housing "dumping ground." Frankie Blackburn, executive director of the Housing Opportunities Commission (HOC), the county's public housing agency from 1987 to 1993, noted a widespread belief that Silver Spring had numerous public housing units during the period. Yet it only had one, she pointed out—Elizabeth House, a complex that served seniors and the disabled. Even so, the idea that downtown was "inundated with affordable housing," resulted in the county denying HOC and private developers permits to build desperately needed units. Even at HOC many "snooty board members from the west side of the county" didn't believe the resistance she faced in getting affordable housing built in East County. By the time Frankie and I met at her house, a couple blocks away from HOC's headquarters in downtown Silver Spring, her frustration over county politics at the time still visibly upset her.[24]

While political leaders and developers tended to characterize Silver Spring as a wasteland, to others it was a community. People not only lived in downtown during the period; they developed a strong sense of community and attachment to it. Dan Reed was among them. I was familiar with Dan before we met in South Silver Spring. I followed his popular blog, *Just Up the Pike,* about planning politics in eastern Montgomery County. For years I heard his name tossed about during faculty meetings, as one of the "star graduates" of the University of Maryland's School of Architecture, Planning, and Preservation. But I didn't know much about his background, which turned out to be important to his interests. Charismatic and outgoing, Dan was not shy to tell his story. At the age of three, he moved into a towering apartment complex in the heart of downtown Silver Spring from Prince George's County. His mother, an immigrant from Guyana, was going back to school at the University of Maryland and wanted to be closer to campus. In the early 1990s, she liked that downtown was "nice and quiet," where she could get her work done. Dan sometimes found the quiet a little lonely, he admitted, but not for lack of community. With multiple family members living in the same building, Dan did not have to go far. He also found community beyond his complex: "There were a lot of people who lived here. A lot of kids in my school lived here. There were people around. I had lots of kids to play with and friends and stuff. We would go to the park and see all the people there." While Dan agreed vacancy rates were high, he held a strong attachment to the community, its residents, and its future.[25]

Dan loved growing up in downtown, he would later reflect, where he could grab a bite to eat at the corner store or peek in to watch drafters hard at work at a nearby architectural firm. He took swimming lessons on the rooftop pool, spent countless hours in the park across the street, and learned to interact with adults through regular conversations with Mr. Ali, the lobby agent who remembered everyone's name, and Ms. Theresa, the leasing agent. While he reflected that "downtown Silver Spring was nowhere you wanted to be back then" and that his parents "spent most of their time in Georgian Towers trying to leave Georgian Towers," a complex prone to disrepair and fires, "we couldn't have stayed in Montgomery County without it." It was a launching pad for his family, which had remained in the prosperous county ever since.[26] While Dan embraced the idea of downtown revitalization, what he had in mind seemed different than county leaders and developers during the period—less a clean slate and more of a process that recognized the existing assets and attachments that held Silver Spring's diverse communities together. This was not the Silver Spring that many county and community leaders saw. Once the "shining leader in modern suburban shopping centers," the *Washington Post* declared, it was now just a "string of tacky stores and gray, litter-dotted streets." In the words of Melvin Tull, it had become "the other side of the tracks."[27]

OLD-SCHOOL SUBURBAN ACTIVISM

Through the 1980s and early 1990s, momentum among Silver Spring's civic and business elite to change downtown's image mounted. Eager to respond to community demands and buffer themselves from the financial impacts of decline, the county adopted a heavy-handed approach to redevelopment. But while projects were proposed, they were opposed by Silver Spring's old-school suburban activists, including middle-class homeowners, civic groups, and business leaders. Called to sit on redevelopment steering committees and advisory boards to represent the "voice of the community," old-school activists were a constitutive part of constructing the vision for downtown's future. In Silver Spring they united over plans that retained downtown's historical value, the character of their sylvan middle-class communities, and their sense of safety, comfort, and place within it.[28] Their dominance over the process pushed out residents and small business owners who stood to lose the most from redevelopment. As the period put in place the bones of large-scale redevelopment, it signaled the many roadblocks ahead for marginalized groups to find a voice at the table and a place in the new downtown.

Middle-class homeowners and private commercial interests often hold sway in suburbs, in part because municipal fragmentation insulates suburban conservatism, while popular governance models legitimize their power over land-use decisions. In Maryland suburban governance and planning often takes place at the county level, leading to less political fragmentation and balkanization than in many suburbs. As regional equity scholars have long argued, fragmentation begets an inefficient and inequitable distribution of resources between cities and suburbs and among suburbs.[29] Often considered a pioneer in suburban planning, Montgomery County's growth-management and affordable housing policies, including its famed Wedges and Corridors Plan, Adequate Public Facilities Ordinance, and Moderately Priced Dwelling Unit (MPDU) policies, are a testament to the power of county planning to support social and environmental goals that defy narrow community interests. Silver Spring's contested redevelopment history, however, underscores the limits of its progressive ideals and the power of old-school activists to control local land-use policy. As development proposals make their way across a web of county agencies, the planning board, and county council for approval, organized and powerful groups with an interest in resisting or controlling the direction of change have often gained ground.[30]

The county's efforts to clean up downtown and spur redevelopment began shortly after the arrival of the Silver Spring Metro Station in 1978.

In anticipation of its opening, the county adopted the 1975 CBD sector plan, zoning much of downtown for high-density office and commercial uses. Following the metro's completion, the county upgraded downtown's infrastructure and provided generous tax incentives to entice new businesses. Their efforts had limited success. While some new office and residential developments occurred adjacent to the metro, the circumference of redevelopment was narrow. As Melvin Tull saw it, "The rest of Silver Spring didn't have much reason to be here."[31] Many private developers and companies viewed downtown as too risky or unworthy of major investment.

By the mid-1980s, White middle-class residents who had "stuck it out" were incensed with the condition of downtown. Some expressed concerns about youth and "loiterers" hanging out in downtown spaces, particularly at City Place Mall, which, Frankie Blackburn said, was sometimes pejoratively referred to as the "Black mall."[32] In 1995 a Silver Spring business owner told the *Washington Journal* that Black youth were in part responsible for downtown's deterioration. "You cannot get away from this," he explained. "Too close to the state line. It'll never go away." Silver Spring was "too close to the inner city" both physically and metaphorically, Dan Reed explained. For more than a decade, such comments proliferated at public meetings about redevelopment, blaming Black youth with making residents and visitors "uncomfortable," contributing to crime, and driving downtown's "decline."[33]

Community advocates saw such concerns as an expression of White middle-class anxieties about downtown's changing race and class composition. To some, people of color had become a "problem" or "nuisance" marring downtown's image. Immigrant and minority-owned businesses only exacerbated the county's image problem and were not those that officials wanted occupying prime real estate, David Rotenstein told me.[34] Ruby Rubens, a longtime Silver Spring resident who worked as special assistant to the county executive in the early 1990s, said race was often the subtext, if not the pretext, of many developers and county officials' concerns about various revitalization proposals. She recalled a conversation with a developer, who remarked, "If we get certain kinds of stores in Silver Spring, we're going to attract people from across the border." Similar comments proliferated in conversations about affordable housing, justifying the need for more "upscale" housing in downtown, she reflected.[35]

The anxieties of old-school activists, developers, and county leaders helped to fuel aggressive redevelopment. Under the leadership of county executives Sidney Kramer (1986–90) and Neal Potter (1990–94), the county cleared hurdles to development. In 1986 it selected downtown Silver Spring as an urban district, creating a special taxing area eligible for a host of county-run services, including increased trash pickup, policing, landscaping, lighting, and signage. In 1992 the county designated twenty-nine acres of downtown an urban renewal area, expanding its redevelopment powers, and established a $53 million redevelopment fund. One of the biggest impediments to redevelopment at the time was downtown's fragmented land ownership. To make redevelopment more attractive, the county used its urban renewal authority to purchase parcels, assemble them, and clear the land. Arguing that downtown had reached an "advanced state of deterioration" and that it was "time to stop Silver Spring's downward spiral," the 1993 Silver Spring CBD plan called for new residential and mixed-use development and increased downtown density, particularly near transit.[36]

The Fall of the Silver Triangle

By the late 1980s, large-scale redevelopment seemed possible, if only because county incentives made it more profitable. In 1989 AT&T relocated its federal system offices from downtown DC to Silver Spring, bringing with it nine hundred employees, which cut downtown Silver Spring's office vacancy rate in half—from 30 to 15 percent. Two years prior Lloyd Moore, the developer of several Silver Spring properties, announced plans for a major downtown anchor, the Silver Triangle. The $250 million, four-hundred-thousand-square-foot complex would span Georgia Avenue and include an upscale hotel, shops, apartments, office space, and an enclosed mall with two major department store anchors. As one observer put it, the new vision for downtown was that of a "super block" for affluent consumers.[37]

While eager for redevelopment, many of Silver Spring's old-school activists fiercely opposed the project. "When the plan was released, all hell broke loose," recalled Gus Bauman, with the fiery frankness I had come to expect. "The press called it the 'Silver Spring War,' and it was a war."[38] Letters flooded the county executive's office, community meetings stretched on well beyond their allotted times, and new neighborhood coalitions took shape. Opponents' primary issues focused on historic preservation and traffic. The project would raze several art deco buildings, including the Silver Spring Shopping Center, Silver Theatre, and Tastee Diner. Preservationists rallied to save these buildings, giving rise to new groups, like the Friends of the Silver Theatre, that threatened to sue the county over their destruction. Among its prime opponents was the Allied Civic Group (ACG), a coalition of civic associations in southeast Montgomery County that included several leaders with connections to powerful preservation groups. ACG's three-term president was indicted for allegedly bribing a council member with ties to the organization to vote against the development plans. Many association members were explicitly racist and antidevelopment, one former representative from ACG explained to me—and the two issues went hand in hand.[39] Another fierce foe, the Silver Spring–Takoma Traffic Coalition (SSTC, formerly known as Citizens to Preserve Old Silver Spring), was composed of twenty-two civic associations that led several antidevelopment campaigns. SSTC forced a referendum to prevent the county's construction of a new downtown parking garage and sued the county for upzoning the CBD. In one lawsuit, filed against the Montgomery County Planning Board, the coalition argued that the board's approval was "erroneous, arbitrary and unlawful." In another they challenged the council's decision to close side streets for the project under the county's adequate public facilities ordinance.[40] These powerful groups were overwhelmingly composed of White middle-class homeowners with a history of opposing development. They had been engaged in county politics for decades and were often called on by political leaders to represent *the* community voice.[41] Old-school activists were not so much antidevelopment as they were interested in controlling the direction of development. The Friends of the Silver Theatre, for instance, described themselves as "residents concerned with the deterioration of the Silver Spring Central Business District."[42]

While a bitterly divided county council passed the Silver Triangle plans by a four-to-one vote in 1988, community opposition led to delays in the permitting process and various concessions. Some claimed that it also led to the unseating of the county executive and several council members.[43]

Figure 9. Tastee Diner, which once excluded Black diners, moved with county support from its original location to a new site in downtown Silver Spring in 2000 to accommodate redevelopment. Photo by Brian Lewis.

The county adopted new traffic plans and regulations that gave neighborhood groups greater control, adjusted growth limits, and worked with the developer to scale back plans. They increased public services and agreed to build a performing arts center; to relocate and expand the Tastee Diner, which once excluded Black diners; and to preserve several art deco buildings, including the Silver Theatre. Historic and neighborhood preservation were priorities of the 1993 CBD plan.

Though not as vocal nor organized as Silver Spring's old-school activists, small business owners, renters, and other vulnerable groups were concerned that new development would have little space for them. By the late 1980s, some property owners were refusing to extend long-term leases to small businesses, forcing some to close their doors. Younger White professionals had also begun moving into downtown, spurring speculation about gentrification. "There are some older people who have lived here for years and years who are being displaced by a lot of younger people," one Silver Spring resident noted during the period. "The people

moving into our neighborhood are almost exclusively young, white professional couples, average age about 30, with one child."[44] Little public
debate focused on these impacts. Instead, it continued to center on the
concerns of old-school activists, who were engulfed in yet another battle
over downtown.

Blair Battles and the Death of the American Dream

The Silver Triangle project enflamed the ongoing war over downtown—a
war that by the early 1990s had become entangled with its schools. I
heard over and over from community leaders that I couldn't understand
the politics of downtown without understanding the history of Blair High
School. Blair was then located in downtown. One of the most populated
high schools in Montgomery County, it was located on one of its smallest
sites and in need of major repair. Blair was also among the county's most
diverse high schools, attended largely by students of color. Parents rallied
for a new school. But in 1993 the county council denied their request,
even as it had recently approved new schools in Bethesda and other
wealthier areas. A diverse coalition of neighborhood and business groups,
labor unions, and civil rights organizations came together to fight for a
new Blair High, rallying around a cry for equitable investments across the
county. "The moment was exploding," Laura Steinberg, former cochair of
Citizens for a Better Blair, the coalition's lead organization, told me. "The
future change of demographics in the county as a whole was showing up
in Silver Spring." The coalition included a host of new-school suburban
activists whose aims were more progressive but whose power over redevelopment had not yet been established. Many wanted redevelopment but
also for their already diverse community to remain so and equitable
investments in educational resources and otherwise.[45]

While attracting a more diverse coalition of interests, the battle for a
new Blair highlighted the unequal power—both within the coalition and
beyond it—among those fighting for the future of downtown. White
middle-class residents led the charge for a new Blair and the fight for
equitable redevelopment in Silver Spring. "The bulk of the White middle
class in all these surrounding neighborhoods, they stayed and they fought.
They fought for a new downtown, and they fought for a new Blair High

School. These were intertwined battles," Gus Bauman explained to me. In 1994 the county finally conceded, agreeing to build a new high school. But not everyone saw this as a victory. Ms. Steinberg explained that the county's decision rested largely on its desire to spur redevelopment rather than address educational disparities. Little in the decision also appeared to be about keeping Silver Spring's newfound diversity intact. "[The county] needed to invest in the schools so that you could, again, continue to attract, first maintain and then attract, a stable middle-class community," she told me. At the time Ms. Steinberg was just getting her start in Montgomery County school politics. When we spoke in late 2014, she was on her way out, having served the school district for nearly a quarter century. But she had not lost the fiery spirit that brought her from a local PTA leader to a central player in downtown's redevelopment politics.[46] While new-school activists like Ms. Steinberg won the battle for a new Blair, they were losing Silver Spring's larger equitable development war.

By the time of the Blair High battles, the fervor for redevelopment had reached a climax. In the mid-1990s, AT&T left downtown, only three years after relocating there. The Silver Triangle was on its last legs. Moore failed to meet multiple county deadlines and scaled back his plans. The project's death knell came with the election of county executive Doug Duncan in 1994. Brought into office by largely White middle-class voters on a platform of restructuring and streamlining county government, Duncan promised voters he would revive downtown Silver Spring "or die trying." One of his first acts as county executive was to kill the Silver Triangle.[47]

Still eager for redevelopment, many old-school activists found their champion in Duncan. A Montgomery County native and former mayor of Rockville, Maryland, Duncan oversaw what he and many others cast as the successful redevelopment of downtown Rockville. For Duncan Silver Spring's redevelopment was needed to not only appease residents but also revive an important economic engine in the county.[48] If not addressed, he claimed, Silver Spring's "blight" would spread. "The fear was, if we don't stop the blight in Silver Spring, it's just going to creep up Georgia Avenue into Wheaton, Olney—and the eastern third of our county would be blighted, and what would we do then?" he asked. The challenge of inner suburbs, he argued, "is they very quickly become part of the center city."[49] Echoing terms used by Silver Spring civic groups, Duncan's biological metaphors reflected the county's and residents' concerns that DC's urban problems were bleeding into the suburbs—a trope used repeatedly throughout the history of US urban policy, with devastating racialized impacts.

With Duncan at the helm, the county took a far more aggressive approach. In 1996 the State of Maryland declared the CBD an Enterprise Zone, increasing tax incentives and other public subsidies for developers and businesses. The county expanded Silver Spring's urban renewal footprint by ten acres and made greater use of eminent domain, purchasing thirty downtown commercial properties. By the end of the decade, it had acquired and cleared most of the urban renewal area, over one-tenth of the CBD, including downtown's most valuable parcels.

Key to Duncan's strategy was to tackle downtown's "image problem" to attract middle-class consumers and residents. "Frankly, we needed to bring back people to Silver Spring, the people who had grown up around there," Duncan explained to me. "We needed to make Silver Spring a destination place again." For these residents to feel safe and comfortable, county leaders adopted a public safety plan and a more visible police presence. Duncan wanted visitors to see people, police, and security everywhere. The county vigorously marketed downtown with a new logo and put the Silver Spring Urban Crew and Corps to work cleaning streets, providing security, and acting as "goodwill ambassadors." "You get them there once, and, if they felt unsafe, they weren't coming back," Duncan said of visitors. The county executive also carefully crafted downtown's media narrative. "Everything we did in Silver Spring, we did a press event," he proudly professed, "because it needed that constant sense that things are happening here; things are changing here."[50] Having cleared the way, the county issued a call for a new downtown developer.

Duncan's strident strategy attracted another major redevelopment proposal—the American Dream. The $585 million, twenty-seven-acre project was proposed in 1995 by Triple Five, Canadian developers who owned the world's two largest malls, including Minnesota's Mall of America. They envisioned a megamall and entertainment complex, replete with a hockey rink, miniature golf course, nightclub, wave pool, indoor roller coaster, and a five-hundred-room themed hotel. "Basically, it was this Hershey Park ... in the middle of suburbia," explained Lily Morgan.

Ms. Morgan was a member of the Greater Silver Spring Committee, a nineteen-member citizens' advisory group composed largely of Silver Spring civic and business elites that endorsed the project. While several members expressed concerns about the proposal, the committee supported it, largely on the grounds that it would change downtown's narrative. "At the end of the day, that task force said, see if we can get to closure with these guys; it's interesting enough," Ms. Morgan told me. "It'll get Silver Spring on the map. It'll let us swoop, overcome, change our brand completely."[51]

Not everyone believed in the American Dream. Several old-school activist groups that fought the Silver Triangle initially appeared to support the proposal but became vocal critics after the developer released project details. Most prominent were the Silver Spring–Takoma Traffic Coalition and Citizens for Sensible Development, a group organized by Woodside Park residents. Together they submitted a petition to Duncan with over 3,600 signatures, urging him to reject the plan.[52] These groups continued to raise fears over the project's size, historic preservation, traffic issues, and other neighborhood impacts, garnering concessions from the developer and county. In late 1995 around eight hundred people showed up at a town hall meeting, only five hundred of which could fit into the packed room. Duncan turned the remaining residents away with a bullhorn, many of whom continued to protest outside. Inside, the developers endured jeers and interruptions. Signs sprouted in front lawns, declaring, "Development, yes. Mega-mall, no." Police on horseback monitored public hearings.[53] Judy Reardon, cofounder of the Silver Spring Historical Society, described the debate as a "battle for the soul of the community"— one that residents were willing to fight.[54] Members of these groups also made their way onto the newly formed forty-seven-member Silver Spring Redevelopment Advisory Board (SSRAB), constituted by Duncan to advise him on the proposal.

Old-school activists also continued to raise fears about the customers the project would attract, again raising the specter of race and class as central issues in the debate. John Robinson, former ACG president, told the *Washington Journal* in 1995, "You do get a lot of code words, like 'teens' and 'troublesome teens,'" noting his concerns about how racist fears played into the debate. Fearing the discussion would derail consensus about redevelopment, SSRAB, which Mr. Robinson cochaired alongside Wendy Perdue of the Silver Spring–Takoma Traffic Coalition, suggested sponsoring workshops for residents with counselors and other specialists in teen behavior.[55] Ironically, while concerned with the language of race, many old-school leaders were allied with organizations that supported policies that had exacerbated racial and class disparities in downtown for decades.

Facing a wall of opposition, the American Dream mall developers went on a public relations tour, hiring a team of well-known civic leaders to sell the project, including Gus Bauman as their local attorney. But like the Silver Triangle, the American Dream ran into roadblocks that eventually killed the project. Developers struggled to find financing and increased their request for county and state subsidies to about half of the project cost, roughly $300 million. Duncan rejected the proposal, stating that it relied too heavily on public dollars. While upsetting many county officials and residents, Duncan quickly pivoted, announcing the county would maintain momentum for redevelopment with a different focus and process. Instead of one massive development, the county would solicit smaller projects to maintain downtown's fabric and character. The developer would work with community groups to come up with a proposal. As Duncan put it, "We didn't pick a project; we picked a partner." And less than a year after the American Dream died, Duncan announced that the county had entered negotiations with a team of developers. The Foulger-Pratt and Peterson Companies, two major county developers and donors to Montgomery County and state political campaigns, would work in partnership with the Argo Investment Company to build a new town center on prime county-owned land.[56]

A SUBURBAN SUCCESS STORY?

In rejecting the American Dream, the county set itself up to play a larger role in downtown redevelopment. Coupled with the desperation felt by many of Silver Spring's business and propertied elites, this propelled a path forward. As signs of redevelopment's "success" slowly emerged, so too did grassroots activism. While old-school activists continued to dominate official planning forums, groups marginalized from the process carved out alternative spaces. Under the umbrella of a new organization, an equitable development movement coalesced for one of the first times in the Maryland suburbs.

To minimize opposition that flared over former proposals, the county required the developer to work closely with the community to come up with a proposal. "The long-standing deeply rooted animosity and poor communication that exists between public- and private-sector groups and agencies in Silver Spring and Montgomery County," concluded a National Main Street Center report on Fenton Village revitalization, was by far the most significant barrier to redevelopment. Distrust and a lack of communication and coordination were such significant issues that downtown's success or failure, the report continued, "ultimately hinges almost entirely on the ability of groups, agencies, and individuals to put past animosity behind them, agree to work collaboratively, and strengthen partnerships with the community."[57] Silver Spring's old-school activists and political leaders had to confront their issues if redevelopment was to go forward.

The primary vehicle for engagement was the newly appointed Silver Spring Redevelopment Steering Committee (SSRSC), with which the county required the developer to confer.[58] Appointed in 1997, the new group adopted members of the disbanded Silver Spring Redevelopment Advisory Board and added many more. SSRSC consisted of around thirty established business and civic leaders and 120 working group members, who advised the county executive on a range of issues facing the CBD. Its members were largely old-school activists. It included several former presidents of the Greater Silver Spring Chamber of Commerce: Sally Sternbach, Steve Silverman, and Charlie Atwell, often known as "the unofficial mayor of Silver Spring"; twenty-one past and present presidents of prominent civic associations, including the Citizens for Sensible Development, Silver Spring–Takoma Traffic Coalition, and Woodside Park Civic Association; and thirteen elected officials as ex officio members. The committee also included a few new-school activists like Laura Steinberg, who cochaired the committee, and Frankie Blackburn. Frankie, a self-described "diehard antipoverty advocate," remembered having to beg her way onto the committee—"a sign of who had the power."[59]

For a committee that was supposed to represent a diverse community, many voices were left out. While some with whom I spoke noted the county's attempts to pay attention to gender, ethnic, economic, and geographic diversity, others were disappointed in the results. Frankie cochaired the Housing Working Group. She noted that the SSRSC included some "token" renters and people of color but that "there was no diversity in the power structure at all." Lily Morgan was less apt to criticize the committee's composition but took issue with the ways that the developer and county cast their recommendations. The issue of community representation clearly struck a nerve, as she spoke in especially frank terms that took me by surprise:

> What would be to me more honest is to say, is a task group of twenty people who were chosen to try to represent the community came up with this recommendation, rather than shortening it [to what] "the community wants." And that's what happened, over and over. "The community wants." Bullshit! You haven't heard from the community.

She added that the committee was not elected and had no public mandate. The redevelopment plans were "created in a vacuum" without broad community consensus or support, she concluded.[60]

While public meetings and other engagement events were held, they continued to be dominated by old-school leaders. Ms. Morgan characterized those who regularly attended public meetings as "president, vice president, or treasurer or something of a neighborhood association." "You have to remember, planning politics largely consists of one hundred people moving from room to room," Royce Hanson reminded me in a professorial manner honed during his long academic career, which stretched back even further than his engagement in Montgomery County planning. His perspective was one I often shared with my own planning students. Many residents involved in Silver Spring redevelopment debates in the 1990s were the same people engaged in its politics during the 1970s, Hanson continued, "largely the White citizens who had long roots."[61]

While some debated why many voices went unheard, few argued that they did. County officials tended to emphasize that new groups, particularly immigrants, had yet to establish a foothold in county politics, were focused on other issues, or were not as affected by redevelopment. Community activists and civic leaders, however, underscored ongoing racial tensions in the county, inequalities in the process, and the county's push to get things done. "What happened to the folks that didn't know how to organize and are more transient, the folks that are renting, the folks that are busy eighteen hours a day running a small business?" asked one county leader. "I'm not sure those voices were considered because we had to get it done! Hey, we had the delusion of inclusion."[62]

The county's lack of attention to diverse voices gave rise to an important player in redevelopment politics: IMPACT Silver Spring. Frustrated with SSRSC's lack of diversity and reluctance to take on affordable housing issues, Frankie Blackburn began hosting meetings about redevelopment in her home. "[SSRSC] was so dysfunctional from a diversity perspective. I just couldn't hold my head up," she recounted. When the county later asked the committee for budget proposals, Frankie seized the opportunity to expand the effort. In less than twenty-four hours, she wrote the template for what in 1999 became the Silver Spring Community Leadership Initiative, which in 2001 was renamed IMPACT Silver Spring. To Frankie's surprise the committee supported her proposal, though she mused, "I think it was partly because people were divided on the other proposals."[63]

With Frankie serving as IMPACT's founding executive director, the organization began providing training and support for diverse community leaders and raising awareness about equity issues among existing leaders. "Our mission is to provide training for community members of diverse backgrounds in order to develop skills and awareness needed to share power and build relationships that cross race, class and cultural lines," read IMPACT's original mission statement. Jayne Park became IMPACT's executive director several years after Frankie left the organization in 2010. "IMPACT has always believed for things to change. It's not just about building power among people who lack power, but it's about getting people with power to shift the way they do things," she explained to me. Jayne had been at IMPACT for less than two years when we spoke in 2016. Like Frankie, she had a legal services background and deep roots working with the county and community. IMPACT's first signature program was its Community Empowerment Program, which cultivated culturally compe-tent community leaders to take important positions on county boards and agencies, including those related to redevelopment.[64] By the time the pro-gram produced its first graduates, however, redevelopment was moving full steam ahead.

Out of a sense of fear and desperation, Silver Spring's old-school leaders had forged common ground on plans for downtown. Some credit the alliance of two influential civic and business leaders, Bruce Lee and John Robinson. Lee was the inaugural president of the Greater Silver Spring Chamber of Commerce and CEO of Lee Development Group, which he ran with his cousin Blair. "[They] said, 'Look, if . . . the commercial community and the civic community doesn't agree on something, Silver Spring is just going to collapse, and it's just going to be bad for everybody,'" explained Royce Hanson. One civic group leader argued that higher-income communities' fears of declining property values associated with Silver Spring's increasing diversity and traffic drove civic groups into what previously seemed an impossible pact with county and business leaders. "Everybody was desperate," he told me. "The county was desperate. [The] business community was desperate. Most of the residents who had property were desperate."[65] Left out of this calculus were the many residential and small business tenants who were concerned with what redevelopment meant for them.

The final plans were more modest than previous proposals, but significant. The $321 million project would span twenty-six acres with over one million square feet of commercial and residential space centered on a major shopping center. It would create a more traditional New Urbanist downtown, with walkable streets and retail frontage centered on a main street. The project included a grocery store, restaurants, retail shops, a movie theater, a civic building, a hardware store, and a public square, alongside two hundred new residential units. The county kept ownership of the land but gave developers a ninety-nine-year ground lease, creating an increasingly privatized and commodified public realm.[66]

The plan was widely supported by Silver Spring's old-school leaders. "It was a big hit," Duncan recounted, referencing both the early plans and the final project. In late 1997 the steering committee voted twenty to zero in favor of the proposal. The county council then unanimously approved $96 million in county funding to support it. "Silver Spring redevelopment is a dream that has been shared for years by community activists, business leaders and government officials," announced the *Washington Post*.[67] It seemed to be a project that could bring many long-standing county and community divides together.

With the county and developers working together, redevelopment began in earnest. After being courted by county leaders, in 1998 two major anchors announced their intent to locate into downtown—the American Film Institute (AFI) and the headquarters of Discovery Communications. Ray Barry, AFI Silver's first director, not only recommended that AFI enter negotiations with the county but also helped to convince Discovery to follow suit. Often described as the cornerstone of redevelopment, Discovery brought 1,500 new workers to downtown. To incentivize these developments, the county spent over $20 million to purchase and restore the Silver Theatre and levied $27 million in county and state tax breaks and subsidies to attract Discovery. By the time I visited the renovated theater to meet with representatives from AFI, its gleaming marquee had once again become a downtown landmark.

Many credit Doug Duncan with making redevelopment happen. "He stood up to all the barriers and said, 'Get out of the way. We're doing this, and if you want to unelect me, fine,'" recounted Robert Wulff, in clear admiration of the former county executive, whose action proved profitable for his firm. Duncan's get-it-done leadership style railroaded past issues that could have derailed the process, including preservation politics that continued to reassert themselves.[68]

Incentives mounted. In 2000 the county adopted a new Silver Spring CBD Sector Plan, calling for public investments to support market-oriented approaches to revitalization. "Silver Spring must be an attractive place; an upgraded urban environment will attract private investment. Local, state, and federal governments must commit public resources to support private investment," it stated.[69] In 2002 the State of Maryland designated downtown Silver Spring an Arts and Entertainment District, making artists and arts organizations eligible for tax credits and other assistance.[70] Two years later downtown became a county "green tape zone," in which businesses building or renovating space could fast-track permitting and licensing. That same year the county invested $165,000 in a Silver SprUng campaign to attract businesses, residents, and shoppers to downtown, with cheery banners declaring that redevelopment was not a hope for some distant future—it was well underway.[71]

By the early 2000s, change was not only in the air but on the ground. In April 2003 Discovery and AFI opened, to much fanfare. Film star Clint

Eastwood attended AFI's lavish opening ceremony. "I remember saying, 'It's the first time in twenty years people in Silver Spring were screaming with joy rather than anger,'" Duncan recounted pridefully. Major retailers followed closely behind—Whole Foods, Strosnider's Hardware, Red Lobster, Austin Grill, Borders Books, Pier One, and Regal Majestic. As in many large cities, Silver Spring's new downtown centered on entertainment and amenities aimed at creative-class professionals and consumers.[72] County leaders touted the flurry of activity as signs of downtown Silver Spring's success. Between 1995 and 2003, commercial vacancy rates in the CBD dropped from 26 to 16 percent.[73] Apartments shot up, with 1,800 new units built in the two decades after 1990. In the first decade of the twenty-first century, downtown's White population rebounded for the first time in decades (see Table 1).

For many White middle-class residents and business leaders, the long-awaited dream of redevelopment had finally come true. Ever the powerful political storyteller, Doug Duncan recalled walking down Georgia Avenue the week after Discovery and AFI opened, talking with a friend and longtime Silver Spring resident. She started to cry, he explained, saying, "I've been here for so long. I never thought this would happen."[74] But not all Silver Spring residents shared this sense of relief. For marginalized residents and business owners, the battle for a place in the new downtown only intensified.

THE QUIET STORM

Redevelopment took a hefty toll on affordable housing and small businesses in downtown Silver Spring, contributing to direct and indirect displacement. While IMPACT brought more diverse voices to the table, new-school suburban activists were hamstrung by capacity and timing issues. And while the county eventually responded to demands to do more for small businesses, their efforts were too little and too late. Many businesses owned by immigrants and people of color closed, moved out of the downtown core, or left Silver Spring altogether. Those that remained struggled to keep their doors open.

Debate over the new plan included little discussion about gentrification and displacement. Activists, however, said displacement was a primary concern for low-income renters and small business owners. Many worried about the loss of small businesses, "third places" to gather outside the home, affordable housing, the diversity of Silver Spring's population, and their sense of place. Ruby Rubens said that many African Americans like herself described the changes as gentrification. They felt left out of the decision-making process and were not optimistic about downtown's future. "I see displacement of families. I see the disappearance of small business people. I see them being kind of wiped out of the Silver Spring market and I don't know where they're going to go," she said in 2003. "We're having more and more upscale restaurants and other stores, retail and all that. Who are the workers? Who can afford to live here? Who's going to work in those places? And the people who work there, can't afford to live here."[75]

Small business owners also worried that redevelopment was proceeding at their expense. "I've been here during the bad times," said Bijan Rashedi, owner of the twenty-year-old Carpet Bazaar. "Now I want to be part of the good times." While Mr. Rashedi was at first excited about the prospects of redevelopment, his business alongside many others was disrupted by construction when the county closed a parking garage attached to City Place Mall. With redevelopment engulfing the downtown core, rents rose quickly. In 2003 Mr. Rashedi was paying twelve dollars per square foot, while the vacant storefront next door was being offered at thirty dollars per square foot. A year later his rent spiked to that of his neighbors, and he lost his lease.[76]

But the county's focus was not on preserving small businesses or affordable housing. It was on attracting large retailers and high-end offices that appealed to middle-class consumers. "By bringing some people with income, people who can afford to shop in the stores, we may have created that balance that was missing," Melvin Tull told me. Many customers were attracted to downtown's traditional look and feel, which included familiar features from the old Silver Spring. High-end retail and entertainment venues also signaled to these consumers that downtown was changing in ways both familiar and desirable to them.[77] County officials also sought to attract upscale housing that would raise its tax base and pacify neighborhood groups' concerns that Silver Spring had become the county's dumping ground for affordable housing, a trope that held stable through decades of redevelopment debate.

By the early 2000s, residential rents were rising, and some property owners were not renewing leases in anticipation of redevelopment. Between 2000 and 2005, the median monthly rent in Silver Spring increased by $312, while the percentage of rent-burdened households, those paying over 30 percent of their income on rent, increased from 37 to 47 percent. Megan Moriarty, an IMPACT organizer, collected stories of rising rents and housing displacement during the period. I was introduced to Megan as a young energetic small business owner who had started a popular marketplace in downtown. Our initial introduction suggested we had more to talk about. Passionate and outgoing, Megan described how her frustrations with the field of international development led her to volunteer for local causes in Montgomery County, where she grew up—and eventually to intern at IMPACT. Her recollections of her time at the organization quickly turned to her frustrations trying to organize Silver Spring tenants. The majority of those affected were older renters living on fixed incomes or receiving housing vouchers. Steep rental increases made many residents feel that they were being "pushed out," she recalled. This included Rachael and her husband, Ainsley, Jamaican immigrants who lived in a downtown apartment complex. When they moved in, their neighbors were a diverse mix of ethnicities, races, and family types. But only three years later, most of their neighbors were White. Their rent had increased year after year, forcing some neighbors to move. With dual incomes, Rachael and Ainsley were able to stay. But prices for new tenants had skyrocketed, preventing them from moving from a one- to two-bedroom unit, as they had long hoped to do. Stories like this stuck with Megan almost a decade later. "That was really sad," she reflected, "and that is still really sad for me, especially because all the buildings that are going up now are high rise, super unaffordable."[78]

Housing prices also rose. Median home values in the CBD before redevelopment were below the county average. By 2007, after completion of the town center, they outpaced the county and the region and continued to rise, reaching $551,000 in 2019. IMPACT's Jayne Park purchased her home for less than $200,000 in North Silver Spring in 1999, when housing prices were "quite affordable." Five years later she sold her home for more than double what she paid. The pace of appreciation in East Silver Spring was even steeper. For instance, a typical 2,800-square-foot Cape

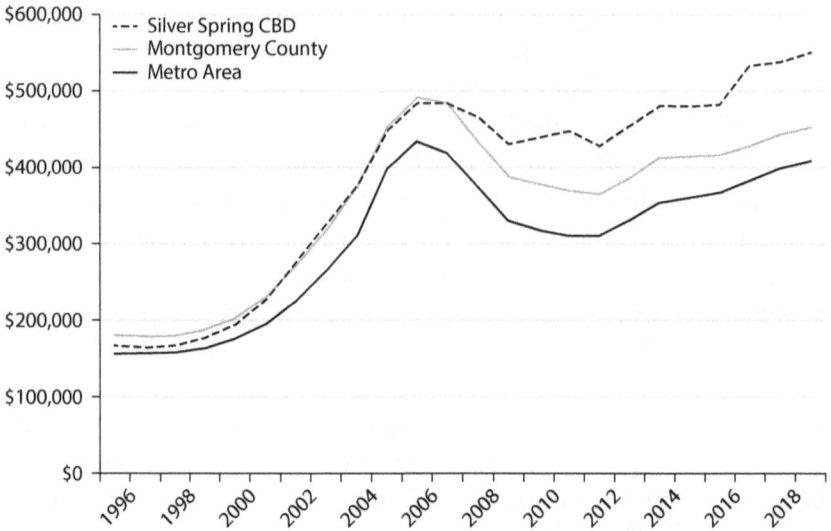

Figure 10. Median home values in downtown Silver Spring rose faster than in the DC Metropolitan Area and Montgomery County after the initial phases of development were complete in the middle of the first decade of the 2000s. The Central Business District as defined here is the 20910 zip code. Data from "Zillow Home Value Index."

Cod that sold for $147,000 in 1993 sold for $800,000, more than five times its previous sale price, in 2007.[79]

Small businesses bore the brunt of redevelopment's impacts. The county directly displaced businesses when it purchased land for the new town center. While some closed or left the area, about half remained in Silver Spring, moving largely to Fenton Village, which sat on the outskirts of the redevelopment area and was an affordable haven for small businesses.[80]

Construction disruptions strained these businesses. Parking was lost, sidewalks blocked, and storefronts made less visible—all of which contributed to lower pedestrian activity. The county made almost no provisions for construction mitigation, which contributed to the loss of some small businesses and increasing tensions between the county and those that remained, recalled Lester Willson. Lester worked for the Maryland Small Business Development Center (SBDC), which partnered with the county to provide technical assistance to Silver Spring businesses in the early

2000s. I was familiar with his work and had invited him to speak to my students about SBDC's work to inform a class project. A chatty guy who had talked his way into many doors during his decades-long career at SBDC, Lester was surprised that several Silver Spring business owners would not even talk to him because they thought he represented the county. "You'd go in to talk to them, they'd throw you out," he told me.[81] The frustration was palpable among business owners like Peter Cho, who blamed construction disruptions and rent spikes for the closure of his store in 2004. "Nobody wants it because the rent is too high," he argued.[82]

Commercial rents often began rising before shovels hit the ground. According to a University of Maryland study, rents rose quickly, in part because of the rapid pace of redevelopment and dominance of a single downtown landlord—the town center developer. Between 1995 and 2003, the average CBD commercial rents increased from fifteen to twenty-two dollars per square foot. Long-term leases were hard to find. Emmanuel Bobga Avaba, a Cameroonian immigrant and owner of Roger Miller, a West African restaurant and popular gathering spot for international soccer fans like Mr. Bobga himself, saw his rent soar from $900 in 1997 to $2,300 seven years later. By that time his landlord had received multiple offers to sell the building. Mr. Bobga persisted in staying in place, but many others did not, threatening the sense of place and community that "third places" like Roger Miller provided for diverse immigrants. By 2005 an estimated eighty businesses had been displaced from the core redevelopment area. Two years later average commercial rents in Fenton Village were only slightly lower than in the CBD, whose rents already exceeded that of downtown Bethesda and were continuing to rise.[83]

Silver Spring's small businesses also competed with large national chains in the town center. While redevelopment attracted new patrons to the town center, few businesses on its periphery saw spillover traffic and instead experienced a loss of customers. The county's investments in streetscaping, sidewalks, and other infrastructure focused largely on the town center, creating an "invisible fence" that clearly distinguished the new and old business districts. One study found that in 2007 businesses in the downtown core experienced fifteen times the foot traffic as those in Fenton Village. "The new Silver Spring developments have not only been unhelpful but have actually *hurt* Fenton Village and its small businesses, forcing higher rents, shop closures, and general discontent among the business owners," the report concluded.[84]

IMPACT Silver Spring rallied to assist impacted small businesses and residents but faced numerous hurdles. They were a new organization with a primarily White staff and few existing community relationships. When Frankie, Megan, and others started going door-to-door to organize tenants, they encountered a diverse community with many internal conflicts, including those between new African immigrants and long-standing African American residents. To rally residents around a common vision for redevelopment, IMPACT needed organizers who could engage diverse residents and navigate hard racial and cultural conversations. "I was scared to death trying to organize these Ethiopian and Eritrean tenants," Frankie humbly recalled. "I didn't know what I was doing." Frankie also participated in a Thirty Door Knocks campaign, focused on improving relations between businesses and residents in Montgomery County, including those in Silver Spring.[85]

Some residents also questioned IMPACT's relationship with the county and developers. IMPACT relied heavily on county funding. Their main office was donated by Foulger-Pratt and the Argo Investment Company. Some argued these ties compromised their advocacy agenda.[86] Frankie didn't speak on the subject but noted that IMPACT struggled to limit county funding in part because it required them to show quantifiable outcomes that could compromise their community-building work.[87] While IMPACT eventually found its footing, it took a while. In 2007 they launched Neighborhood IMPACT, an initiative to work in Silver Spring and nearby neighborhoods to identify tenant leaders and foster collective action. The campaign that Megan Moriarty led, Silver Spring Loves Renters, collected stories about housing conditions, rents, and impacts of redevelopment to advocate for greater tenant protections and affordable housing.

With only a few organizers, however, IMPACT's neighborhood work was limited. They also lacked other nonprofits in Silver Spring and the county with which to partner. Founded in a Montgomery County church basement in 1985, CASA de Maryland, an immigrant rights organization that grew to be among the largest in the mid-Atlantic region, was an ally but had yet to focus its work on local redevelopment issues. Gustavo

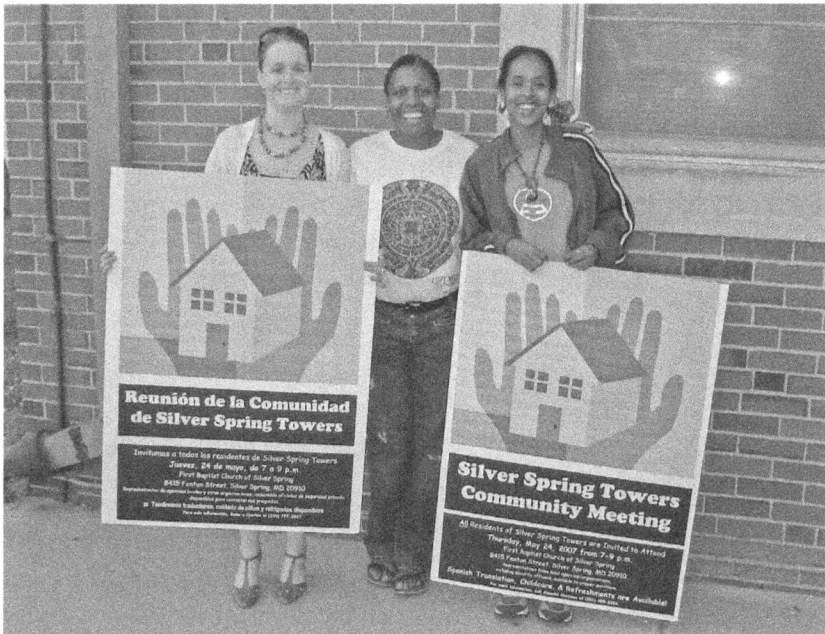

Figure 11. IMPACT Silver Spring staff organizing tenants at Silver Spring Towers as part of their Silver Spring Loves Renters campaign, which advocated for tenant protections and affordable housing. Courtesy of IMPACT Silver Spring.

Torres, CASA's executive director, sat on the redevelopment steering committee's housing work group with Frankie, but the two upstart organizations did not work closely together during the period. With a front seat to the redevelopment debates and IMPACT's organizing efforts, however, Torres was learning critical lessons he would apply in the CASA-led campaign to prevent displacement along the International Corridor more than a decade later.

IMPACT did less to organize small business owners, who were just as diverse and fragmented as residents. "The small business issue was deeply troubling to all of us," explained Frankie, "but the people we worked with didn't have the time or bandwidth to contribute to the capacity building that we wanted to create." IMPACT was unable to get small business leaders to attend their meetings.[88] The Greater Silver Spring Chamber of Commerce represented the interests of large employers and, some said, was unwelcoming to Black and Brown business owners. Silver Spring had no small business associations to represent their interests.

Capacity-strapped and lacking strong community connections, IMPACT shifted its attention away from redevelopment. While its Community Empowerment Program produced several leaders who went on to serve in high-ranking government positions, the program lasted only eight years. Even before it ended, Frankie explained, IMPACT had long since stopped encouraging its graduates to sit on county redevelopment boards:

> They'd get on these things, and they either had no power or they were run in such a domineering way. In their pure essence, they weren't meaningful. Why do I want to encourage people, especially people who were really trying to change something, [to] go on to these limp advisory boards?[89]

Hard-hit by the recession and subsequent budget cuts, IMPACT's tenant-organizing efforts were even more short-lived. The Neighborhood IMPACT program ran for three years, and the Silver Spring Loves Renters campaign was just getting started at its close. "That was definitely when we were getting somewhere," recalled Frankie, clearly disappointed about the program's short lifespan, which roughly corresponded with her departure from the organization.[90] After landing a contract with the Department of Health and Human Services, IMPACT turned its focus to the creation of small neighborhood support networks throughout the county. Jayne Park explained that around the time of Frankie's resignation, funding challenges left the organization short-staffed and forced them to make hard choices about its direction. When we spoke in 2016, she was clear that IMPACT's work was neither about redevelopment nor advocacy. "We're not an advocacy organization," Park clarified in response to my question about issues that they had supported in recent years. "Our work is really to go deep into neighborhoods and to knit together the social fabric."[91]

IMPACT's early organizing efforts also began too late to significantly influence the trajectory of redevelopment plans. "The decisions were already made, and then IMPACT started," explained Megan Moriarty, fiercely rejecting the idea that the county supported IMPACT as a way of bringing more diverse voices to the decision-making table—a statement I heard from county leaders more than once. "IMPACT was there trying to pick up the pieces after everything had happened," Megan countered. Frankie was more attuned to IMPACT's challenges in building strong community connections. "We didn't do the organizing that was needed," she reflected in our second conversation, nearly five years after the first. By then she had cofounded a new nonprofit focused on collaborative community change and relocated out of the region. "All the moments of leverage—none of us were ready for them."[92]

While IMPACT failed to significantly shift the redevelopment terrain, the county made some concessions. In response to my questions about residential displacement, county leaders often touted their increased investments in the county's affordable housing trust fund and downtown developments with below-market rate units. Between 2000 and 2004, the county's Housing Initiative Fund went from around $4 million to $21 million. Between 1992 and 2004, the county also helped to secure about 270 units of housing for low- and moderate-income families in downtown Silver Spring.[93] Many advocates, however, said these investments were insufficient. "These steps didn't really serve the people who were being displaced," argued Frankie. CASA's Gustavo Torres agreed. "I don't see that the government is planning to ensure there is not that kind of gentrification that we are concerned [about], that the people who are poor are going to be removed from those areas," he argued in 2003. "If you ask a Latino or an African American how we feel it's going in Silver Spring, we don't see how we are going to be involved, and how we are going to benefit," Mr. Torres said.[94]

The county's response to commercial displacement was more direct. Under county law businesses displaced by eminent domain could apply for compensation and relocation assistance. Responding to early complaints, the county mitigated construction disruptions by providing "open for business" and wayfinding signage, customer shuttle services to nearby parking, marketing to promote local businesses, and public events to keep visitors coming to downtown. As Discovery was being planned, they negotiated with developers to not include a cafeteria and instead encourage employees to frequent local restaurants. And in 2004, after the town center opened, they launched a countywide business-impact assistance program and a separate program to assist Silver Spring small businesses.

The former provided grants and loans to small businesses negatively impacted by county-led redevelopment. The latter, the Silver Spring Small and Minority Business Retention Initiative, was meant to assist and strengthen small businesses indirectly impacted by eminent domain. It established retention and "strike" teams to visit and assist small businesses, a Silver Spring small business assistance guide, a business-relocation assistance program, and increased technical assistance and training for Silver Spring businesses.[95]

The county's response would not have been possible without Tom Perez, the first Latino Montgomery County council member representing District 5, which included Silver Spring. Before his election in 2002, Perez was a civil rights lawyer, an immigrant rights advocate, and board member at CASA. "It was a Godsend when Tom Perez was elected to represent Silver Spring," Frankie professed.[96] Shortly after taking office, Perez worked with IMPACT to conduct small business listening sessions, door-to-door needs assessments, and business tours for county leaders. As council president in 2005, Perez placed small businesses among his top priorities. He pushed to implement the countywide impact-assistance and Silver Spring small business programs and cosponsored a bill requiring the county to award a portion of contracts to local small businesses. But just as Perez's efforts in Silver Spring were gaining ground, he moved on. In 2007 he became Maryland's secretary of labor, licensing, and regulation and went on to serve as the assistant attorney general for the US Department of Justice's Civil Rights Division and then as US secretary of labor.

County assistance was slow to take hold and insufficient for many businesses. Some directly displaced by eminent domain complained that more compensation was needed for them to restart elsewhere, even as county officials stressed that assistance often exceeded their legal requirement. The county's impact-assistance and business-retention programs had many more critics. Advocates and even some county officials pointed out that many businesses had already closed by the time the programs began, and that the programs were underfunded, difficult to access, and short-lived. Silver Spring's small business retention initiative lasted only two years. Like many with whom I spoke, then county council member Ike Leggett pointed to gaps in outreach, timing, and funding levels in the county's impact-assistance program: "I think we did not put enough money up, we didn't have enough outreach, and we did a poor job in all of these things. We didn't get to the people early enough. They were not included . . . That's just it. We failed."[97]

Businesses had been the "life blood of downtown," Leggett told me candidly. "When the revitalization came in, and it was gentrified in some ways, they lost." Funding for the program was capped at $20,000 per business and appropriated only for five years. Between 2005 and 2010, twenty-six businesses received assistance, less than half of which were in downtown Silver Spring. A 2005 University of Maryland survey of downtown small businesses found that only about half had received visits from county officials, and many remained unaware of county resources available to assist them. Business owners faced language barriers and a lack of time and knowledge about how to apply.[98] One former county employee I spoke to who helped to coordinate the county's business retention team at the time characterized the county's response as sporadic and uncoordinated.[99]

In contrast, county officials and other redevelopment advocates often characterized Silver Spring's residential and commercial displacement as negligible or as simply the cost of doing business. Several dismissed the notion that Silver Spring had gentrified. "This is not gentrification," offered Melvin Tull, comparing the area to other neighborhoods that, to his mind, had gentrified. "This is improving Silver Spring back to what Silver Spring was."[100] Several argued that more businesses were lost to "natural" attrition and turnover than redevelopment. They recounted tales of businesses that closed for reasons other than redevelopment or took county buyouts to do something different. Some argued that displacement was unavoidable and necessary for Silver Spring to "evolve" or "progress." "Some [redevelopment] did occur at the loss of some businesses," one government official told me. "Sometimes it takes a little pain to move things along." In refrains reminiscent of urban growth-machine theory: all growth was good, change was inevitable, and losses were unavoidable.[101]

Doug Duncan did not worry too much about the complaints he received about rising property taxes. "I knew we were successful in Silver Spring when the homeowners around the downtown started complaining to me about their property taxes," he told me, clearly bemused. Several county leaders touted stories of thriving small businesses that used county assistance to attract a new clientele, such as Kefa Café, a coffee shop owned by two sisters from Ethiopia, which was many times offered to me as a model of the county's success in retaining small businesses. Melvin Tull offered another, Marco's, an established Italian restaurant. "Little by little [Marco] tried things—he moved the cash register back, he put some tables up front, he moved the cash register further back, put a few more tables up front," Mr. Tull explained. "He's a smart guy, and so he's adapted." It was neither feasible nor even "healthy," some county leaders suggested, to try to keep the community unchanged. While the "transition" was tough, county leaders admitted, those willing to adapt would benefit in the long run.[102]

Community advocates countered that such successful examples were limited. Adapting to the new Silver Spring was difficult, if not impossible, for many small businesses owned by immigrants and people of color that lacked the business networks and capital to adjust their product lines and prices to compete with national chains. Like many businesses he knew in downtown, Dan Reed's family restaurant struggled to survive. Construction disruptions reduced their foot traffic, and they lost many regular clients after the town center was complete.[103] "If your clientele changes you have two choices—you can either adapt or wither," Dan concluded, repeating the mantra of many county leaders. He encouraged his aunt to choose the former by marketing to new clients but said she largely stuck to what she knew. Her saving grace was that she owned her building, a rarity among Silver Spring businesses, Dan noted.[104]

Advocates also pointed out that redevelopment's impacts were often missed because they defied traditional concepts of gentrification. David Rotenstein argued that residents' declining sense of place, culture, and character went hand in hand with residential, commercial, and industrial displacement. These shifts were difficult to see in data about displacement, but residents, particularly those of color, felt them every day in the loss of familiar faces and places. Because Silver Spring's displacement largely affected its retail and industrial sectors, it did not always register as gentrification, David remarked. Frankie Blackburn characterized the process as "silent gentrification." "I am so clear that we had silent gentrification of a magnitude that no one really knows to this day," she said in 2015. Over the two decades after redevelopment began, Frankie lamented that she hardly recognized the downtown businesses that she once knew well.[105]

Community advocates and county leaders tended to agree on one point—many small businesses were an uneasy fit within the new mold of downtown Silver Spring. Those that thrived before redevelopment operated on a different model than new businesses, some said. But while community advocates felt that more county resources should help businesses stay in place and promote a diverse local economy, county leaders tended to characterize the losses as inevitable. Gary Stith served as the director of the Silver Spring Regional Development Center from 2000 to 2009, where he represented the county in redevelopment and managed its redevelopment investments. Though many early interviewees suggested that I speak to him, Mr. Stith was among the last people I spoke to about Silver Spring redevelopment in 2019, as he was nearing retirement from a long career in planning and real estate development. His opinion on a process he oversaw for nearly a decade carried great weight. Despite the many county efforts to retain existing businesses, Stith argued, many businesses were simply not viable given Silver Spring's new market. "The change in the market—some businesses just couldn't deal with that. Their business models were based on low rents. There wasn't any way we could keep that from happening," he told me. "You have to ask, are the lease rates the real issue?" Melvin Tull asked in 2004. "Or is it just not in their business plan to be in Silver Spring."[106]

Recalling the early fights over Clarendon's downtown, the long and bitter battle in Silver Spring left many residents and small business owners feeling that, after they stuck it out through the hard times, they did not have a place in the new downtown. "Many of these small business owners—along Bonifant, Thayer, and parts of Georgia, Colesville and Fenton—are left with the impression that those pulling the strings would prefer that they simply fade away," concluded Bruce Johansen, in his dissertation on the politics of downtown Silver Spring.[107]

THE FATE OF WASHINGTON'S "MOST DIVERSE SUBURB"

Downtown Silver Spring's redevelopment was one of the largest—and widely touted as one of the most successful—urban renewal efforts ever undertaken in the state of Maryland. It is proclaimed as a national model of suburban retrofit projects and among the most diverse suburban communities in the United States. But as my research came to a close in early 2020, it appeared that residents and business owners who historically bore the brunt of redevelopment's impacts continued to do so. As redevelopment marched forward, marginalized groups struggled for a place in a downtown that was more ethnically than economically diverse. Affordable housing and commercial spaces were lost, and that which remained was precariously hanging on. And while redevelopment still threatened downtown's fragile diversity, the organizing that once spurred engagement among diverse communities had waned. Many were left wondering how to keep the fight for equitable development alive in Silver Spring.

When judged solely by its economic revenue, redevelopment paid off. Between 2000 and 2010, the county invested around $450 million in public funds in the CBD, which supported around $2 billion in private investment. Between 1995 and 2007, its tax base grew by 62 percent.[108] Dozens of trendy restaurants and shops located in downtown, as did three new hotels. United Therapeutics constructed their $10 million headquarters and state-of-the-art laboratory across from City Place Mall. The Fillmore, a twenty-three-thousand-square-foot live music hall, opened in the old JCPenney building, preserved through a public-private partnership between the county and Lee Development Group. Luxury condominiums and apartments popped up all over town, and several older apartment buildings were given new life.

Economic revenue, however, was not the county's only measure of success. County officials often pointed to Silver Spring's racial and ethnic diversity that, by several indicators, was among the most diverse in the region and country.[109] Some said that redevelopment provided a platform for people to see the diversity that already existed. Others argued that redevelopment attracted more diversity, including White middle-class professionals. Laura Steinberg recounted the story of a family friend who moved from New York to the region and chose to live in Silver Spring because of its diversity—a distinct difference from a time when young professionals were leaving downtown, she noted. "She's like, 'Yeah, I want to live in Silver Spring.' . . . This is where things are happening. This is where the *edge* is." In DC and other gentrifying neighborhoods, multiple scholars have associated the desire of young residents to live in hip, cool, and diverse neighborhoods with various forms of displacement.[110]

Redevelopment advocates often praised Silver Spring's multicultural mix. Mantras abound about the multiple languages one hears on the street and the popular ethnic festivals that crowd the central plaza. Doug Duncan praised how White seniors, Black families, and teenagers gather at the downtown Red Lobster. "[It's] just amazing to watch how different groups come in at different times," he told me. "And everybody's comfortable and happy and all that." "This has turned [out] to be this mixing bowl," concluded Mel Tull.[111] From melting pot to mixing bowl, county leaders' common terms of reference underscored their perceptions about the ease with which diverse groups shared space in downtown.

Community advocates questioned this rosy picture. Black and Latinx populations declined in downtown after 2000, while the White population rose. Silver Spring was now more ethnically than economically diverse but also highly racially and economically segregated between its northwest and southeast neighborhoods, many said. Frankie Blackburn argued that Silver Spring's redevelopment contributed to the county's widening income gap.[112] While the median household income rose in downtown after 2000, so too did the percentage of families living in poverty (see Table 1).

Advocates also argued that while diverse groups sometimes share space in downtown, they rarely mix, and that people of color are still often made to feel unwelcome. Several pointed to the response to a 2011 gang-related stabbing in downtown, an incident that sparked outrage from community members, who Laura Steinberg characterized as being uncomfortable with youth hanging out in downtown. They perceived the youth as "coming from DC," a popular complaint that withstood three decades of redevelopment debate. Despite data showing reduced youth- and gang-related crime in the county in recent years, county executive Ike Leggett proposed a countywide youth curfew. The proposal was backed by the town center's developers, with the help of Doug Duncan, whom they hired as a consultant. While the proposal was later rejected by the county council, to community advocates the incident was symptomatic of the lingering hostility of residents, county officials, and developers to the presence of Black and Brown youth in downtown.[113] Incessantly monitored and policed, they were still questioned and feared in the new Silver Spring, just as it had been in the old.

The question of whether downtown's diversity could be sustained gave many community advocates pause. Erin Ross, an active member of the East Silver Spring Civic Association, explained that while her neighborhood remained ethnically diverse, the affordability that once allowed residents and small businesses to get a foothold was no more. Fellow East Silver Spring resident Megan Moriarty shared Ms. Ross's concerns. Her personal network, which was rooted in part in the neighborhood, had significantly shifted since she first moved there in the mid-2000s. While her "friend/professional group" was still racially and ethnically diverse, it was less so economically. "I definitely don't have the same connections I used to have to people who were just really living in different circumstances than I was," Megan told me.[114] Downtown's density and county investments in affordable housing provided some relief, but advocates worried it was not enough. Downtown still had few public housing units. And the county's renowned inclusionary zoning program served only those making at or below 65 percent of area median income. Its regulations were difficult for many low-income families to navigate, and its units were in high demand.[115]

Small businesses continued to be what Jerry McCoy called the "victims of the success of the revitalization of downtown Silver Spring." Rising rents, property neglect, and speculation still threatened many businesses, particularly those in Fenton Village. Once the most neglected part of downtown redevelopment, Fenton Village became its center. In 1997 the county's Department of Housing and Community Affairs designated it a commercial revitalization area, prioritizing it for streetscape, facade, and other infrastructure improvements. When we spoke in 2015, Megan Moriarty was looking for a space for her jewelry business in the neighborhood but had nearly given up. "The speculation going on right now is ridiculous. I mean, people are sitting on properties that are falling apart. The landlords here don't give a shit!" Megan raged, referencing a fire that recently displaced three long-term small businesses, including Kefa Café. Because few property owners live in or near Silver Spring, she added, business owners have no one to appeal to about their concerns. Characterized by the county as "Silver Spring's own global village," Fenton Village is often marketed as a diverse "urban" neighborhood. But advocates worried that the branding could displace the neighborhood's existing diversity, as its "cool factor" attracted higher-end businesses and wealthier residents.[116]

Figure 12. Small businesses along Bonifant Street in Fenton Village, which became the county's focus of redevelopment following the "successful" redevelopment of the town center. Photo by the author.

Silver Spring's light industry is also disappearing, due in large part to land-use changes and rising rents. For decades commercial services and industrial businesses, especially auto repair shops owned by immigrants and people of color, clustered at the southern end of Fenton Village. As light-industrial zones shifted to commercial and mixed-use, Jerry McCoy pointed to the loss of automotive repair and supply shops that used to line Georgia Avenue. While he still gets "giddy after twenty-two years" from being able to walk home after dropping off his car for maintenance, many of these places were "just destined to disappear," he speculated.[117] Not far from where we met in South Silver Spring, a new fifteen-story mixed-use apartment building had recently replaced a former car dealership and auto repair shop.

As residents and businesses struggle to find a place in the new downtown, activism has dimmed. IMPACT Silver Spring no longer engaged in downtown redevelopment politics, and no organizations had filled its critical role. After Tom Perez moved off the county council in 2007, there was also less sustained pressure from the top. Old-school business and civic leaders continued to dominate Silver Spring's redevelopment politics. Dan Reed pointed out that "older retirees, people with money, people who are worried that something bad could happen" showed up repeatedly to public meetings, while "young, immigrant, minority communities, people of lower income, people who are just busy," did not.[118]

Dan and others noted that activism and community engagement shifted forms but did not completely stop. Despite decades of top-down planning, Dan was excited about the conscious and creative community of young, diverse residents that he saw beginning to flourish in Silver Spring, who were actively building bridges across their differences and with established groups. His comments reminded me of Frankie, who spoke to IMPACT's struggles to build bridges across differences and get diverse communities engaged in conversations about the future of Silver Spring. Dan seemed convinced that the spirit of that mission was still very much alive in Silver Spring. Their efforts had taken on a life of their own, he explained, sometimes with the help and permission of the county but oftentimes without it.[119] Megan Moriarty agreed that she still saw hope in the future of organizing in Silver Spring. "That's why I want to stay here, 'cause I think there's a lot of potential to organize people in a different way," she told me.[120]

Dan's and Megan's comments reflected the hopes of many Silver Spring residents that a new equitable development politics was emerging in downtown, but many advocates also questioned whether the hard lessons of redevelopment had been learned. They wondered if the county would step up to bring more voices to the table and prevent future displacement. They questioned whether marginalized residents and businesses had the capacity and power to press the county for needed changes—or whether they were going to be left to fill considerable gaps on their own. As Frankie Blackburn asked, "Is there a vision that is shaping this rapid growth? What is redevelopment going to look like looking back? Did we really achieve diversity?" While offering no definitive answers, she noted her skepticism that significant power shifts in the county and community had yet to come about.[121]

.   .   .   .   .

Much has changed in downtown Silver Spring since I lived there in the late 1990s. While I still often shop at City Place Mall, it is now packed with Latinx families patiently lining up outside the Chinese buffet on Saturday mornings. I dine with friends at popular Caribbean and Burmese restaurants in Fenton Village and meet up for writing dates across a rotation of my favorite cafés, owned largely by people of color and new immigrants. I watch classic movies at the renovated Silver Theatre or a more recent release a couple blocks away at the Regal. Occasionally, I catch a nationally renowned hip-hop or R&B artist playing at the Fillmore or a local favorite at the Society Lounge's live reggae night. On weekends I drop in on one of the many cultural festivals and markets at the central plaza. I wade through traffic to pick up my teenage son, who prefers to hang out in downtown Silver Spring rather than in many gentrified neighborhoods in DC. As I watch Black and Brown youth skateboard through downtown's main street and splash one another in the fountain, I can understand why.[122] To many well-to-do suburbanites, Silver Spring is too urbane. For many millennials flooding into DC, it is too suburban. But to regulars like myself, it offers the best of both worlds, and many amenities that defy the false lines between city and suburb.

Had I not taken the time to investigate its history, I could easily have missed the unequal processes and politics that have gone into the making of this diverse suburban downtown. Silver Spring's redevelopment was set into motion by the flight of White capital and by community and county leaders' increasing discomfort with its fate. The departure of White middle-class residents and the businesses that followed opened opportunities for communities of color, including one of the largest Ethiopian populations outside of Ethiopia. These new suburbanites started businesses and built a sense of place from the scraps others left behind. But to many White residents—those who left and those who stayed—the condition of *their* downtown became unacceptable. It was blighted, diseased, and damn near empty. The story that they told themselves, one another, and county leaders justified redevelopment's means and ends. It necessitated the use of vast public resources to remake downtown, bring back the missing middle-class, and make them feel secure and comfortable to live and shop in Silver Spring again. Their desires defended a process that marginalized the voices and needs of residents and businesses that had kept downtown afloat.

This story did not happen just anywhere. It happened in a suburb where the tools and practices used by county and civic leaders to systemically exclude African Americans were refined by decades of suburban public policy and private practice. When the floodgates could no longer be held by such means, White residential and commercial flight were also common to suburbs. Suburbia's old-school activists gained ground as ideas about what good suburban development looks like changed. Suburbia's segregated land uses prefaced calls for robust public and private interventions to make redevelopment happen.

Suburbia's social, political, and institutional context also compounded community advocates' struggle for equitable development. Like in many suburbs, the in-migration of immigrants and people of color did not simply reproduce urban segregation patterns. Neighborhoods like East Silver Spring were more racially and ethnically diverse than their central city counterparts. But they were also less organized. By the time redevelopment began, African immigrants, African Americans, Latinx Americans, and other suburban newcomers were still finding their footing—socially, politically, and economically. Marginalized and excluded from Silver Spring's traditional power structure, they lacked the time and resources to develop institutions of their own. They did not have established community-based organizations with the trust and rapport of residents and the capacity for sustained organizing. They also lacked progressive political leaders to bring their voices to the policymaking table. Though grassroots and grasstops leaders and small business protections emerged out of the redevelopment battles, the most critical policies hit ground after redevelopment's impacts were already borne out.

As many questioned what county and community leaders learned from one of the region's most significant suburban redevelopment projects, I put the question to county executive Ike Leggett, who succeeded Duncan. "We learned some lessons, but it was painful what we went through in Silver Spring," he responded. But Leggett added, under his administration the county had begun to turn the tide by engaging in more extensive outreach, anticipating the challenges facing small businesses, and providing more direct assistance during construction.[123] A key test of Leggett's proposition was the county's response to the Purple Line, a new sixteen-mile light-rail line proposed to run directly through the heart of downtown

Silver Spring and other vulnerable neighborhoods—a case that I discuss in Chapter 5. The more immediate test was in Wheaton, a neighborhood just up the road, where many former downtown Silver Spring residents and businesses had once fled. As redevelopment took hold in Silver Spring, Leggett began to build his own urban legacy in Wheaton. And, as the county set its sights on its next major redevelopment project, a growing community of suburban equitable development advocates turned their attention there as well.

4 Resisting the Suburban Retrofit

On Georgia Avenue, north of downtown Silver Spring, Wheaton is the next major destination and only two stops away on the metro's Red Line. Just outside the station, a mural harkens back to the community's rural roots. Across the street low-slung strip malls host hundreds of small businesses selling Peruvian chicken, pupusas, pho, and countless curry dishes serving the neighborhood's fast-growing immigrant populations. This colorful corner of Montgomery County, only four miles north of the DC line, is now known for its rich mix of multiethnic residents and small businesses.

This trek is a familiar one. It is a straight shot on Georgia Avenue from my home in DC through downtown Silver Spring to my in-law's house in Wheaton, where they have lived since the mid-1980s. This multicultural vision of Wheaton was not the one they had always known but one they had grown attached to. For them the initial draw was simply the ability to purchase a new, larger home, away from the violence of the city. While my husband complained about its quiet streets, long walk to the metro, and multiple bus transfers that extended his commute to school in DC from less than fifteen minutes to over an hour, his parents were happy with the move. Homes on their winding, tree-lined street were bought by Korean,

Jamaican, Nigerian, and Eritrean families. Raised in segregated urban neighborhoods, they surprisingly found comfort and community in their diverse middle-class suburb.

But this multiethnic mix was not necessarily sustainable. Following the redevelopment of downtown Silver Spring, Wheaton became the focus of county revitalization efforts. As redevelopment has taken hold, the fate of many small, ethnic enterprises that define downtown as well as the residents they serve has been thrown into question. Rising property values have been coupled by an influx of young professionals who helped drive downtown's booming new residential market, which raised the prospects of gentrification and the displacement of many small, immigrant-owned businesses. But, as in Silver Spring, community-based organizations, residents, and businesses came together to fight for their right to remain.

This chapter takes a serious look at the process that gave rise to calls for equitable development in Wheaton, where organizers attempted to hold the line on large-scale redevelopment. Its redevelopment story continues to demonstrate the dense layers and complex forms of public planning, investment, and subsidy that make suburban renewal possible and profitable. It highlights the critical nexus of neoliberal suburban public policy in transforming disinvested communities through public-private partnerships, in which county-led redevelopment clears the way for private investment and gain. Just as in Silver Spring, though redevelopment was slow to get off the ground, with the power of the public purse and policy, it soon proceeded at a fast clip.

But the reaction of a generation of new suburbanites was different than old-school suburban activists who dominated Silver Spring's redevelopment politics. Having learned some hard lessons from Silver Spring, new-school suburban activists were more of a force in Wheaton. Some sat on redevelopment boards and committees. Others headed local civic groups that rallied for redevelopment. Some even made their way onto the county council. Unlike those of their old-school counterparts, the interests of newer residents who rallied around redevelopment were not simply in historic preservation or protecting their sylvan middle-class communities. Largely made up of people of color, these residents had intertwined interests to keep Wheaton diverse and its multicultural character intact. They fought to project a more inclusive redevelopment process and vision from the outset. Suburban boosters, including elected representatives and developers, meanwhile sought to capitalize off the visible expressions of difference in the landscape. Wheaton's ethnic retail and cultural spaces served as a kind of symbolic capital they could exploit to attract new residents, visitors, and businesses, reflecting the multicultural marketing tactics used in many gentrifying urban neighborhoods.

While acknowledging Wheaton as a multiethnic community, both new-school activists and suburban boosters rallied around visions of redevelopment that continued to leave many voices out. Their visions also obscured the "actually existing" diversity of residents and the protections needed by those most vulnerable to displacement, including many Latinx and immigrant residents and businesses.[1] These elisions gave rise to the Coalition for the Fair Redevelopment of Wheaton, which would push past the goals of new-school activists toward a bolder vision of equitable suburban development. Building on lessons from Silver Spring, the coalition reached residents and businesses earlier in the process and built stronger partnerships among organizations inside and outside the neighborhood. They allied with county leaders and new-school activists to assert a more robust vision of development without displacement and to guarantee affordable housing, workforce, and small business protections. And they leveraged and strengthened policy tools initiated in downtown Silver Spring.

But many challenges remained. While led by a higher-capacity, established urban nonprofit, Wheaton's coalition still struggled with capacity issues among its partners and inside its lead organization, the Latino Economic Development Center (LEDC). Working within Wheaton's "ecology of scarcity," including its dearth of nonprofit, social-serving, and community-based organizations, LEDC struggled to build a robust coalition and political will to advance its progressive agenda. Though LEDC had been engaged in battles over gentrification in DC for decades, it was new to Wheaton and struggled to find its footing. Latinx Americans were still underrepresented in county leadership and on redevelopment boards. While the political winds shifted with the election of a Latina county council member who would take up parts of their platform, many "policy blind spots" had to be filled—and quickly—to meet their demands.[2] In the end the coalition failed to achieve its robust aims, as it fought to keep the momentum alive through the fits and starts of nearly three decades of redevelopment.

For suburban equitable development activists, Wheaton represented a step forward, but one that foreshadowed the long road ahead. It showed a movement still very much struggling to define itself and test its own limits, while simply surviving to fight another day.

DIVERSIFYING WHEATON'S DOWNTOWN

An unincorporated community in Montgomery County, Wheaton was widely considered part of the greater Silver Spring area for much of its early history. With a population of fewer than thirty thousand through the mid-1940s, most residents lived on large estates and farms. As noted in Chapter 2, after World War II Wheaton's population ballooned with White federal government workers and veterans and, with them, a more unique neighborhood identity. As ethnic exclusions waned in the postwar boom, the neighborhood became particularly popular among Jewish families, with one of the largest populations in the county at the time. Many families who left Langley Park settled just across the county border in Wheaton. Several subdivisions, like Kemp Mill Estates, were being built by Jewish developers, and synagogues clustered in the neighborhood.[3] Jewish developers also built Wheaton Plaza. After its opening in 1960, Wheaton Plaza attracted businesses fleeing downtown Silver Spring and competed with those that remained, with its popular department store anchors and abundance of national chains.[4] Outside Wheaton Plaza the historical downtown more closely reflected the community's character. In the late 1950s, downtown hosted more than four hundred small businesses and professional offices.[5] Located at a major crossroads, known as the Wheaton Triangle, downtown had long been a popular commercial area, with streets extending to DC, Baltimore, northern Virginia, and beyond. Several businesses were run by Italian and Jewish owners.

Ethan Walker lived in Wheaton since the early seventies, working at Barbarian Comics in the heart of downtown since 1981, roughly a decade after the shop opened. Sitting in the store, surrounded by overflowing shelves of new and used comic books and action figures, I could see what had kept

Figure 13. Small businesses along Wheaton's Triangle Lane in 2015, before redevelopment began. Photo by the author.

Mr. Walker there for so long. As we talked, he paused frequently to greet customers and make recommendations, with many of his favorite picks tucked neatly away but close at hand. He recalled coming to the store as a young hobbyist when the strip of stores along Triangle Lane was quite different. While the small business character had not changed, their ownership had, with few remnants of the old. Mr. Walker pointed me to one of the few, Filippo's, just a few doors down.[6] The popular Italian deli had been in the neighborhood since 1955. The owner, Filippo Leo, who immigrated from Italy in the 1970s, sat behind the counter, greeting and serving his loyal customers. Filippo took over the store from his uncle, Thomas Marchone, for whom the deli was formerly named.[7] Today Barbarian Comics and Filippo's are surrounded by a host of immigrant-owned businesses, most of whom serve the neighborhood's rapidly growing Latinx population.

Wheaton changed quickly after 1970. As it began to sprout new subdivisions, planned and unplanned, it also became a popular neighborhood for African Americans and diverse working-class immigrants. Many newcomers were attracted by amenities that drew generations of working-class White Americans before them—affordable housing, good schools, and robust retail spaces and services.[8] With the opening of the Wheaton metro in 1990, the neighborhood became even more popular, with ready access to downtown DC. Born in Ecuador, David Fraser-Hidalgo grew up in Wheaton in the 1970s and early 1980s. His parents, one from Ecuador and the other from Philadelphia, bought into the neighborhood for its accessible location and affordability. As the parents struggled to raise David and his two brothers—all born within a four-year span—on his father's federal government salary, Wheaton "just made sense."[9] Increasingly, part of the attraction for families of color like David's and my own became the diversity of its residents and small businesses. As White-owned businesses closed, mirroring the decline of Wheaton's White population, businesses owned by people of color and new immigrants took their place.

Marian Fryer, who is African American, moved with her family to Wheaton from downtown Silver Spring in 1974. Their motivation was simple—to get a bigger house that included office space for her husband. In Wheaton she moved into a contemporary split-level house on a cul-de-sac just off University Boulevard. While few other African American families lived in Wheaton at the time, the area was changing. There were also a few historical African American areas surrounding Wheaton, including Wheaton Lane, where Ms. Fryer attended church. The diversity that was to become Wheaton's calling card was reflected on her street, which included an Asian American family, two Black families, and a Jewish family who had survived the Holocaust. Each of these neighbors helped Ms. Fryer feel at home. She remembered Wheaton during the period as a place with a strong sense of community. "It was so nice. The neighbors were friendly. People were really, really neighbors. It was like what I remembered when I was growing up in another place." A federal government employee, Ms. Fryer commuted to DC until she retired in 1995 and decided to stay put. By that time she had grown attached to her neighbors and the shops she frequented in Wheaton's downtown, only blocks from her home. "That was one of the other reasons I liked it, because you had this diversity of businesses and restaurants and things like that that you could go to and just feel comfortable," she told me, as we sat in the compact single-family house she purchased around the time of her retirement, just down the street from her former home.[10]

By the time Ms. Fryer retired, the character of downtown had changed considerably, with many new Asian-owned businesses. Between 1980 and 1990, Wheaton's Asian American population grew from just over 5 to 11 percent, holding relatively steady after that. Beyond the typical factors drawing working-class immigrants to the neighborhood, Wheaton was also near other popular Asian American suburbs like Rockville, and it had cheap commercial rents. "In the nineties, if you wanted Chinese food, you could have five different Chinese restaurants in Wheaton," recalled David Fraser-Hidalgo, who in the early 2000s returned to his old stomping grounds, buying a condo with his brother within walking distance of downtown Wheaton.[11] Others remembered a host of Vietnamese, Korean, and Thai restaurants.

Stephanie Wang grew up in DC's Chinatown as a first-generation American, born to immigrant parents. In mid-1960s, after her parents started a Chinese restaurant in downtown Silver Spring, the family moved to Wheaton. With so few Chinese people in Wheaton at the time, Ms. Wang found herself often returning to DC's Chinatown, where most of her friends still lived. But things changed as families were pushed out of DC in the various waves of gentrification (explored in Chapter 2). Many residents and businesses landed in Wheaton, including popular restaurants like Wong Gee and Kam Fong, which in Wheaton was renamed the New Kam Fong. Ms. Wang joined the mix. Having worked in her parents' restaurant most of her young life, she was a natural entrepreneur. In the mid-1990s, she opened her own restaurant, specializing in Cantonese and Hong Kong cuisine, in Wheaton's downtown, where it remains today. It opened just as the era of Wheaton's "small Chinatown" was coming to a close.[12]

After the 1990s downtown changed yet again, reflecting the area's rapidly growing Latinx population. Between 1990 and 2000, Wheaton's Latinx population more than doubled to become a quarter of the population. For those who got their start in suburbs like Langley Park, this was a step-up, with better schools, larger homes, and better transit and employment access.[13] By 2010 Latinx Americans were by far the largest ethnic group, comprising 42 percent of the population. Just off Viers Mill Road, the post–World War II homes built for returning White veterans were turned over to largely Latinx residents, who crafted a new suburban landscape.[14] They rented out basements and back bedrooms; packed front lawns with cars, flowery tropical gardens, and ornate iron fences; and raised chickens and vegetables that reminded them of the rural places that many had left behind. Latinx families also crowded into the affordable garden-style apartments across from the metro, run by Montgomery Housing Partnership, a nonprofit housing developer for whom I once worked. A rush of Latinx-owned businesses started up in downtown, particularly after the Great Recession, as commercial rents became even more affordable.

By the first decades of the twenty-first century, downtown had come to reflect both old and new. In 2021 more than one hundred stores were owned by immigrants or people of color, making up almost half of its retail.[15] On the corner of University Boulevard and Georgia Avenue, Wheaton's main intersection, is the sign for the Anchor Inn, a landmark restaurant that was torn down in 2006 to make way for a new mixed-use development. That's where my family gathered every so often for special occasions. It was also a restaurant that African Americans could not eat in until 1962.[16] Less than a block away, along University Boulevard, sat the remnants of Wheaton's "small Chinatown." Among its lasting treasures are my favorite Vietnamese restaurant, a karaoke bar where I have been known to scream my heart out, my son's go-to ramen noodle shop, and one of the only restaurants I have found in the region that sells crossing-the-bridge noodles, a dish I ate obsessively during my yearlong travels through southern China. Tucked among the many auto repair shops across the street are stores representing the diverse character that has become Wheaton's trademark—a Creole restaurant, an Irish pub, a Thai restaurant, Brazilian and Chinese grocers, a Taiwanese restaurant, a Salvadoran *pupusería*, an Ethiopian market, a Peruvian restaurant and sports bar, and a Japanese tea shop and spa. A familiar pattern of immigrant-run shops—hair and nail salons, check cashiers, accountants, sporting goods stores, dollar stores, restaurants, and bakeries—are tangled among its narrow streets and alleyways.

For many residents who arrived after 1970, my family included, Wheaton's "eclectic" character, which they often referenced, helped to define their suburban sense of place and identity. They felt at home in a place in which difference pervaded, such that theirs did not stand out. "When I found this place, I just fell in love," Ms. Fryer recalled of her current house. "I said, 'No, I'm not leaving Wheaton.'" Ms. Fryer's attachment to Wheaton was not just to her house but also to the sense of community she found amid diversity that she could not find elsewhere. "That's the main reason why I moved here—the sense of neighborhood I wanted to have," she told me.[17] Indeed, downtown closely matched the character of the Wheaton community. By 2010 nearly half of Wheaton's population was foreign-born, and nearly three quarters were non-White. No racial or ethnic group was in the majority. The population was a mix of middle-class professionals and working-class immigrants. Between 1990 and 2000, poverty rates more than doubled, as education rates declined.

Wheaton's diverse mix, however, was not neatly reflected in its emerging redevelopment politics. Khalid Afzal worked as a Montgomery County planner, overseeing the Wheaton sector plan since 1997. We first met in 2013, when he attended a presentation my students gave to Wheaton residents, county officials, and planners on ideas for retaining small businesses in downtown. My first semester as a new assistant professor, I had started the project as an ambitious attempt to expose students to the real world of planning politics. At the time I was just beginning to learn about Wheaton redevelopment, unsure of where the research might land. That meeting, attended by many with whom I later interviewed, was a turning point. Soft spoken and sincere, Khalid was one of many passionate community advocates who helped convince me of the urgency of issues facing Wheaton. When we spoke two years later, Khalid referred to the neighborhood as being in its "established community phase," typical of many communities. This is when older residents are in control, even as they are declining in population. In Wheaton these older residents were a mix of those who had moved in when the neighborhood was largely White.[18] It also included David Fraser-Hidalgo, Marian Fryer, and Stephanie Wang—all people of color. In Wheaton these diverse interests were activated as the county sounded the call for downtown redevelopment.

A NEW SCHOOL OF SUBURBAN ACTIVISTS

Efforts to redevelop Wheaton began in earnest around 1990, when the metro's Red Line was completed. That year the Montgomery County Planning Board issued the Wheaton Central Business District and vicinity sector plan, laying out a vision for a more dense, walkable downtown.[19] Many Wheaton residents supported the idea of redevelopment but also wanted control and voice in the process. Compared to Silver Spring, Wheaton redevelopment advocates were more diverse—and so was their vision for downtown. Their efforts drove conversations about the county's commitment to retaining diversity alongside redevelopment.

Not only did the Wheaton sector plan establish a vision for downtown; it prioritized retaining small businesses. Speculation around the arrival of the metro had already caused rent spikes that displaced several downtown businesses.[20] In community meetings held in anticipation of the plan, residents voiced concerns about the impact of redevelopment on downtown's character, especially small businesses. Responding to these concerns, the plan aimed to permit growth "without sacrificing the qualities of livability that give Wheaton its special character." It recommended the county adopt "policies and programs that would help to retain as many existing businesses as possible," including a Retail Preservation Overlay Zone.[21] Adopted by the county council in 1990, the overlay applied strict height limits, added requirements for assembling parcels, and did away with a process that had previously streamlined redevelopment, making it harder and less profitable for developers to rebuild. Khalid explained that residents' fears about redevelopment drove the new restrictions. Many expected redevelopment to happen quickly and that "Wheaton as they knew it would be wiped out."[22]

That fear, argued many county leaders, was unfounded. "There was no market for redevelopment in Wheaton," Khalid told me.[23] While the county upgraded infrastructure to spur new development as it had in Silver Spring, improving sidewalks and lighting, by the early 2000s they had yet to see a return on their investment. Redevelopment proponents argued that the county was not doing enough. "Wheaton has pretty much been a forgotten case," argued Ray Morrison, a local business owner and resident, in 1999.[24]

As in Silver Spring, some longtime homeowners, businesses, and county leaders argued for the need to clean up Wheaton, restore the neighborhood's reputation, and improve conditions that they perceived as declining alongside diversity. This group included large businesses and older property owners who did not see much value in the current character of downtown. "You would hear that [we have] a lot of these ethnic stores, that we don't have any special restaurants; we don't have nighttime business," noted Khalid. The media propelled the neighborhood's narrative of decline. The *Washington Post* characterized Wheaton during the period as "still trying to shake its reputation as a blue-collar suburb that was decaying because of crime and encroaching urbanization."[25] By the 1990s David Fraser-Hidalgo was working as a county police officer in training. He noted that, at the time, Wheaton had several high-profile murders and a relatively high crime rate (for a county with little crime). But, he clarified, it also had many residents and small businesses that cared for and avidly fought the neighborhood's negative stereotypes.[26]

While sharing some characteristics with the old-school suburban activists who drove downtown Silver Spring's redevelopment politics, David was part of a new generation of suburban community leaders. These new-school suburban activists were more diverse and attuned to the concerns of small businesses and marginalized residents. Nearly all the residents I spoke to who were active in redevelopment had either moved to or grown up in Wheaton after 1970. There they found a uniquely diverse community that they had grown to appreciate. While they were generally middle-class homeowners, they were largely people of color. Their race and class interests did not fall neatly in line with the old-school preservation and NIMBY politics that overwhelmed discussions about the future of downtown Silver Spring.[27] Their vision was not to restore Wheaton to some nostalgic suburban past in which they did not exist. It was of a more diverse and inclusive Wheaton. As people of color and longtime residents, they also did not face the same challenges as new-school activists in Silver Spring. These residents were deeply connected to the community they sought to mobilize. Though wary of the traffic and environmental impacts, many characterized redevelopment as something the community deserved and had been unjustly denied. Their statements recalled those of Lakeland residents, who had once claimed urban renewal as a civil right. While the county had invested heavily in west-side neighborhoods and in downtown Silver Spring, they had ignored Wheaton. And some reasoned that the slight had much to do with neighborhood's diversity and lack of political power.

Marian Fryer was part of this new school. The sense of community that Ms. Fryer found in Wheaton inspired her passion to learn and share the neighborhood's diverse past and to invest in its future. By the time we met, she was "president for life" of the Wheaton Citizens Coalition, an organization that gives voice to residents' concerns and opinions about community issues, including redevelopment. The coalition started in 1995, a year before Ms. Fryer became president—a title she still held when we spoke two decades later. By 1999 they were 350 members strong.[28] As we sat in her tidy kitchen, the coalition's meeting headquarters, Ms. Fryer picked through neatly organized boxes she kept tucked away in a nearby room, which constituted the organization's archives. Her home was also her business, out of which Ms. Fryer ran a consignment boutique for women. Occasionally pointing to an old photo or planning document, Ms. Fryer pieced together the history of the coalition and the larger neighborhood. She explained that the coalition included leaders from several local civic associations who initially came together in response to a development proposal for a new high-rise condominium just outside the Central Business District (CBD). The project did not fit the "character of the neighborhood," she argued, and would have brought a lot of traffic, overcrowded schools, and "all kinds of crazy things that the community was not happy with." Seemingly aware that her response sounded like many NIMBY suburbanites who rarely looked like her, she quickly added that the coalition did not simply oppose the project. They worked with the Montgomery Housing Partnership, the nonprofit developer, to advocate for new funding to rehabilitate existing apartment buildings instead. With help from the county, the Montgomery Housing Partnership purchased over 250 units in downtown Wheaton between 1998 and 2002, which it preserved as affordable housing.[29] Another early coalition campaign sought to prevent the county from using eminent domain to close several small businesses to expand parking downtown. The latter launched Ms. Fryer into the heart of Wheaton redevelopment politics, which was heating up at the time.[30]

In 1999 Ms. Fryer was appointed by county executive Doug Duncan to the Wheaton Urban District Advisory Committee (WUDAC). By the mid-1990s Wheaton was one of the three county urban districts, including downtown Silver Spring, eligible for a host of county-run services. Ms. Fryer recalled the frustration of committee members over the condition of downtown. Nearly a decade after the metro opened, little had been done to realize the sector plan. "There was no vision; it was just little strip malls and little low-rise buildings. It just looked terrible, and nothing was happening," she told me. David Fraser-Hidalgo was appointed to WUDAC not long after Ms. Fryer, the first of his many political appointments that would land him a seat as a Maryland state delegate by the time we spoke. The committee, he recalled, shared concerns both about inspiring redevelopment and retaining small businesses—but the central dilemma was how to do both. To spur action and ensure community voice, WUDAC urged the county to engage in a series of studies and community conversations to reimagine downtown.[31]

The county hired the National Main Street Center in the early 2000s to conduct a study of downtown and spark ideas for investment. The report sought to raise investor confidence in redevelopment, noting that no new building permits had been approved in downtown Wheaton in the prior decade. Laura Adkins, a senior policy analyst for the National Main Street Program, painted Wheaton as facing an "unpleasant future":

> Several key businesses owners had begun looking for new locations because their customers didn't want to come to Wheaton. The downtown trend in retail was attracting more adult bookstores and check-cashing facilities. Property owners were holding onto properties in the hope of some future development boom, but the area had not seen any major reinvestment in more than a decade.[32]

Overlooked in this bleak portrait were the many small businesses owned by and catering to the neighborhood's rapidly growing immigrant population. While many were struggling to stay afloat, these businesses defined the unique character and culture of downtown.

CAPITALIZING ON WHEATON'S "FUNKY" BUSINESSES

By the late 1990s, however, the political climate for Wheaton redevelopment had shifted. Having just played a major role in downtown Silver Spring, Doug Duncan turned his sights on Wheaton. His approach was similarly heavy-handed, but less intense, with the county investing fewer funds to spur redevelopment. To incentivize private investment, in 1998

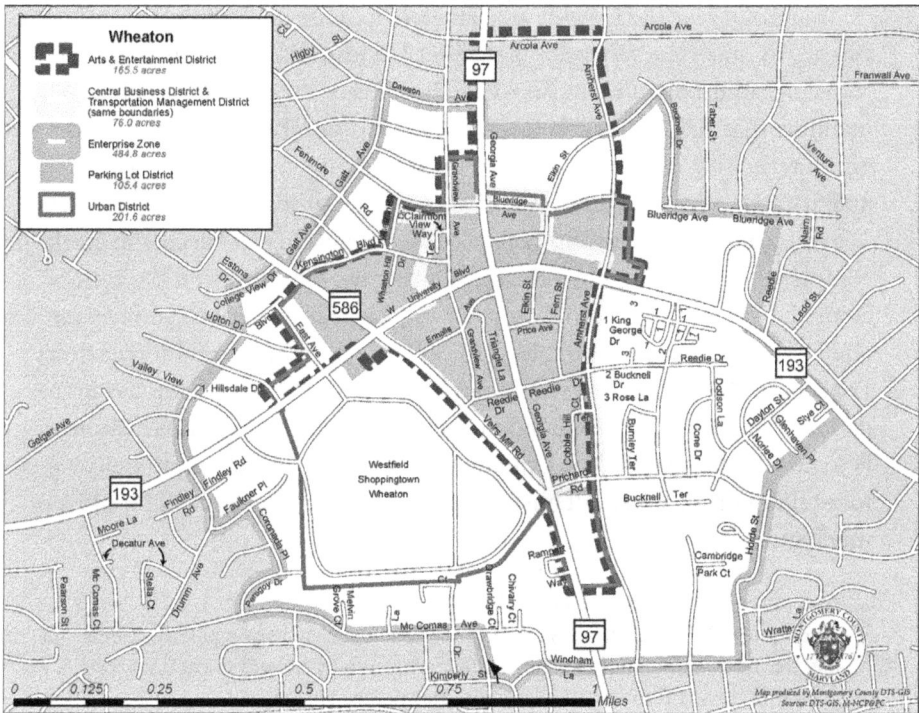

Figure 14. Montgomery County used various incentives to spur redevelopment in downtown Wheaton, including the designations shown here. Courtesy of Montgomery County, Maryland.

the State of Maryland designated downtown Wheaton as Montgomery County's second enterprise zone, after Silver Spring. Two years later the county executive created the Wheaton Redevelopment Program, with the mission to encourage private development through public investments. Shortly thereafter the state designed the CBD as a Maryland Arts and Entertainment District—one of only three in the state, including downtown Silver Spring. Finally, and perhaps most important, in 2006 the county essentially did away with the Retail Preservation Overlay Zone, which many blamed for frustrating redevelopment. Within the zone the county allowed, for the first time, developers to have the option of building above four floors—moving the height limit in much of the CBD from less than 50 feet to around 125 feet.[33]

That same year Ike Leggett was ushered in as the new county executive, vowing to finish the redevelopment that Duncan did not.[34] Sitting in his towering suburban office in Rockville, I could see the confident but casual qualities that helped launch Leggett from his humble southern roots to become the first African American on the Montgomery County Council and its first Black county executive. Seeking to leave his own legacy, Leggett prioritized Wheaton redevelopment, painting its success in stark contrast to downtown Silver Spring. During his four terms on the county council, beginning in 1986, Leggett witnessed Silver Spring's many wins and losses. Small businesses, he said, were among the latter. In Wheaton Leggett vowed the process would not be repeated. "What we are trying to do now—and this is the connection between Silver Spring and Wheaton— is to avoid that mistake," he explained to me, "to be much more inclusive to retain many of the small business."[35] Three years earlier he had said as much publicly:

> The plans to develop the small businesses in Silver Spring, I think were inadequate. Many of them were shoved aside because they could no longer pay the rent or stay in Silver Spring, even though they were there for a long period of time. I don't want to see that happen in Wheaton.[36]

Under Leggett Wheaton redevelopment became a clear political priority, supported by county policy and funding. "Anything to create incentives for the private sector to invest their own money, we have certainly supported," noted Nancy Floreen, a fifteen-year veteran of the Montgomery County Council. I sat with her in the same towering office building where I had met county executive Leggett, but we had none of the same casual conversation. She got right down to business, describing her support for redevelopment in Silver Spring and then Wheaton. She took the position that no one was negatively affected by Silver Spring redevelopment—a familiar mantra that seemed to reflect her feelings about Wheaton as well, though, she reminded me, redevelopment had only recently begun.[37] Council member Tom Perez took a different stance. Having pushed legislation to protect small businesses in Silver Spring, he hoped to do the same in Wheaton. "Redevelopment that replaces small businesses and undermines the community is not revitalization," he said of Wheaton in 2006.[38] Perez introduced the legislation that did away with the retail overlay zone but added a provision requiring developers who took advantage of increased height limits to set aside a portion of street-level spaces appropriate for small businesses.

Residents, from both the old and new schools, continued to rally for redevelopment. As in Silver Spring, community engagement occurred largely through county-appointed advisory boards. The two main groups were the eleven members of WUDAC and the twenty-member Wheaton Redevelopment Advisory Committee (WRAC). Both committees were appointed and approved by the county. One resident who served on WRAC under county executive Duncan complained publicly that decisions were made in a top-down fashion, with the committee "expected to give its unqualified endorsement."[39] WUDAC members represented small and large businesses in Wheaton, the Wheaton and Kensington Chamber of Commerce, residents, and the Mid-County Citizens Advisory Board (MCCAB), which was established in 1979 to advise the county on policy and planning issues for the larger midcounty area. WRAC was founded in 2000, in part because of a push by WUDAC to have more community input in the redevelopment process. The group included Wheaton businesses and residents who advised the county on all phases of downtown redevelopment. In addition the county hosted community-wide charettes and visioning sessions to try to establish a unified vision for downtown, including those hosted by the National Main Street Center.

The process produced little consensus. One unifying theme, however, emerged: Wheaton did not want to be like downtown Silver Spring. "Wheaton is so unique and different from other areas in Montgomery County, especially Silver Spring, Bethesda, and those areas. Wheaton is nothing like them," argued Marian Fryer. "That was really kind of the focus—that Wheaton was unique, and we needed to keep it that. It was really a neighborhood and not an urban town." Redevelopment advocates rallied against the high-rise office towers and dense development of downtown Silver Spring and in favor of a smaller-scale neighborhood look and feel that matched its existing character. To Ms. Fryer and other new-school activists, this also meant retaining the character, if not the actual small businesses, in downtown. "Our goal was to make sure that we always advocated for businesses, for small businesses," she noted, referencing her role as an early WUDAC member. Ms. Fryer went on to serve a slew of other organizations engaged in redevelopment, including WRAC, MCCAB, and the Wheaton and Kensington Chamber of Commerce.[40]

County leaders got the message but wavered on how they would respond. "They're very concerned about . . . the county or others building gleaming steel skyscrapers overshadowing these *funky* businesses. We have got to be aware of that," acknowledged David Dise, referring to Wheaton residents. Dise was director of Montgomery County Department of General Services (DGS), the county office that oversaw redevelopment planning. After taking on the role in 2008, Dise oversaw redevelopment in downtown Silver Spring and Wheaton. As I sat in a tight conference room with him and two other DGS employees, his confident air was that of a man used to being in charge. While recognizing residents' concerns, Dise noted that the county had to strike a balance between avoiding the density of Silver Spring and maintaining a "viable and commercially successful downtown." "We are not quite there yet," he told me in 2015.[41]

Dise's reference to Wheaton's "funky" businesses was an oft-cited way of describing businesses in the CBD—and another rallying point for redevelopment advocates. While some older residents were critical of the character of the businesses, the new-school suburban activists I spoke to saw the diverse small businesses as critical to Wheaton's unique character. One county planner working on Wheaton's redevelopment noted that his initial meetings with WUDAC and WRAC quickly gave him a sense of their central concerns. "There is a general sense that there is a very funky, interesting mix in Wheaton," he explained. "They didn't want to lose, you know, the texture they had in their community." This vision was somewhat at odds with that of the county, he pointed out, which saw Wheaton's potential as a major employment center.[42]

County leaders downplayed the conflict, presenting Wheaton's diversity instead as an opportunity. Speaking to the county's commitment to retaining the character of small businesses, David Dise noted, "The ethnicity that makes Wheaton distinctive is its cultural diversity, which is demonstrated in the restaurants and some of the boutiques that are popping up in the CBD. That's fine. Let's exploit that. Let's maximize that and not try and make it something it isn't." Dise saw the county's redevelopment efforts as well aligned with "maximizing" and "exploiting" that character, particularly the area's designation as an Arts and Entertainment District.[43] Other county leaders saw Wheaton's diversity in a similar light. In 1999, when county executive Doug Duncan first set his sights on Wheaton as the "next critical area for Montgomery County" redevelopment, he noted, "Diversity is a real selling point and a tremendous asset. It's one of the strongest things that Wheaton has going for it." In his pitch to redevelop Wheaton, Duncan and other county leaders repeatedly referred to the neighborhood as "Adams Morgan," helping to solidify the neighborhood's oft-cited nickname, which highlighted its ethnic diversity as a "selling point."[44]

The county's new suburban renewal tactics were not new. Their roots could be traced to strategies used by many cities to leverage arts and culture and multicultural marketing and branding to make way for capital reinvestment. Just as in the city, developers, municipalities, and others who stand to profit from redevelopment often exploit signs and symbols of ethnic difference in the suburban landscape to promote cultural consumption among new residents and tourists that seek the allure of an authentic urban experience. While Black culture has been marketed and consumed by newcomers in many DC neighborhoods, in Wheaton county leaders put another kind of diversity on display.[45] Wheaton's eclectic mix of mom-and-pop shops helped to testify to the suburb as a global marketplace, open and available to all. Its funky character was called on by boosters as evidence that Wheaton was inclusive of many cultures—one packaged within the look and feel of a quaint and quiet suburban American Main Street. This image not only forgot the racialized exclusions that had attended the making of downtown Wheaton but also failed to protect the small businesses that produced the character county leaders sought to exploit.

The county's stated commitment to retaining the character of diverse small businesses and that of the larger community amid redevelopment would be put to the test as proposals emerged. After nearly a decade of county investments, a major redevelopment proposal arrived for the county-owned parcel known as Parking Lot 13 in the Wheaton Triangle from the Bozzuto Group, an established local real estate developer. Unfortunately for redevelopment advocates who widely supported the plan, with the Great Recession underway Bozzuto dropped their proposal in 2009, citing poor market conditions and an inability to secure anchor tenants. That same year an Urban Land Institute report warned county leaders that the rush to redevelop Wheaton could negatively impact small businesses. "Wheaton's strengths, such as its eclectic retail mix, are also quite fragile, and could be irreparably harmed by any redevelopment projects that are ill-conceived or rushed." Any "attempt to force a desired result," it argued, "would not only fail but would also end up undermining the unique identity that Wheaton already possesses."[46]

The county, nonetheless, pivoted quickly to find an alternative, issuing a Request for Proposals for developers to engage in a public-private partnership for the Triangle's redevelopment. The selected developer, the B. F. Saul Company, promised nearly a million square feet of mixed-use retail spaces and dining, high-rise apartments, class A office space, a hotel, and a new town square. Robert Wulff, a former executive with the Peterson Companies, the firm that built Silver Spring's new town center, would lead B. F. Saul's efforts in Wheaton. Based in Bethesda, B. F. Saul was the parent company to Chevy Chase Bank, which owned various large office and shopping center complexes throughout the region. It was one of two public companies chaired by B. F. Saul, one of Washington's largest real estate moguls.[47] For those who held doubts about whether redevelopment would ever come to Wheaton, it now appeared that strong county support would make it happen. But what would aid those whom the county had promised to protect? That was still very much an open question.

THE PUSH FOR FAIR REDEVELOPMENT

Despite the engagement of new-school activists on county commissions and civic groups, there were many voices left out of the redevelopment conversation. Among them were new immigrants, particularly Latinx residents and businesses. Their lack of representation led to the rise of a new equitable development coalition that would help to further define what fair development could look like in Wheaton.

Wheaton residents complained to the county about the lack of engagement and limited representation of non-White and lower-income communities. Some argued that county advisory boards were not representative of the interests of its diverse neighborhood. Others argued that outside of these groups, the county was not effectively engaging marginalized groups. Most notable was the absence of Latinx Americans, including small business owners and residents, the area's fastest-growing group. WUDAC pushed the county to respond to questions about a lack of voice among these groups and their plans to retain Wheaton's diverse small businesses. In response the county hired the Latino Economic Development Center (LEDC), an established nonprofit known for its work with Latinx small businesses in Washington, DC. In Wheaton LEDC was tasked with engaging small businesses and providing them with technical assistance that could help them adjust to redevelopment.

In 2006 LEDC established its first offices outside of DC in Wheaton. Manuel Hidalgo, LEDC's executive director, noted that the decision to start a new office was not driven just by their contract with the county. Latinx-owned small businesses were increasingly starting up or moving to Montgomery County. The county's immigrant-friendly policies, including those focused on immigrant health, employment, and legal services, helped to attract a large Latinx population and facilitate immigrant-owned small businesses and start-ups.[48] "That's where things were happening," explained Manny, as most knew him and he suggested I call him. Manny had a jovial and casual manner but was a fierce immigrant rights advocate. A Miami native and son of Cuban immigrants, he had grown up in Silver Spring. Attracted by the diversity of the community and strong family ties to the region, he moved his expanded family back to his old stomping grounds in Silver Spring shortly after graduating from Georgetown. In the early 2000s, he served as development director for CASA de Maryland and was an early member of IMPACT's Community Empowerment Program. Manny was among several activists I met whose long engagement in the region's equitable development politics connected debates about redevelopment in downtown Silver Spring to that of Wheaton.[49]

LEDC's first step was to get to know Wheaton business owners. Daniel Parra was a manager at LEDC in its DC office before being called on to help set up the new Wheaton office. By the time we met, Mr. Parra had moved on to a new role but continued to engage Wheaton businesses as executive director at the Hispanic Chamber of Commerce of Montgomery County, a nonprofit started by and to promote Latinx businesses. In the early days of LEDC's Wheaton office, he recalled being one of the only staff members working out of a small cubicle in the county-run Gilcrest Immigrant Resource Center. His initial goal was to build trust with businesses owners. Parra began by going door-to-door, asking businesses about their needs and concerns. He then helped to launch a campaign to educate business owners about redevelopment and to offer microloans to assist them with start-up and working capital. LEDC also helped to launch Local First Wheaton, a campaign run by a group of small business owners that LEDC hoped would become a self-sustaining business association.[50]

But not long after LEDC began working in Wheaton, its focus shifted. Staff became increasingly concerned that the technical assistance they were providing was insufficient to help small businesses remain after redevelopment. Ash Kosiewicz began working for LEDC in 2009 as a communication and development manager, quickly graduating to director of communications and advocacy. He sat with me in LEDC's main headquarters in DC's Adams Morgan neighborhood, excited to tell the story of his time in Wheaton. It was clear from the start of our conversation that his work was a passion project, deeply connected to his identity as a community advocate and organizer. Beyond Ash LEDC had a long history of organizing. Founded in Mount Pleasant after the 1991 uprisings that followed the police shooting of a Latino man, LEDC began in an effort to rebuild the neighborhood by enabling low-income Latinos to build assets through small business development, homeownership counseling, and tenant organizing. By the time LEDC opened its Wheaton office, its staff had been organizing for over two decades to help keep residents and businesses in place in DC's rapidly gentrifying neighborhoods.

Ash recalled one of his first meetings in Wheaton, in which B. F. Saul was seeking community input on their draft concept plan. "There were no Latinos in the room," he noted. "It was a huge wakeup call for us that there's a huge part of this community not participating in this process." That realization sparked LEDC's aggressive outreach to Wheaton businesses and their changed focus from that of a service provider to an advocate. "We just decided we can't just do technical assistance and microlending and do training here if it's all for naught—because redevelopment is going to displace all of them," explained Manny in a spirited tone that matched that of Ash.[51] I sensed the two made a good team.

A catalyzing moment came in late 2010, when county officials signaled support for B. F. Saul's requested $66 million in infrastructure upgrades that would aid its construction of high-density office buildings. LEDC questioned why such deep subsidies were going to the developer when many feared that the project would result in rising rents that would displace many businesses and residents. As Ash explained, LEDC had asked,

> How can we make this project happen but put assurances within a general development agreement that would make clear that in return for $66 million in public taxpayer money, the community will have a series of benefits that will ensure it with local jobs, protect small businesses, preserve housing, and these sort of standalone wonderful examples of how you get fair redevelopment done in this new age of transit-oriented development?

Ash charged that, amid the fervor to attract private investment, the county was making too many concessions to developers and not asking enough for the community in return.[52]

LEDC was not alone. By 2011 it had organized a group of more than fifty community leaders, businesses, and nonprofit organizations, with the goal of ensuring that redevelopment met the needs of established businesses and residents. The organization was known as the Coalition for the Fair Redevelopment of Wheaton.[53] Its partners included IMPACT Silver Spring and CASA de Maryland, which had supported IMPACT's efforts in Silver Spring and was just beginning its own redevelopment battle in Maryland's International Corridor. In an early statement, the coalition argued that if the county did not put protections in place, redevelopment would be borne off the backs of Wheaton residents and businesses. "We don't want Wheaton's strengths—its people of diverse incomes and cultures, its small businesses, and its broad array of housing options to accommodate individuals and families alike—to be sacrificed in the process," it stated.[54]

The coalition came together slowly, largely out from the persistence of its lead organizer, Ash Kosiewicz. As a White guy trying to organize largely Latinx businesses, he did not have an easy challenge. Ash went door-to-door to businesses every day—sometimes several times a day—to earn their trust. Marco Rivera, an immigrant from El Salvador, started his business selling electronics in Wheaton in 2000. Wheaton was close to his home and had affordable commercial rents and the strong Latinx customer base he needed. Wheaton was, as Mr. Rivera informed me, the "Latino Capital of Maryland" and a place many Latinx-owned businesses thrived by catering to residents. Like many business owners I met, Mr. Rivera was excited about the prospect of redevelopment but concerned about what it would mean for his ability to remain in Wheaton. As we sat in his storefront, facing a bustling Georgia Avenue, he explained his strong attachment to Wheaton and that he had always wanted to help his community outside of his business. But Mr. Rivera had not gotten involved until he met Ash: "He was knocking doors, delivering little fliers, saying, 'We have a meeting this time.' Then, he would deliver the fliers. And then the day of the meeting he will go, 'OK, the meeting is in two hours.'" While few business owners related to county representatives who sometimes came around, Ash was different. Not only did he speak Spanish; he spoke the language of small business owners. "He found a way to make people become interested in what we needed to be prepared for," noted Mr. Rivera, conveying the gratitude many business owners invoked when talking about Ash.[55]

The Coalition for the Fair Redevelopment of Wheaton's initial concerns were largely over parking, rental increases, and competition from larger commercial chains.[56] "Over two years of construction, taking away that parking. That's it. Nobody is going to survive," predicted Filippo Leo in 2011, in response to the plans that eliminated 168 parking spaces adjacent to Triangle Lane, which his customers relied on. Some struck a more hopeful tone at the time. "We have to be thinking about a new and different type of clientele, and we have to target that clientele, and we have to do the changes necessary for that," one owner said at the time. "We have to be ready." Many in the county agreed, preaching the same mantra of individual business adjustment and adaptation as they did in downtown Silver Spring. "Part of what businesses need to do is they need to expand their horizons," Peter McGinnity, the manager of business development with the Wheaton Redevelopment Program, said to businesses during a WRAC meeting in late 2011. "It's not simply the issue of redevelopment." But Georgia Bennet, longtime owner of a salon along Triangle Line, retorted that the county held a significant responsibility for what was happening. "We understand about broadening our horizons, but the thing is you have to understand what you have now and what you're going to lose," Bennet said, arguing that the county was focused on making a profit and less so on communicating and working with existing small businesses.[57]

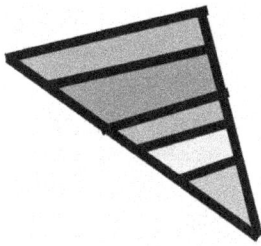

Coalition for the
Fair Redevelopment
of Wheaton
Community Benefits for a Stronger Wheaton.

Figure 15. The Coalition for the Fair Redevelopment of Wheaton's logo emphasizes their campaign for a community benefits agreement. Courtesy of the Latino Economic Development Center.

The Coalition for the Fair Redevelopment of Wheaton organized business owners and residents to attend redevelopment meetings. With the support of about five hundred county residents and small businesses, the coalition urged the county executive and council to include a community benefits agreement in their development contract with B. F. Saul. Community benefits agreements are legally binding tools used to balance the scales of development by requiring developers to address community needs.[58] The county, Manny argued, wanted redevelopment without community accountability. "They didn't want to have to give [B. F. Saul] any strings. Of course, we were insistent on the strings," he explained, lightheartedly, but in a way that conveyed his serious intent. In Wheaton the proposed agreement included provisions for job training and local hiring, small business support, affordable housing, the relocation of community services displaced by redevelopment, and a new multicultural community center and town square. According to the coalition, "without these benefits, Wheaton's spirit and identity could be lost forever. Small businesses could be displaced and go out of business during construction, the cost of housing could increase beyond the means of Wheaton residents, and important community services could disappear from the area."[59] The features that had brought diverse residents together and shaped the community's character, the coalition charged, were under threat.

The agreement was meant to counter the negative impacts of development and establish a more equitable and inclusive framework for Wheaton after redevelopment. As Manny saw it, the county's interest was in producing a far different kind of community than what existed in Wheaton.

> Basically, [they] want to reengineer Wheaton to be something completely different. What happens to the people here? There was a lack of concern for the displacement that was going to happen. . . . There was no commitment to do anything but the tried and, in their opinion, true method of traditional economic development, which is like putting in a DC USA in Columbia Heights and saying this is good for the community.

Manny's reference was to a DC neighborhood whose redevelopment had forced many Latinx residents out of the city to places like Wheaton—and more particularly to a suburban-style shopping mall whose big-box stores were often blamed with forcing small businesses to close their doors. LEDC had recently helped immigrant tenants in Columbia Heights purchase an apartment building, using DC's Tenant Opportunity to Purchase Act to combat rising rents. For Manny keeping immigrant businesses in place was another key component of diverse and equitable neighborhoods.[60] "Redevelopment without gentrification," he believed, was possible in Wheaton.[61]

Early meetings between the coalition, county, and developer indicated little support for the community benefits agreement. Finally, in a response letter to the coalition's request, Steve Silverman, director of the Department of Economic Development, and David Dise stated unquestionably that the county would not enter into an agreement with the coalition. It would be "inequitable for Montgomery to create an established relationship with one specific interest group as there are numerous interest groups involved with Wheaton redevelopment," the letter stated.[62] Silverman was an outspoken advocate for downtown Silver Spring redevelopment, the former president of the Greater Silver Spring Chamber of Commerce, and former cochair of the Silver Spring Redevelopment Steering Committee. After being elected to the Montgomery County Council, he oversaw the redevelopment of both Silver Spring and Wheaton. Before that he was involved in the group that supported the new Blair High School and in 2006 ran against Ike Leggett for county executive, which he lost. Wesley Graham, who worked closely with both county leaders and Wheaton businesses at the time, spoke to the county's reasoning.

"I think the concern at that point was were you really going to be able to attract development in here if someone's going to have to negotiate with a wide variety of community organizations in order to do it." Taking me on a brief tour of the Triangle, a beat that he walked regularly for nearly a decade, Wesley spoke knowledgeably and personally about the businesses we passed. Perhaps more than anyone else in the county, he knew what was at stake in the county's decision about whether and how to support small businesses.[63]

County leaders' lack of support for the coalition's CBA was hardly surprising, given their failure to support a related countywide community benefits bill. Introduced in late 2011, the bill responded to community concerns about several proposed big-box stores in the county, including a new Costco at Wheaton Plaza. "We saw this as a sort of tool for stabilizing Wheaton and also providing a new potential base of customers for small businesses," one county leader who was involved in negotiations over the bill explained of Costco, not mentioning countywide controversy over its presence. The bill would have required large retail stores to enter community benefits agreements with civic organizations or demonstrate that they had made a good faith effort to do so. While supported by many members of the Coalition for the Fair Redevelopment of Wheaton, it was strongly opposed by developers and local chambers of commerce. Opponents claimed that the bill would make the county's already time-consuming, complicated, and expensive permitting processes even more so, discouraging new businesses from starting up in the county. County executive Leggett promised to veto the bill if it came to his desk. With no action taken, the bill expired. And in 2013 Costco opened its 148,000 square-foot store in Wheaton, underwritten by $4 million in county funds.[64]

By then the coalition's efforts had hit another snag. Countering early indications, the county council unanimously voted in 2012 to deny B. F. Saul the requested subsidy. The county's explanation for the change was that there was no market for the significant office space, the key to their plans. "It was a lot of money going to a private player, and we didn't see that ... they had a clear path to success," council member Nancy Floreen told me.[65] In a scathing report to the council, one senior legislator questioned why the county was offering up one of its most valuable parcels in Wheaton to invest in an expensive project unlikely to return much economic or community value. "Unlike a school or a train, the platform does not teach any child to read and does not take anyone to work. If it is not generating revenues, then it probably is not a good investment."[66] With ongoing pressure from various stakeholders to make redevelopment happen, the county simultaneously announced that it would instead pursue a counterproposal. Under the new plan, the county would partner with private developers to relocate the county's main planning offices to Wheaton and fund a new town square on Parking Lot 13. The county would retain control of its prime parcel and spur redevelopment through its own investments. Many county leaders touted the proposal as win-win for the county, which needed a new park and planning building, and for residents, who wanted a revitalized Wheaton.

Residents who had pushed for redevelopment were incensed. Henroit St. Gerard, a native of Silver Spring who was appointed to WUDAC in 2011 and a few years later became its chair, explained the committee's disappointment with the decision. Council members who attended the WUDAC meeting after the vote received an earful of complaints. Mr. St. Gerard said the sentiment shared by most members was "we're not going through this whole entire process if we're going to have to wait another five, ten years for redevelopment to happen because you just took the whole thing away from us." St. Gerard did not appear the patient kind. An MBA and experienced senior business analyst, he had agreed to meet me during his lunch break near his executive-level job at a management consulting and recruiting firm in downtown DC.[67]

Stephanie Wang sat on WUDAC for six years and decided to leave the committee shortly after the county's decision. We met in her restaurant in Wheaton Plaza, surrounded by her signature dishes, which she prodded me to try while explaining her disappointment in the county's decision:

> You get a little frustrated after a while when they keep talking about things and talking about things, and you make decisions on certain projects and things, and then all of a sudden [the council] decides, "No, we don't want to do this. But this is good, and we're going to do it this way, and what you were doing for the past three years is not good, and we're not going to do it this way." You could get fed up with it. I said, "You know what? They can do what they want to do. I don't want to have anything to do with it."

Like St. Gerard, Ms. Wang lacked patience with the county, but for other reasons. As the mother of four and a business owner, she had her hands full. She was also worn from years of battling the county and developers about her business. Wheaton Plaza was her restaurant's third location in Wheaton. In the first she had run up against the county's restrictive permitting process that prevented her from renovating and expanding. In the second her landlord sold the building and canceled her lease after she had invested over $700,000 in renovations. After ten months of being out of work while outfitting the new location, she finally opened in the mall. Her trials had inspired her activism but exhausted her patience.[68]

For the Coalition for the Fair Redevelopment of Wheaton, however, the county's new plans meant something very different. It was a final blow to their proposed community benefits agreement and hurt the momentum of their organizing. Ash explained that before B. F. Saul and the county parted ways, the coalition had more holistic and hopeful discussions about the equitable development gains that might be achieved. But afterward the ground shifted.

> I'd say the capacity, or lack of capacity, has made it increasingly difficult to stay intensely involved in these processes. I'd say especially so when B. F. Saul left the project. It really opened up a vacuum. The most challenging thing, I think, about that moment was that it confirmed in some people's minds that [redevelopment] may never, ever happen.[69]

While many coalition members feared the impact of redevelopment on marginalized businesses and residents, they had made significant progress in framing an alternative vision of what equitable development could look like. But that vision and the engagement it inspired for a different kind of redevelopment became less clear, as downtown plans shifted focus yet again.

THE REBIRTH OF THE FAIR REDEVELOPMENT MOVEMENT

As the movement for fair redevelopment in Wheaton hit new stumbling blocks, development ramped up. In 2012 the county passed a new CBD

Figure 16. Redevelopment in downtown Wheaton took hold in the early 2010s, including many new apartment buildings around its metro station. Photo by the author.

sector plan that proposed greater density in downtown and an increased mix of residential uses.[70] Between 2000 and 2019, housing units in the CBD grew nearly three times—from just over 800 to nearly 2,300. This included new buildings like the prominent seventeen-story, 486-unit Exchange, an apartment complex situated atop of a new grocery store built with around $5 million in county subsidies. Between 2008 and 2014, roughly $163 million in private investment and 1.5 million square feet of new development was built in the CBD.[71] Further incentivizing development, the county modernized Wheaton High School and invested $70 million in a new library and recreation center.

Demographics in the CBD began to shift. Between 2000 and 2019, as the population in the CBD nearly doubled, the median household income rose as the percentage of those with college and advanced degrees nearly doubled. Growth was accounted for largely by increases in Black and mixed-race populations, while the proportion of Latinx and foreign-born residents declined sharply. And Whites finally reversed their five-decade-long decline. Trends in the CBD differed from the larger Wheaton population, where the percentage of Latinx residents grew, Whites continued their steady decline, foreign-born residents held steady, and median incomes declined (see Table 2).

Amid the flurry of redevelopment, new plans took shape. In 2013 the county contracted with StonebridgeCarras and Bozzuto, a joint venture of local-based companies that included the developers that had proposed to redevelop downtown six years earlier and had built dozens of apartment and condominium complexes in Wheaton. Their plan would create a 308,000 square-foot government office building with ground-floor retail space, a new town square, and a two-hundred-unit mixed-income apartment complex on four publicly owned sites in the heart of downtown. The county would invest about $144 million in the plans, including funds to rebuild the Mid-County Regional Services Center displaced by the new town center. The partnership included a land swap, in which the county gifted the developer the site of its old planning office in downtown Silver Spring, which would move to Wheaton. In its place the developer would build a new mixed-use complex that would serve as a gateway to downtown Silver Spring, aiding redevelopment in both places.[72] Construction for Wheaton's new downtown would begin in late 2016 and last three years.

While the Coalition for the Fair Redevelopment of Wheaton's hopes for a community benefits agreement were dashed, they continued to organize and found an ally in public office. In 2009 Nancy Navarro became the first Latina on the Montgomery County Council, representing Mid-County's District 4, which included Wheaton. Born in Venezuela, Navarro previously lived in Wheaton and was known for her work as an immigrant rights advocate. Before being elected to council, she founded a nonprofit promoting the economic and educational development of immigrant communities and served two terms on the board of education, where she created a unit that provided translation for non-English-speaking parents. On the council Navarro championed various immigrant and equitable development issues. She fought to allow undocumented immigrants to be eligible for in-state tuition and opposed a federal program requiring local police to share arrest data with US Immigration and Customs Enforcement. She campaigned on a promise to bring additional services and resources to

Table 2 Demographic and housing data for Wheaton Central Business District (CBD) and Census Designated Place (CDP), 1970–2019

	1970		1980		1990		2000		2010		2019	
	CBD	CDP	CBD	CDP	CBD	CDP	CBD	CDP	CBD	CDP	CBD	CDP
Population	1,389		1,112	48,598	1,537	53,720	2,070	57,694	3,141	45,079	3,756	50,229
					Race, ethnicity, and immigration							
White (%)	93		86	79	58	61	33	40	29	27	30	23
Black (%)	5		4	10	11	16	13	18	29	17	34	15
Hispanic or Latinx (%)[1]	4		4	5	20	12	39	26	29	42	15	44
Asian (%)	—		6	6	11	11	9	12	10	12	10	13
Other (%)[2]	0		0	1	0	0	6	4	3	3	11	5
Foreign-born (%)	26		18	15	29	25	49	40	51	45	28	44
					Income							
Adjusted median household income[3]	$91,690		$48,777	$84,689	$70,828	$95,067	$69,370	$91,140	$63,267	$81,091	$71,360	$85,617
Families in poverty (%)	0		13	3	8	3	2	6	10	8	10	8

Education

High school or less (%)	73	64	52	47	40	51	43	34	49	14	44
College (%)[4]	27	36	48	41	47	33	42	40	37	59	40
Advanced degrees (%)	—	—	—	12	14	16	16	26	15	28	16

Housing

Total housing units	465	495	17,262	669	19,977	836	20,125	1,251	15,080	2,273	16,257
Renter occupied (%)	54	61	98	56	34	64	32	73	30	82	35
Renters' cost burden (%)[5]	23	41	22	45	38	37	24	55	54	54	56

SOURCES: US Census Bureau, *Census 1970*; US Census Bureau, *Population and Housing, 1980*; US Census Bureau, *Population and Housing, 1990*; US Census Bureau, *2000 Census of Population*; US Census Bureau, *2006–2010 Summary File*; US Census Bureau, *2019 ACS 1-Year*.

NOTE: The Wheaton Central Business District is defined as Census Tract 7038.

[1] The "Hispanic or Latinx" group was double-counted in 1970. All other groups are Non-Hispanic from 1980 onward.

[2] "Other" consists of American Indian, Alaska Native, Native Hawaiian, other Pacific Islander, some other race alone, and two or more races. The year 1970 includes Asian groups.

[3] All years have been indexed to 2019 values.

[4] The years 1970 to 1980 include advanced degrees.

[5] The cost burden from 1970 to 1980 is more than 35 percent of income spent on rent; from 1990 to 2019, it is more than 30 percent.

the Mid-County area and to close the county's investment gap between disinvested neighborhoods in Mid- and East County compared to those in West County. Navarro cosponsored the failed countywide CBA bill and, after the B. F. Saul project failed, helped to ensure that county funds for Wheaton redevelopment were available to support the new plans.

After several meetings with the coalition, Navarro stepped in to ensure that at least some of the community benefits it had fought for were realized. Responding to its demands for more affordable housing, she worked to secure a county commitment of up to 30 percent of affordable housing in the new development.[73] To stem the loss of displaced community organizations, she helped to ensure commitments that organizations disrupted by redevelopment would have space in the new Mid-County Regional Services Center or elsewhere in Wheaton. Picking up the call for a new multicultural center, she fought to bring a county-run combined health and human services and arts and humanities center to Wheaton. The county in turn promised that the Department of Health and Human Services would be among nine county agencies located in their new Wheaton office building and that it would conduct a feasibility study for a new Wheaton Arts and Humanities Center. Responding to the coalition's concerns regarding local hiring, Navarro cosponsored Bill 48-14, which amended the county's minority-owned business-purchasing program to increase the number of participating firms. Finally, and of significant importance to the coalition, Navarro introduced Bill 6-12, a resolution to establish a Small Business Assistance (SBA) program. The program would provide training as well as technical and financial assistance to small businesses adversely impacted by county redevelopment projects. The council passed the bill unanimously in mid-2012.

I met Adam Fogel, Navarro's chief of staff, in the towering county office building in Rockville that was by now familiar turf, with a long list of questions about the bill. He explained the bill's goals were intended in part to ensure that Wheaton redevelopment did not repeat the mistakes of downtown Silver Spring:

> The understanding, the perception, and, I think, reality was there were a lot of businesses displaced during Silver Spring's redevelopment. We wanted to learn those lessons and not repeat mistakes. . . . In putting forward the concept of a small business assistance program, we wanted to alleviate those

concerns that these businesses wouldn't be ignored this time around—that there would not just be lip service but there would actually be a concrete program in place that served their interests and their needs.[74]

However well-intentioned the bill was, advocates recognized that the devil lay in the details. For the bill's vision to become a reality, the program needed to be ironed out, and they needed to be at the table.

The Coalition for the Fair Redevelopment of Wheaton pressed for the bill's passage and to ensure it worked for Wheaton small businesses. At a public hearing in early 2012, Ash told the council that the bill was a "step in the right direction" but required adequate funding and regulations to allow broad participation and should be part of a comprehensive approach to helping small businesses.[75] Following the bill's passage, the coalition created a Small Business Pledge, signed by 1,200 supporters, calling for business access and visibility during construction, public comment on the program regulations, and full program funding and staffing, among other things. WUDAC also pushed the county to commit to implementing the program, maintaining transparency in decision making, mitigating construction impacts on businesses, and addressing businesses' concerns for parking, safety, and rising rents.

With coalition activism and that of Wheaton's new-school activists who sat on various committees and boards, the final SBA program regulations, approved in December 2015, addressed several of these concerns. The county agreed to provide grants of up to $75,000 that could be used to offset increased rents, among other things. Priority was given to businesses most heavily impacted, included those with lost parking and obstructed views near the new town center.[76] The county hired four technical assistance providers—LEDC, the Maryland Small Business Development Center, the Greater Washington Hispanic Chamber of Commerce, and the Hispanic Chamber of Commerce of Montgomery County—to help small businesses qualify for assistance. The county also agreed to sponsor an Open for Business campaign, to conduct a parking study, and to create a parking-mitigation plan. They would promote small businesses through ongoing events like Taste of Wheaton, Local First Wheaton, and the Wheaton Small Business Innovation Center, a county-run incubator for early-stage businesses. The county also established retail priority streets in the CBD, where they would encourage mixed-use development and street-level activity through urban design.[77]

But the coalition also lost some battles, including a provision of the SBA program that limited funding to healthy businesses. Adopted to address county officials' concerns of subsidizing businesses unlikely to succeed regardless of redevelopment, the program defined healthy businesses as those that could show profit in at least one of the last three years of tax returns. Coalition advocates argued that the definition left aside many businesses that would be hardest hit by redevelopment that the bill was intended to help. In a letter responding to the proposed regulations, the coalition wrote,

> Many [businesses] have spent decades driving Wheaton's economy, have made critical decisions to facilitate their continued operation despite the economic downturn, and are committed to staying in Wheaton. Now, these definitions establish obstacles to financial assistance for some business owners who are seeking assistance in the face of an external shock.

Navarro and other council members, however, were intent that the language remain. "It's this idea that you don't want to throw good money at bad," said Adam Fogel, explaining Navarro's support for the regulations.[78]

Ultimately, the hopes that the coalition once held for what could be achieved in Wheaton were tempered not only by such losses but also by its own struggles to survive. Shortly after the passage of Bill 6-12, shake-ups at LEDC led to the loss of staff who had once led the coalition. Manny, who actively supported LEDC's organizing activities in Wheaton, stepped down as executive director in 2013 after disputes with the nonprofit's board, which he characterized as increasingly conservative and White.[79] Ash's position was reduced to part-time, and in 2014 he left LEDC. With his departure the coalition largely became defunct.

Some said that the demise of the Coalition for the Fair Redevelopment of Wheaton was largely due to waning engagement in the redevelopment process caused by multiple project delays and a lack of trust between the county and community. After Manny left LEDC in 2013, the coalition was not particularly active in Wheaton. One LEDC leader I spoke to reasoned its declining momentum was due largely to the many failed redevelopment proposals and current project delays:

I think what was challenging about the work with the coalition, really, was the timing of the development. It would be announced there's something that was imminent, and then the plans would pull back. And now it looks like we're starting groundbreaking at the end of this calendar year. But this is four years later.

By the time we spoke in early 2016, two major proposals for downtown Wheaton had come and gone, and the proposed groundbreaking for the new town center had just been pushed back nearly a year.[80]

Regardless of the cause, the fragile coalition that had been built around the active efforts of an organization that was still gaining its foothold in a new community became exhausted by a long redevelopment battle. Reflecting on his time as the coalition's lead organizer, Ash somberly noted that the hope he once had for what could be accomplished had died long before the coalition itself:

> We really hoped and tried everything we could to get this to work out. What would be on one hand a very bold vision for Wheaton and bring all the things people had been wanting for years, but also . . . the first-ever community benefits proposal that would sort of marry the fruits of redevelopment with economic justice. We wanted Wheaton to be the shining example of that. . . . I had visualized in my mind what it would have been like for B. F. Saul, the county, the coalition, and community members to come up and be like, "We did it. We got this redevelopment proposal. We feel like redevelopment can work if there are certain things put in place." I wanted to see that vision happen, and it never did.[81]

While Ash was disappointed to not see his vision fully realized, parts of it were carried forward by the coalition and its allies, including those in public office. And while the coalition lost momentum as the process of redevelopment wore on, other groups stepped in to try to carry the torch forward.

KEEPING THE FIGHT ALIVE

As the Coalition for the Fair Redevelopment of Wheaton faded, signs of renewed activism arose. In 2015 a group of Latinx business owners founded La Voz Latina de los Empresarios de Wheaton (The Voice of the

Latin American Businesses in Wheaton). Still, small business engagement in the redevelopment process ebbed as shovels broke ground on the new town center. Meanwhile, questions remained about whether the protections the coalition had helped to secure were enough to keep small businesses in place. As rents rose and construction disruptions hit businesses hard, some closed while many others worried and waited to see what the future would bring.

Latinx business owners who were active in the coalition started La Voz to fill the void left behind by the loss of LEDC as the coalition's lead organizer and advocate on behalf of Wheaton small businesses. Marco Rivera, one of La Voz's founding members, explained that Ash's departure from LEDC left a big void. "He was the engine of this," he told me soberly. "That was confirmed when he left."[82] By this time Mr. Rivera had come to play a larger role in county redevelopment politics as a member WUDAC and MCCAB but still felt there were important voices missing from the conversation.

Without the same organizing capacity as LEDC, La Voz struggled from the start. When Mr. Rivera and I spoke in 2015, the year of La Voz's founding, the organization had few businesses attending meetings and no clear position on redevelopment. Three years later, when I spoke to Richard Cisneros, LEDC's small business coach, he reported that the group was no longer meeting. I had been trying to meet Richard for over a year when I finally caught up to him at a Fair Development Coalition meeting at CASA.[83] We later sat together at LEDC's Wheaton office, which had grown from its humble origins in the Gilcrest Center to an office suite in a building adjacent to Wheaton Plaza. By then Richard had been working with Wheaton small businesses for three years, picking up where Ash left off, though not under the umbrella of the now-defunct Coalition for the Fair Redevelopment of Wheaton. In trying to help La Voz get started, Richard noted that the business owners leading the organizing lacked the credibility of more established owners and that the diversity of Wheaton's businesses challenged their organizing. "There's a lot of conflict because it's so diverse," he noted.[84] Few county redevelopment leaders I spoke to had even heard of La Voz.

Equitable development advocates also struggled to engage Wheaton small businesses in ongoing redevelopment talks—a sign of their waning momentum and limited capacity. The long process of redevelopment, its many fits and starts, and the battles lost along the way all frustrated participation. As Isabel López saw it, many businesses no longer saw redevelopment as an immediate crisis or had simply resigned themselves to the fate of what was to come. Isabel joined my meeting with Richard at his request, as her work in Wheaton predated his. She interned at LEDC in 2011 and later became the program manager for small business development in its Wheaton office. Uncertainty in the process and the county's lack of communication with businesses affected the coalition's work and the engagement of businesses over time, she explained.

> I was an intern at LEDC when there was a redevelopment coalition with Ash, and I think there was momentum there because I remember being part of us going to hearings and sort of voicing the small business opinion. And then it never, construction never happened. There were no updates, so there was a loss of momentum with the organization. And I think that was also a factor in businesses losing that trust, and I think they lost out on also them being a group or staying as a group of committed business owners.

As redevelopment proposals came and went and with no business association in place, LEDC had to repeatedly reestablish relationships with small businesses—each time trying to build back the trust and momentum lost in the process.[85]

The waning engagement of small businesses was notable, as the county tried to qualify businesses for its SBA program. In 2005 a county survey of Wheaton small businesses had a 73 percent participation rate, while a similar survey conducted in 2012 had a response rate of only 36 percent.[86] Three years later the county hired the Maryland Small Business Development Center to conduct small business financial assessments to qualify businesses for the SBA program and determine funding needs. Only about a fourth of eligible businesses participated.[87] Marisela Villamil, the center's senior business consultant, said that there was a lot of confusion and frustration among businesses about the program's terms, including whether funding would be a grant or a loan. Ms. Villamil worked out of the same office building as LEDC, which also hosted the Wheaton Small Business Innovation Center that included several immigrant entrepreneurs with whom she worked. She spoke fast and feverishly in an accent that I had a hard time placing. "I am Cuban, but I am from Ireland," she clarified with a laugh. Her experiences growing up in multiple countries was an asset, she noted, in working with Wheaton's diverse small business owners, including their frustrations in qualifying for the SBA program.[88] The county later engaged multiple organizations to help businesses qualify and to clarify the program's terms. But many said that the process was still confusing, and skepticism among businesses ran high.

While funding for the SBA program eventually came through, some advocates said it was too late to help the most vulnerable businesses. One LEDC representative reflected on a provision that required businesses to show losses due to construction after they suffered the damage, which she likened to home insurance. "You can access the insurance payment once your house has burned down but you're kind of screwed once your house has burnt down."[89] The requirement disparately affected businesses that had little savings and needed immediate relief.

Advocates were also concerned about the county's timeline for establishing program eligibility. When Adam Fogel and I spoke in late 2015, the program regulations were not yet in place, while groundbreaking for the town center was less than a year away. "It's deeply concerning," he said, noting a provision in the bill stating that businesses would be eligible for the program a year before construction began. Council member Navarro had proposed a two-year advanced timeframe. The county, Mr. Fogel stated brusquely, needed to get the program up and running quickly to be true to the bill's intent.[90]

As it turned out, groundbreaking was delayed shortly after we met, until June 2017, giving additional time for the county to determine program regulations. Funding for the SBA program was finally budgeted for the 2018 fiscal year and program regulations set by late 2015, specifying that businesses could apply for assistance starting the quarter after construction began. Still, uncertainty about the program guidelines left many businesses in limbo for years, questioning whether and how much relief they could receive. Multiple redevelopment proposals and delayed construction timelines also left many doubting whether redevelopment was even coming to Wheaton. But by late 2017 cranes hovered in the skyline and construction barrels blocked access to several downtown streets and parking spaces, doing away with all speculation to the contrary.

Beneath those cranes many diverse businesses that characterized Wheaton's funky downtown struggled to remain open. Several were victims of predatory leasing practices. Reflecting the experiences of businesses in Silver Spring, business owners and advocates noted that landlords intentionally kept spaces vacant in anticipation of redevelopment. Many business owners had signed onto predatory leases that made tenants responsible for basic property repairs. Immigrants who did not understand the contracts they signed and could not afford to hire lawyers to help with negotiations were particularly vulnerable. On my regular visits to downtown Wheaton, I noted familiar green and white "for lease" signs that remained on buildings for months, if not years. The real estate company referred to in the ads, I was told, was among the largest property owners in downtown and infamous among small businesses.

Mr. Rivera didn't tell me the name of his former landlord, but his story was similar to others I heard in Wheaton. Before Mr. Rivera moved to his current space, his landlord had tried to charge him $30,000 for a broken air-conditioner. The neighboring business was charged $33,000 for a roof leak that led the business to close. As in Silver Spring, after construction began landlords increasingly refused to renew leases or provide tenants with long-term leases. Businesses also complained that landlords were not honoring existing leases and were setting them to expire just after construction ended, with the expectation of raising rents or selling the building. "So [businesses] stayed here and endured the hardships of construction," Richard Cisneros reflected, looking at the cranes hovering outside LEDC's fifth-story window. "What assures them that they're not going to be kicked out as soon as this construction is done?"[91]

For businesses that had hung on, parking, signage, and other construction disruptions continued, despite county mitigation efforts. Isabel López offered a personal example. After construction began her mother invited close family and friends to her favorite Bolivian restaurant in downtown Wheaton to celebrate a traditional holiday. But when her guests arrived, some of whom drove from Virginia, no one could find nearby parking. Many were confused by signs directing them to park elsewhere—signs not written in Spanish and so small that many missed them altogether. Embarrassed and frustrated, her mother asked guests to instead meet up at Wheaton Plaza. Isabel complained directly to the county but noted that the issue was neither easily nor quickly resolved, which, she added, many are not. Bureaucracy among the state, county, and developers resulted in communication lapses with businesses and customers about construction updates.[92]

Some businesses were also frustrated that they did not get county contracts to make up for construction losses. Richard Cisneros said businesses feared that the county and developers were bringing in outside vendors to provide services during construction instead of relying on the many small businesses in Wheaton that provided the same services. "The reality is if they are losing clients because of the parking, they should be able to capitalize on the people that are there, the workers and other people in the area," he argued. Priority hiring for Wheaton small businesses was a goal of the coalition that council member Navarro fought for. But for many businesses, the path was not clear, and the protections insufficient.[93]

Business owners also worried that if they were not directly displaced by rising rents, they would be indirectly displaced by the loss of customers. As one business owner told the county, "Our business depends on the Latino population, so if the population falls, so does our business."[94] The reverse is also true. Immigrants tend to locate in or near communities that provide services and amenities they need. The residents moving into the new high-end apartments and condominiums in downtown Wheaton hardly resembled the clientele who were the mainstay of many small businesses. In contrast, county leaders' beliefs about the benefits of redevelopment for small businesses echoed Silver Spring—those that could survive the "transition" would benefit in the long run. "You've got an entire new market of folks you're going to be adjacent to," one county leader projected. "You'd be crazy to be going someplace else, if we can help you through this period."[95] While the county saw new customers that redevelopment attracted as an asset, many businesses saw them as a threat.

Meanwhile, the grassroots activism that once spurred residents, businesses, and nonprofits to come together and demand that government rethink the process and purposes of development—those it hurts and those it helps—dimmed just as redevelopment finally arrived. Ethan Walker told me that LEDC once played a critical role in taking the concerns of small businesses to the council and helping businesses unify around plans to stay open. While noting that LEDC had recently become more active in helping businesses qualify for the SBA program—praising Richard's efforts—Mr. Walker was skeptical about whether many businesses would survive, including Barbarian Comics. The possibility of closure was not one that he took lightly. As an older disabled adult who had worked in the store most of his life, his prospects of getting another job were dim. The loss would not just be personal but felt acutely by his loyal customers of more than forty years. "There are other places they could actually shop and get the same merchandise, but they come here because they're comfortable. It feels like home, basically," he quietly reflected. I asked organizational leaders working in Wheaton how they would measure the success of Wheaton's small business survival. "To me, 50 percent would be a resounding success," one answered. Somberly she added, "Because I actually fear that the number will be much lower than that."[96]

Business owners like Marco Rivera were busy trying to figure out how to be one of the lucky 50 percent, with or without county assistance. When we met, he was scrambling to do what he could to prepare for a changed clientele, more competition, and higher rents. Pointing to the wall filled with DJ equipment, car stereos, and alarms, he explained how he moved from product retailing to offering services, including computer and electronic repair and accounting. "That's something that we tried to encourage our colleagues around here, try to do business in a different way," he noted. "If we're going to stay in the old-fashioned way, you might not survive."[97] As in Silver Spring, these individual adjustments to a changing Wheaton are what many county officials and redevelopment advocates say offer businesses the greatest prospects for keeping their doors open.

But the Coalition for the Fair Redevelopment of Wheaton once offered an alternative vision. Their vision did not rely on the adaptive capabilities of individual businesses but was instead founded on the collective right of businesses and residents to remain. It recognized that diverse, small businesses constituted the cultural heart and soul of Wheaton and that redevelopment that came at their expense was fundamentally flawed and inequitable. While fragments of that vision remain in ongoing efforts of grassroots and grasstops advocates, the fullness of that dream dimmed as redevelopment forged full steam ahead.

·　·　·　·　·

Figure 17. Downtown Wheaton in early 2020, with redevelopment of the Wheaton Triangle Business District nearly complete. Photo by the author.

In the fall of 2020, the county celebrated the opening of the Wheaton Triangle Business District, anchored by its fourteen-story LEED Platinum office building, with four hundred underground parking spaces. This mixed-use, transit-oriented, one-stop shop for county services could be seen from anywhere in downtown—a towering symbol of one of the county's largest investments in redevelopment since downtown Silver Spring. County leaders declared that the building was not an end but a beginning of many things to come in Wheaton. The new district, they pronounced, was a win for which residents and small businesses had been waiting a long time.

Months earlier the former county council member and Silver Spring Redevelopment Steering Committee member Marc Elrich, who replaced Leggett as county executive in 2018, touted the county's success in keeping small businesses in place:

> While we were looking toward the future with the construction of the new building that will help revitalize Downtown Wheaton, from the start, we always had concern for the small businesses that have been part of this

community for so long. It was important for us to provide these businesses with help to make sure that they made it through the disruptive construction period and the Small Business Assistance Program has worked as designed.

Elrich's comments came alongside the county's announcement that the SBA program had distributed over $1 million to twenty-three Wheaton small businesses and that "most have remained open during construction."[98]

Across the street the town plaza with an amphitheater and outdoor stage was nearing completion. It was named for Marian Fryer, who passed away in 2017, three years after I sat at her kitchen table, blocks away. Council member Nancy Navarro led the plaza's dedication. "To me this plaza really embodies what Ms. Fryer was all about. She was about making sure that everyone would be heard, making sure that Wheaton's diversity could converge," Navarro said to a diverse but older crowd, who had gathered for the start of the county's summer concert series.[99]

Since then I've passed downtown countless times on the way to my in-laws. Each time I am left with nagging questions and concerns about the future of this diverse suburban downtown and the dire predictions of many I spoke to. I wonder if this is truly the inclusive vision that Ms. Fryer and other new-school suburban activists fought for and what could have been, had the coalition's vision for a more equitable Wheaton been achieved. Did the small businesses that survived against countless odds to remain along Triangle Lane look across the street at the fourteen-story office building with a sense of relief or with fear for the future? I suspect a bit of both.

As in Silver Spring, Wheaton demonstrated the county's consistent role in spurring large-scale redevelopment and its associated impacts on vulnerable small businesses. Using a host of similar tactics, county government and planning agencies enticed private capital investments through heavy public investments. Redevelopment was vigorously courted by county programs, policies, and economic incentives to feed the suburban growth machine. But, unlike Silver Spring, redevelopment advocates did not position the neighborhood as a blank slate. Rather, its diversity was read by some as an opportunity to be marketed and exploited to promote new investment.

The county-led redevelopment process was pushed by a new generation of suburban activists. As communities of color moved to the suburbs, they brought different visions of the suburban good life than earlier generations of White suburbanites. In Wheaton many saw the fight for a new downtown as the attainment of benefits and opportunities they had long been denied. These new suburbanites sought assurance that county investments would be attended by an inclusive process and that the diverse character of their community would not be lost.

While more diverse, established community leaders who pushed for redevelopment still left many voices out. The Coalition for the Fair Redevelopment of Wheaton provided a critical platform for these marginalized voices and a bolder vision of fair development. Its successes in helping to protect and increase affordable housing, workforce development, public amenities, and small businesses showed the increasing power of suburban activists to push more comprehensive goals than those imagined by an earlier generation of activists. Critically, this push was driven from both the grassroots and the grasstops. Like Tom Perez, council member Nancy Navarro pressed the county to take the concerns of the coalition and Wheaton's small businesses seriously. As the first Latina on the county council, she highlighted the importance of political representation in bringing the concerns of marginalized communities into the policy arena.

But while the coalition achieved many things, its work was still perilously incomplete. Like IMPACT Silver Spring, LEDC's advocacy was limited by Wheaton's thin network of community-based organizations, their need to build trust in a new community, and complex ties to county government. While able to rely on their established urban roots in ways that IMPACT could not, LEDC struggled to transfer their rich organizing capacity and social capital to the suburbs. The coalition's fate rested in the hands of a few people within an organization that was still wrestling with questions about its own role in the community and the county.

Effective anti-displacement strategies require not just grassroots capacity but also the right tools at the right time. Even with the policy foundation for Wheaton's SBA program established during earlier redevelopment battles in Silver Spring, the county still struggled to adapt the tool in the face of community pressure. The program's eligibility criteria, funding, and delayed implementation left many gaps for businesses most in need— and too many hanging in the balance for far too long.

The coalition's vision was more ambitious than what ultimately came to pass in Wheaton. Equitable development, it argued, required a comprehensive approach and vision that clearly centered the needs of the most vulnerable from the outset, one reflected in its proposed community benefits agreement. This was a fight lost in Wheaton, but it was not forgotten. CASA de Maryland, a critical partner in the redevelopment battles in both downtown Silver Spring and Wheaton, took up where the Coalition for the Fair Redevelopment of Wheaton left off. Just as cranes began to dot the Wheaton skyline, decades-old plans for a new light-rail line that would connect some of Maryland's most advantaged and disadvantaged suburbs finally came to fruition—threatening the stability of the latter. In response CASA quickly mobilized, leveraging the lessons learned and partnerships forged over decades of organizing in the Maryland suburbs. Emboldened by recent wins in Wheaton, they helped to build one of the region's largest equitable development coalitions, whose mobilization signaled the start of a new and more mature phase of the movement.

5 Somos de Langley Park

We are not against progress. But how good is it going to be
if we're not there to enjoy it?

—Jorge Sactic, Langley Park small business owner

In September 2017, around the time of the groundbreaking for Wheaton's
downtown, the Purple Line also broke ground. By 2022 the sixteen-mile,
$3.3 billion project was proposed to become the region's first suburban
light-rail line—connecting some of Maryland's highest-income neighborhoods to some of its most impoverished. This new connection raised new
possibilities for historically disinvested Maryland suburbs. Many hoped
that it would improve the lives of low-income residents by motivating
neighborhood investment and increasing access to employment, education, and other opportunities. But the line would also likely raise land values, burdening vulnerable residents and small businesses with higher
rents, which could result in widespread residential, commercial, and cultural displacement.

Langley Park faced the most acute threats. This inner suburb sits in
Prince George's County, just over a mile from the northeast border of
Washington, DC—and a few miles east of downtown Silver Spring and
Wheaton. Alongside Long Branch, an adjacent neighborhood in
Montgomery County, locals often refer to the area as the International
Corridor. The corridor is widely considered the heart of the Latinx com-
munity in the DC region, home to Maryland's largest concentration of

immigrants and many immigrant-owned small businesses.[1] In the previous three decades, this "arrival suburb" for diverse immigrants saw rapidly
rising poverty alongside deteriorating housing, retail conditions, and
neighborhood infrastructure, as explored in Chapter 2.[2] With new Purple
Line stations being built in the heart of the community, Langley Park residents and business owners feared that they would not be there to enjoy
the benefits that the line could bring. Years of construction disruptions,
speculative real estate practices, and higher rents were certain to follow
the line's completion.

Langley Park was where the fight for fair redevelopment in the
Maryland suburbs took on a new maturity. Two groups formed to ensure
that the Purple Line benefited and did not disparately burden or displace
established residents and small businesses throughout the corridor: the
Fair Development Coalition (FDC), a grassroots group of community-
based organizations in the International Corridor; and the Purple Line
Corridor Coalition (PLCC), a grasstops group providing outreach and
technical assistance across the corridor. The former was led by CASA de
Maryland, an immigrant rights group that fought alongside IMPACT and
the Latino Economic Development Center (LEDC) in downtown Silver
Spring and Wheaton. The PLCC was led by the University of Maryland's
National Center for Smart Growth Research and Education (NCSG).

My engagement with Langley Park did not start at NCSG, where in
2014 I served as faculty affiliate and three years later took on the title of
director of community development. Langley Park had been my familiar
stomping ground since I was a graduate student in the mid-2000s in the
University of Maryland's Urban Studies and Planning Program. At the
time I worked as a graduate assistant with Dr. William "Bill" Hanna, a
longtime neighborhood advocate. I helped Bill prepare his self-published
newsletter, *Barrio de Langley Park,* an incendiary monthly circular that
reflected his fiery personality and penchant for political writing. The newsletter was a product of the nonprofit Bill began in 1998, Action Langley
Park, a volunteer group that advocated for residents and organized health
and job fairs, an afterschool program, and cultural performances in the
neighborhood. A White man who spoke stilted Spanish, Bill was the first
to admit that he was an unlikely community leader. After Bill learned
about the struggles of immigrant families from a student, however, Langley

Park became his passion project. For nearly three decades, he was a fierce fighter for neighborhood schools, affordable housing, and small businesses in Langley Park—and against displacement due to the Purple Line.[3]

When I returned as a faculty member to my alma mater in 2013, Bill had retired but could still be found chatting with faculty and students in the hallways, which is where we reunited. I invited him to coffee. At Bill's suggestion we met at a bustling *pupusería* in Langley Park. Irene's Pupusas began as a food truck in the 1980s, run by a Honduran immigrant, entrepreneur, and mother of seven, for whom the restaurant is named. Irene opened her first brick-and-mortar store in Langley Park in 1996. By the time Bill and I met, she had three locations throughout the region, including one in Wheaton.[4] While filling me in on Irene's history and prodding me to try another pupusa, Bill also pressed me about the work I was planning to do in Langley Park. I didn't have an answer. Less than a year into the job, I was overwhelmed by the many demands of faculty life, including completing my first book. While I had heard that NCSG had recently launched the PLCC, I was not yet engaged. An outspoken critic of the Purple Line, Bill urged that there was important work to be done, and I was uniquely positioned to help. I couldn't say no.

I began by introducing myself to Zorayda Moreira-Smith, the CASA staff member who ran the FDC. Over the next decade, I would work with Zorayda and other CASA and NCSG staff on multiple efforts to resist displacement and improve the neighborhood, including projects related to affordable housing, code enforcement, asset mapping, and crime prevention. In 2019 I accepted an invitation to sit on the PLCC steering committee. While my research on the Purple Line ended in early 2020, before the line was complete, my work in Langley Park continued.[5]

From these multiple and intimate vantages, I watched how the FDC and PLCC advanced equitable development in the International Corridor. Together they built strong partnerships across county lines and engaged hard-to-reach residents around an equitable development platform that received significant buy-in from county and state political leaders. They advanced new plans and policies for quality, affordable housing, small business retention, workforce development, and neighborhood investments. And they created metrics and mechanisms to hold regional leaders responsible for implementation.

Their fight shows the maturation of more than two decades of organizing in the Maryland suburbs. Compared to Silver Spring and Wheaton, the battle was fought by coalitions with far greater organizational capacity, community and political connections, and anti-displacement tools. While still incomplete, the achievements of these coalitions show how new-school activists and organizers built on the lessons of earlier suburban struggles. Their strong cross-sector coalitions were led by high-capacity organizations that got ahead of the redevelopment curve. They tackled key political and planning challenges that made communities vulnerable before, during, and after construction. They built on anti-displacement tools handed down to them by activists in other suburbs, and they brought community-based organizations across both counties that represented a robust mix of race and class interests into their fold, including LEDC, which had led the fight in Wheaton.

But like the Purple Line itself, FDC and PLCC's work in Langley Park is incomplete. The community's social, spatial, and political structures and conditions underlie the need for new investment but also make residents highly vulnerable to the impacts of those investments. There are no easy fixes. The neighborhood's declining infrastructure, bicounty location, low-capacity nonprofits, and thin anti-displacement policies are not easily remediated or repaired. While two relatively robust suburban coalitions have made important inroads in addressing the gaps, they have also sometimes struggled to stay afloat as pressure has increased for residents and businesses to move.

A COMMUNITY AT THE CROSSROADS

Langley Park is a vibrant immigrant neighborhood with a mix of local small businesses, dense multifamily housing, and a strong sense of community. Like many suburbs, the neighborhood lacks clear borders. Residents often see it as the unincorporated area spanning Prince George's and Montgomery Counties, which share similar demographics, housing, and retail characteristics. For planning purposes, however, it is a one-square-mile Census Designated Place in Prince George's County, just beyond DC's northeast border.

As noted in Chapter 2, Langley Park was a White working-class neigh-borhood in the postwar era, before briefly becoming majority Black, and a popular way station for diverse immigrants from Central and South America, the Caribbean, Asia, and Africa. Today Langley Park is a pre-dominantly Latinx immigrant community and one of the most densely populated neighborhoods in Maryland. Among its roughly twenty thou-sand residents, two-thirds are foreign-born. About 84 percent are Latinx, the overwhelming majority of which are recent arrivals from Central America, largely Guatemala and El Salvador (see Table 3).[6]

In fact, Langley Park has the highest percentage of residents born in El Salvador of any community in the United States, who make up nearly a quarter of the neighborhood. Most settled in Langley Park after a decades-long civil war that left over seventy-five thousand dead.[7] The neighborhood has one of the largest concentrations of undocumented Latinx immigrants in Prince George's County. Among non-Hispanics, over half are Black, including a large West African population from Cameroon, Nigeria, and Ghana. New migrants arrive daily, fleeing vio-lence and deep poverty across the deserts of Texas, Arizona, or California, to make their way to friends and relatives in the Washington, DC, region. The trip is brutal and difficult. Most arrive scarred—some with wounds you can see, many with those you cannot.[8]

The draw for many Latinx Americans is the comfort that only an immi-grant community can provide. "It's an area where they feel comfortable enough because it has a critical mass of Latinos," one Prince George's County elected official explained. "There's a large Guatemalan community that's coming that speak Mam. Nobody knows Mam except them."[9] Langley Park residents are intimately connected to their home countries, with fluid lines between their multiple homes. Many have close family members abroad, including children, spouses, and parents whom they support. Children, more so than their parents, regularly cross the south-ern border for school, childcare, and their parents' desire to give them a deep sense of culture. More than three-fourths of Langley Park families provide financial support to relatives abroad. "They send back like $100 or $200 per month to support their families at home. It's a way of life. It's a must that community members do," explained Zorayda Moreira-Smith, CASA's housing and community development manager. Zorayda worked

Table 3 Demographic and housing data for Langley Park Census Designated Place, 1970–2019

	1970	1980	1990	2000	2010	2019
Population	11,576	11,123	17,474	16,214	18,159	19,520
Race, ethnicity, and immigration						
White (%)	96	43	11	5	4	2
Black (%)	4	36	40	25	16	11
Hispanic or Latinx (%)[1]	11	12	39	64	77	84
Asian (%)	—	7	9	3	2	2
Other (%)[2]	1	2	1	3	1	1
Foreign-born (%)	16	25	60	65	68	61
Income						
Adjusted median household income[3]	$65,251	$52,070	$59,030	$58,398	$50,759	$63,105
Families in poverty (%)	7	11	11	11	13	11
Education						
High school or less (%)	72	60	64	75	78	82
College (%)[4]	28	40	31	20	19	16
Advanced degrees (%)	—	—	5	5	3	2
Housing						
Total housing units	4,599	4,781	5,792	4,716	4,888	4,930
Renter occupied (%)	82	79	73	78	70	73
Renters' cost burden (%)[5]	25	29	35	35	50	50

SOURCES: US Census Bureau, *Census 1970;* US Census Bureau, *Population and Housing, 1980;* US Census Bureau, *Population and Housing, 1990;* US Census Bureau, *2000 Census of Population;* US Census Bureau, *2006–2010 Summary File;* US Census Bureau, *2019 ACS 1-Year.*

[1] The "Hispanic or Latinx" group was double-counted in 1970. All other groups are Non-Hispanic from 1980 onward.

[2] "Other" consists of American Indian, Alaska Native, Native Hawaiian, other Pacific Islander, some other race alone, and two or more races. The year 1970 includes Asian groups.

[3] All years have been indexed to 2019 values.

[4] The years 1970 to 1980 include advanced degrees.

[5] The cost burden from 1970 to 1980 is more than 35 percent of income spent on rent; from 1990 to 2019, it is more than 30 percent.

at CASA for over six years, beginning as a staff attorney. We sat in a crowded conference room in their mid-Atlantic headquarters, in the sprawling twenty-thousand-square-foot former McCormick-Goodhart mansion, where we had met many times. Not far away, check-cashing facilities like La Chiquita, which offer international wiring services, dot University Boulevard, the neighborhood's major arterial and unofficial Main Street. Lines are long most weekends, as residents send their weekly wages to loved ones abroad, whether to build a house they dream of one day moving back to or pay for their children's education. "My work is here, but my heart is in two places at once," explained one resident, who left her children in El Salvador with family as she fled the civil war and was unable to visit or retrieve them. "It is not El Salvador, but neither is it America. It is somewhere between the possible and the impossible, a place of suspension," wrote a Langley Park observer.[10]

With residents migrating largely for economic opportunity, the neighborhood is disproportionately young and male. About 60 percent of the population is male, with a median age of just over thirty years old. Households average about four people, over a point higher than the county or state, often including many related and unrelated individuals that crowd into apartments to make the rent. Life in Langley Park is one of tough decisions, sacrifices, and trade-offs. Many hold memories, desires, and regrets for the life they left behind but also hope of reinventing themselves in a new place. Their mantra is *borron y cuenta nueva*—"erase the past and start over"—a refrain difficult to realize with many operating on temporary work visas or none at all.[11]

Roughly half of Langley Park homes are overcrowded, a rate five times higher than the county or state. Apartments are packed with beds, couches, and cribs—bedrooms often defined by a thin curtain or sheet. Residents struggle to pull together the documents to sign a lease, including a driver's license and proof of steady employment, let alone the down payment. Illegal sublets provide additional income that keeps many in their homes. Zorayda reflected that overcrowding affects other aspects of life. "There's so many people in the household, so many adults sometimes, where it can be really challenging to have that quiet homework space for the kids."[12]

Langley Park youth face many other challenges. Less than half of those over five years of age speak English only or "very well." Gangs recruit in local high schools, including the notorious Salvadoran street gang MS-13.[13] Dropout rates at the local high schools are high, with many leaving school to help their families make ends meet. Schooling is often disrupted by frequent moves, whether back to their country of origin or simply because their parents' circumstances changed—sometimes for the better, sometimes for the worse. Parents tend to have low levels of education and English proficiency. Only about one in five adults over twenty-five has a high school diploma or equivalent. Many lack basic literacy.

Adults often work in low-wage, low-skilled positions outside of the formal labor market. Many hold intermittent, part-time, or seasonal jobs with few benefits, often working multiple jobs to get by. Most are employed in construction as day laborers, with others commonly working in retail, health care, food services, and waste management. Men take on jobs as roofers, gardeners, and carpenters, while women frequently act as health-care providers or house cleaners, working late in other people's homes. Many run businesses out of their apartments, whether preparing pupusas or sewing textiles. When I asked Zorayda what residents' employment struggles look like, she offered a tragic tale about a migrant worker who traveled over an hour to work on a farm. While working, she lost her finger. Unable to work, she was also ineligible for unemployment, disability, or other benefits that could support her.[14] Day-labor sites like CASA's Welcome Centers in Langley Park, Long Branch, and Wheaton help residents safely find temporary employment and negotiate fair wages and hours. Following the recession, those employed in construction and related sectors had difficulty finding jobs. In 2011 Langley Park's unemployment rate of 13.4 percent was double that of the state's.[15]

Poverty rates are high, and household incomes are low. Nearly one half of households earn incomes below the DC metropolitan-area median, and nearly a quarter percentage lower than that of Prince George's County. Roughly one in six residents live below the poverty line.[16] Zorayda explained that most residents, particularly those who are undocumented, live day-to-day with little security. "They can't work on a budget. They don't know what they're making tomorrow or the next day." Income precarity adds stress to families and the entire neighborhood. Many dream of one day moving out of Langley Park to more spacious suburbs or returning to their home countries in style. For some the calculus works out after years of hard work and patient sacrifice. Many remain for decades—unable to get ahead.[17]

Community health is poor, and safety concerns abound. Residents suffer from high rates of conditions linked to poverty like heart disease and diabetes, and over half lack health-care coverage. Teen pregnancy rates are high, and many women lack prenatal care, resulting in high rates of infant mortality and low birth weights.[18]

The neighborhood has been labeled a county "crime hotspot," with crime rates nearly twice the statewide average and frequent complaints of gang activity, alcoholism, domestic violence, and police harassment. Yet crime often goes unreported, given language barriers and residents' lack of trust of police, especially among the undocumented. "Because of fear, many community members won't call the police because there's a lot of stress, and there's a lot of ugly history around immigration and police enforcement," explained Zorayda. Crackdowns on immigrants in Langley Park and in Prince George's County during the Obama and Trump presidential administrations exacerbated these issues. Many live in a constant state of precarity. "One comes here to work and grow tired. I think all the time about my daughters, how I can help them, but if immigration catches me, poof," explained one resident, making a gesture of vanishing into thin air.[19]

Compounding the neighborhood's vulnerabilities is a lack of quality, affordable housing. About four in five households rent one of the neighborhood's 5,200 housing units, the vast majority of which are over sixty years old and have not seen reinvestment in decades. Nearly all are "market-rate affordable" apartments that receive no subsidies to ensure their affordability. In 2010 the neighborhood's principal zip code was a "foreclosure hot spot," with rates 135 times higher than the state average. The COVID-19 pandemic exacerbated these conditions, with the neighborhood experiencing some of the highest infection rates in the state alongside spiking unemployment.[20]

Despite these challenges, Langley Park is a strong, connected community. As in many low-income immigrant neighborhoods, residents rely on one another for everyday support. Residents give and take favors freely—laundry coins, platters of food, assistance in filling out visa forms, carpools, or childcare. Their interdependence and tight social networks help to sustain the neighborhood's strong sense of community. Zorayda remarked that because residents lack a basic social safety net, "their system of support is themselves."[21] Churches, nonprofits, and other community institutions help to fill the human and social service gap. CASA's headquarters located in the heart of the neighborhood provides popular health, legal, social, education, and employment services.

Small businesses also connect the neighborhood. Of the neighborhood's roughly 1,500 businesses, many serve locals and are family run and immigrant owned. Despite multiple county attempts to shut them down, street vendors line the sidewalks selling popular Central American street foods and drinks like tamales, *chuchitos*, and atole.[22] Stores like Atlantic Market provide residents with fresh fruits and vegetables and other products from their home countries, sustaining Langley Park's vibrant local and transnational economy. Parking lots are community-gathering spaces in a neighborhood with little public space. They are also employment centers, where men congregate and catch up with friends, while waiting to see if they are one of the lucky ones among the rush of workers that swarm vehicles looking for temporary laborers.

The neighborhood is constantly abuzz. Women push strollers along Langley Park's oversized superblocks on their way to meet their kids at crowded school bus stops. Ice cream trucks and makeshift vendors pushing carts from nearby shopping centers congregate nearby, hoping to catch a slice of the midday rush. Men lean on bare trees, some drinking from loneliness and traumatic memories. They gather around beat-up cars, constantly under repair, blaring bachata, merengue, and reggaeton. Friends and neighbors stop on their bicycles, snacks hanging from the handlebars. They greet one another while hopping out of the back of paint-splattered pickup trucks. In the evening exhausted women struggling under the weight of cleaning supplies exchange quick greetings. Kids pass soccer balls across patched lawns filled with neighbors who have pulled out folding chairs and card tables to pass the time and escape their crowded apartments. Parents perch watchfully on balconies or windowsills, sometimes turning their attention to televisions blaring news from El Salvador.

Langley Park's deep sense of community and cultural identity draws residents to the neighborhood. "We don't feel at home anywhere else," said Eva Yesenia Martinez, a Guatemalan immigrant who stayed in Langley Park, even after losing her son to gang violence. The neighborhood, she said, reminded her of her hometown, where neighbors know one another, residents take afternoon breaks at the plaza, and street vendors abound. "Everything is around the corner. It is so convenient."[23] This community, so deeply rooted in culture and place, also feared its ability to withstand the threats posed by yet another disruption—the Purple Line.

The Purple Line was the locus of political struggle for decades. Discussions about a trolley or light-rail running east-west through Montgomery and Prince George's Counties connected to the metro system had been underway since the 1980s. Backlash to early proposals came mainly from residents in Chevy Chase, a neighborhood of wealthy, White, well-organized residents upset that the route would run through a popular golf course and hiking trail. Proponents claimed that the line was needed to connect major job and populations centers in the Maryland suburbs.

As discussions evolved, Parris Glendening, who served for three terms as Prince George's County executive, became Maryland's governor in 1995. During his two terms, the Purple Line, as it would come to be known, was a cornerstone of his planning agenda. Purple Line plans, however, lay dormant during the administration of his successor, Republican governor Robert Ehrlich, who opposed the line.[24] But in 2006 they emerged again in the gubernatorial campaign of Martin O'Malley, whose sound defeat of Ehrlich was often credited to his strong backing from Purple Line supporters. After years of discussion about the line's alignment and the election of a new governor, Republican Larry Hogan, who again threw the fate of the line in question, Purple Line construction finally began in 2017. Old-school suburban activist groups like Chevy Chase's Friends of the Capital Crescent Trail and Columbia Country Club continued to file multiple lawsuits. One suit led to a critical decision by a Chevy Chase–based federal judge that cut off nearly $1 billion in Federal Transit Administration funds to the project. Columbia Country Club also contributed heavily to the election campaigns of Governors Ehrlich and Hogan, as well as Montgomery County executive Doug Duncan, all of whom opposed the line.[25]

Two years behind schedule, Purple Line construction had an ambitious five-year schedule for build out under a $5.6 billion public-private partnership between the Maryland Transit Agency and a concessionaire, the Purple Line Transit Partners, a consortium of private companies that partnered with the state to design, build, finance, and operate the Purple Line.

Its majority partners, Meridian and Star American, were global subsidiaries with a combined portfolio of more than $13 billion.[26] While the state touted the Purple Line as a national model of how public-private partnerships could advance public transit, in late 2020 the Purple Line Transit Partners' design-build contractors halted construction. They blamed the state and other contractors with cost overruns and project delays, including those caused by Purple Line opponents. After the state paid around $250 million to settle the suit, it selected new contractors, pushing back the timeline yet again to 2026 and substantially raising the cost to taxpayers.

When finally complete, the sixteen-mile light rail will become the region's first intersuburban line and east-west, circumferential connection in the metro system that will link to other commuter rail and bus routes. Unlike most major transit lines built in a "hub and spokes" model designed to bring suburban commuters into downtown, the Purple Line recognizes the United States' "new suburban reality," in which many people live and work in suburbs. "People travel from one suburb to another," explained a member of the Maryland Transit Agency's Purple Line Outreach Team, noting that the amount of jobs in the Purple Line Corridor is the same as in downtown Boston.[27] I met members of the team outside on a warm spring day in Baltimore near MTA's headquarters to learn about their efforts to build the line and mitigate its anticipated impacts.

The Purple Line will transect a diverse and divided region, highlighting the vast inequalities among Maryland suburbs. It will connect some of the region's wealthiest communities in Montgomery County to some of its most distressed in Prince George's County. On the west side, the line will start in Bethesda–Chevy Chase, a low-density, largely White, upper-income area with some of the state's highest-performing and fastest-growing employment centers. On the east side, it will terminate at Riverdale–New Carrollton, a largely Black, working- and middle-class neighborhood. Langley Park sits in the middle of the line in the International Corridor. Among the corridor communities, the International Corridor has the lowest property values and median household incomes, highest density of households, and largest immigrant and Latinx populations (see Table 4).

The Purple Line is poised to radically reshape Langley Park and the larger International Corridor. Nearly all of Langley Park's housing and small businesses are located within a half mile of the neighborhood's two

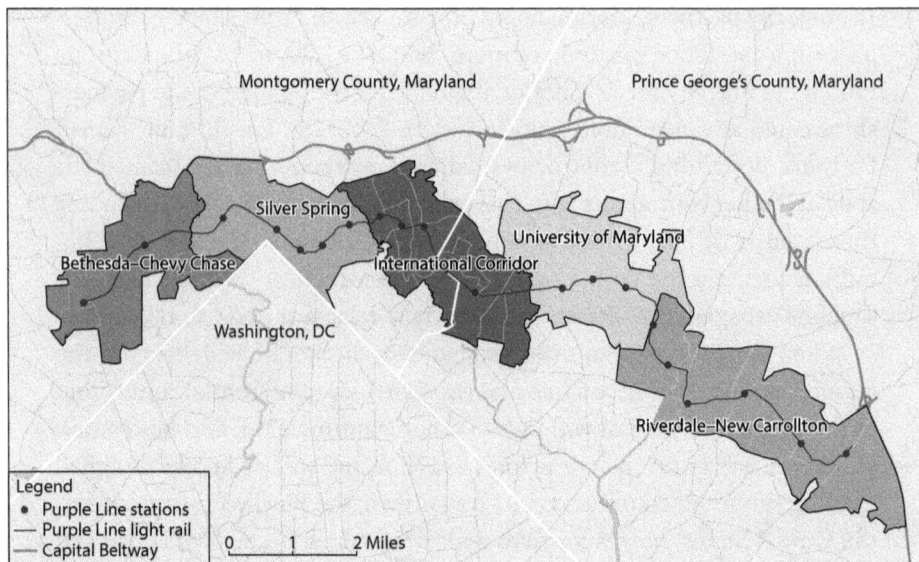

Map 4. Communities along the Purple Line light rail. Table 4 highlights the disparities between west- and east-side communities, particularly the International Corridor. Map by Nohely Alvarez. Inspired by a similar map by the National Center for Smart Growth Research and Education.

proposed Purple Line stops. While currently characterized by mid-rise apartment complexes and low-slung retail centers, Prince George's County plans imagine a denser future. Its 2009 sector plan calls for transit-oriented development to "create future hubs of activity" around Purple Line stations and a higher density, mixed-use, and pedestrian-friendly environment.[28] The new designation proposes increased commercial and residential densities, new design guidelines, and other policies to improve walkability and biking, decrease crime, improve public spaces, and introduce green infrastructure. Approved in 2021, despite multiple protests from Langley Park residents, the new zoning shifted the neighborhood's land uses from largely midrise residential and commercial shopping centers to mixed-use, with maximum building floor-to-area ratios between 1.8 and 2.5, or sixty and eighty feet. Plans also outlined major roadway reconstruction to accommodate the new line.[29]

The central concern of Langley Park residents and business owners was displacement. New transit lines often raise land values, triggering rent

Table 4 Demographic characteristics for communities along the Purple Line light rail, 2011

	Bethesda–Chevy Chase	Silver Spring	International Corridor	University of Maryland	Riverdale–New Carrollton
Population	19,045	33,343	56,527	21,703	28,782
Number of jobs	41,091	30,043	7,636	22,204	28,639
Median household income	$141,331	$82,900	$62,220	$62,977	$64,096
Population using public transit (%)	12	17	26	9	13
Non-White population (%)[1]	23	53	87	34	89

SOURCES: US Census Bureau, *2007–2011 Summary File;* US Census Bureau, *Longitudinal Employer Household Dynamics.*

[1] This category does not include the Hispanic or Latinx population.

and tax increases and tenure conversions.[30] Given the Purple Line's proximity to Langley Park housing and retail spaces, the threats are vast. Rising land values triggered by changing land uses and new transit could make housing further unaffordable to residents. With large parcels held by only a handful of owners, the decision of a single landlord to raise rents or convert their property to condominiums could have a large impact. Rising land values would also raise commercial rents, impacting local small businesses that already operate on slim margins. Guy Johnson, attorney for CASA, warned in 2008 that, unless protections were put in place, residential and commercial property values could double or triple when the line began operating, incentivizing landlords to displace poor residents.[31]

With a loss of businesses and residents, neighborhood advocates feared Langley Park's strong sense of community and cultural identity would be lost. "You don't want the character of the community to change," argued Paul Grenier, economic and cultural development specialist for

Montgomery Housing Partnership, an FDC and PLCC partner that managed affordable units in Wheaton and Long Branch. Paul worked in the International Corridor for more than a decade, helping businesses to grow. With his passionate and persuasive personality, Paul reminded me of the new-school suburban activists I met in Silver Spring and Wheaton like Frankie Blackburn and Ash Kosiewicz, who were not from the neighborhood but had become ardent advocates when they saw the need and what was at stake. When Paul referred to preservation, he was not talking about buildings or history; he was talking about protecting vulnerable people and a fragile cultural mix. We met at a popular Latin American restaurant in Long Branch, where Paul was clearly a regular, greeting many of the staff by name. Much like the conversation I had with Manny Hidalgo about Wheaton, Paul had also witnessed the transition of DC's Columbia Heights neighborhood after the metro station opened and worried that the same could happen in Langley Park. "The rents went up really quickly [in Columbia Heights]," he explained. "Even where they didn't go up, a lot of people felt, 'This neighborhood is not for me anymore. This isn't my culture. I can move to Langley Park or somewhere.'"[32] Langley Park inherited many displaced DC residents who were now facing another wave of redevelopment and possible displacement.

Despite these concerns, the overall reaction to the Purple Line in Langley Park was positive. Many community advocates supported the line because of the neighborhood's highly transit-dependent population. In an area lacking reliable, fixed-route transit, the Purple Line promised to improve residents' access to goods, services, and employment across the region and reduce their commute times and costs. Many residents lack a driver's license, and about a quarter of Langley Park households do not own a vehicle. "They mostly prefer to ride buses, even if that means taking more than two buses in the morning to get to work," explained one MTA Purple Line Outreach Team member. Takoma Langley Crossroads is one of the state's busiest bus-transfer stops, with over fifteen thousand passengers getting on and off its nine bus routes a day. Over a third of employed adults carpool as their primary means to work, and one in five rely on the neighborhood's poor public transportation. The lack of reliable, affordable transit limits everything from church service attendance to job opportunities in distant suburbs or even those only a few miles away.[33]

Figure 18. The Takoma Langley Crossroads Transit Center, completed in 2016 in anticipation of the Purple Line, was the largest public investment in the neighborhood in decades. For many residents it symbolized both their hopes and fears about the new line. Photo by Jordyn Battle.

The Purple Line could stimulate other needed neighborhood improvements. Despite its crumbling sidewalks and long superblocks, Langley Park residents walk at all hours of the day and night. Bordered by busy state highways, many jet across six-lane roads to shops and bus stops, sometimes jumping fenced medians designed to prevent crossing. Langley Park has one of the state's highest pedestrian fatality rates.[34] Without a car, residents commonly haul groceries and navigate the neighborhood by bike, but without bike-friendly infrastructure. Taking cars off Langley Park's clogged streets could reduce congestion and clean up the environment. An increased tax base could be reinvested in dilapidated schools, public safety, and open spaces. It could create opportunities for long-term, protected affordable housing and spur a more stable local economy by bringing new clients to small businesses. The Purple Line is key to the economic-development plans of both Montgomery and Prince George's Counties. "It's an opportunity for investment in the north side," one county elected official told me, referring to the northern suburbs of Prince George's County, which have seen little investment in recent decades compared to suburbs farther south.[35] Much like what council member Nancy Navarro said of Wheaton, the county official believed that promoting investment in Langley Park was key to closing the uneven investment gap in Prince George's County.

Langley Park's new transit center, completed in 2016, symbolizes the possibilities and potential pitfalls of redevelopment. The $34.8 million, 130-foot structure sits at the neighborhood's main intersection, one of the busiest bus-transfer points in the region. The transit center is one of the neighborhood's largest public investments in decades. It will soon connect to the Purple Line, allowing residents to smoothly transfer from the bus to the light rail. To many residents and small business owners, the towering structure is a reminder of the possible benefits of the new line. For others it inspires fear that they may not be there to reap the rewards.

ORGANIZING FOR EQUITABLE REDEVELOPMENT

Given the potential costs and benefits of the Purple Line, advocates organized to ensure that the interests of residents and businesses in the International Corridor were represented at the planning table. In 2009 MTA identified the potential path of the line and began holding community meetings. Residents from higher-income, west-side communities came out in large numbers. Their concerns primarily centered on crime, noise, and the line's effect on property values and open spaces. In contrast, residents of the International Corridor and much of Prince George's County who stood to bear the brunt of the project's negative impacts were often absent.[36]

Advocacy groups stepped in to fill the void. Zorayda recalled that when she began working on the Purple Line in 2011, MTA showed little concern for the line's impact on low-income communities. They narrowly defined displacement to a property taking, she explained, rather than viewing transit as a catalyst for larger neighborhood changes.[37] Under her leadership CASA organized local community groups and residents to respond to MTA's draft Environmental Impact Assessment and county sector plans being redrawn in Langley Park and Long Branch to accommodate the line. They did so under the banner of a new organization, the Fair Development Coalition, a grassroots advocacy group composed of about forty community, labor, faith-based, business, and educational leaders focused on the Purple Line's impacts on the International Corridor.

FDC organizers were inspired by transit advocates in Baltimore. Like the Purple Line, the proposed new Red Line light rail would connect some of the lowest-income neighborhoods in the city of Baltimore to its higher-income suburbs. The Red Line Compact, an agreement signed and adopted by state, city, and local officials and community-based organizations in 2008, came about because of grassroots advocacy over the potential impacts of the new line on low-income communities. The resulting agreement committed its seventy signatories to creating new jobs, improving the environment, investing in community-centered design, and mitigating construction impacts. Though CASA was not a signatory to the agreement, it had been involved in statewide transportation issues, including advocacy for a state-wide tax that helped to fund transit lines like the Red Line and Purple Line. These victories inspired CASA to launch the FDC, with the Red Line Compact serving as both a template and inspiration for what was possible for the Purple Line.[38]

Slow to take hold, the FDC received a boost with the formation of the Purple Line Corridor Coalition in 2013. The PLCC was a more grasstops group of county and state leaders, developers, civic organizations, foundations, businesses, and universities focused on ensuring active and equitable planning and policymaking in communities across the line. Led by the University of Maryland's National Center for Smart Growth Research and Education, director Dr. Gerrit Knaap cofounded the PLCC. Gerrit was the last person I spoke to about the Purple Line, in part because I was nervous about interviewing my close colleague. His friendly and familiar manner quickly put me at ease. I was curious about the history of the PLCC that predated my engagement. As Gerrit told it, its origins could be traced to a trip he took to Minneapolis–Saint Paul, where he learned about advocates' efforts to ensure that a new $1 billion light rail served low-income neighborhoods and the critical role of local universities in the process. Inspired, Gerrit returned to Maryland with a new vision for NCSG's engagement in the Purple Line, slated to run directly through the University of Maryland campus.[39]

The main distinctions between PLCC and FDC were their geographic foci, membership, and politics. The PLCC focused on corridor-wide planning and policymaking. PLCC's initial advisory group included representatives from state, regional, and county agencies and elected officials, developers, and large nonprofits and was explicitly "not an advocacy organization," Gerrit explained. "My vision for the coalition was less threatening, more mainstream, would include the governments, would include the businesses, would include chambers of commerce," he continued, comparing the PLCC to FDC. The contrast between the organizations seemed to match the personalities of their leaders. "A reformed economist" with three degrees in economics, Gerrit had spent most of his forty-year academic career analyzing housing markets, the economics of land-use policies, economic-development instruments, and environmental policies. He did not consider himself a community-based researcher or a scholar-activist. His manner was severe and analytic—the mark of someone more comfortable with graphs, maps, and spreadsheets than at a community meeting. Zorayda, on the other hand, was every bit the steadfast community advocate. "We would be willing to walk away and everything if there was a negative impact on the community. We would oppose the Purple Line publicly. There's strong values there," she told me convincingly. The FDC did not include government officials. "We didn't want to have our hands tied," Zorayda explained.[40] CASA, however, was not apolitical. In 2018 it started a political action committee to organize for and endorse political candidates who shared its values.

The two coalitions complemented each other, as did Gerrit's and Zorayda's leadership styles. "I'm the bad cop, because I get to push buttons," Zorayda joked, comparing herself to Gerrit. CASA's alliance with PLCC helped it partner with government agencies, while keeping community needs at the forefront of its agenda. For PLCC the partnership gave it credibility it otherwise lacked among community residents, businesses, and nonprofits. "I wasn't prepared to go to Langley Park and engage the community," explained Gerrit. "We all have different strengths, and I think we can use that to our advantage." What Gerrit had that CASA lacked was strong relationships with state and county agencies, built during his two decades as NCSG director. Gerrit sat on the Maryland Smart Growth Subcabinet and Sustainable Growth Commission, and under his leadership the center conducted countless studies for Montgomery and Prince George's Counties and state agencies, including MTA. NCSG also had the credibility that came from being a part of a flagship state university physically located in the center of the Purple Line and widely perceived as politically neutral, especially compared to groups like CASA. In conversations with the state about the compact, Gerrit noted that he could be the "straight man and the less threatening voice," while CASA could "play hardball."[41] Together FDC and PLCC fought to address key challenges posed by the Purple Line, focusing on areas most impacted by the line, including Langley Park.

CONFRONTING THE CHALLENGES OF CHANGE

In Langley Park the FDC and PLCC worked to identify and combat the conditions that made residents and small businesses vulnerable to displacement. Among them were the neighborhood's interjurisdictional location, large stock of naturally occurring affordable housing, underresourced immigrant-owned small businesses, and lack of community capacity for sustained advocacy. The coalitions' efforts to close these gaps highlighted promising pathways and likely stumbling blocks for the growing suburban equitable development movement.

Planning across County Lines

The International Corridor spans Montgomery and Prince George's Counties. For many Langley Park residents, their sense of community also straddles the invisible line dividing the two counties, including parts of the city of Takoma Park.[42] The neighborhood's location at the crossroads of multiple jurisdictions complicates county officials' and advocates' ability and willingness to work together. Langley Park's location in the unincorporated inner suburbs of Prince George's County lends itself to a lack of representation and political will. Compared to DC and Montgomery County, Prince George's County Council has fewer at-large representatives—only two among its eleven members. "They're all just answerable to their voters," explained Cheryl Cort, director of Smart Growth America, a regional advocacy organization and PLCC partner.[43]

Deni Taveras represents District 2, which includes Langley Park, and was, at the time of her election in 2014, the only Latinx member on the Prince George's County Council. The daughter of Dominican immigrants, Ms. Taveras was raised by her grandmother in a hardscrabble Harlem neighborhood. While her grandmother had only a first-grade education, Ms. Taveras managed to receive two Ivy League degrees and was en route to a PhD in theoretical physical chemistry before being drawn into public affairs and eventually public service. After relocating to the DC area, she grew her political roots when her condominium building near Langley Park was facing bankruptcy after years of mismanagement and neglect. Ms. Taveras became a tenant organizer to improve its conditions and eventually took over management of the building. Seeing her organizing skills put to good use, she got more serious about politics, serving as chief of staff for State Senator Victor Ramirez, the first Latinx state official representing Prince George's County. After a hard-fought battle that included significant outreach to new Latinx voters by groups like CASA, she won her first election by a mere six votes.[44]

Most other Prince George's County Council members are African American and represent wealthier "outside the Beltway" neighborhoods with more homeowners, less immigrants, and less poverty. Political representation for African Americans in a county that was once majority-White was hard-won. To many within and outside the county, its Black leadership symbolized the possibilities of political incorporation to advance racial equity in suburbia. But the narrative of Black suburban power also obscured the diversity of African American interests that varied significantly along class and ethnic lines—and between African Americans and other groups. By 2019 Latinx Americans made up 18 percent of the county's population. But, as in other edge gateways throughout the region and the nation, their battle for political representation was very much a work in progress.[45] Council member Taveras was only the second Latinx American to hold her seat on the council. The county's political makeup and Latinx Americans' low voter turnout have made it difficult to get elected leaders to care about issues that affect Latinx Americans in Langley Park, noted one elected official.[46]

Working across county lines is even more difficult, complicating everything from decision making to outreach. I sat with Rosalind Grigsby and

Sara Daines in my favorite Indian restaurant in Langley Park, one of the few reminders of the neighborhood's history as a haven for working-class Asian Americans. Both worked a few blocks away in Takoma Park's Division of Housing and Community Development, as they had for years. The two made a good team, often completing each other's thoughts or affirming their statements as we spoke about the challenges of planning for the area. They noted that most Takoma Park residents do not think about themselves as part of Langley Park. Takoma Park's profile looked very different, with Latinx Americans making up only 11 percent and White residents composing 46 percent of its population. While conducting outreach, they refer to the area as "Takoma/Langley" to clarify that parts of the neighborhood are included in the city and to emphasize their allied interests. But it is a difficult sell. On issues of crime, Takoma Park residents are hypervigilant, often perceiving Langley Park as being high crime. In contrast, many see gentrification as a "Prince George's conversation," explained Ms. Daines. In Takoma Park the focus is instead often on enhancing development, improving "marginal" businesses, and the line's potential to boost property values.[47] Takoma Park's status as an incorporated municipality in Montgomery County fostered residents' sense of distance from Langley Park and their political power to enact their disparate economic-development priorities. Though the city does not hold zoning or permitting power, it plays a significant role in guiding local planning and development reviews.[48]

Langley Park's location in an unequal fragmented region further complicates its politics. While one of the wealthiest African American counties in the country, Prince George's County has only about 60 percent of the tax base of neighboring Montgomery County, which ranks among the wealthiest counties in the nation. As sociologist and urban studies scholar Angela Simms notes, "The *virtuous fiscal cycles* of majority- and plurality-White jurisdictions are intricately tethered to the *vicious fiscal cycles* of those majority-Black."[49] These inequalities are evident in Langley Park, as the county line cuts directly through the neighborhood along University Boulevard. Sidewalks are better maintained on the Montgomery County side, with colorful banners hung by the Takoma/Langley Crossroads Development Authority, a business association that markets and promotes businesses in Montgomery County. "Both sides of the street don't look the same. You can tell where the wealthier county ends and the poor county begins," noted one Prince George's County elected official.[50] Judith Stephenson, Montgomery County small business navigator, worried that the Purple Line will exacerbate these inequalities. When we met in her office in Rockville, Ms. Stephenson still seemed to be enjoying her title, which she had created for herself two years earlier to describe her role in guiding small businesses through the county's maze of requirements and regulations. From her work in the International Corridor, she worried about the lack of bicounty coordination. Without strong state leadership, "each county is going to end up doing their own thing," she speculated, causing tensions among businesses and exacerbating existing inequalities.[51]

Coordination across county lines had already proved difficult. Anticipating the Purple Line, Prince George's County passed the *Approved Takoma/Langley Crossroads Sector Plan* in 2009. Three years later Montgomery County passed a plan of nearly the same name, along with the *Long Branch Approved and Adopted Sector Plan* the following year. While county leaders tried to develop a bicounty crossroads sector plan, the effort quickly fell apart. The resulting plans, argued one MTA representative, "aren't really in sync." The *Long Branch* sector plan, for instance, calls for a "no net loss of affordable housing." To reach this goal, the county suggests no zoning changes to existing multifamily housing areas, except those with county-subsidized housing, prioritizing the latter for new affordable housing. In contrast, Prince George's County's *Crossroads Sector Plan* proposes raising densities on all of Langley Park's existing multifamily housing areas and emphasizes reducing the concentration of "distressed housing" and providing housing types for a range of incomes.[52] The counties also have disparate tools to reach their goals. Montgomery County's *Takoma/Langley Crossroads Sector Plan* notes that its inclusionary zoning program would produce upward of 230 new affordable housing units in the area. In contrast, while Prince George's plan aims to "give existing residents the option of remaining" as the neighborhood redevelops, the county lacks inclusionary zoning and many other housing policies to produce new affordable units.[53]

As bicounty collaboratives, FDC's and PLCC's interjurisdictional planning and policymaking roles have been critical. FDC was a major force in the sector plans passed in both counties. Its advocacy around the *Long*

Branch sector plan helped to defeat previous plans many felt would lead to displacement. "[The plan was] so focused on the new community, the community members that [the county] would like to come in. It was not so much for the community members that lived there," Zorayda explained, clearly proud of the work that it had done. Through its organizing, FDC helped to secure the county's commitment to a "no net loss" of affordable housing. FDC members rallied to secure similar commitments in the Prince George's County *Crossroads Sector Plan* but failed. Their advocacy, however, pushed the planning office to develop affordable housing and small business strategies for the neighborhood and a requirement for developers to go through a public process to make use of proposed transit-oriented development density bonuses.[54]

In 2017 the coalitions scored one of their largest victories—the signing of a community development agreement by both counties' executives and other county officials, cities, towns, and nonprofit organizations along the corridor. Led by the PLCC, "Pathways to Opportunity: A Community Development Agreement for the Purple Line Corridor" defines key corridor goals, including revitalizing and stabilizing neighborhoods through affordable housing preservation and production, supporting small businesses, connecting local workers to jobs, and creating healthy and vibrant communities.[55]

The tiring process to reach the agreement, however, highlighted the challenges of working across such diverse stakeholders and interests and the tough landscape of Purple Line politics. First envisioned and led by CASA as the Purple Line Compact, the agreement was modeled after community benefits agreements for transit projects in Baltimore and elsewhere. But talks had stalled by the time the PLCC launched in 2013. PLCC renewed conversations with municipal, county, and state leaders and nonprofit partners and held community engagement sessions to set priorities for the agreement. It struggled to find middle ground among these different stakeholders. For community residents and advocates, the priority was preventing displacement. For some county and state leaders, however, even raising the issue of gentrification could shut down conversations. "Gentrification is a nonnegotiable for our county government," argued Zorayda, noting her disappointment that the word did not appear in the final agreement.[56]

Figure 19. Fair Development Coalition meeting, featuring
Maryland's lieutenant governor Anthony Brown *(left)*, who lost
the 2014 gubernatorial election to Larry Hogan, who did not
support the Purple Line Community Compact. Courtesy of
CASA de Maryland.

After over a year of negotiation, the Purple Line Compact failed to gain
support from state leaders. Under Maryland Democratic governor Martin
O'Malley, the state appeared to be an active partner and signatory. But the
2014 election that brought Republican governor Larry Hogan into office
led to cutbacks in state funding for the Purple Line and the loss of state
support for the agreement. Appealing largely to rural White voters, Hogan
touted new roads as a solution to the state's transportation challenges. One
of his first acts as governor was to cancel funding for the Baltimore Red
Line and reduce state funding for the Purple Line.[57] Discussions about the
compact came to an abrupt halt. "We [were] no longer invited to negotiate
or be at the table with the state," recalled one PLCC member who was
active in the negotiations. Hogan's opponent, Maryland lieutenant governor Anthony Brown, who served as state delegate representing Prince
George's County, was a staunch supporter of the compact and endorsed by
several of its advocates, including CASA. "Had Lieutenant Governor

Brown been elected, the course of the signing a compact with the state at the table, something that looked a lot like Baltimore's, probably would have been pretty smooth," the member lamented. By the time we spoke, I had heard this story many times, as it had defined so much of PLCC's early work.[58]

Hogan's decision meant that the counties had to pick up more costs for building the Purple Line and would be the primary signatories of the compact, resulting in a significantly watered-down agreement. PLCC engaged county and nonprofit leaders in various iterations before the agreement's signing in 2017. In the process it went from a fifteen- to two-page document, losing much of its specificity. The counties were reluctant to make hard commitments, noted Gerrit, explaining the changes. One elected official I spoke to was more critical, stating that the Prince George's County Council's concern was that they were "going to be held to account to what the compact says."[59] Instead of using legally binding language, the community development agreement was a statement of intent, outlining principles for working together toward its broad goals. To create greater accountability, PLCC established an online data dashboard and bicounty housing, economic development, and neighborhood working groups to develop specific plans and recommendations.

After a lengthy process, Purple Line construction began in August 2017. Months later the Purple Line Community Development Agreement was signed, establishing shared equitable development goals and pathways to achieve them. While the agreement was a victory, most PLCC and FDC leaders recognized that it was just a starting point. "Words on papers don't mean nothing. What will happen and what will be more important is the work that goes behind that," Zorayda told me.[60] And that work was just beginning.

Protecting "Naturally Occurring" Affordable Housing

One of the primary goals of the Purple Line Community Development Agreement is to protect and produce quality, affordable housing. In Langley Park this goal is challenged by housing conditions typical of many inner suburbs. Its apartment complexes are composed of largely naturally occurring or market-rate affordable housing, accessible to low- to

Figure 20. A typical Langley Park garden-style apartment complex, many of which are in poor condition and lack affordable housing protections. Photo by the author.

moderate-income households in the region. Even so, over half of Langley Park households cannot afford them, spending more than 30 percent of their income on rent. Langley Park has no public or subsidized housing projects, and, between 2009 and 2010, there were only fifty-two Housing Choice Voucher recipients in the neighborhood's primary zip code.[61]

Like in many inner suburbs, Langley Park's housing conditions have declined in recent decades. Its apartment complexes are old and dense, with nearly three hundred units in each. The majority of its thirteen complexes are owned by a handful of out-of-state companies or their subsidiaries, including various real estate investment trusts. Few corporate landlords invest in property upkeep, contributing to what Cheryl Cort called Langley Park's "slumlord market." Their hazardous environmental conditions range from asbestos and lead to mold, bedbugs, and rodents. As of August 2018, Langley Park was home to two of the county's six "distressed properties," multifamily properties with multiple and repeated code violations that make up around nearly a fifth of neighborhood homes. Though tenants pay market-rate rents, Langley Park apartments "are not in market-rate living conditions," remarked one county elected official.

Describing a recent visit to one apartment complex, one nonprofit housing developer representative recalled,

> I saw exposed wires, electrical wires. I saw a gas stove in the kitchen that was in the middle of the room that had no ventilation. It's such a huge code violation; there's no exhaust duct by it. It was not by a window. There was no way to exhaust from this gas stove. Completely, totally illegal. There [were] water stains on the walls; obviously there's water penetration coming in— that's mold. Those are just things I visually saw in a few minutes in there. Clearly the windows were old and leaky.

As a veteran of the affordable housing world, the representative had seen a lot in nearly a quarter century of working in the field. Even so, she was taken aback. "There are some real life-safety issues in many of them," she told me somberly.[62]

Residents pack into homes with several related and nonrelated individuals to afford the rent. With occupancy limits sometimes exceeding housing codes, residents, particularly those who are undocumented, are reluctant to call county code enforcement to report poor conditions. As of January 2018, the county's code-enforcement office had only one Spanish-speaking inspector. "If your status is illegal, but let's say you leased a two-bedroom unit, and there's supposed to be three of you in that unit, and you have six people living there instead, you're not going to call," Ilana Brand told me. Ilana worked with Paul Grenier as Montgomery Housing Partnership's policy and neighborhood development manager, whose mission was to provide quality affordable housing. Given existing housing conditions, she noted, code enforcement was a double-edged sword that could easily lead to eviction. "It's a really tough position to be in to try to be ensuring that the housing is safe in quality but then also knowing in the back of your mind that the decisions you're making are impacting the affordability and the access that some of those people might have to housing," she reflected on the tough decisions facing code-enforcement officers.[63]

Landlords often take advantage of residents' precarious legal status to avoid making repairs. Residents frequently complain of landlord retaliation or intimidation for calling code-enforcement officials, making maintenance requests, or organizing tenants. As of 2019, there was only one tenant association in Langley Park, which CASA recently helped to organize.

Tenants frequently complain about leasing practices that require them to pay excessive late fees for basic services, such as complex-wide extermination fees. These charges add up. "[Rents are] going up every single year. Then when you don't pay on time, they tack on fees that are fifty, seventy-five, one hundred dollars, that accrue," explained one county elected official.[64] As speculation heated up around the Purple Line, rents rose without substantive property improvements. In 2020 more than one hundred Langley Park households went on rent strike, withholding rent to protest a recent wave of eviction notices during the pandemic and to demand better living conditions. The buildings' owners, Bedford United, were linked to a Manhattan-based real estate investment firm that held over $1.75 billion in multifamily properties across the country. In Langley Park they owned two complexes encompassing nearly six hundred units.[65]

While Prince George's County could intervene to protect this valuable affordable housing stock, it has few tools and little political will to do so. Like many suburban counties, it lacks many of DC's robust affordable housing protections. Compared to neighboring suburban counties like Arlington and Montgomery, its investments have also lagged. Prince George's officials have long argued that the county serves as a regional affordable housing warehouse and that racial bias contributed to its depressed housing values, predatory lending, and inequitable share of low-quality housing. With a lower tax base than its wealthier and Whiter neighbors, Prince George's County has less to invest in producing affordable housing. Officials charged that the county's wealth of "naturally occurring" affordable housing made up for a region unwilling to share the burden. Prince George's County politicians' common mantras, said Cheryl Cort, are "We already have enough affordable housing"; "We have a disproportionate portion of affordable housing"; and "We have our fair share."[66] These were all statements I had heard many times.

Langley Park housing advocates, however, argued that this perspective is misleading and shortsighted. Some pointed out that the county lacks similar numbers of protected affordable units as its neighboring jurisdictions and an increasing number of cost-burdened households. Others charged that county officials' desire to retain their status as a wealthy Black county hampered their investments. Even so, most acknowledged the county had to wrestle with historical and ongoing racial discrimination in its housing market. Cheryl Cort noted the county's poor tax base often pits the priorities of middle-class residents against those of the poor, leading to a zero-sum political game. Majority-Black jurisdictions often face "cascading fiscal constrictions" and lack the same ability as majority-White jurisdictions to support high-quality goods and services, "even when majority-Black locales have middle-class resources," argued Angela Simms.[67]

Nonprofit housing developers have struggled to intervene. With little county funding available, few nonprofit developers work in Prince George's County. Those who do have a tough time addressing the scale of the problem. Given the degree of deferred maintenance in large complexes, few nonprofits have the capacity to rehabilitate apartments to an acceptable standard. A preforeclosure portfolio sale of six properties with over one thousand units, including many in Langley Park, illustrated the challenge. Recognizing the unprecedented opportunity to preserve affordable units in the Purple Line Corridor, the Housing Initiative Partnership (HIP), the county's largest nonprofit housing developer and an FDC and PLCC partner, worked with the county, Enterprise Community Partners, a national affordable housing organization, and other partners to make an offer. But the sale terms, including price and closing period, were infeasible for HIP—or any nonprofit, noted one PLCC member. The apartments were in such poor condition that they needed to be torn down or condemned, one housing leader said. Because of overcrowding issues, to purchase and renovate the buildings to county standards would require HIP to evict "tons of people, probably largely undocumented," she noted. Had the county invested in proactive code enforcement, she pointed out, conditions would have never gotten to that point. Another member added that the county's lack of tools and funding hampered their ability to intervene.[68] Instead, an out-of-state real estate investment trust purchased the properties.

PLCC and FDC have pushed Montgomery and Prince George's Counties to address these housing challenges, including expanding Prince George's affordable housing toolkit. Following advocacy by CASA, HIP, and other FDC partners, in 2013 Prince George's County initiated its first housing trust fund. That same year it adopted the Conversion of Rental Housing Act. Introduced by council member Taveras and pushed by coalition partners, the act allows the county to purchase multifamily properties being sold or converted to condominiums or nonresidential uses, commonly known as the right of first refusal. When backed by housing trust funds, similar policies have been effective affordable housing preservation tools in DC and Montgomery County.[69] While the county refused to adopt countywide inclusionary zoning, PLCC and other advocates convinced the county to conduct a Purple Line inclusionary zoning study in 2020, which could create a mechanism for its targeted application.

The coalitions have also advanced new housing-quality regulations. Following a natural gas explosion at an apartment complex in Long Branch in 2016 that killed seven people and injured forty, FDC and PLCC partners advocated for better code-enforcement regulations in Montgomery County. Three months later the county unanimously passed a bill requiring annual inspections of all rental complexes, new fines for landlords that violate housing codes, and new lease provisions, including those related to rent increases. It also initiated an apartment-assistance program, run by the Montgomery Housing Partnership, to help owners of small apartments improve and manage their properties. Inspired by these victories, council member Taveras introduced and passed four new bills in Prince George's County in 2017. These bills instituted new fines for multifamily rental facilities, increased protections for tenants from retaliatory landlords, and increased property standards for multifamily housing, including those related to overcrowding.[70]

PLCC's Housing Action Team, which includes housing leaders from Prince George's and Montgomery Counties, also advanced bicounty coordination and investments in affordable housing. In 2019 it published a corridor-wide housing plan, laying out actions to preserve and produce a diverse mix of housing across the corridor, improve housing quality, work across sectors and jurisdictions, and engage local communities.[71] Just months before the release of the plan, JPMorgan Chase and Company awarded $5 million to three PLCC partners—Enterprise Community Partners, LEDC, and National Housing Trust—to expand access to economic opportunity for residents and small businesses along the line. The grant supported the Housing Action Team's planning work and allowed Enterprise and National Housing Trust to issue loans and technical assistance to affordable housing providers to accelerate new investments. In

2021 Kaiser Permanente, a major anchor institution in the corridor and housing–working group coleader, invested $5 million in a new loan fund to support PLCC's affordable housing goals.

Still, housing advocates anticipated obstacles ahead. Those who fought for the Prince George's County's housing trust fund also had to fight for the county to fund it. Those who celebrated the county's adoption of the right of first refusal had to push the county to make use of it. Even with the right tools in place, advocates need political will and funding to make effective use of them. And the ability of Langley Park residents to stay put is deeply intertwined with that of its many small businesses.

Preventing Small Business Displacement

The Purple Line places pressures on Langley Park small businesses that rent space in strip malls that, as in many inner suburbs, serve as affordable havens for immigrant enterprises.[72] With the Purple Line, many advocates expect commercial rents to rise and years of construction to disrupt business parking and pedestrian activity. The loss of these businesses would threaten the neighborhood's culture, economic life, and sense of community.

Like residents, Langley Park small businesses are already on the edge. Many are immigrant-owned and family-run businesses that operate on thin margins with limited cash flow. They cluster in retail and service-sector industries that have a low cost of entry but are vulnerable to economic downturns and produce below-average returns. They also compete with liquor stores, check-cashing facilities, and dollar stores that cluster in the neighborhood and, advocates say, prey on poor people.

Paul Grenier and I sat facing the businesses along Flower Avenue, Long Branch's main street. Over the years Paul had worked diligently to provide businesses with technical assistance and improve their facades, including a colorful mural on the side of the building in which we sat. While some were now thriving, Paul did not take credit for their success. Rather, he praised the small business owners who were exceptionally creative and diligent in differentiating their products, adjusting their prices, and changing their look and feel to attract customers. He suggested I visit LA Mart to see for myself, which I did a couple months later.[73] I sat in a tight

Figure 21. A Langley Park strip mall filled with immigrant-owned small businesses, many of which are struggling with how to adjust to the Purple Line. Photo by the author.

makeshift office behind the counter with the owner, James Chang, who recalled how the store had evolved alongside the neighborhood. In 1989, when Mr. Chang first started his store in Long Branch, it was called Maxim and primarily oriented to the neighborhood's large Vietnamese population. I was familiar with it then, as I had occasionally stopped in for its unique mix of Asian groceries, music, jewelry, fabrics, and other products. I had not been back since. Under its current name, LA Mart, the store began serving more Hispanic products and today is one of the area's largest African markets, with three stores throughout the region. When I asked Mr. Chang what made him successful, he said paying attention to the changing needs of customers was key. Paul worried that there were not enough business owners like Mr. Chang who could quickly pivot in the face of the rapid changes taking place.[74]

As I heard many times in Silver Spring and Wheaton, Langley Park businesses also face lending discrimination and have less capital and access to credit than their White counterparts. They borrow from friends and family or use personal savings to launch and grow their businesses. For some their immigrant status presents barriers to getting a business loan or simply starting a bank account. For others language, education, and cultural barriers frustrate access to needed capital. A county elected official pointed out that some Langley Park businesses lack the documentation to initiate a loan. "They build what they build, and they're just going from paycheck to paycheck, from pay period to pay period." Other business advocates I spoke to noted that few immigrant business owners want to take on new debt, even if they are able.[75]

Advocates also emphasized the barriers businesses faced in accessing technical assistance. As sole proprietors with few employees, many must shut their doors to attend trainings or apply for a grant. Others lack the knowledge of available resources, language skills, social networks, time, or the documentation to apply. I first met Mayra Bayonet at a PLCC community engagement event, when she was working for Montgomery County's Hispanic Chamber of Commerce, the organization run by Daniel Parra that had helped businesses qualify for Wheaton's Small Business Assistance program. We met up again at Irene's Pupusas after she had left the chamber but was continuing to work with businesses in the International Corridor as a consultant. Lively and cheery, Mayra's energy matched that of the restaurant. Not surprisingly, as a city planner, she found her passion in engagement. After emigrating to the United States from the Dominican Republic, she noted the lack of engagement among Latinx immigrants. "When we go to the meetings, no one Hispanic went to the meeting, no one," she recalled. Determined to fill the gap, Mayra began volunteering with the chamber, where her job was to spread awareness of county resources, connect businesses to one another, and bring resources closer to them. Many Langley Park business owners, she explained, lack basic resources like business plans and knowledge about available resources needed to manage or grow their business.[76]

As in Wheaton, Langley Park businesses tend to rely on foot traffic from local clientele who are themselves vulnerable to displacement. As Jorge Sactic, a Langley Park small business owner, put it, "If the residents go away, businesses will go into bankruptcy." Mr. Sactic fled war-torn Guatemala and landed in the DC area as an undocumented immigrant in 1985. After nearly two decades working in the construction industry, first as a laborer and then owner of his own company, he decided to start a business in Langley Park because he "had to go where the people are." With many forced to emigrate because of economic or political disruptions, Mr. Sactic recognized migrants desperately missed food and other familiar reminders of home. While the focus for many was on staying and figuring out how to survive, he believed that remaining connected to their home countries was core to their sense of stability. In 2004 he opened Chapina Bakery in La Union, a mall named after a province in El Salvador from which many Langley Park residents hail. As he saw it, the bakery offered far more than familiar, affordable food. "We don't sell bread; we sell sentiments," he told me. His products offered comfort and helped to ease the pain of migrants who could not otherwise return home. "Eat it and then start to remember. The trip is free." Mr. Sactic was more than a business owner; he was a trusted counselor who some dubbed "The Mayor of La Union" or "Don Jorge." From behind his counter, he helped customers fill out leases, send money back home, and deal with mundane problems such as parking tickets. Small businesses like his, he noted, were constantly operating in survival mode, where even one sale could make a big difference.[77]

Small business associations help to fill critical gaps in many neighborhoods, but not in Langley Park and not for lack of effort. After launching his business in La Union Mall, Mr. Sactic began hearing complaints from other businesses about their landlord, which led him to help organize a business association for mall tenants. The process proved powerful, as the association began addressing common lease issues, providing legal and financial assistance, and sponsoring weekend musical festivals. But in 2011 the property owner filed for bankruptcy and sold the building. The new owner did not support the association's events, frustrating their organizing. Two years later the association was defunct. As Purple Line discussions ramped up, Mr. Sactic saw an opportunity to revive and expand the association. Many small business trainings he went to about the line were not in Spanish and many trainers "did not understand the mentality of Langley Park business owners." He and other business owners started knocking on doors, and by 2014 about fifty business owners were engaged in the Langley Park Small Business Owners' Association, with Mr. Sactic as its founding president. But running the association was taking time away from Mr. Sactic's business, and after several attempts it failed to attract funding and 501(c)(3) nonprofit status. By the time we spoke in late 2015, the organization was struggling, with few business owners regularly attending meetings.[78]

Other established small business associations surround Langley Park but do not represent its owners. The Takoma/Langley Crossroads Development Authority and Long Branch Business League represent businesses only on the Montgomery County side of the line. The Long Branch Business League, started in the late 2000s with the help of Montgomery Housing Partnership's Paul Grenier, exemplifies the power of small business associations. When Paul began working in the neighborhood, many businesses had faded and broken signage and high-vacancy rates. "There were people hanging around the streets getting drunk. There was trash everywhere. People didn't take care of the area. You [could] just tell, if someone tried to plant flowers, within a week they'd be trampled, or they would be gone." His vision for the business league was to revitalize the neighborhood in a way that would preserve its character and serve the community. Few people showed up to the initial meetings. Paul said the typical reaction of business owners was "we're not interested. Nothing ever changes here." Frustrated but determined, Paul finally broke through, after several years of going door-to-door—reminding me of the persistence, passion, and patience that drove Ash's organizing efforts in Wheaton. Today he calls the business league a "model of collaboration," noting its success in strengthening businesses and their connections to one another and the community. Their recent events included business trainings, signage- and facade-improvement campaigns, a "superblock party," and murals celebrating the neighborhood's arts and culture. One of Paul's favorites is the Flower Face Lift, an annual spring planting event to brand and beautify Flower Avenue, where, he noted with delight, no one steals the flowers anymore.[79]

The league also works with the nearby Washington Adventist University, where Kimberly Pichot runs a service-learning program that is clearly her pride and joy. Pictures of their work plaster her office walls, as she pulled out examples to show me from her packed shelves. In Long Branch Ms. Pichot described the power of connecting businesses to the community through her work with a local laundromat, Rainbow Laundry. The owner, a Korean immigrant, was struggling to survive when Ms. Pichot and her students helped give the laundromat a fresh look by repainting the interior. In the process they noticed that it served as a daily gathering place for youth, who sat with their parents for hours with little to do. With the owner's permission, the students started what is now a popular after-school tutoring program at the laundromat. The owner has since become active in the business league and community—even throwing a Christmas party for the neighborhood kids. Paul reflected that little things like this add up to larger changes that shift people's attitudes about the neighborhood and foster business collaboration.[80]

But Paul and others neighborhood advocates worried that these changes were not happening fast enough to keep up with redevelopment. Carlos Perozo, president of the Long Branch Business League, has run his accounting business along Flower Avenue since 2007, to serve what he called an underserved Latinx community. The power of any business league depends on the engagement of its members, he pointed out, and that power has been difficult to sustain. Looking out his large window at the businesses across the street, Mr. Perozo worried that for all that the business league had accomplished, it was not enough. He had already seen his rent rise and worried that, after the Purple Line was complete, he would be priced out. Just down the street, LA Mart's James Chang, a member of the business league and the example of success that Paul had pointed me to, was even more doubtful. "Twenty years later, this area [is] going to be developed. The high-rise[s] and none of our business members are going to be here," he predicted.[81]

As in Wheaton and Silver Spring, few businesses own their properties. In Langley Park commercial tenants, like residents, tend to lease space from large out-of-state corporate owners. "The owners of the strip malls aren't invested in it, aren't invested in that community, and are probably just waiting to sell the property to the highest bidder," argued one county elected official. With low profit margins and little savings, many business owners spend a sizable proportion of their income on rent in what is already a high-rent commercial area. "When people say, for example, that you're going to put all these small businesses out of business because the rents are going to increase, they're already paying twenty-five to thirty dollars per square foot," Sara Daines said. "Or more," Rosalind Grigsby quickly added.[82]

Like in Wheaton, many business owners are locked into predatory, triple-net leases that require them to make significant capital improvements. Paul Grenier was incensed after looking over the leases of Long Branch business owners:

> Property owners in some parts of the county, including some cases in Long Branch, get away with leases that are beyond belief. The way the law is written, if it's in the fine print of the contract and the property owner owns the property, there's no recourse for the small businesses. None. No matter how irrational or exploited it might be, there's no one there to help.

Jorge Sactic helped small business owners negotiate their leases as, he noted, many have language issues and do not understand what they are signing.[83]

Cumulatively, these conditions make it hard for Langley Park small businesses to adapt to the realities already evident in the corridor. A few businesses, like the popular Mega Mart grocery and thrift shop, closed as their buildings were torn down to make room for the line. Many more have been disrupted from the construction that started in late 2017, after three years of construction for the Takoma Langley Crossroads Transit Center. Streets have been closed or reduced in capacity, sidewalks blocked, medians replaced by traffic barrels, and parking lots taken over by construction equipment. Many businesses have lost customers and space for deliveries and faced water and electricity shutoffs. Even before construction began, Paul worried that there were insufficient mitigation efforts underway.

> There's going to be a lot more trucks, a lot more congestion. It's going to be more of a hassle to drive through here. There's the psychological barrier and physical barriers that that creates, and that's a big concern, and rightfully so. . . . If a year into the construction, because of the dust and the mud and the congestion, someone's business has gone down 50 percent, there is nothing available to compensate for that.[84]

In late 2020, when the Purple Line Transit Partners' design-build contractors stopped their work, with streets and sidewalks already torn up in the International Corridor, construction had been ongoing for three years and would take at least another six years to complete.[85]

Many feared the worst was yet to come, after construction is finally complete, customers would change, and competition would increase. Paul worried that the years he and the business league had invested in changing perceptions of Long Branch could be upended. "If someone comes along and says, 'Ah, the Purple Line is here. Let's knock all of this down. We'll sell it.' Someone will knock it all down, and they'll put up some cookie-cutter stuff that just kicks out the whole community," he speculated. One county official with whom I spoke was more reserved but no less concerned about the prospects. While big-box retailers would help increase the neighborhood's tax base, the official had a tough time imagining a future in which new businesses moved in without displacing at least some established Langley Park small businesses. "I don't know how possible that is. Not everybody is going to be able to survive."[86]

Prince George's County has limited resources to protect and promote small businesses, in part because of its history of commercial redlining, which Montgomery County officials also argued affected downtown Silver Spring's commercial mix. Similar to housing, Prince George's County officials have long claimed that it has been bypassed by major employers and large chains because of racial bias. Instead, popular white-tablecloth restaurants and entertainment complexes locate in the favored quarters on the region's west side, leaving the county with an abundance of small, low-value businesses and a lack of major anchors. Prince George's County's approach to economic development has centered on trying to attract large retailers and national chains, at the expense, some argue, of small businesses. Compared to its neighbors, the county lacks a robust stream of small business grants, loans, and technical assistance programs, including a business-impact-assistance fund like that which helped small businesses in Silver Spring and Wheaton.

PLCC and FDC have secured additional resources and greater protections for Langley Park small businesses. Before the state's withdrawal from the Purple Line Compact, PLCC members helped to convince the Maryland Department of Labor, Licensing and Regulation to cofund construction-disruption mitigation efforts. After the department pulled out of negotiations, FDC and PLCC continued to work with MTA, which initiated an Economic Empowerment Program to provide information and assistance to businesses during construction. Its services include assistance with advertising, "open for business" signage, and campaigns to encourage Purple Line staff and contractors to patronize local businesses.

MTA also established a Workforce Development Program, giving priority to small and disadvantaged businesses in Purple Line contracts—another goal of the compact. Council member Taveras led the county's effort to create a business assistance and outreach center in Langley Park that connects businesses to financing opportunities, grant programs, and technical assistance.

By late 2020 PLCC's Business Action Team, cochaired by LEDC and CASA, were finalizing its small business action plan. The plan's priorities were to provide marketing for small businesses to help boost customers and sales, educate state and county legislators on protecting small businesses during and after construction, and coordinate among service providers to serve small businesses. That same year the Maryland General Assembly allocated $2 million to help stabilize affected Purple Line businesses. The $5 million JPMorgan Chase award boosted the business team's work, enabling LEDC to provide direct technical assistance and loans to businesses and support greater access to the federal Paycheck Protection Program. Nationally Black- and Latinx-owned businesses were the most vulnerable to closure due to the pandemic but the least able to access the wealth of federal and local resources.[87] LEDC's work built on the lessons learned assisting businesses in Wheaton, including their approach that coupled deep outreach and direct assistance with policy advocacy.

In another important victory, PLCC, in partnership with MTA, won a $2 million grant in 2018 from the Federal Transit Administration for the coordination of transit-oriented development, infrastructure, and accessibility along the Purple Line. The funds supported the development of a Purple Line economic-development strategy, corridor-wide transit-oriented development planning, and data and monitoring tools. While the work was just getting started when I spoke with Gerrit, he was excited about the possibilities the grant offered to push PLCC's goals and stabilize the organization. "There have certainly been times when I wondered if we were going to survive," he noted. "But now, I mean, we do have credibility; we actually can show some stuff on the ground that we're doing. We've been around for a while. The big national foundations are aware of us. So, you know, I'm optimistic," he continued, striking an unusually upbeat tone.[88] In 2020 PLCC hired its first full-time director, a sign of how far the fledgling organization had come.

Building Community Capacity for Sustained Advocacy

Like business owners, Langley Park residents struggle to find the time and resources to participate in everyday community events, let alone decades-long transit planning. In some neighborhoods community-based organizations help to fill the gap. But Langley Park organizations struggle with high demands and limited capacity. And while PLCC and FDC have helped to fill critical gaps, the coalitions have sometimes struggled to stay afloat, while wrestling with tough questions about their roles.

Since early discussions about the Purple Line, Langley Park has fought to gain the visibility and voice of west-side communities. "[Participation] is *the* challenge that I have, not just in the Purple Line, but for everything: schools, development, parent engagement," explained one county elected official. Immigrants sacrifice a lot to get to the United States and simply want to put their heads down and work, the official noted. Many come from countries where democratic decision-making processes are lacking or repressed. "A lot of these people have left El Salvador as the result of a civil war," the official explained. "That left a bad taste in people's mouths, and they're not as politically engaged here as you would like them to be." Zorayda added that, while some residents are willing to speak out in public hearings, "they're like a needle in a haystack."[89]

Fear casts a long shadow over undocumented residents and their families. One MTA Purple Line Outreach Team member told me that undocumented immigrants carry a perpetual fear that follows them to work and into their homes and schools, affecting every aspect of their daily lives. Benjamin Mason said that the anti-immigrant climate of the past decades exacerbated fear in the corridor, distracting attention away from the Purple Line. Benjamin ran a popular restaurant in Long Branch, where we met during one of his breaks. The son of a Salvadoran farmer who fled during the early years of the civil war, Benjamin and his family were a success story. They moved from grocery store owners in DC's Mount Pleasant neighborhood, where he was raised, to become owners of five Tex-Mex restaurants in the region. Admittedly, by the time Benjamin got to high school, he could scarcely relate to the waves of Central American migrants flocking to the region. But during regular visits to his uncle in Long Branch, he hung out with kids with very different lives than his, including many who were undocumented. This connection later drove Benjamin to move to the neighborhood, take up the family business, and get engaged with the Long Branch Business League (with some prodding from Paul). In an era of mass deportations, legal-status issues for undocumented residents left little time or room for Purple Line participation. "They're here to try to provide for their families and try to get their green card," Benjamin argued. "Anything about Purple Line is like, 'What's it going to do for me?'"[90]

For residents willing to speak out, language, cultural, and resource barriers often frustrate their efforts. One MTA Purple Line Outreach Team member questioned why they were unable to generate more participation in Langley Park around the Purple Line. "The PowerPoint presentations are in Spanish. The website is in Spanish. We have a Spanish phone line," she puzzled. Mayra Bayonet countered that simply translating materials was not enough. They needed people who could meet residents where they are, speak their language, and tailor information to their needs. Like Langley Park business owners, residents lack the time, resources, and networks to navigate local planning bureaucracies. In many families both parents work, often at multiple jobs and in distant locations. "That's what's hard—for me to reach out to the person that's got two or three jobs, and they have no free time," noted one county elected official. Families also often lack a car, childcare, home computers, and reliable internet.[91]

Langley Park's thin network of community-based organizations struggles to fill the communication gaps. A member of the Purple Line Outreach Team noted that MTA traditionally works through local organizations to conduct outreach, but Prince George's County's lack of institutional infrastructure makes that difficult. Instead, they typically reach out through citizens' advisory boards and churches, though, the representative admitted, "We're not always very successful." For the Purple Line, MTA created community advisory teams composed of civic and business leaders in each Purple Line neighborhood to act as local liaisons. But advocates say these official channels are insufficient and often ineffective. "I've never seen the task force, or whoever's involved, send out a newsletter to the houses and be like, 'Look, there's a meeting happening in this neighborhood,'" noted Benjamin Mason.[92] One PLCC member with whom I spoke compared the infrastructure of housing organizations in Montgomery and Prince

George's Counties to DC, noting that the counties lacked similar numbers, capacity, and umbrella organizations.[93] Prince George's and Montgomery Counties also often compete for limited state funds with cities like Baltimore, which have clearer poverty-related challenges.

As was the case with LEDC in Wheaton, Langley Park's nonprofit service providers have also struggled to establish satellite offices as they extend out of their urban headquarters.[94] The Latin American Youth Center (LAYC), a nonprofit supporting low-income youth, established their first suburban satellite office in 2005 in Hyattsville, adjacent to and serving Langley Park. By the time we met in 2016, Luisa Montero-Diaz, LAYC's former managing director, was working as the Mid-County Regional Service Center director, helping to oversee Wheaton redevelopment. When I sat down with her, I was surprised to hear about how her leadership at LAYC prefaced her understanding of the struggles of businesses and nonprofits in Wheaton. She was yet another example of the many people that connected the experiences of multiple case studies to one another. Ms. Montero-Diaz explained that LAYC's expansion from its office in the Columbia Heights neighborhood of DC was needed because its clients and staff could no longer afford to live in the neighborhood where the organization was founded. Setting up a new suburban location, however, proved difficult. "Suburbs were so different in terms of how you deliver services," Ms. Montero-Diaz explained. LAYC's capacity was stretched thin by the county's dearth of service providers, the lack of public transit, and their need to deliver services across a wide geographic area, including county lines. LAYC established offices in both Montgomery and Prince George's Counties in part because of its inability to administer county-funded programs across municipal lines.[95]

FDC and PLCC have bolstered participation in Purple Line planning. PLCC engaged more than 550 political leaders, community residents, and business and property owners in public events designed to identify goals, strategies, and actions for the Community Development Agreement. Its Housing Action Plan was informed by county agencies, housing developers, civic groups, and over 500 residents. Gerrit was clear, however, that PLCC's mission was to engage local organizations who have the interests of communities in mind and can reach out to them when needed. PLCC's larger success, he pointed out, was in building political leadership and political will, including a recently formed caucus of elected officials, whose job it was to advocate for the corridor at the county and state levels.[96]

FDC, in contrast, is driven by the grassroots. As a high-capacity and long-standing community institution, CASA holds trust and rapport with Langley Park residents and hosts regular programs that serve as platforms to collect and share Purple Line information. As a nationally known immigrants' right group, CASA still holds a focus on local community development, as evidenced by Somos de Langley Park, the community development organization it founded. "This is bread and butter. This is our community. This is our base. This is where we live. This is what we breathe, we walk," explained Zorayda. CASA's strong community connections allow it to uplift concerns in countywide conversations and nimbly activate residents when needed. To overcome transportation challenges, CASA sometimes provides shuttle vans to bring residents to planning meetings.[97]

Local churches are also active in FDC and serve as Purple Line engagement venues. St. Camillus Catholic Church, which is based in Silver Spring, holds services in Langley Park. It collaborated with CASA and FDC to hold rallies at the church in support of the Purple Line Compact. They also teamed up with Catholic Community of Langley Park to form United for the Common Good, an effort to engage faith-based communities in Montgomery and Prince George's Counties to advocate for vulnerable communities along the line. "In a way, the Purple Line is a test—it is a moral test of what kind of people are we," argued St. Camillus's Friar Jacek Orzechowski, an FDC member. "The development can't happen on the back of the poor."[98]

While run by high-capacity organizations, FDC and PLCC have still struggled to stay afloat. Purple Line plans emerged over more than four decades, with multiple delays that hurt the coalitions' momentum and funding. The PLCC did not receive any major funding until 2018 and kept the coalition together, in Gerrit's words, "largely on the good will of its partners." PLCC's survival relied heavily on NCSG's established infrastructure and ability to operate the coalition with almost no money. Their recent funding successes, Gerrit told me, were also largely a credit to NCSG's established relationships with local and state agencies.[99] Capacity-strapped nonprofits within the coalition with few political ties have struggled to find funding to support their engagement.

Many coalition partners also face an uncertain fate. Small nonprofits are especially vulnerable to displacement because of Purple Line construction, rising rents, and the loss of established residents. These same forces can also affect larger, more established nonprofits, like CASA. "If anything happens to the community, it's going to happen to us too," Zorayda explained. "Organizations who serve the community understand that they can't be far away from the community to truly serve the community. We move with the community."[100]

Adding to these challenges are questions about FDC's and PLCC's role in Langley Park. Some residents and business owners charge that PLCC and FDC do not represent the diversity of Langley Park residents. One resident with whom I spoke argued that PLCC and CASA's work on the compact was "taking credit for what other groups have done" and "taking over the agenda." Both organizations, he argued, were too political and sometimes proposed agendas not vetted by or grounded in the community.[101] Others charged that CASA's focus on national immigration politics took attention away from their work on issues affecting Langley Park.

Debates about voice, agency, and strategy have also created fissures within the coalitions. A critical debate focused on PLCC's decision to engage with the county around a "community development agreement" rather than a "compact." Some argued that after the state pulled out, the agreement was not viable without greater compromise with the counties on the language and terms. To others the decision was a "huge disappointment," noted one PLCC member, as they felt that the compromise made it harder to hold parties accountable. This member's organization chose to be agnostic in the debate that provoked strong feelings on either side.[102]

Despite these struggles, FDC and PLCC have survived and continue to grow. They have attracted significant funding, inserted themselves into the heart of Purple Line politics, and put several new anti-displacement policies and plans in place. Though their role has sometimes been questioned, they have boosted engagement among residents who might not otherwise have been heard and given hope to many that a more equitable future is possible. Gerrit was positive about what the PLCC has achieved, while also acknowledging its limitations:

I think the reality will be better because of the work that we're doing. What we want is a sustainable and equitable corridor, so what does that mean? It means something about not having displacement and having affordable housing and having a corridor that works well in every dimension you can think of. Will we have made a contribution to that? I think so. Will there be gentrification? Will there be displacement? Yeah, probably, it's probably already happened. Will small businesses go out of business because of construction and disruption? Yeah, probably so. We will never achieve our goals completely, but I'm pretty confident that we will have made progress toward them.

As usual, Zorayda struck a more defiant chord. While agreeing that the coalitions made a difference in ensuring that the International Corridor remain a vibrant, diverse community, she argued that questions of equity and displacement need to be more front and center as the coalitions' work moved forward. "Until we stop sugarcoating it, I think we're not doing enough. I think we have a lot more work to do."[103]

·   ·   ·   ·   ·

The Purple Line is one of the largest public infrastructure investments in the Maryland suburbs in the past several decades. And while its impacts are not completely known, they are certain to be unequally felt. Communities on the east side of the line, like Langley Park, that are most in need of its benefits are also most vulnerable to its threats. Cross-sector and community-based coalitions have tempered these threats by building an ambitious equitable development agenda and working across municipal lines to advance it. In doing so PLCC and FDC have become central players in the region's growing suburban anti-displacement movement— one that activists in Silver Spring could hardly have imagined when they began their fight more than a decade earlier. Still, the coalitions in the International Corridor have encountered significant setbacks that fore-shadow the struggle ahead for the growing movement.

Disinvested suburbs like Langley Park desperately need new transit. As diverse migrants flock to this quiet corner of Prince George's County, they encounter predatory slumlords that take advantage of residents struggling to pay the rent in run-down properties. While rich in entrepreneurs and willing workers, the neighborhood lacks employment opportunities, robust pathways to economic mobility, and protections for small businesses that act as vital community institutions. While it has a strong sense of community and cultural identity, Langley Park lacks a sturdy social safety net, public spaces, and a network of community-serving institutions. Many residents depend on public transit but lack reliable options. The Purple Line could help improve these conditions, making the neighborhood safer and more walkable. It could increase residents' access to opportunities in and beyond the neighborhood—but only if equity is at the core of Purple Line planning.

PLCC and FDC have changed the prospects for disadvantaged communities across the line. By leveraging the policies, partnerships, and lessons from activists in Silver Spring, Wheaton, and other communities inside and outside the region, they built robust suburban coalitions that worked across counties and sectors. Led by high-capacity anchor institutions, CASA and NCSG used their platforms to build the capacities of smaller nonprofits, residents, and small businesses to engage in sustained activism. They advanced new plans and policies for affordable housing, small businesses retention, and workforce development, and they created mechanisms to hold regional leaders accountable. Along the way they increased their own capacity and stability. Their advocacy continued to highlight the conditions that make inner suburbs vulnerable to displacement, and they offered critical place-based tools and strategies that can create pathways to equitable suburban development—and a glimpse at how far the region had come in doing so.

The fight is far from over. While FDC and PLCC brought county leaders across a rigid county divide to the table, they struggled to align policies and priorities and gain state support. Although they improved both counties' affordable housing toolkits and put forth a bold housing plan, many holes remain in funding, tools, and capacity to achieve their goals, particularly in Prince George's County. Given inequalities across the region, some political leaders remain unwilling to invest in the coalitions' plans, while serious gaps remain in philanthropic and nonprofit capacities. While providing vital technical assistance to vulnerable small businesses, the coalitions have yet to gain support for more comprehensive protections. And while increasing community participation and the capacity of

Figure 22. A future Purple Line stop by the new Silver Spring Library in Fenton Village. Photo by the author.

local organizations, the coalitions struggle with questions about voice, internal politics, and funding that threaten their long-term viability and legitimacy.

Langley Park is one of a string of struggling Purple Line communities that face similar threats. Early Purple Line plans located its main maintenance depot in Lyttonsville, continuing the neighborhood's long history of environmental injustice. Residents pushed back, defeating the proposal, but failed to save the historical bridge that once connected African Americans to White Silver Spring and protected the residents from neighbors hostile to their presence. From Lyttonsville the line will continue through downtown Silver Spring, running along Bonifant Street, Fenton Village's main boulevard. Small businesses that once found refuge there after being displaced from the town center are still fighting the impacts of redevelopment that began more than three decades ago. Now the Purple Line will run directly outside their front door, prompting construction disruption and raised rents. At the end of the street, the line will run directly next to the new Silver Spring Library as it heads toward Long Branch and on to Langley Park. There colorful signs remind visitors that, despite construction, small businesses remain open for business.

Silver Spring community leaders have joined the PLCC, including Reemberto Rodríguez, who in 2009 became the first Latino director of the Silver Spring Regional Development Center. Many activists I spoke to credited him with changing the culture of engagement among small businesses in Silver Spring. A Cuban-born immigrant, Reemberto came to the position with a background in community development and organizing. He was a familiar and friendly figure at community meetings, which is where we first met. I asked Reemberto what he expected the Purple Line would mean for both Silver Spring and the International Corridor. Perpetually positive, Reemberto turned somber when considering my question. He predicted that in connecting the neighborhoods, the Purple Line would help to boost the visibility of Langley Park, which he called an "undiscovered country." It would redefine the culture "with a little *c*" of Silver Spring in similarly significant ways as downtown redevelopment. But he remained ambiguous as to what direction that change would take. "What we're in the middle of right now, we ain't done yet. There's a lot of redevelopment to occur." His comments reminded me that redevelopment, like the Purple Line itself, extends over a vast expanse of time and space—and that the struggles of communities for an equitable piece of the pie were likewise decades in the making.[104]

Other Silver Spring advocates were clear that the changes were not likely to be positive. Among Erin Ross's many hats, she served various local and county Purple Line advisory groups. Since 2006 she fought the threats the line posed to East Silver Spring and its businesses. We sat together at Kefa Café before Purple Line construction began and before a fire in the neighboring property temporarily displaced the coffee shop. Ms. Ross politely introduced me to the owners, two Ethiopian sisters, before sharing her concerns about the café's fate. In her brash tone, she noted, "Four feet from the front door, there'll be a train. If you trip going out the front door, you die." Her narrative about the fate of this community grew more impassioned as we walked along Bonifant Street toward the library, with Ms. Ross rolling off the histories of each business we passed. She shared her concerns about the impacts of years of blocked or lost parking, a planning process that left many voices out, and politics that continued to prioritize developers and wealthier west-side communities. "There is an enormous inequity with the money they will spend to mitigate in Bethesda than here. You take all our trees. Can't we get a tree?" she asked.[105]

While construction of the line had not yet hit Bonifant Street, as it soon would, speculation was already apparent when Megan Moriarty and I met a couple of blocks away. Megan was quick to point out that Ms. Ross's advocacy has been central to protecting small businesses and providing a greater voice for the community. But Megan worried it was not enough. The writing was on the wall in Fenton Village, with property owners positioning themselves to capitalize not only on the ongoing "successes" of the initial phase of Silver Spring redevelopment but also on the Purple Line. "Bonifant Street, all of that stuff, will be torn down in the next five years, ten years max," she predicted. Even so Megan and other neighborhood activists remained intent to fight for another kind of future.[106] And after decades of equitable development struggle in the region, they were now more equipped than ever to do so.

6 Place Matters

> The right to the city is, therefore, far more than the individ-
> ual liberty or group access to the resources that the city
> embodies: it is a right to change and reinvent the city more
> after our hearts' desire. It is, moreover, a common rather
> than an individual right, since reinventing the city inevita-
> bly depends upon the exercise of a collective power over the
> process of urbanization.
>
> —David Harvey, *Rebel Cities*

In 2020 the brutal police slayings of unarmed young Black men, women, and LGBTQ Americans prompted widespread uprisings amid global health and economic crises that hit Black and Brown communities hardest. Calls to end racialized policing, police violence, and systemic anti-Black racism surged. Protests arose in cities, small towns, and suburbs across the United States. In the DC suburbs, demonstrators in Manassas, Virginia, which had a history of brutal policing of Latinx immigrants, blocked a state highway. Police tear-gassed and shot protesters with rubber bullets. Along River Road nearly one hundred protesters rallied at a historically Black church, calling for accountability for Black men fatally shot by Montgomery County officers. In June 2020, in one of many demonstrations in downtown Silver Spring, over two hundred protesters gathered at Veterans Plaza, alongside a county council member and three state delegates who kneeled in solidarity with those killed by police. Just over a month after the first demonstration erupted in downtown DC, Dan Reed counted over two dozen Black Lives Matter protests in Montgomery County alone.[1]

These rebellions reflect the new suburban reality in which Black and Brown people do not live predominantly in urban centers. Likewise, the

Figure 23. Black Lives Matter protest in downtown Silver Spring during the summer of 2020. Julia Nikhinson/*The Diamondback.* Used by permission. All rights reserved.

places in which they encounter police violence are not primarily urban.[2] Yet so much of the discourse about policing frames central cities as the locus of state-led violence. As uprisings aim to reveal the logics and tactics of structural violence against people of color, and Black people in particular, the conversation too often ignores the spatial origins of the Black Lives Matter movement—a movement born in Sanford, Florida, after the killing of seventeen-year-old Trayvon Martin in a gated suburban community. It forgets that the movement grew into a global force following the police murder of Michael Brown in Ferguson, Missouri, a declining inner suburb.[3] For organizers, scholars, and abolitionists seeking new forms of racial redress and justice in and beyond policing, confronting the deep suburban roots of the movement and the contemporary suburban reality of police violence is critical to imagining and enabling different futures.

The same is true of gentrification. I have argued that the popular notion that gentrification happens largely, if not solely, in the city has obscured scholars, community advocates, and policymakers' views about how gentrification takes place, whose lives are disrupted, and what communities can do to achieve more equitable outcomes. This final chapter reflects on lessons of this analysis of the new suburban renewal in moving toward a right to the city—but in the suburbs. It asks what this rallying cry that inspired generations of anti-displacement advocates means for marginalized suburbanites. Following David Harvey, what does it mean for them to "reinvent" the suburbs after their "hearts' desire," and how can they generate the "collective power" to shape the processes of suburbanization?

This book has given a glimpse of what the fight for that right looks like. A right to suburbia that recognizes marginalized groups as critical suburban constituents must acknowledge their right to stay put and benefit from investments in their communities. It requires activists, grassroots and grasstops alike, who can help to shift narratives about gentrification and suburban redevelopment, clarifying gentrification's expansive reach and the harmful consequences of the new suburban renewal. It demands close attention to the physical, emotional, and financial investments that marginalized groups have made in suburbia and to why and how place matters to gentrification processes and politics that threaten their bonds to their beloved communities. And it requires advocates who can rally people, resources, and collective hope around visions of a more just future. "Place is security and space is freedom: we are attached to the one and are longing for the other," wrote the acclaimed geographer Yi-Fu Tuan. The spaces in which people collectively invest their time and meaning become valued places that provide a stabilizing force intimately bound up in a larger freedom struggle.[4]

Across the three case studies in this book, place mattered as to how redevelopment played out, what activists were able to achieve, and what was at stake in the fight. Suburban social, political, institutional, and spatial conditions frustrated marginalized groups' ability to effectively mobilize. Segregated land uses made redevelopment highly disruptive, requiring vast public and private investments to make it happen and to balance the scales for affected communities. The low capacity of community-based organizations and lack of existing organizing infrastructure challenged advocates' ability to engage residents and businesses in sustained redevelopment battles. Suburban fragmentation and a lack of political incorporation left marginalized communities with few progressive policymakers to push new anti-displacement policies.

But these communities also dreamed of different suburban futures. In charting the slow but steady rise of an equitable development movement in the Maryland suburbs, *The Right to Suburbia* illustrates how community leaders and activists generated new forms of collective power and inspired a new politics of suburban redevelopment. This final chapter looks back on what activists achieved and by what means. It highlights how they built vital institutional capacity, organized diverse coalitions, grew progressive political leadership, and established timely and targeted protections to counter redevelopment's most damaging effects. It shows how community leaders reshaped dominant development discourses and how the battle was fought and on whose terms. Their victories and struggles offer practical lessons for communities elsewhere, as they fight for their own right to suburbia and fortify themselves for the long battle ahead.

DISPLACING *THE URBAN* IN GENTRIFICATION DISCOURSES

Suburban gentrification is not limited to the neighborhoods I explored. While I directed my attention to three Maryland communities, I might have instead shifted my gaze to the suburbs of northern Virginia. I could have spent time in Nauck and Arlington View, communities that sit in the shadow of Amazon's sprawling new campus, which threatens to displace many residents. These were the communities where, only decades earlier, the federal government shuffled African Americans into public housing complexes after repeatedly displacing them from other Virginia suburbs. Instead of following the struggles of communities along the Purple Line, I might have told the stories of those impacted by the Silver Line, a new metro route being built in Fairfax and Loudon Counties in Virginia that will soon cut across DC and Maryland. Or I could have traveled to Denver, Minneapolis–Saint Paul, or Atlanta, where new light-rail lines have been built and where low-income communities of color—immigrants and nonimmigrants alike—have struggled to stay in place across city and suburban lines.

Gentrification knows no municipal bounds. It moves alongside public policy, private capital, and privileged people. As municipalities adopt policies to motivate new development, real estate actors find profit in new places. As they do, people privileged by race, class, or otherwise find new value in underinvested neighborhoods. Though historically these neglected neighborhoods were largely located in cities, as these chapters affirm, they existed in suburbs too. Today there are many more. Suburbs have and can gentrify.

Gentrification also makes little distinction among suburban geographies. Though inner suburbs in the United States have seen more dramatic patterns of disinvestment that make them particularly vulnerable to large-scale reinvestment, gentrification also happens in outer suburbs.[5] As new places come under the metropolitan fold, increased development pressures can disrupt long-standing communities that once existed intact—whether established Black townships or new immigrant neighborhoods.

In 2014 I brought my urban studies and planning students to Frederick, Maryland, an exurban town about forty miles north of Washington, DC. At the time the city was experiencing its first major wave of immigration, with increasing Latinx and Asian American populations. Many immigrants and immigrant-owned businesses clustered around the Golden Mile, a popular retail hub that served as the city's main gateway. As immigrants moved in, the city targeted the area for redevelopment, threatening the viability of small businesses and affordability of nearby homes. The city, still 80 percent White, was also in the throes of an anti-immigrant backlash. Just two years earlier, the Republican-led Frederick County legislature passed an ordinance declaring English the official language, requiring all official documents and government business to be in "English only." My students worked with community advocates and the city to propose strategies to keep businesses and residents in place. Their efforts made clear that a lack of trust between immigrants and the city blunted communication and engagement.[6] By 2015 small steps were being made in a new direction. Immigrant rights groups successfully repealed the English-only law, and the city's Department of Economic Development staff began holding office hours in the Golden Mile to better respond to the needs of immigrant-owned businesses in the redevelopment process. Anti-displacement activism and policy were needed in the exurbs too.

Racialized patterns of development are a more pervasive feature of metropolitan growth than the illusive urban-suburban divide. The link between people of color and the devaluation of homes and neighborhoods reinforced through public policy, private practice, and collective violence are deeply intertwined in US systems, structures, and institutions—so too are the links between Whiteness and value that boost investments in certain neighborhoods and strip it from others.[7]

The new suburban renewal is not all that new. It took shape and proceeded alongside decades of public policy and private practices that displaced generations of suburbanites. As I show in Chapter 2, slum clearance did not happen just in the city; it happened in suburbs. Racially restrictive covenants and redlining did not entirely keep people of color out of suburbs; they segregated and further isolated communities within suburbs. Racial steering, blockbusting, and exclusive zoning were not just strategies of suburban exclusion; they were directed at Black towns and industrial suburbs that White communities feared would encroach on their privileged spaces. While largely taking shape in urban areas, where the crisis of disinvestment and the people scapegoated as its cause were most visible and easily contained, predatory underinvestment and reinvestment also ravaged suburbs. The same is true of gentrification today.

The contemporary back-to-the-city movement has not been limited to the city. While a new generation of the US middle class may be leaving the suburbs they grew up in, they are rediscovering the joys of urban life in the city as well as in walkable, transit-oriented suburbs. In the process places that generations of low-income residents, immigrants, and communities of color once thought of as places of opportunity are instead becoming targets of new and old forms of real estate speculation, predation, and racialized reinvestment.

While previous iterations of racist public policy and private profiteering produced large-scale displacement, this metropolitan moment is different. The new urban and suburban renewal, characterized by neoliberal patterns of investment—public-private partnerships, the use of public policy for private gain, and the gradual rescission of the welfare state and social safety net—has increased the economic and geographic divide between rich and poor, Black and White, native- and foreign-born. It has also widened the scope of the damage wrought by redevelopment policies. Displacement has become an endemic part of the metropolitan development process—one that extends well beyond the United States.

But scholars and policymakers alike still too often fail to call these processes by their proper name. While many balk at the term, "gentrification" underscores the political nature of redevelopment processes and their uneven consequences. It causes people to sit up and pay attention, particularly in suburbs, where a veil of invisibility has long lain across redevelopment discourses. Discussions of suburban retrofitting, smart growth, and New Urbanism rarely call to mind the dispossessed communities that often are left in their wake. If we do not recognize their harms, they cannot be remedied or repaired.

CONTESTING THE NEW SUBURBAN RENEWAL

The movement of people of color, immigrants, and impoverished communities to suburbs has been celebrated by some who suggest that it has opened opportunities for those long denied its benefits.[8] While true for some, for others suburbanization has deepened inequalities. The *Right to Suburbia* offers a cautionary tale, charging scholars as well as political and community leaders to ask who bears the burden of suburban redevelopment—and what is owed to those who are harmed.

Scholarly and popular political discourses often position suburban redevelopment, whether inspired by retrofitting, smart growth, or New Urbanism, as a rather banal process that should be welcomed by suburbs. They claim that it helps to correct the wrongs of decades of irresponsible policies that led to sprawling, disconnected suburbs that are environmentally and socially damaging. In Silver Spring, a national model for smart growth, county and community leaders used the rhetoric of revitalization and rebirth to justify one of the state's largest urban renewal projects. It has since become a national poster child of the suburban retrofit. But those who tout new models of suburban redevelopment rarely acknowledge the suffering they can cause. They fail to see redevelopment processes as deeply politicized and racialized, as many residents and businesses are violently displaced.

This view requires not just a look forward but also a view back to the roots of suburbs now undergoing a rebirth. Early White suburbs grew as protected places bolstered by a tight web of racist policies and practices—restrictive covenants, redlining, blockbusting, steering, police violence, and much more. When these protections could no longer be justified, White residents and businesses fortified their privilege and power in new places and ways. In Silver Spring the opening of downtown to African Americans and later to new African, Latinx, and other immigrants prompted massive White flight to farther-out suburbs that drained its tax base and dimmed investment prospects. While some middle-class White residents refused to leave, they increasingly sealed off their neighborhoods, growing Silver Spring's racial and class divide and prefacing the unequal dynamics of future redevelopment battles. In Langley Park the migration of African Americans and diverse immigrants to the neighborhood prompted a more wholesale departure of White residents and businesses, including Jewish residents who were once subject to similar restrictions. As housing and employment opportunities continued to open for more upwardly mobile people of color, many followed their White peers, leaving close-in suburbs like Langley Park for new developments farther away. As had happened in inner-city neighborhoods, in inner suburbs poverty became more entrenched, crime rose, schools declined, and infrastructure began to fail.

Whether settling in inner or outer suburbs, Black and Brown suburbanites found that their new neighborhoods became less economically valuable simply because of their presence. The places they once saw as communities of hope—places to build out of their disparate circumstances—became targets for new predatory forms of suburban inclusion. As White businesses left, neighborhoods were commercially redlined by large businesses that did not see their traditional customer base reflected in the faces of new residents. In Langley Park predatory and low-cost businesses moved in to fill the gap: check-cashing facilities, dollar stores, and the like. Commercial landlords exploited underdeveloped suburbs, overcharging tenants for repairs and escalating rents while refusing basic property maintenance.

In housing the Great Recession ravaged communities of color, especially Black neighborhoods in Prince George's County, with skyrocketing foreclosures. As homes lost value, landlords took the opportunity to exploit and harass tenants, while the county tended to turn a blind eye.

Langley Park became a "slumlord market," ripe for multinational real estate corporations and complicated financial conglomerates to nickel-and-dime residents, especially the undocumented. Slumlords thrived in environments where housing regulations were lax and tenants were vulnerable.[9] They lined their shareholders' pockets while patiently waiting for higher-paying tenants certain to arrive after the state and county invested in a new light-rail line. It was not just private disinvestment but also public neglect that devastated places like Langley Park. The sidewalks did not get fixed; potholes were not filled. Parks and public spaces were almost nonexistent or so run-down that many residents avoided them, seeing them as more of a hazard than an amenity. The public transit that residents relied on was inefficient at best. As is often the case for Black and Brown communities, they were left with the *use value* of their communities—the joy, memories, and hard work that they invested in places undervalued by others. They were not given the *exchange value* of White communities that were deemed viable and invested in simply because of the racialized value attached to their residents.[10]

Narratives about these struggling suburbs fueled further disinvestment. Race and risk are tied in an inexorable link. In Silver Spring decline was likened to a disease to be surgically removed and contained, lest it infect nearby communities with the violence and vacancy it wrought. These narratives placed blame on those who lived through disinvestment, not the systems and structures that caused it. To many who sat in city hall, board rooms, or comfortable middle-class neighborhoods, these communities were black holes—unsafe and unlivable for legitimate suburbanites who had once made them vibrant communities. They painted them as places of death and despair or as blank canvases ripe and ravenous for investment, where something, anything, would do. Their narratives justified massive public and private intervention and its side effects, intentional or not, large or small. Someone always has to lose, they said. It is the price of progress. In the end, we will all be better off. Those who had invested their time, sweat, and limited funds to keep these neighborhoods afloat while starved of the resources they needed to do so were not lauded, rewarded, or protected when redevelopment came. Like the many Black- and immigrant-owned businesses that closed in Silver Spring, they were treated as necessary casualties of a war for the survival of the suburbs or as obstacles to progress.

Just as there was nothing natural about the processes that prompted suburban decline, there was nothing natural about the vast funds poured into these communities to make redevelopment happen. County and state governments led the way through planning, policies, and public investments meant to entice private investment. As Silver Spring and Wheaton vividly revealed, their efforts were layered and robust: enterprise zones, urban and art districts, eminent domain, tax breaks, parcel assemblage, parking regulations, new transit investments, and infrastructure. Public agencies created new market pressures that directed and enabled profitable private development. They served as the promotional arm of private corporations, advertising new suburban downtowns as safe for middle-class consumers and residents. They were critical actors in creating displacement pressures and were, as many activists argued, responsible for their redress. But for the millions of dollars in tax breaks, incentives, and assistance that developers were given, what was asked in return for those who lost their homes, businesses, and sense of community? What was gained for those who had lived with broken sidewalks and run-down playgrounds for decades? Were they the beneficiaries of this progress or was the development, as many suspected, for someone else?

As visions for new suburban downtowns emerged, long-standing communities could scarcely see themselves in the sketches of shiny new plazas and pedestrian streets. As in downtown Silver Spring, these images projected futures that allowed for the comfortable return of the White middle classes, catering to their tastes and preferences for what an authentic and safe urban experience looked and felt like. They did not honor marginalized groups' deep histories, struggles, or valued places. If suburban boosters dared to look back at all, their visions sugarcoated the past in ways that did not trouble their present plans. Even diversity became a selling point. In Wheaton, multicultural festivals crowded the downtown plaza and colorful art displays featured faces from across the world. Yet many wondered whether its fragile diversity was simply a transition to a future in which they no longer existed.

This is gentrification—and it is suburban. While the language of retrofitting or renaissance may be much more genteel, their processes are no less brutal nor disruptive. They affect the lives and livelihoods of countless neighborhoods and threaten the sense of place that people of color and new immigrants have fought to establish and protect, sometimes with, but largely in the absence of, White neighbors and public support. Urban scholars, policymakers, planners, and community advocates must challenge the racial inequalities that these processes produce and on which they were built. They must ask, "What is lost?" and "What is owed?"[11]

In some cases the consequences are not fully known. Redevelopment is an ongoing process that is perhaps never complete. But failing to reckon with these questions leaves the victims unaccounted for, the ledger more unequal, and racialized structures intact. To stop the bleeding and begin to repair the damage, public policy and urban development practices must carefully account for what has been taken and by whom. As with other reparative processes, they must seek solutions with those who have been harmed and must invest in their visions.[12] And they must reconcile questions about why place matters to the unequal processes of investment and disinvestment that repeatedly take shape across metropolitan landscapes.

WHY PLACE MATTERS

For marginalized communities to remain in place in redeveloping suburbs requires confronting myriad challenges. *The Right to Suburbia* exposes how struggling suburbs were made especially vulnerable to displacement by suburban spatial divides, a dearth of community-based organizations and organizing capacity, a lack of political representation, and political fragmentation. Their battles illuminate key arenas for other suburban advocates fighting to ensure that marginalized communities benefit from development taking place in their backyards.

Spatial Divides and Private Profit

Redevelopment is highly disruptive in suburbs with segregated, neatly separated land uses. Massive redevelopment plans and zoning changes are required to shift these sprawling, disparate suburban landscapes into compact communities. Across all the cases, local and state governments targeted areas for reinvestment and applied a range of new policies and incentives to spur private investment. Height limits went up, and mixed-use and transit-oriented zones were adopted. Multifamily housing, not the norm in many places, was permitted. Parking minimums and setbacks were reduced or removed. In Silver Spring the county took control of prime downtown land, using eminent domain to assemble parcels with a ferocity not seen since the days of urban renewal.

But suburbs were still stubbornly resistant to the urban lifestyles municipal leaders tried to promote. Traffic had to be directed away from downtowns; pedestrian and main streets were crafted where they never existed. Sidewalks had to be repaired and widened. Medians had to be planted, crosswalks painted, and traffic bollards installed. Protected bike lanes were built along busy state highways. In Wheaton public land was leveraged in partnership with developers to jumpstart redevelopment. Parking lots were refashioned into public spaces that became the center of new public events and festivals. Public art appeared in new plazas and on the sides of towering new apartment buildings. Safety was assured with bright lighting and security patrols on constant watch. Like Silver Spring a decade earlier, media campaigns announced the birth of its "new downtown," with politicians on standby for photo ops and ribbon cuttings. As former Montgomery County executive Doug Duncan proudly professed in reflecting on Silver Spring, without large public-sector investment, none of this would have been possible.[13]

After generous public investments, private development followed, facilitated by a land-use structure that allowed for grand makeovers and quick profits. Large-lot zoning meant that extensive redevelopment was not just possible but probable. Broad swaths of commercial, office, and residential land were held by only a few owners, the state, or the county. Primed by public investments that raised property values, owners were incentivized to work with municipal leaders to market their parcels as ripe for redevelopment. As Wheaton demonstrated, where land was more fractured, tenants stood a better chance of survival. But landlords used any number of speculative means to make them available to new tenants. They held properties vacant and refused long-term leases or renewals. Where tenants lacked language skills, education, or legal documentation, as some did in Langley Park, they tied them into predatory leases or threatened them with eviction or deportation.

The legacy of suburbia's segregated land uses left former downtowns and central business districts filled with auto-oriented strip malls. In Langley Park and Wheaton, these run-down retail centers offered affordable havens for immigrant-owned businesses, start-ups, and entrepreneurs, as well as a host of community services and institutions—childcare and health-care centers, ESOL and driving schools. Few businesses, however, owned their properties and few tools were available to help them do so. In Langley Park nearby residents lived in large blocks of multifamily housing traded in large portfolios on the stock market and managed by investors who never stepped foot in the neighborhood. Large-lot zoning contributed to the financialization of Langley Park's housing stock, making redevelopment more likely and communities more susceptible to speculative development.

Organizing from the Ground Up

Many suburbs lack organizations that can effectively mobilize residents and businesses around redevelopment. With few nonprofits and service providers to support residents' basic needs, established organizations often have the upper hand. In suburbs these tend to be old-school suburban activists: homeowners and civic associations, chambers of commerce, and historic preservation boards that support the interests of higher-income residents. As I demonstrated in Silver Spring, this traditional power structure often wields control over redevelopment. Groups like IMPACT Silver Spring that represent a new school of suburban activists began with the aim of countering their power by elevating the voices of marginalized groups. But as new organizations, they struggled to build the community trust and capacity to realize their ambitious goals.

Suburban community-based organizations often lack critical capacity. If they are not new start-ups like IMPACT, they are often recent suburban arrivals like the Latino Economic Development Center (LEDC) that borrow capacity from their urban headquarters. These urban transplants struggle to relocate staff, find new funding, and build partnerships in new suburban satellite offices. They survive on shoestring budgets with little support from foundations and suburban municipalities. Many are there to provide critical health and human resources and scramble to deliver a range of services to communities with discrete needs spread out across a sea of incorporated and unincorporated places.[14] Few have skilled organizers at the ready. Others like LEDC, with a legacy of organizing, can endanger their own funding and survivability by standing alongside the communities they serve. To fill capacity gaps, they may seek out other like-minded organizations but lack a slate of potential allies. As the Purple Line Corridor Coalition and Fair Development Coalition showed, some compete for limited funding or may simply not be used to working together. They may have different priorities and politics. While they need umbrella organizations and established coalitions to bring them together and bridge their divides, few exist in suburbs.

To mobilize communities, activists must assemble the infrastructure communities need to organize on their own. Unlike cities, suburbs rarely have existing tenant and small business associations or even neighborhood associations that have the interests of marginalized groups in mind. As IMPACT and LEDC emphasized, suburban organizers too often start from scratch, working to build community and a sense of shared purpose with residents and business owners from different parts of the world, with diverse customs, languages, and business practices, and in neighborhoods deeply divided by race and class. The differences can be stark—between established middle-class homeowners and newer working-class renters, established businesses owners who rally in support of redevelopment, and new immigrant entrepreneurs who struggle under their weight. Advocates are charged with creating a sense of urgency in a redevelopment process that can easily span decades. As IMPACT Silver Spring found, if they start too late, the battle has already been lost. But when they start early, as LEDC and CASA de Maryland did, they must find ways to sustain long-term engagement among communities apt to believe that neither the process nor the people in charge have their best interests in mind.

Suburban Fragmentation and (Mis)Representation

Suburban activists who overcome these hurdles still often struggle to find the political support to bring residents' issues to higher decision-making tables. A lack of political representation for marginalized communities exists at many levels, from redevelopment boards and county councils to state transportation agencies, affecting activists' ability to push for needed anti-displacement policies. Political representation is intimately tied to regional fragmentation and inequality. The three case-study communities are unique among US suburban municipalities. As explained in Chapter 3, in Maryland suburban governance and planning takes place at the county level, offering more opportunities to address inequalities among municipalities than in more balkanized, fragmented suburban areas. But for activists trying to gain ground in counties whose governance structures still largely represented the interests of established civic and business groups, the cases showed a complex range of governance and policy challenges they had to confront to gain recognition for their cause.

Langley Park highlighted the challenge of cross-jurisdictional planning and policymaking. As an unincorporated area at the crossroads of two counties, Langley Park found itself caught in a policy gap with different planning priorities, tools, and visions. Coordination was hampered by the complicated relationship between one of the highest-income counties in the state and one of the lowest in the region. Bicounty efforts were stilted or nonexistent. State and regional leadership was lacking. Political fragmentation and inequality made it difficult for community leaders to garner attention to their needs, as the struggles of one community became less visible and connected to others.

Where progressive political leadership emerges, more progress is possible. But political leaders who come to the fore to represent marginalized groups and communities often do so against incredible odds. Suburbs rarely have the same slate of progressive leaders as central cities. Political incorporation typically lags behind population movement. While county governance may act as a bulwark to balkanized suburban politics, it can stymie the process of gaining representation for marginalized groups in suburbs. Slow to emerge, new leaders are typically the first and only of their kind. The council members I profiled—Tom Perez, Nancy Navarro, and Deni Taveras—were motivated to represent the interest of the communities that elected them and from which they came, but suburban political structures frustrated their aims. They represented large and diverse constituents and interests that did not always match those of the larger jurisdictions of which they were a part. Often outvoted, to get what they want they had to compromise. To the communities that brought them to office, such compromises could easily be read as selling out.

Political leaders had to fight not only their fellow policymakers but also old-school activists who still hold sway in many suburbs. In Silver Spring these activists showed up to public meetings, knew how to organize, and had tight political connections. They were called to sit on redevelopment steering committees and advisory boards and to represent the voice of the community. New-school activists, like those that emerged in Silver Spring and Wheaton, could balance their power and influence but often struggled to start new organizations, learn the political process, and build power with like-minded leaders.

Progressive political leaders, like their grassroots counterparts, often have few tools from which to build bold visions. Many suburban municipalities lack the anti-displacement policies built over decades of struggle in cities, including a robust stock of affordable housing, tenant rights, and small business protections. Needed well in advance of redevelopment, these tools are too often built during times of crises and lack the regulations, funding, or timing for impactful implementation. The results are unsurprising. Those most likely to survive are those who start with the most—the most capital, good credit, networks, and know-how. But as anti-displacement activists across city and suburban lines have long argued, these losses are not inevitable. While redevelopment threatens the viability of struggling suburbs, communities are fighting back—and, increasingly, they are winning.

NEW POSSIBILITIES FOR STAYING PUT

The Right to Suburbia illustrates how activists, from the grassroots to the grasstops, built their organizing capacities and new leadership, grew their anti-displacement toolkits, and built power among marginalized groups to push bolder equitable development agendas. For gentrifying suburbs across the country, their victories can inspire and ignite new possibilities for how to enact their right to stay put.

Strengthening the Grassroots

To effectively intervene in redevelopment processes, communities must be organized. When redevelopment plans are adopted or development pressures arise, affected groups must respond quickly and with a unified voice. Organizations capable of mobilizing diverse constituents are key. Effective organizers hold deep political and community connections. They can call on diverse voices, community-based partners, and political allies when needed. Residents and small businesses must be equally prepared to articulate their interests and concerns. While this community capacity is lacking in many struggling suburbs, it is being built.

As low-income communities of color have grown in suburbs, so too have community-based organizations that serve their interests, including those focused on equitable development. IMPACT Silver Spring underlined the critical role of suburban organizers in developing platforms of engagement and representation in redevelopment processes. The case also emphasized that activist organizations need time to take root and funding to support their organizing aims. While their capacity is being built, suburbs can pull on established urban nonprofits. In Wheaton LEDC leveraged their resources, networks, and decades of organizing experience in the city to mobilize small businesses in the suburbs. They showed that established organizations and organizers can more quickly pivot to respond to community needs and hold local governments and developers accountable. Linkages between city and suburban organizations fill critical capacity gaps among suburban nonprofits and promote stronger city-suburban coalitions that serve their shared interests.

Still, effective coalitions need high-capacity suburban nonprofits with deep community roots. CASA's critical role in launching the Fair Development Coalition and pushing the Purple Line Community Development Agreement showed the power of established suburban nonprofits and strong intersuburban alliances. Their work leveraged longstanding connections and partnerships with other major anchor institutions, foundations, government agencies, political leaders, and grassroots organizations inside and outside the neighborhood. They also drew on the trust built over decades of working in Langley Park to mobilize residents and businesses. Compared to LEDC and IMPACT, CASA had a more robust organizing infrastructure, established partnerships with large institutions and community-based groups, and funding that supported their organizing—all of which enabled them to better sustain the fight and push their demands.

Marginalized residents and businesses also need robust platforms for direct engagement. Across all three case studies, organizers tried to build self-sustaining tenant groups and small business associations. And, while many failed, the Long Branch Business Association showed the power of community associations to generate voice and collective action to improve neighborhood conditions and put vital anti-displacement protections in place. Opportunities to organize must be protected and supported in suburbs by public and private funding, technical assistance, and robust tenant protections, especially for the undocumented.

Building the Suburban Anti-Displacement Toolbox

Advocacy is needed at all phases of redevelopment and policymaking processes. Struggling suburbs need community and political leaders at the table. Across the case studies, grasstops leaders and new-school activists on county councils, redevelopment advisory boards, and civic associations were critical to bringing visibility to marginalized communities and advancing policies to address their concerns. These advocates pushed for more inclusive processes, new protections, and regulations to ensure new policies worked for those who needed them most.

Suburban governance structures need to better account for the systems that fail to represent the interests of marginalized communities. Montgomery County's Urban District and Regional Services Center offers a model for more direct engagement on redevelopment issues that can efficiently target resources, especially to unincorporated communities. But urban district officials and their advisory boards lack decision-making power and the structures that would make them accountable for equitably representing their diverse constituents. Local control must be balanced by more effective regional and cross-jurisdictional planning and policymaking bodies to address disparities among suburbs. The Purple Line Corridor Coalition's vital coordinating role in Langley Park highlighted the potential role of non-profits coalitions in areas with a vacuum of layered regional leadership.

With or without such structures, communities must organize to put progressive leaders in place up and down the ballot. This includes not only city councils but also redevelopment, historic preservation, and citizen-advisory boards. They must gain power in new and existing civic, tenant, homeowner, and small business associations. IMPACT Silver Spring's work to train progressive political leaders to serve on county boards and commissions was widely recognized as some of its most impactful work and a model that other suburbs could learn from.

But progressive suburban leaders cannot do it alone. To be effective advocates, they must be supported by other elected and community leaders. In the Bay Area, the Regional Suburban Organizing Project brings housing justice groups from suburbs across the region together to shift power toward equitable, affordable, and inclusive housing. Groups that work across municipalities and organizations are rare in suburbs but are growing, as organizers bring greater visibility to their shared problems. The Purple Line Corridor Coalition highlighted the important role of cross-jurisdictional organizations, as municipalities struggled to address uneven regional patterns of residential and commercial development in the absence of regional leadership that could have promoted fair-share solutions.

Even without the support of regional alliances, however, progressive leaders advanced new anti-displacement protections. On the housing front, LEDC and council member Nancy Navarro fought for greater requirements for affordable housing in Wheaton's downtown. In the International Corridor, coalitions and council members in Montgomery and Prince George's Counties pushed multiple new policies to keep vulnerable residents in place. They resisted the upzoning of already-dense residential areas. They adopted new code-enforcement regulations, protections against landlord intimidation, and a host of new affordable housing policies and plans. They strengthened tenants' rights, including eviction protections and residential lease requirements, critically needed in many suburbs.

Given the lack of existing tools, the challenge of keeping small businesses in place in redeveloping suburbs may be even greater than that of affordable housing. Across the case studies, however, advocates made inroads, while also highlighting unmet needs. In Silver Spring they built the county's first impact-assistance fund for small businesses and, with continued advocacy, strengthened the program in Wheaton. They built protections to help existing businesses compete with new larger businesses and attract customers with new facade-improvement grants, marketing programs, technical assistance, and local hiring requirements. They pushed to mitigate construction disruptions, helping small businesses weather the storm of torn-up streets and lost parking with new signage requirements and parking plans. Though few long-term affordability or commercial tenant protections were put in place, advocates brought these conversations into the public discourse, offering examples from elsewhere that expanded policymakers' views about what is possible.[15]

Building off the lessons of and in partnership with other suburban advocates, the Maryland suburbs now offer examples of comprehensive equitable development that other advocates are looking to. In the International Corridor, the Fair Development Coalition and Purple Line Corridor Coalition created new platforms for cross-sector and cross-jurisdictional planning and policy that targeted the needs of the hardest-hit communities. They coordinated planning priorities and tools among municipalities and agencies to ensure that assistance was timely and targeted and that protections were in place before, during, and after construction. Their plans came together through deep engagement with communities and the support of political leaders at various levels, from local agencies to state officials. Though they failed to obtain the legally binding community benefits agreement many hoped for, they advanced a community development agenda that included protections for affordable housing, small businesses, workforce development, and new neighborhood investments. Their plans are bold and comprehensive and will undoubtedly leave a lasting imprint on the region as the Purple Line moves forward. By bringing visibility to their struggles of vulnerable corridor communities, they have charted new domains that activists elsewhere can use to carry the movement forward.

Envisioning New Suburban Futures

Suburbia's many boundaries and divides often isolate the struggles of one community from another. This lack of visibility and recognition of communities' linked fates makes it difficult to build political will within and across municipalities. Organizers in the Maryland suburbs did not accept the celebratory redevelopment rhetoric handed down to them by planners and politicians. They refused the idea that some must win and others must lose—when those who would lose seemed so predictably clear. Instead, they questioned how to prevent the damage before it occurred and how to turn the expected losses into wins for marginalized communities. The stories they told shifted the focus away from the privileged and powerful and centered on the voices of the dispossessed and the excluded in narratives about redevelopment.

These activists showed that equitable development organizing cannot just be about *the what* but must also address *the why*. In mobilizing around needed policies to keep vulnerable residents and small businesses in place, advocates must also show why these protections are needed in suburbs to begin with. They must challenge narratives about progress or revitalization that fail to recognize or account for the harm done to the most vulnerable and must instead center their stories to paint a different picture about what success looks like. Reframing the story expands the possibilities for collective action. It builds power in new places, shifting the focus from questions of private profit and middle-class comfort to questions about inclusion, equity, justice, and reparation.

The stories that need telling differ from suburb to suburb. I have focused on three Maryland communities that have learned lessons from one another and collectively built power to push their shared interests. The efforts of the central organizations were led by impassioned community leaders like Frankie Blackburn, Ash Kosiewicz, and Zorayda Moreira-Smith. While fierce fighters for their neighborhoods, they also cared deeply about racial and immigrant justice across the region and beyond. Their local battles were part of a larger equitable development war, and their tactics carried forward lessons of how to build community power and political will from one struggle to the next. Their organizations signed one another's petitions, stood beside one another at county council hearings, wrote grants together, and served alongside one another on working groups and advisory committees. Collectively, their stories conveyed warnings about the harm wrought by redevelopment on the people and places they cared deeply about as well as messages of hope about the possibilities of what could be achieved that inspired future leaders. These pivotal players also tried to build a leadership bench and organizational capacity to ensure that there were others ready to pick up the torch. Their efforts ensured that the movement grew over time and space, with each iteration raising the odds that their increasingly bold demands would be met.

In many ways their stories diverged. Political leaders had multiple redevelopment goals in mind and followed varied paths to achieve them. Neighborhoods were in differing stages of development or decline. They had different tools and funding available to meet the moment. Communities had diverse demographics, immigrant histories, and organizing capacities. But they were also bound together in distinct ways. They were located within a historically Black-White region that has only recently experienced new immigration. The metropolitan area had grown rapidly for decades, with the federal government providing a stable and relatively high regional economic base. They sat in some of the wealthiest suburban counties in the country, both Black and White, that held countywide planning and policymaking authority, a rare form of suburban governance.

In other places these dynamics will look different. In Rust Belt suburbs the pace of change may be slower, allowing activists more time to get ahead of the redevelopment curve. In West Coast ethnoburbs, activist organizations and affected communities may have different demographic profiles, raising unique challenges to building community power and agency. Far exurban places may not have the same wealth or even the basic toolkit that existed in Prince George's County. Their politics may be more conservative and their elected leaders less inclined to fight for the interests of marginalized communities or even to listen.

Had my attention been directed elsewhere, I might have come to different conclusions about the factors that matter most to the politics of suburban gentrification and the capacity of communities to respond. That is to be tested. I suspect that aspects of these cases are unique to Maryland suburbs, while others are quite representative of suburban conditions elsewhere. Struggling suburbs exist in every state and region in the United States and beyond. Some have changed in a few short decades, as White residents and capital fled and Black and Brown communities moved in. Underdeveloped communities are beginning to, or have already seen, a rush of reinvestment. These places are hailed by suburban boosters, where the disparate impacts are left unchallenged.

Advocates—whether political leaders, planners, community organizers, or scholars—must pay acute attention to the many forms that gentrification takes across the distinct geographies. They must be aware of why place matters to gentrification's uneven impacts and what communities can do about it. There is much work to be done to tease out how these factors differ among diverse metropolitan regions, suburban typologies, and neighborhoods. Future studies will hopefully continue to look across the multiple dimensions of metropolitan and neighborhood inequality to move the equitable development needle in varied urban, suburban, and rural places.

Advocates will also hopefully tell stories that link the concerns of one community to another and show how those who are often pushed to the margins have a critical stake in their metropolitan futures. Indeed, the problems of one neighborhood affect the economic, environmental, and social vitality of an entire region. If one neighborhood suffers and another succeeds, those on the "winning" side may count themselves lucky. But in fact both lose.[16] To speak of gentrification as a process connected across time and space is to disrupt the racialized institutions that create, maintain, and condone separate and unequal neighborhoods and to become an accomplice in defending the right of communities to remain in cities and suburbs.

The stories of multiple metropolitan futures are most powerful when they are connected to the lives of people who have cared for and sustained them through good times and bad. Evocative tales that speak to a community's place meanings and attachments inspire collective action and change collective narratives. My story honors my own family's legacy in Chocolate City and its suburbs. The stories my in-laws shared around their dining room table carried a heavy sense of what meant to lose their home and sense of community in their former and current neighborhoods as well as their place in the region's future. As marginalized communities are pushed farther beyond the urban edge, they are pushed out of sight and out of mind. Their stories become harder to tell and see. Their daily rhythms and order seem ever more out of step with the changing times. Their dreams and desires no longer hold sway in their former communities. In turning a blind eye to these challenges, we lose the capacity to respond. We miss the ability to resolve existing funding and policy gaps and the innovative solutions emerging among community institutions and leaders. We lose a sense of urgency and our connected fates.

Activists are not fighting for pie-in-the-sky ideas; they are pushing for thoughtful plans that articulate new possibilities. When we listen to marginalized communities and invest in their visions, we invest in futures in which it is possible to move up in one's neighborhood without moving out. We give life to the promise that groups who have fought for communities can remain in them and build long-term wealth, opportunity, and a sense of place. We invest in and fight for the just futures that all communities—urban and suburban—deserve.

APPENDIX   On Choosing the Suburban
              Margins

I came to theory because I was hurting—the pain within
me was so intense that I could not go on living. I came to
theory desperate, wanting to comprehend—to grasp what
was happening around and within me. Most importantly, I
wanted to make the hurt go away. I saw in theory then a
location for healing.

—bell hooks, *Teaching to Transgress*

For many scholars of color, particularly women, scholarship is self-care. It is a
pursuit of our truth and desire to see ourselves reflected in stories that engage the
multiple marginalized worlds we inhabit. While we may engage in "choosing the
margin," it is not because we accept being relegated to otherized and denigrated
spaces, as bell hooks reminds us. It is an act of resistance that invites new ways of
knowing and seeing other possibilities for people and places forced to the margins.[1] Like so many women of color, my scholarship is deeply personal and
political.

The communities I have focused on are beloved communities—not just to
myself but to the many who cared for and tended to them when others looked the
other way or actively denied them critical resources. *The Right to Suburbia* offers
these stories in search of new pathways to personal and collective healing and
shows communities of resistance that are imagining and "planning otherwise."[2]
It refuses the "damage centered research" and "pain narratives" that too often fail
to posit marginalized communities as agents in envisioning and realizing their
own futures.[3] As cultural historian Saidiya Hartman poignantly describes, urban
reformers in the early twentieth century studied Black "slums" in ways that
refused to see beauty, with powerful consequences:

The surveys and the sociological pictures left me cold. These photographs never
grasped the beautiful struggle to survive, glimpsed alternative modes of life, or illu-
minated the mutual aid and communal wealth of the slum. The reform pictures and

249

the sociological surveys documented only ugliness. . . . The social worlds represented in these pictures were targeted for destruction and elimination. The reformers used words like "improvement" and "social betterment" and "protection," but no one was fooled. The interracial slum was razed and mapped into homogenous zones of absolute difference. The black ghetto was born.[4]

Similar lenses are applied to racialized spaces today, with equally damaging results. *The Right to Suburbia* aims to show the "beautiful struggle" of marginalized communities to remain in their beloved communities and what is at stake in their loss.

I began the book in 2013 by exploring the histories and characteristics of redeveloping suburbs throughout the DC region. My research was broad and diverse, covering neighborhoods in Virginia and Maryland—Black and White, immigrant and nonimmigrant. Among those that were redeveloping or had undergone redevelopment within the past several decades, I compared their social, spatial, political, and economic conditions. I settled on three communities that were diverse in character, demographics, and redevelopment histories but closely connected geographically and otherwise. As noted in Chapter 1, my exploratory research and interviews in the selected cases repeatedly referenced the lessons learned from or employed by other cases. The connected case-study idea emerged as one that mirrored the collective aims of organizers. The activists I spoke to had tales they wanted told not only about their neighborhoods but also about the growing regional equitable development movement. *The Right to Suburbia* seeks to capture and celebrate their collective aims.

My exploration of these three communities was also guided by my familiarity with them. They were communities near and dear to my heart—places that I had lived and worked in and fought for, places of my past that I saw connected to my future. They were communities in which I knew residents, business owners, and advocates fighting for the right to remain, in ways big and small. In them I sensed a foreboding that inspired my research: my desperation to serve as a coconspirator and to tell their stories so that they would not be forgotten.

In each neighborhood I sought out people who could speak to their redevelopment politics from an intimate vantage. In most cases I began with community activists who led the battle for equitable development; their voices are most prominent in these chapters. My initial interviews led to others, as I sought out multiple perspectives from community-based organizations to political leaders involved in the redevelopment processes and politics. This resulted in a robust snowball sample of community leaders, business owners, nonprofit organizations, government-agency representatives, elected representatives, and planners. The number of interviewees varied for each of the three cases: nineteen for Silver Spring, thirty-one for Wheaton, and twenty-four for Langley Park. Because of the connected nature of the cases, interviewees were often aware of and sometimes intimately involved in more than one case study.

I conducted semistructured interviews between 2014 and 2020. They tended to last between one to two hours, though some extended well beyond that. I asked most interviewees questions about the process and politics of redevelopment related to a single case study. Those who had knowledge about multiple cases informed comparisons among them. I conducted nearly all interviews in-person, with a few conducted by phone at interviewees' request. All were recorded with the permission of participants, transcribed, and coded using qualitative analysis software to locate themes within and across the case studies. I followed up with only a few interviewees, usually to ask clarifying questions or as critical issues arose that we had not previously discussed.

Some interviewees I knew well; others I did not. In Silver Spring I had not previously worked with any interviewees but had met a few in professional settings. In Wheaton I was more familiar with multiple interviewees, as I had regularly engaged my class in neighborhood walking tours and led a class project about protecting small downtown businesses. Langley Park was the neighborhood where I held the closest connections. As described in Chapter 5, my work in Langley Park predated my research and continued throughout the research period. I held strong connections with various members of the Purple Line Corridor Coalition (PLCC), led by the National Center for Smart Growth Research and Education, where I served as director of community development, and with the Fair Redevelopment Coalition, led by CASA de Maryland. Though I sat on the PLCC steering committee, I rarely attended meetings but was a familiar face at early PLCC events. During the research period, I organized a class forum on the Purple Line's potential impact in Langley Park with invited community leaders, engaged students in numerous neighborhood walking tours, and hosted a class project on protecting neighborhood affordable housing. I collaborated on several projects with CASA directly and indirectly related to the Purple Line. I am the lead author of *Preparing for the Purple Line: Affordable Housing Strategies for Langley Park, Maryland,* a 2017 report coauthored with CASA, which informed some of their housing-policy advocacy. That same year I coauthored with CASA *Engaging Communities around Opportunity through Story Mapping* and *Mapping in Action: Engaging an Immigrant Community in Planning for a New Light Rail,* which highlight community assets that could be threatened by the new line. I was the lead author of *Housing Matters: Ensuring Quality, Safe, and Healthy Housing in Langley Park,* a 2019 report that details a two-year CASA-led collaborative, in which I participated. The report made recommendations to improve housing quality and code enforcement in the neighborhood. Between 2018 and 2020, I also served on the Langley Park Crime Prevention Collaborative, a group led by CASA to plan and implement multiple community-driven crime prevention and safety projects. Through these activities, I built close working relationships with various people featured in Chapter 5, including grassroots community activists as well as county and state representatives.

My connections helped me to locate interviewees and build rapport but also charged me to reflect on my positionality. In line with critical ethnographic scholars, my engagement challenges the illusion of "critical distance" as a useful tool for understanding and interpreting my or others' lived experiences.[5] Knowledge is socially and culturally situated, and thus my aim has been to clearly position myself within the story and to fairly do the same for those who shared their perspectives with me.

In each community I dug into the history of race and redevelopment, using a variety of archival and secondary sources. Community and municipal archives were vital. In Silver Spring and Wheaton, those held by Montgomery History, including the Mary Kay Harper Center for Suburban Studies, proved particularly helpful. In Langley Park, Bill Hanna's archives, held by the University of Maryland's Latin American and Caribbean Studies Center, were an unexpected treasure trove on the neighborhood's history. Local and regional blogs and news sites offered essential insights, especially *Greater Greater Washington,* the *DCist,* Dan Reed's *Just Up the Pike,* and David Rotenstein's *History Sidebar.* In many cases interviewees opened their personal and organizational archives to me. I am especially indebted to IMPACT Silver Spring's Frankie Blackburn, Latino Economic Development Center's Ash Kosiewicz, Wheaton Citizens Coalition's Marian Fryer, and PLCC's Gerrit Knaap. To understand the history of segregation and inequality in DC and across its suburbs, Prologue DC's "Mapping Segregation" and community archives held by the Lakeland History Project were especially useful sources.

For each case I also reviewed various municipal planning and redevelopment documents, including county master and sector plans, special district-designation applications, requests for proposals, development reports, market analyses, environmental-impacts statements, public-meeting transcripts, and more. My understanding of their redevelopment histories and politics benefited greatly from regional and national newspaper archives, especially those of the *Washington Post, Washington City Paper, Washingtonian,* and Maryland's *Daily Record,* which I reviewed dating back as far as the 1920s. I also carefully tracked US census data numbers for each community from 1970 to the present, including data associated with race, income, immigration, housing, and employment.

While *The Right to Suburbia* organizes these as sequential case studies, the research was conducted simultaneously, largely between 2014 and 2018. Wheaton and Langley Park were the most current case studies, where the process of redevelopment was still very much incomplete when I finished research in early 2020. Then COVID-19 hit, radically reshaping the conditions on the ground for residents and businesses. While I kept up with the redevelopment processes and politics in these communities after my research ended, I chose not to update the case studies. Only minor details have been added for context. Just as redevelopment is a process that is never done, the battle for equitable development remains ongoing in these communities. As a scholar-activist and community-engaged researcher, it is difficult to know when and how to leave the field. To me this is not a question of leaving communities behind or shifting focus from their struggle. It is a decision to move from data collection to analysis and from collecting to telling stories about their struggles. My hope is that this book sheds light on the ongoing fight of marginalized communities to remain in redeveloping suburbs and aids them in realizing the right to the suburbs of their American dreams.

Notes

INTRODUCTION

1. I first encountered this idea about the joys of city life in Amin, "Ethnicity."

2. The term "beloved community" refers to a concept popularized by Dr. Martin Luther King as a society based on principles of justice, equal opportunity, and love.

3. The notion of "city of my heart's desire" comes from Harvey, *Rebel Cities*, 4.

4. It turns out that the story was already eloquently told by native Washingtonian scholar and artist Sabiyha Prince, in *African Americans*.

5. The terms "Black" and "Brown" may not be familiar outside of a US context, but they generally refer to non-White racialized groups. They highlight the disparate experiences of groups, particularly Black people, in racial hierarchies within the US and internationally. I also sometimes reference people or communities of color. I chose not to use "BIPOC" (Black, Indigenous, and People of Color) or "minority," both terms with which I do not personally identify (though for the former, I agree with its use). I capitalize White to highlight the ways people racialized as White benefit from and affirm their status in institutions and communities.

6. hooks, "Choosing the Margin," 16.

7. This reference to suburbs comes from the 1962 song by Malvina Reynolds, "Little Boxes."

8. This is, of course, before the release of the 2021 version of *The Wonder Years,* which centered on the life of a Black family in the suburbs.

9. On racialized suburban tropes, see Rios, *Black Lives;* and Schafran, "Discourse and Dystopia."

10. Lung-Amam, *Trespassers.*

11. I credit planner and blogger Dan Reed's post about the "Wonder Years" with this insight.

12. The language of "Silver SprUng" and the banner that accompanied it were from a county-led marketing campaign to bring more residents into its Central Business District. See Craig and Barr, "Bill on House Heights."

1. THE FIGHT TO STAY IN PLACE

1. The notion of "asset stripping" in Black communities in the name of redevelopment comes from Woods, "Misérables of New Orleans."

2. Harvey, *Rebel Cities;* Lefebvre, *Writings on Cities,* 63.

3. Lees, "Reappraisal of Gentrification"; M. Phillips, "Other Geographies of Gentrification."

4. On class-based definitions of gentrification, see Glass, *London;* and Smith, *New Urban Frontier.* My definition pulls from Rucks-Ahidiana, "Theorizing Gentrification."

5. On the "new urban renewal," see Hyra, *New Urban Renewal.*

6. Glass, *London.* On other common definitions of gentrification, see Lees, Slater, and Wyly, *Gentrification;* and Zuk et al., "Role of Public Investment."

7. Smith, "Gentrification and Uneven Development"; Smith, "Toward a Theory"; Smith, *New Urban Frontier;* S. Stein, *Capital City.*

8. The idea of serial displacement refers to its original conceptualization in Fullilove and Wallace, "Serial Forced Displacement."

9. On two previous waves of gentrification in the United States, see Hackworth and Smith, "Changing State of Gentrification."

10. On neoliberalism, see Harvey, *Brief History of Neoliberalism.* On HOPE VI reforms and gentrification, see Lees, Butler, and Bridge, "Introduction."

11. Keil, *Suburban Planet;* Lees, Shin, and López-Morales, *Planetary Gentrification.*

12. Florida, *Cities,* 1; Zukin, *Cultures of Cities;* Zukin, *Naked City.*

13. Hackworth and Rekers, "Ethnic Packaging and Gentrification"; Hyra, *Race, Class, and Politics;* Lindner and Sandoval, *Aesthetics of Gentrification;* Loukaitou-Sideris and Soureli, "Cultural Tourism"; Summers, *Black in Place;* Zukin, *Naked City.*

14. On the characteristics and preferences of White gentrifiers, see Brown-Saracino, *Neighborhood That Never Changes;* Hamnett, "Gentrification"; Ley,

New Middle Class; and Zukin, *Loft Living.* For perspectives on the Black middle class in gentrifying neighborhoods, see Boyd, "Downside of Racial Uplift"; Freeman, *There Goes the "Hood";* Moore, "Gentrification in Black Face"; Pattillo, *Black on the Block;* and M. Taylor, *Harlem.*

15. On the displacement measurement debate, see Slater, "Eviction of Critical Perspectives"; and Zuk et al., "Role of Public Investment."

16. Marcuse, "Abandonment, Gentrification, and Displacement."

17. Chapple and Jacobus, "Retail Trade"; Meltzer, "Gentrification and Small Business"; Meltzer and Schuetz, "Bodegas or Bagel Shops"; Zukin et al., "New Retail Capital."

18. Curran, "Gentrification"; Curran, "Frying Pan."

19. On cultural displacement, see Howell, "It's Complicated"; Hyra, "Back-to-the-City Movement"; and Zukin, *Cultures of Cities.* On microsegregation in gentrifying neighborhoods, see Hyra, *Race, Class, and Politics;* Lees, "Gentrification and Social Mixing"; and Tach, "Diversity, Inequality, and Microsegregation."

20. Howell, "It's Complicated"; Hyra, *Race, Class, and Politics;* Modan, *Turf Wars.*

21. Baker and Lee, "Light Rail Transit"; Chapple and Loukaitou-Sideris, *Transit-Oriented Displacement;* Dawkins and Moeckel, "Transit Induced Gentrification"; Rayle, "Investigating the Connection."

22. Lefebvre, *Writings on Cities.* On the Right to the City Alliance, see Fisher et al., "We Are Radical."

23. Ramírez, "Take the Houses Back"; Roy, "Dis/possessive Collectivism." On "defensive development," see Boyd, "Defensive Development." On Black business improvement districts and cooperatives, see Sutton, "Rethinking Commercial Revitalization." On equitable transit-oriented development, see Cho, "People's Plan"; and Sandoval, "Planning the Barrio."

24. Lees, Annunziata, and Rivas-Alonso, "Resisting Planetary Gentrification," 346. On strategies, see, for example, Drew, "Listening through White Ears"; Lung-Amam and Dawkins, "Participatory Story Mapping"; Newman and Wyly, "Right to Stay Put"; Slater, "North American Gentrification"; and Villanueva, "Designing a Chinatown."

25. See, for instance, Chapple and Zuk, "Forewarned"; "Equitable Development Toolkit"; Finio et al., "Regional Planning Process"; and Pollack, Bluestone, and Billingham, *Maintaining Diversity.*

26. For examples of these approaches in the Bay Area and Portland, see Bates, "Gentrification and Displacement Study"; and Gordon et al., *Rooted in Home.* On DC, see Howell, "Planning for Empowerment."

27. On diverse definition of suburbs, see Airgood-Obrycki, Hanlon, and Rieger, "Delineate the U.S. Suburb"; and Forsyth, "Defining Suburbs."

28. Archer, Sandul, and Solomonson, *Making Suburbia;* Fong, *First Suburban Chinatown;* González, *Mexican Beverly Hills;* Kruse and Sugrue, *New*

Suburban History; Lung-Amam, *Trespassers;* Nicolaides and Wiese, *Suburb Reader;* Wiese, *Places of Their Own.*

29. Frey, *Diversity Explosion;* Price and Benton-Short, *Migrants to the Metropolis.*

30. Kneebone and Garr, *Suburbanization of Poverty;* Orfield and Luce, "America's Racially Diverse Suburbs."

31. Holliday and Dwyer, "Suburban Neighborhood Poverty"; Kneebone and Berube, *Confronting Suburban Poverty;* Lucy and Phillips, *Confronting Suburban Decline.* On the ravages of the Great Recession, see Martin and Niedt, *Foreclosed America;* Raphael and Stoll, *Job Sprawl.*

32. Kneebone and Holmes, *U.S. Concentrated Poverty.*

33. K. Taylor, *Race for Profit,* 5. On high-poverty suburbs, see Kneebone and Holmes, *U.S. Concentrated Poverty;* and Suro, Wilson, and Singer, *Immigration and Poverty.*

34. Alba et al., "Immigrant Groups"; Clark, "Race, Class, and Place"; Farrell, "Immigrant Suburbanisation"; Logan, "Separate and Unequal"; Pfeiffer, "Racial Equity"; Schafran, *Road to Resegregation;* Vallejo, *Barrios to Burbs.*

35. On ethnoburbs, see Li, *Ethnoburb;* and Li, *From Urban Enclaves.* On Asian-White conflict in ethnoburbs, see Fong, *First Suburban Chinatown;* and Lung-Amam, *Trespassers.*

36. Definitions of inner suburbs and outer suburbs vary. For common definitions, see Airgood-Obrycki, Hanlon, and Rieger "Delineate the U.S. Suburb." The definitions used in this book related to the DC region are those previously defined by Lung-Amam, Anacker, and Finio, "Worlds Away in Suburbia." Neighborhoods that lie in counties directly bordering Washington, DC, are termed inner suburbs. Those that lie beyond the inner suburbs are considered outer suburbs. I sometimes refer to areas as "exurban" to indicate that they are located on the fringes of the metropolitan area.

37. Hanlon, "Older Inner Suburbs"; Hanlon, *Once the American Dream;* Hanlon, Short, and Vicino, *Cities and Suburbs;* Puentes and Orfield, *Valuing America's First Suburbs;* Puentes and Warren, *One-Fifth of America;* Vicino, *Transforming Race and Class.*

38. Cooke and Marchant, "Changing Intrametropolitan Location"; Kneebone and Berube, *Confronting Suburban Poverty.*

39. Anacker, *New American Suburb;* Covington, Freeman, and Stoll, *Suburbanization of Housing Choice;* Felland, Lauer, and Cunningham, *Suburban Poverty;* Lo et al., *Social Infrastructure and Vulnerability;* Logan and Alba, "Locational Returns"; Mahler, *Salvadorans in Suburbia;* Murphy and Wallace, "Opportunities"; Holloway, "City to the Suburbs"; Schneider and Logan, "Suburban Racial Segregation."

40. Murphy, "Social Organization," 1. On suburbia's dearth of social service capacity and struggles of suburban nonprofits, see Allard, *Places in Need;* Allard

and Roth, *Strained Suburbs;* Holloway, "Suburban Safety Net"; Murphy, "Symbolic Dilemmas"; and Roth, Gonzales, and Lesniewski, "Stronger Safety Net."

41. Puentes and Warren, *One-Fifth of America,* 1.

42. Hanlon, "Fixing Inner-Ring Suburbs"; Kneebone and Berube, *Confronting Suburban Poverty;* Lucy and Phillips, *Confronting Suburban Decline;* Pendall, Weir, and Narducci, *Governance;* Puentes and Orfield, *Valuing America's First Suburbs;* Vicino, "Quest to Confront."

43. Dreier, Mollenkopf, and Swanstrom, *Place Matters;* Finio et al., "Metropolitan Planning"; Keating and Bier, "Greater Cleveland's First Suburbs"; Orfield, *American Metropolitics;* Pastor, *Regions That Work;* Weir, Wolman, and Swanstrom, "Calculus of Coalitions."

44. Boyles, *Suburban Policing;* Gordon, *Citizen Brown;* Oliveri, "Setting the Stage"; Rios, *Black Lives.*

45. Lung-Amam and Schafran, "From Sanford to Ferguson."

46. Boyles, *Suburban Policing;* Gordon, *Citizen Brown;* Lung-Amam and Schafran, "From Sanford to Ferguson."

47. See, for instance, Ewing and Hamidi, *Costs of Sprawl;* Ross, *Dead End;* and Squires, *Urban Sprawl.*

48. Dunham-Jones and Williamson, *Retrofitting Suburbia;* Tachieva, *Sprawl Repair Manual.* On New Urbanism, see Calthorpe and Fulton, *Regional City;* Duany, Plater-Zyberk, and Speck, *Suburban Nation;* and Duany, Speck, and Lydon, *Smart Growth Manual.*

49. Lung-Amam and June-Friesen, "Growing Together." On critiques of smart growth by urban and environmental justice advocates, see Bullard, *Growing Smarter;* Gearin, "Smart Growth"; and powell, "Urban Sprawl."

50. On critiques of New Urbanist and mixed-income developments, see Bridge, Butler, and Lees, *Mixed Communities;* and Day, "New Urbanism." On Atlanta, see Immergluck, *Red Hot City;* Lanari, "New City Center"; Markley, "Suburban Gentrification"; and Markley, "New Urbanism and Race."

51. See, for example, Vitiello, "Politics of Immigration." On debates over single-family homes, see Charles, "Understanding the Determinants"; Hanlon and Airgood-Obrycki, "Suburban Revalorization"; Lung-Amam, "Monster House"; and Sweeney and Hanlon, "Old Suburb to Post-suburb."

52. On suburban revanchism and neoliberal suburban tactics, see Markley and Sharma, "Gentrification," 57; and Niedt and Christophers, "Value at Risk." On Baltimore, see Niedt, "Gentrification and the Grassroots"; Hanlon and Airgood-Obrycki, "Suburban Revalorization"; and Vicino, "Quest to Confront."

53. Peck, "Neoliberal Suburbanism"; Phelps and Wood, "New Post-suburban Politics"; Teaford, "Post-suburbia."

54. On critiques of early suburban histories, see Kruse and Sugrue, *New Suburban History;* Nicolaides and Wiese, *Suburb Reader;* and Wiese, *Places of Their Own.* For historical and contemporary studies of progressive politics in suburbs,

see Greason, *Suburban Erasure;* D. Harris, *Second Suburb;* B. Haynes, *Red Lines;* Johnson, *Black Power;* and Vicino, *Suburban Crossroads.*

55. Carpio, Irazábal, and Pulido, "Right to the Suburb," 189.

56. Carpio, Irazábal, and Pulido, "Right to the Suburb," 189.

57. Lewis-McCoy, "Changing Face." On recent suburban uprisings, see Boyles, *You Can't Stop;* Lung-Amam and Schafran, "From Sanford to Ferguson"; and Rios, *Black Lives.*

58. Lanari, "New City Center"; Lung-Amam, *Trespassers;* Rios, *Black Lives.*

59. For a review of gentrification from the Global North and Global South, see Lees and Phillips, *Handbook of Gentrification Studies.*

60. Keil, *Suburban Planet,* 15.

61. Kruse and Sugrue, *New Suburban History;* Nicolaides and Wiese, *Suburb Reader;* Schafran, "Discourse and Dystopia."

62. On suburbia as a "promised land" and its many false promises for Black and Brown suburbanites, see Lewis-McCoy, *Inequality;* Nicolaides, *My Blue Heaven;* Straus, *Death;* and Wiese, *Places of their Own.*

63. O'Connell, "Catching Fish."

64. O'Connell, "Echoes of Little Saigon."

65. By 1989 about half of the Clarendon's seventy-six businesses were Asian-owned. Arnett, "Arlington Losing Ethnic Flavor"; Ayres, "Arlington Journal"; O'Connell, "Echoes of Little Saigon."

66. O'Connell, "Echoes of Little Saigon"; Scannell, "Clarendon Easing toward Rebirth."

67. Ayres, "Arlington Journal," A18; Ginsberg, "Virginia"; Scannell, "Clarendon Easing toward Rebirth."

68. Ayres, "Arlington Journal"; Hsu, "Plan Would Reshape Clarendon."

69. Ayres, "Arlington Journal," A18.

70. Quoted in Arnett, "Arlington Losing Ethnic Flavor," A1; and Ayres, "Arlington Journal," A18.

71. Arnett, "Arlington Losing Ethnic Flavor"; Ayres, "Arlington Journal."

72. Meyers, "Eden Center"; O'Connell, "Echoes of Little Saigon."

73. See Hyra and Prince, *Capital Dilemma,* and its multiple authors in what they call the "DC School of Urbanism."

74. Asch and Musgrove, *Chocolate City;* Gale, *Washington, DC;* Gillette, *Between Justice and Beauty;* Jaffe and Sherwood, *Dream City;* Ruble, *Washington's U Street.*

75. On DC's status at the "most intensely gentrified city" in the United States, see Richardson, Mitchell, and Franco, *Shifting Neighborhoods,* 4.

76. Gallaher, *Politics of Staying Put;* Golash-Boza, *Before Gentrification;* Howell, "Preservation"; Huron, *Carving Out the Commons;* Hyra, *Race, Class, and Politics;* Hyra and Prince, *Capital Dilemma;* Modan, *Turf Wars;* Prince, *African Americans;* Summers, *Black in Place.* Quote from Franke-Ruta, "Urban Comeback."

77. On racial and immigration in the DC suburbs, see Friedman et al., "Race, Immigrants, and Residence"; and Manning, "Multicultural Washington, DC." On poverty, see Kneebone and Berube, *Confronting Suburban Poverty;* and Lung-Amam, Anacker, and Finio, "Worlds Away in Suburbia."

78. Garreau, *Edge City.*

79. Dunham-Jones and Williamson, *Retrofitting Suburbia;* Williamson and Dunham-Jones, *Case Studies.*

80. Hanson, *Suburb.*

81. Center on Urban, *Region Divided;* Kneebone and Berube, *Confronting Suburban Poverty.*

82. Unless otherwise noted and with their permission, I use interviewees' actual names. Those whom I anonymized were largely community residents, small business owners, and people who asked to remain as such. I generally refer to people by their last names and with Mr. or Ms. or their titles. Only when interviewees are close acquaintances or similarly aged peers or younger do I refer to them by their first names. A more detailed discussion of methods can be found in the appendix.

83. The notion of "long engagement" comes from Plath, *Long Engagements.* Other ethnographers whose long engagements with racial issues in urban and suburban spaces have informed my own include Mitchell Duneier, Karyn Lacy, Elliot Liebow, Mary Pattillo, and Carol Stack. See, for example, Stack, *All Our Kin;* Stack, *Call to Home;* Duneier, *Ghetto;* Duneier and Carter, *Sidewalk;* Pattillo, *Black on the Block;* Pattillo, *Black Picket Fences;* Liebow, *Tally's Corner;* and Lacy, *Blue-Chip Black.*

84. Pierre, "Comparative Urban Governance"; Robinson, "Comparative Urbanism"; Ward, "Toward a Comparative (Re)turn."

85. Kaba, *We Do This,* 48, 106.

2. DC SUBURBAN SHUFFLE

1. Building Bridges, "11th Street Bridge Park."

2. E. Haynes, "Currents of Change."

3. Here I am pulling Chris Asch and George Musgrove's analysis of four distinct periods of gentrification in Washington, DC. See Asch and Musgrove, "We Are Headed."

4. See, for instance, Archer, Sandul, and Solomonson, *Making Suburbia;* Kruse and Sugrue, *New Suburban History;* and Nicolaides and Wiese, *Suburb Reader.*

5. Scholars have written about various arenas of racialized inequality in suburbs, including education, housing, health care, electoral politics, and criminal justice. For a review, see Lewis-McCoy et al., "Resisting Amnesia."

6. Manning, "Multicultural Washington, DC," 328.

7. Tyler Morgan, quoted in Asch and Musgrove, *Chocolate City,* 176.

8. Ruble, *Washington's U Street.*

9. Borchert, *Alley Life in Washington;* Weller, *Neglected Neighbors.*

10. On DC's urban design history, see Gillette, *Between Justice and Beauty.*

11. Riis, quoted in Gillette, *Between Justice and Beauty,* 116.

12. Levy, "Washington."

13. Flanagan, "Battle of Fort Reno."

14. Prologue DC, "Federal Housing Administration"; Shoenfeld and Cherkasky, "Strictly White Residential Section."

15. Gale, *Washington, DC;* Lesko, Babb, and Gibbs, *Black Georgetown Remembered;* Green, *Secret City.*

16. Levy, "Washington."

17. Kelly and Maryland-National Capital Park, *Places from the Past;* Virta, "County with Rich History."

18. On the history of rural Black towns and "freedom colonies," see Roberts, "Texas Freedom Colonies"; Slocum, *Black Towns;* and Wiese, *Places of Their Own.* On those in Montgomery County, Freedman's Village, and other Black towns in Arlington, see "Historic African American Communities."

19. Lubar, "Trolley Lines"; Walston, "Commercial Rise"; Hanson, *Suburb,* 15.

20. "Woodside Park," R2; Hanson, *Suburb;* Lubar, "Trolley Lines," 323. On Silver Spring's racial covenants, see Rotenstein, "Silver Spring"; and Rotenstein, "Fairway."

21. "Silver Spring Shopping Center," S1.

22. Hanson, *Suburb;* Longstreth, "Silver Spring"; Oshel, "Home Sites of Distinction"; Walston, "Commercial Rise."

23. Getty, "Silver Spring Area," 9.

24. Rotenstein, "Silver Spring, Maryland"; Johansen, "Imagined Pasts."

25. Wiese, *Places of Their Own.*

26. Rotenstein, "Early History of Lyttonsville"; Rotenstein, "Other Side"; Shaver, "Montgomery Bridge."

27. Bestebreurtje, "Built by the People."

28. Lewis, *Washington;* Yellin, *Racism.*

29. Shoenfeld and Cherkasky, "Strictly White Residential Section."

30. Abbott, "Dimensions of Regional Change," 1384.

31. Jackson, *Crabgrass Frontier.*

32. Prologue DC, "Federal Housing Administration."

33. On national statistics, see Jackson, *Crabgrass Frontier.* For DC regional statistics, see Prologue DC, "Federal Housing Administration"; and Manning, "Multicultural Washington, DC," 328.

34. Prologue DC, "Federal Housing Administration."

35. On Veterans Administration mortgages nationally, see Katznelson, *Affirmative Action.* On local impacts, see Lewis, *Washington.*

36. Kijakazi et al., *Color of Wealth;* Jaffe and Sherwood, *Dream City.*

37. Clarke and Brown, *Black Public Schools;* Hedlund, "Public School Desegregation."

38. Hirsch, *Making the Second Ghetto;* Rothstein, *Color of Law;* K. Taylor, *Race for Profit.*

39. "In Memoriam"; May, "Integrating Suburbs"; Shoenfeld, "Race and Real Estate."

40. "Conversation with James Baldwin"; Cantwell, "Anacostia"; Gillette, *Between Justice and Beauty.*

41. On the Emergency Committee on the Transportation Crisis and the North Central Freeway, see Levey and Levey, "End of the Roads." On the freeway revolts, see Jaffe, "Insane Highway Plan"; and Schrag, "Freeway Fight."

42. Lewis, *Washington.*

43. Bachman and Hedlund, *Suburban Boom.*

44. The term "community builders" comes from Weiss, *Community Builders.*

45. Longstreth, "Silver Spring"; Doug Duncan, interview with the author, March 26, 2015.

46. Harriston, Keith. "Drugs Erode Community's Closeness," A1.

47. KCI Technologies, "Suburbanization Historic Context"; Pearl, *National Register;* Prince George's County, *Crossroads Sector Plan.*

48. On Viers Mill Village, see Callcott, *Maryland and America;* Clouse, *Maryland Historical Trust Determination; Investigation of the Viers Mill Village Veterans' Housing Project, Montgomery County, MD: Hearings before a Subcommittee of the Committee on Expenditures in the Executive Departments.* 80th Cong., 2d sess. (1948) (testimony of Loren L. Murray); Fleishman, "Changing Lives"; and Kyriakos, "In Veirs Mill Village," E14. On Levittown, see Kelly, *Expanding the American Dream.*

49. Simpson, "My Old Neighborhood."

50. Anderson, "Largest Shopping Center"; Bachman and Hedlund, *Suburban Boom;* "NAACP Pickets New Store."

51. Bachman and Hedlund, *Suburban Boom.*

52. On River Road, see Kathan, Rispin, and Whitley, "Tracing a Bethesda." On Black population decline, see Bachman and Hedlund, *Suburban Boom.*

53. On the impacts of urban renewal in other cities and across the nation, see Hirsch, *Making the Second Ghetto;* and Sugrue, *Origins.* On DC, see Asch and Musgrove, *Chocolate City;* and Gillette, *Between Justice and Beauty.*

54. Asch and Musgrove, *Chocolate City;* Gale, *Washington, DC.*

55. On the national politics of public housing, see J. Bauman, *Public Housing.* On DC, see Barnes, "Battle for Washington."

56. Longstreth, *Housing Washington.*

57. Rotenstein, "Fairway."

58. Bestebreurtje, "Built by the People"; Libertz, *African American Heritage.*

59. "Scholar's Guide."

60. Lakeland Community Heritage Project, *Lakeland.*

61. Conway, "Lakeland Plan Upsets Residents"; Lakeland Community Heritage Project, *Lakeland;* Wynter, "Lakeland"; Wysolmerski, "Fight for a Neighborhood."

62. Massey and Denton, *American Apartheid;* Sugrue, *Origins;* US Department of Labor, *Negro Family.*

63. Jaffe and Sherwood, *Dream City;* Schaffer, "1968 Washington Riots."

64. Kerner Commission, *Report,* 1, 262.

65. Fauntroy, *Home Rule;* Jaffe and Sherwood, *Dream City.* Congress maintained veto power over the city's budget and legislation. It controlled the court and penal system and prohibited the district from raising revenues through a commuter tax.

66. Castaneda, *S Street Rising;* Jaffe and Sherwood, *Dream City,* 249; Kofie, *Struggle for Neighborhood.*

67. Golash-Boza, *Before Gentrification,* 87; Gillette, *Between Justice and Beauty.*

68. Asch and Musgrove, "We Are Headed"; Gale, *Washington, DC;* Lee, Spain, and Umberson, "Neighborhood Revitalization"; Lloyd, "Fighting Redlining and Gentrification," 1096; McGovern, *Politics of Downtown Development.*

69. Asch and Musgrove, "We Are Headed"; Lloyd, "Fighting Redlining and Gentrification"; Schuster and Bullard, "Tenant Activism."

70. Gallaher, *Politics of Staying Put;* Huron, *Carving Out the Commons.*

71. Kathan, Rispin, and Whitley, "Tracing a Bethesda"; Levine, "Resurrection of 'Scotland'"; Rathner, "Generations of Residents," G1.

72. Integration was heavily fought. Two human relations commissioners resigned in opposition to the Open Accommodations Act, which was also opposed by Silver Spring's Board of Trade and many area chambers of commerce. One year after its adoption, a Republican-dominated county council lobbied unsuccessfully to repeal the ordinance, and many businesses used the act's tavern exemption to avoid desegregation.

73. Brack, *Twenty Years.*

74. Milgram, *Good Neighborhood.*

75. McCoy and Silver Spring Historical Society, *Downtown Silver Spring.*

76. Carter, "City's Shadow," B1.

77. Tolbert, "In Montgomery."

78. On sundown suburbs in the DC region, see Denny, *Proud Past,* 89; Loewen, *Sundown Towns;* and Mann, "Avowed Minuteman Spokesman."

79. Dent, "New Black Suburbs"; Harrell, "Understanding Modern Segregation."

80. Manning, "Multicultural Washington, DC."

81. Rowland, "1970s Tax Reform Initiative." In 1984 the county eliminated the cap on the total property taxes collected but maintained a freeze on the property tax rate.

82. Harriston, "Drugs Erode Community's Closeness," A1; Ifill, "Langley Park."

83. Sandosharaj, "Ghetto Proclivities," 174.

84. Harriston, "Drugs Erode Community's Closeness"; Ifill, "Langley Park."

85. Harriston, "Drugs Erode Community's Closeness," A1; Naughton, "Hispanics Carve Niche"; Sandosharaj, "Ghetto Proclivities," 121, 126; Wiese, *Places of Their Own.*

86. Lacy, *Blue-Chip Black;* Manning, "Multicultural Washington, DC."

87. Repak, *Waiting on Washington.*

88. Singer, "Latin American Immigrants."

89. Manning, "Multicultural Washington, DC"; Singer, *At Home.*

90. Hathaway and Ho, "Small but Resilient"; McGovern, *Politics of Downtown Development;* T. Morgan, "Wrecker's Ball."

91. Modan, *Turf Wars;* Price and Singer, "Edge Gateways," 137.

92. Friedman et al., "Race, Immigrants, and Residence"; Li, *Ethnoburb;* Singer, *At Home.*

93. Friedman et al., "Race, Immigrants, and Residence"; Lacy, "What Happens."

94. Lung-Amam et al., *Housing Matters;* Singer, "Metropolitan Washington."

95. Garreau, *Edge City;* Friedman et al., "Race, Immigrants, and Residence."

96. Chacko, "Washington, DC"; Chang, "Asian and Latino."

97. Saunders, *Arrival City.*

98. Sandosharaj, "Ghetto Proclivities," 133, 257.

99. Castillo, "Langley Park Market"; Naughton, "Hispanics Carve Niche"; Reeves, "Langley Park School"; Stewart, "Ethnic Entrepreneurship."

100. Erin Ross (pseudonym), interview with the author, October 13, 2014.

101. Chacko, "Ethiopian Ethos"; Reed, "Little Ethiopia."

102. US Census Bureau, *2000 Census of Population.*

103. Wang, "Urban Enclave to Ethnoburb," 101–2.

104. Arocha, "Wheaton Is Waiting"; Perez-Rivas, "Huge Growth Spurt"; Wang, "Urban Enclave to Ethnoburb."

105. Gilmore, "Fatal Couplings," 15.

106. Cohn and Morin, "Dispersion Decade."

107. "The Plan" was a concept popularized by Lillian Wiggins in the *Washington Afro-American* newspaper in 1979 (see Jaffe, "So-Called 'Plan'"). The finding on gentrification is based on a measure of neighborhoods that experienced gentrification between 2000 and 2013, from Richardson, Mitchell, and Franco, *Shifting Neighborhoods,* 4.

108. On terminology, see Ehrenhalt, *Great Inversion;* and Hyra, *New Urban Renewal.* On the waves of gentrification in DC, see Asch and Musgrove, "We Are Headed."

109. US Census Bureau, *2000 Census of Population;* US Census Bureau, *2019 ACS 1-Year.*

110. De Vita, Manjarrez, and Twombly, *Poverty in the District;* P. Stein, "DC's Poorer Residents."

111. DC Fiscal Policy Institute, *DC's Two Economies;* Kijakazi et al., *Color of Wealth;* Naveed, *Income Inequality.*

112. Zheng, "Rise and Fall."

113. Crockett, "Brixton"; Hyra, *Race, Class, and Politics.*

114. Summers, *Black in Place,* 22. See also Summers, "H Street."

115. Gallaher, *Politics of Staying Put.*

116. Debonis, "DC Public Housing"; Paden, "Disappearing Act"; Tatian, *Preserving and Expanding.*

117. Richardson, Mitchell, and Franco, *Shifting Neighborhoods;* Ruble, *Washington's U Street.*

118. On DC's changing food culture, see Reese, *Black Food Geographies.*

119. Hyra, "Back-to-the-City Movement."

120. Golash-Boza, *Before Gentrification;* Hopkinson, *Go-Go Live;* Howell, "It's Complicated"; Hyra, "Back-to-the-City Movement"; Maher, "Capital of Diversity"; Prince, *African Americans.*

121. Richardson, Mitchell, and Franco, *Shifting Neighborhoods.*

122. Lung-Amam, Anacker, and Finio, "Worlds Away in Suburbia"; Turner and Hayes, *Poor People.*

123. Kneebone and Garr, *Suburbanization of Poverty;* Kneebone and Holmes, *U.S. Concentrated Poverty;* Lung-Amam, Anacker, and Finio, "Worlds Away in Suburbia."

124. Chacko, "Washington, DC"; Friedman et al., "Race, Immigrants, and Residence"; Price et al., "World Settles In"; Singer, "Metropolitan Washington"; Singer, *At Home;* Singer et al., "Nation's Capital Reveals."

125. DeRenzis, Singer, and Wilson, *Prince William County Case.* The housing ordinance was repealed shortly after it was adopted under pressure from the American Civil Liberties Union and residents.

3. TROUBLE ON MAIN STREET

1. Reemberto Rodríguez, interview with the author, March 27, 2014.

2. On decline, blight, and forced removals, see Beauregard, *Voices of Decline;* Fullilove, *Root Shock;* Thomas, *Redevelopment and Race;* and Wacquant, "Three

Pernicious Premises." On city efforts to appeal to the White, middle class, see Zukin, *Cultures of Cities.*

3. Peck, "Neoliberal Suburbanism," 884.

4. Peck, "Neoliberal Suburbanism."

5. Gus Bauman, interview with the author, November 4, 2014; G. Bauman, "Silver Spring War."

6. David Rotenstein, interview with the author, November 9, 2016.

7. Reed, "These 1970s Plans."

8. Jerry McCoy, interview with the author, November 7, 2014; McCoy and Silver Spring Historical Society, *Downtown Silver Spring.*

9. Oshel, "Home Sites of Distinction," 16; Walston, "Commercial Rise," 337; Hanson, *Suburb.*

10. Leinberger, *Option of Urbanism,* 36; Orfield, *American Metropolitics.*

11. Robert Wulff, interview with the author, February 26, 2015.

12. On the politics of the plan, including developers' opposition to it, see Hanson, *Suburb.*

13. Royce Hanson, interview with the author, November 24, 2014.

14. Fenston, "Silver Spring War"; Silverman, "Dream Come True."

15. G. Bauman, interview.

16. McCoy, interview.

17. Boudreaux, "New Silver Spring," B8.

18. Melvin Tull Jr., interview with the author, March 9, 2015.

19. Hooker, "Ghost Town"; Meyer, "Still Awaiting the Renaissance," C1; P. Morgan, "Dream On." On DC, see Kofie, *Struggle for Neighborhood.*

20. Hanson, *Suburb,* 91; Doug Duncan, interview with the author, March 9, 2015; Wulff, interview.

21. Brown-Saracino, *Neighborhood That Never Changes;* Smith, *New Urban Frontier.*

22. Boudreaux, "New Silver Spring," B8.

23. Duncan, interview.

24. Frankie Blackburn, interview with the author, April 2, 2015.

25. Dan Reed, interview with the author, April 21, 2015.

26. Reed, "It Shouldn't have Happened"; and Reed, "They Used to Call."

27. Seaberry, "Sprucing Up Silver Spring," quoted in Johansen, "Imagined Pasts"; Tull, interview.

28. Hanson, *Suburb,* 13.

29. Orfield, *American Metropolitics;* powell, "Urban Sprawl"; powell, "Addressing Regional Dilemmas"; Rusk, *Cities without Suburbs.* On Maryland and Montgomery County, see Hanson, *Suburb.*

30. In Montgomery County land-use decisions are made by a five-member planning board, appointed by the county council. Board members also serve on

the Maryland–National Capital Park and Planning Commission (M-NCPPC), which ensures coordination between Montgomery and Prince George's Counties. Aided by planning staff, the board considers proposals for new development and provides guidelines for future development through new zoning ordinances and master plans. Projects must also meet other permitting and transportation requirements regulated by agencies under the county executive. The county council holds the final authority on all land-use matters. The Office of Zoning and Administrative Hearings assists the council in zoning decisions.

31. Tull, interview.

32. Frankie Blackburn, quoted in "Look at the Past," 1; G. Bauman, interview.

33. Reed, interview; Jensen, "'Dream' Mall"; Reale, "Race a Hidden Issue."

34. Johansen, "Imagined Pasts," 211; Reale, "Race a Hidden Issue"; Rotenstein, interview.

35. Quoted in Johansen, "Imagined Pasts," 348–49.

36. *Silver Spring CBD*, 6.

37. Sinclair, "County Tries to Turn," B1. On AT&T, see Meyer, "Still Awaiting the Renaissance."

38. G. Bauman, interview. See also Fenston, "Silver Spring War."

39. Anonymous, interview with the author, December 9, 2014.

40. Armao, "Citizens Group Sees"; Asayesh, "Judge Delivers Setback"; "Lawsuit Filed over Mall," 27. On the former suit, the coalition lost their three-year court battle, which ended at the Maryland High Court in 1991.

41. Hanson, *Suburb*, 33.

42. Quoted in Friends, "Business Plan," 2.

43. Hanson, *Suburb*.

44. Meyer, "Still Awaiting the Renaissance"; Sinclair, "Silver Spring Renaissance"; Richburg, "Silver Spring," B1.

45. Laura Steinberg, interview with the author, November 21, 2014.

46. G. Bauman, interview; Steinberg, interview.

47. Shin, "Silver Spring Development"; Silverman, "Arresting Suburban Blight"; Barr, "Silver Spring's Soul," B1.

48. Duncan, interview.

49. Cohn, "Inner Suburbs Fall," A7.

50. Duncan, interview.

51. Lily Morgan (pseudonym), interview with the author, February 9, 2015.

52. Perez-Rivas, "Megamall Foes Deliver Petition."

53. Aguilar and Spinner, "Residents and their Fears"; Jensen, "'Dream' Mall"; V. Phillips, "Mulling the Mall"; Wilson, "As Change Begins."

54. Reardon, "Battle for the Soul," C8.

55. Jensen, "'Dream' Mall"; Reale, "Race a Hidden Issue." Both Mr. Robinson and Ms. Perdue would go on to serve on the Montgomery County Planning Board.

56. Duncan, interview; Turque, "Cracks in Silver Spring."

57. Ochoa, *Assessment Report*, 16, 6.

58. Rivas, "Fresh Look."

59. Perez-Rivas, "Fresh Look at Future"; Blackburn, interview, 2015.

60. Blackburn, interview, 2015; L. Morgan, interview.

61. L. Morgan, interview; Hanson, interview.

62. Anonymous, interview with the author, March 27, 2014.

63. Blackburn, interview, 2015.

64. IMPACT's mission statement quoted in Johansen, "Imagined Pasts," 91; Jayne Park, interview with the author, August 9, 2016.

65. Hanson, interview; anonymous, interview, December 9, 2014. See also "Look at the Past."

66. On the privatization of the Silver Spring's public square, see Williamson, "Protest on the Astroturf."

67. Duncan, interview; Shen, "Council Approves Funding."

68. Duncan, interview; Wulff, interview.

69. Montgomery County Planning Department, *Approved and Adopted*, 15.

70. On the effects of such designations on gentrification and displacement, see Chapple, Jackson, and Martin, "Concentrating Creativity."

71. Craig and Barr, "Bill on House Heights," S2.

72. Duncan, interview. For more on the "creative class" and gentrification, see Florida, *Cities;* Landry, *Creative City;* Zukin, *Cultures of Cities;* and Zukin et al., "New Retail Capital."

73. Cottman, "Some Minorities."

74. Duncan, interview.

75. Rubens, quoted in Johansen, "Imagined Pasts," 349.

76. Rashedi, quoted in Cottman, "Some Minorities"; Perez-Rivas, "Silver Spring's Welcome Mat"; Shin, "Silver Spring Development." Mr. Rashedi was one of the lucky few able to take advantage of the new county small business program that started that same year to help in the move.

77. Tull, interview. On the importance of retail and commercial amenities in attracting middle-class consumers to gentrifying neighborhoods, see Brown-Saracino, "Social Preservationists."

78. Moriarty, *Real Stories;* Megan Moriarty, interview with the author, March 9, 2015.

79. Park, interview; "Real Property Data Search."

80. Urban Studies, *Minimizing Small Business Displacement.*

81. Lester Willson, interview with the author, May 19, 2015. On other effects of construction disruptions, see Urban Studies, *Minimizing Small Business Displacement.*

82. Cho, quoted in Shin, "Silver Spring Development," E10.

83. Cottman, "Some Minorities"; Hedgpeth, "Redevelopment Carries a Price"; "Mom-and-Pops"; Urban Studies, *Minimizing Small Business Displacement*; Wrigley, "Fenton Village"; Zibart, "Roadside Café."

84. Urban Studies, *Minimizing Small Business Displacement*; Wrigley, "Fenton Village," 31.

85. Blackburn, interview, 2015.

86. Johansen, "Imagined Pasts," 89. Johansen also argued that the organization's Christian leanings and philosophical roots did not resonate well with many of the immigrant communities it sought to organize.

87. Blackburn, interview, 2015.

88. Frankie Blackburn, interview with the author, December 5, 2019.

89. Blackburn, interview, 2015.

90. Blackburn, interview, 2019.

91. Park, interview.

92. Moriarty, interview; Blackburn, interview, 2019.

93. "Montgomery County Affordable Housing."

94. Blackburn, interview, 2019; Torres, quoted in Cottman, "Some Minorities," B9; and "Look at the Past."

95. Kosmetatos, "Making Sure Everyone Gains"; Shin, "Big Boost."

96. Miller, "Subtle Force"; Blackburn, interview, 2019.

97. Ike Leggett, interview with the author, April 30, 2015. On the perspective of small businesses, see Johansen, "Imagined Pasts," 146.

98. Leggett, interview. "Montgomery County Economic Development," 17; Urban Studies, *Minimizing Small Business Displacement*.

99. Anonymous, interview with the author, July 17, 2015.

100. Tull, interview.

101. Anonymous, interview with the author, May 7, 2015; Beauregard, *Cities*; Fogelson, *Downtown*.

102. Duncan, interview; Tull, interview; Cottman, "Some Minorities."

103. Cottman, "Some Minorities."

104. Reed, interview.

105. Rotenstein, interview; Blackburn, interview, 2015. Similar arguments have also been made by many scholars, who point out the narrow ways that gentrification and displacement are defined and the difficulty of measuring indirect and cultural displacement. See, for instance, Atkinson, "Measuring Gentrification and Displacement."

106. Gary Stith, interview with the author, December 19, 2019; Tull, quoted in Shin, "Silver Spring Development."

107. Johansen, "Imagined Pasts," 141.

108. G. Bauman, "Silver Spring War."

109. See, for instance, McCann, "Ethnically Diverse Cities," which ranked Silver Spring the fourth "most culturally diverse city" in the United States; and

"2019 Most Diverse Suburbs," which ranked Silver Spring as the forty-third "most diverse suburb" in the United States in 2019.

110. Steinberg, interview (emphasis added). For other examples, see Caulfield, *City Form;* Grier and Perry, "Dog Parks"; Hyra, *Race, Class, and Politics;* Ley, "Gentrification and the Politics"; Ley, *New Middle Class;* Ley, "Artists"; Summers, *Black in Place;* and Zukin, *Loft Living.*

111. Duncan interview; Tull, interview.

112. Blackburn, interview, 2015.

113. Steinberg, interview; Reed, "Teens Need Things"; Turque, "Cracks in Silver Spring."

114. Erin Ross (pseudonym), interview; Moriarty, interview.

115. Wong, Lung-Amam, and Knaap, "Moderately Priced Dwelling Units."

116. McCoy, interview; Moriarty, interview. For a larger discussion about the branding of diversity in Silver Spring, see Johansen, "Imagined Pasts." On Fenton Village, see Montgomery County Planning Department, *Approved and Adopted,* 60.

117. McCoy, interview. On industrial gentrification elsewhere, see Curran, "Gentrification"; and Curran, "Frying Pan."

118. Reed, interview.

119. Reed, interview.

120. Moriarty, interview.

121. Blackburn, interview, 2019.

122. Although downtown Silver Spring has been a hub for skateboarders and Black and Brown youth since the 1990s, a recent proposal by developers to put astroturf on its main street and replace the splash pad was viewed by some residents as an attempt to push them out of downtown yet again. See Reed, "After 15 Years."

123. Leggett, interview.

4. RESISTING THE SUBURBAN RETROFIT

1. My reference is to Neil Brenner and Nik Theodore's classic article "Cities and Geographies of Actually Existing Neoliberalism," which notes discrepancies between free-market narratives based on the neoliberal ideal and the uneven ways in which its practices and policies play out. Likewise, my use of the term "'actually existing' diversity" signals the divergence from an ideal vision of multicultural inclusion to its reality, which often leaves many people and voices aside.

2. On suburbia's "ecology of scarcity," see Murphy, "Social Organization." On its "policy blind spots," see Puentes and Warren, *One-Fifth of America.*

3. Hogle, "Exodus."

4. Anderson, "Largest Shopping Center"; Hogle, "Exodus"; "Gudelsky, Lerner Built Center."

5. Wheaton and Kensington, "History of Wheaton."

6. Ethan Walker (pseudonym), interview with the author, April 21, 2016.

7. Davenport, "Wheaton's Challenge"; Goldreich, "Marchone's Italian Deli."

8. Price and Singer, "Edge Gateways."

9. David Fraser-Hidalgo, interview with the author, January 5, 2016.

10. Marian Fryer, interview with the author, March 31, 2014.

11. Fraser-Hidalgo, interview.

12. Stephanie Wang (pseudonym), interview with the author, March 3, 2016. On Wheaton's "small Chinatown" era, see Wang, "Urban Enclave to Ethnoburb."

13. Perez-Rivas, "Huge Growth Spurt."

14. Based on analysis from US Census Bureau, *2019 ACS 1-Year*, for block groups commonly associated with Viers Mill Village.

15. &Access, Partners for Economic Solutions, and Ochoa Urban Collaborative, *Montgomery County*.

16. Johansen, "Imagined Pasts."

17. Fryer, interview.

18. Khalid Afzal, interview with the author, January 27, 2015.

19. Montgomery County Planning Board, "Comprehensive Amendment."

20. Hankin, "Higher Rents Squeeze Retailers."

21. Montgomery County Planning Board, "Comprehensive Amendment," 2.

22. Afzal, interview.

23. Afzal, interview.

24. Perez-Rivas, "Wheaton Aims," M1.

25. Afzal, interview; Davenport, "Wheaton's Challenge."

26. Fraser-Hidalgo, interview.

27. NIMBY stands for "Not in My Backyard," a common reference for exclusionary land-use politics often associated with middle- and upper-class communities, particularly suburbs.

28. Perez-Rivas, "Wheaton Aims."

29. Montgomery County's Housing Initiative, *Permanent Source of Funding*.

30. Fryer, interview.

31. Fryer, interview; Fraser-Hidalgo, interview.

32. Adkins, "Building Consensus," 2.

33. With the adoption of a new Wheaton CBD sector plan in 2012, the county officially did away with the overlay.

34. By this time Doug Duncan had set his ambitions on the Maryland governorship, announcing in 2005 his decision to run for the Democratic Party nomination.

35. Ike Leggett, interview with the author, April 30, 2015.

36. Kraut, "Montgomery County Proposes."

37. Nancy Floreen, interview with the author, November 3, 2015.

38. Davenport, "Wheaton's Challenge," C1.

39. "County Is Moving Forward," T4.

40. Fryer, interview.

41. David Dise, interview with the author, April 2, 2015 (emphasis added).

42. Anonymous, interview with the author, January 27, 2015.

43. Dise, interview.

44. Perez-Rivas, "Downtown Wheaton Ripe," B1.

45. On marketing the global suburb, see Lung-Amam, *Trespassers*. On DC, see Hyra, *Race, Class, and Politics;* and Summers, *Black in Place*.

46. Office of Planning and Capital, *Technical Assistance Panel Report*, 13.

47. "Saul Centers."

48. Singer, *At Home*.

49. Manuel Hidalgo, interview with the author, November 24, 2015. Some notes on Manny's biography are taken from Johansen, "Imagined Pasts."

50. Daniel Parra, interview with the author, November 20, 2014; "Local First Wheaton."

51. Ash Kosiewicz, interview with the author, March 11, 2014; Hidalgo, interview.

52. Kosiewicz, interview, March 11, 2014.

53. Lazo, "Wheaton's Downtown."

54. Coalition for the Fair Redevelopment, "Petition to Tell."

55. Marco Rivera (pseudonym), interview with the author, August 28, 2015.

56. Kosiewicz, interview, March 11, 2014.

57. Kraut, "Longtime Wheaton Triangle Businesses"; Kraut, "Small Businesses Gear Up."

58. Baxamusa, "Empowering Communities through Deliberation."

59. Coalition for the Fair Redevelopment, "Petition to Tell"; Hidalgo, interview.

60. Hidalgo, interview.

61. Quoted in Reed, "Costco and Safeway Proposals."

62. Steve Silverman and David Dise to the Coalition for the Fair Redevelopment of Wheaton, January 31, 2012, Montgomery County Planning Department Archives, Wheaton, MD.

63. Anonymous, interview with the author, November 18, 2014; Wesley Graham (pseudonym), interview with the author, February 6, 2015.

64. French, "Business Leaders Speak Out"; Neibauer, "Nine Years to Recoup"; Anonymous, interview, November 18, 2014.

65. Floreen, interview.

66. Sesker, *FY13-18 Capital Improvements Program,* 7.

67. Henroit St. Gerard, interview with the author, March 12, 2015.

68. Wang, interview.

69. Kosiewicz, interview, March 11, 2014.

70. Montgomery County Planning Department, *Wheaton CBD and Vicinity* (2012). County planning staff initially recommended that, in exchange for the loss of retail-zoning overlay, the county explore a moderately priced retail-unit program to ensure the retention of affordable small business spaces in new developments. This recommendation, however, was not included in the final sector plan. See Montgomery County Planning Department, "Memorandum."

71. "Leggett, StonebridgeCarras and Bozzuto."

72. Reed, "Montgomery Picks Developers."

73. This is a higher percentage than typically required by the county's inclusionary zoning program, known as the Moderately Priced Dwelling Unit program, of 12.5 percent. The county continued to invest in affordable housing in Wheaton. In 2019 the county began the construction of Wheaton Gateway, a county-owned development with seventy-five thousand square feet of ground-floor retail space and eight hundred new rental units, 30 percent of which would be affordable.

74. Adam Fogel, interview with the author, December 3, 2015.

75. Ash Kosiewicz, public testimony at Montgomery County Council, February 28, 2012.

76. Montgomery County Council, *Bill 6-12.* Businesses were eligible for reimbursement of revenue losses if they could demonstrate an adverse financial impact during construction. The original limit of payments in the program was $75,000 per business over the three-year period, but the maximum payment was later increased to $125,000. See "Montgomery County Small Business."

77. Montgomery County Planning Department, *Wheaton CBD and Vicinity* (2012); Montgomery County Planning Department, *Wheaton CBD and Vicinity* (2011).

78. Montgomery County Council, *Bill 6-12*; Fair Redevelopment of Wheaton, "Response to Draft Regulations," 1; Fogel, interview.

79. Hidalgo, interview.

80. Anonymous, interview with the author, February 1, 2016.

81. Ash Kosiewicz, interview with the author, May 14, 2014.

82. Rivera, interview.

83. See Chapter 5 for a discussion of the Fair Development Coalition.

84. Richard Cisneros, interview with the author, February 16, 2018.

85. Isabel López (pseudonym), interview with the author, February 16, 2018.

86. Montgomery County Department, *Overview of 2012 Wheaton.*

87. Anonymous, interview with the author, July 14, 2015.

88. Marisela Villamil, interview with the author, March 9, 2015.

89. Anonymous, interview with the author, February 25, 2016.

90. Fogel, interview.

91. Rivera, interview; Cisneros, interview.

92. López, interview.

93. Cisneros, interview. Navarro introduced legislation (Expedited Bill 25-19) in 2019 that added even stricter criteria designed to increase the number of local businesses awarded county contracts. It was unanimously adopted by the county council in 2020.

94. Quoted in Montgomery County Department, *Overview of 2012 Wheaton*, 7.

95. Anonymous, interview, November 18, 2014.

96. Walker, interview; Anonymous, interview, February 25, 2016.

97. Rivera, interview.

98. "Montgomery County Small Business."

99. Quoted in Queen, "Marian Fryer Plaza."

5. SOMOS DE LANGLEY PARK

1. Scott et al., *From Cradle to Career.*

2. The term "arrival suburb" is an adaptation of the concept of "arrival city," which refers to spaces that act as a launching pad for immigrants; see Saunders, *Arrival City.*

3. Bill passed away in 2015. The legacy of his work at Action Langley Park is held at the University of Maryland's Latin American Studies Center, including archives of his newsletters.

4. Feola, "Langley Park"; Rapuano, "Pupusa Queen."

5. See the Appendix for more on my relationship to this and other case-study sites.

6. Unless otherwise stated, all demographic statistics come the from US Census Bureau, *2019 ACS 1-Year,* for the Langley Park Census Designated Place.

7. Constable, "On the Border"; "Top 101 Cities."

8. Constable, "On the Border"; Park and McHugh, *Immigrant Parents.*

9. Anonymous, interview with the author, May 18, 2016. Mam is an indigenous group from Guatemala who speak Mam as their mother tongue. Many also speak Spanish.

10. Scott et al., *From Cradle to Career;* Zorayda Moreira-Smith, interview with the author, May 13, 2016; quoted in Constable, "On the Border," 1.

11. Constable, "On the Border."

12. Moreira-Smith, interview.

13. Hanna, "Mobility and the Children."

14. Pan, "Honorable Work"; Moreira-Smith, interview.

15. US Census Bureau, *2007–2011 Summary File.*

16. Census undercounts likely inflate the neighborhood's picture of economic well-being by failing to account for its high undocumented population and households that are often composed of unrelated adults.

17. Moreira-Smith, interview; Constable, "On the Border."

18. Scott et al., *From Cradle to Career.*

19. Lung-Amam, Alvarez, and Green, "Beyond Community Policing"; Moreira-Smith, interview; quoted in Constable, "On the Border," 1.

20. Lung-Amam et al., *Purple Line;* Lung-Amam et al., *Housing Matters;* Scott et al., *From Cradle to Career;* Gallaher, "Park Has Been Hit."

21. Moreira-Smith, interview.

22. Pan, "Honorable Work."

23. Quoted in Lazo, "In Langley Park."

24. Governor Ehrlich instead wanted to build a bus rapid-transit line, which he argued would be more cost-efficient. He was heavily critiqued by Purple Line advocates for his support of the Intercounty Connector, a new $2 billion highway in suburban Maryland that redirected potential Purple Line funds to new roadway construction. For more, see Ross, *Dead End.*

25. Action Committee for Transit, "History"

26. "Purple Line Transit Partner."

27. The term "new suburban reality" comes from Orfield, *American Metropolitics;* anonymous, interview with the author, May 12, 2016.

28. Prince George's County, *Approved Takoma/Langley Crossroads,* 5.

29. Schweitzer, "Langley Park Residents."

30. Dawkins and Moeckel, "Transit-Induced Gentrification."

31. Davis and Shaver, "Pr. George's Pushes."

32. Paul Grenier, interview with the author, November 19, 2015.

33. Anonymous, interview, May 12, 2016; Hanna, "Mobility and the Children."

34. Rainey et al., "Pedestrian Casualties Mount."

35. Anonymous, interview with the author, May 19, 2016.

36. Lung-Amam, Pendall, and Knaap, "Mi Casa."

37. Moreira-Smith, interview.

38. "Red Line Community Compact"; Moreira-Smith, interview.

39. Gerrit Knaap, interview with the author, December 20, 2019.

40. Knaap, interview; Moreira-Smith, interview.

41. Moreira-Smith, interview; Knaap, interview.

42. Lung-Amam and Dawkins, "Participatory Story Mapping."

43. Cheryl Cort, interview with the author, July 6, 2015.

44. Hernandez, "Deni Taveras Wins"; Lopez-Bernstein, "Sky's the Limit."

45. Cort, interview; Johnson, *Black Power;* Price and Singer, "Edge Gateways."

46. Anonymous, interview, May 19, 2016.

47. Ms. Daines emphasized that the perception of crime was worse than the reality; crime rates in Takoma/Langley are often lower than in other parts of the city. Rosalind Grigsby, interview with the author, June 20, 2016; Sara Daines, interview with the author, June 20, 2016.

48. Both counties have their own planning and zoning authority and operate under the Maryland–National Capital Park and Planning Commission, which coordinates park and land-use planning between the counties. The city of Takoma Park has its own city-planning department but designates zoning authority to Montgomery County.

49. Simms, "Fiscal Fragility," 205.

50. Anonymous, interview, May 19, 2016.

51. Judith Stephenson, interview with the author, February 20, 2015.

52. Anonymous, interview, May 12, 2016; Montgomery County Planning Department, *Long Branch,* 22; Prince George's County, *Crossroads Sector Plan,* 64.

53. Montgomery County Planning Department, *Takoma/Langley Crossroads Sector Plan;* Prince George's County, *Crossroads Sector Plan,* 65.

54. Moreira-Smith, interview.

55. "Pathways to Opportunity."

56. Moreira-Smith, interview.

57. Following Hogan's decision to cancel the Baltimore Red Line, a host of civil rights groups filed a complaint alleging discrimination under the 1964 Civil Rights Act. In early 2017 the Obama administration's Department of Transportation announced that it would expand the investigation, but when Donald J. Trump took office later that year, his administration closed its investigation with no finding. See Shaver, "Federal Officials."

58. Anonymous, interview with the author, January 30, 2017.

59. Knaap, interview; anonymous, interview, May 19, 2016.

60. Moreira-Smith, interview.

61. Lung-Amam et al., *Purple Line.*

62. Lung-Amam et al., *Purple Line;* Cort, interview; Lung-Amam et al., *Housing Matters;* anonymous, interview, May 19, 2016; anonymous, interview with the author, July 29, 2015;

63. Ilana Brand, interview with the author, November 9, 2016; Lung-Amam et al., *Purple Line;* Lung-Amam et al., *Housing Matters.*

64. Lung-Amam et al., *Housing Matters;* Lung-Amam et al., *Purple Line;* anonymous, interview, May 19, 2016.

65. Swenson and Schmidt, "It's Time to Unite"; Schweitzer, "Conditions Were Bad."

66. Cort, interview.

67. Cort, interview; Simms, "Fiscal Fragility," 205.

68. Anonymous, interview, July 29, 2015; anonymous, interview, January 30, 2017.

69. While the county adopted these regulations, it was slow to make them effective. Its trust fund did not receive a budget until 2017, when it was allocated $5.1 million. The Conversion of Rental Housing Act had almost no funding and was limited to certain areas of the county. With continued advocacy, however, the county extended the program through the entire county and in 2021 purchased its first building to preserve a 245-unit building in Hyattsville. Pointer, "Prince George's County Launches."

70. Lung-Amam et al., *Housing Matters*.

71. Purple Line Corridor Coalition, *Housing Action Plan*.

72. Loukaitou-Sideris, "Urban Commercial Strips."

73. Grenier, interview.

74. James Chang, interview with the author, April 7, 2016; Grenier, interview.

75. Anonymous, interview, May 19, 2016; anonymous, interview with the author, January 8, 2016. For more on the struggles of businesses owned by immigrants and people of color, see Alvarez, Andrews, and Lung-Amam, *Small Business Anti-displacement Toolkit*.

76. Mayra Bayonet, interview with the author, April 12, 2014.

77. Jorge Sactic, interview with the author, December 8, 2015; Hendrix, "Prince George's Hispanics."

78. Sactic, interview.

79. Grenier, interview.

80. Kimberly Pichot, interview with the author, January 19, 2016; Grenier, interview.

81. Carlos Perozo, interview with the author, June 29, 2015; Chang, interview.

82. Anonymous, interview, May 19, 2016; Daines, interview; Grigsby, interview.

83. Ajayi, Carballo, and Moreira-Smith, *International Corridor*; Grenier, interview; Sactic, interview.

84. Grenier, interview.

85. Shaver, "Purple Line Will Open."

86. Grenier, interview; anonymous, interview, May 19, 2016.

87. Edmonds et al., *Year 1 Evaluation*; Fairlie, *Immigrant Entrepreneurs*.

88. Knaap, interview.

89. Anonymous, interview, May 19, 2016; Moreira-Smith, interview.

90. Anonymous, interview, May 12, 2016; Benjamin Mason (pseudonym), interview with the author, January 7, 2016.

91. Mayra Bayonet, interview with the author, April 15, 2014; anonymous, interview, May 12, 2016.

92. Anonymous, interview, May 12, 2016; Mason, interview.

93. Anonymous, interview, January 30, 2017.

94. Allard, *Places in Need*.

95. Luisa Montero-Diaz, interview with the author, June 23, 2016.

96. Knaap, interview.

97. Moreira-Smith, interview.

98. Lazo, "For Low-Income Communities."

99. Knaap, interview.

100. Moreira-Smith, interview.

101. Anonymous, interview with the author, December 8, 2015.

102. Anonymous, interview, January 30, 2017.

103. Knaap, interview; Moreira-Smith, interview.

104. Reemberto Rodríguez, interview with the author, March 27, 2014.

105. Erin Ross, interview with the author, November 25, 2014.

106. Megan Moriarty, interview with the author, April 1, 2015.

6. PLACE MATTERS

1. Nikhinson, "Hundreds Marched"; Reed, "Across Maryland and Virginia"; Reed, "Suburban Protestors Speak Out."

2. Sinyangwe, "Police Are Killing Fewer."

3. Lung-Amam and Schafran, "From Sanford to Ferguson."

4. Tuan, *Space and Place*, 3.

5. See, for instance, Walker and Fortmann, "Whose Landscape?"

6. Urban Studies, *Golden Mile*.

7. C. Harris, "Whiteness as Property"; Lipsitz, "Racialization of Space."

8. One formulation of this thesis was suggested by early scholars of the "urban underclass," including in the popular writings of William Julius Wilson: *When Work Disappears* and *Truly Disadvantaged*.

9. For a similar example, see MacGillis, "Real Estate Empire."

10. Lipsitz, "Racialization of Space."

11. The phrasing comes from advocates of reparations for Black Americans. See, for instance, Hannah-Jones, "Time for Reparations"; and Jones, "What Is Owed."

12. Williams, "Racial to Reparative Planning."

13. Doug Duncan, interview with the author, March 9, 2015.

14. Allard, *Places in Need*.

15. For examples from elsewhere, see Alvarez, Andrews, and Lung-Amam, *Small Business Anti-displacement Toolkit*.

16. In Chicago researchers showed that high levels of racial and economic segregation are associated with lost income, lost lives, and lost potential for the
entire metropolitan area. See Acs et al., *Cost of Segregation.*

APPENDIX: ON CHOOSING THE SUBURBAN MARGINS

1. hooks, "Choosing the Margin."
2. Bates et al., "Race and Spatial Imaginary," 254.
3. Tuck, "Suspending Damage," 409; Tuck and Yang, "R-Words," 226.
4. Hartman, *Wayward Lives,* 19–20.
5. Foley and Valenzuela, "Critical Ethnography."

Bibliography

"2019 Most Diverse Suburbs in America." Niche Best Places to Live. Accessed October 2019. www.niche.com/places-to-live/silver-spring-montgomery -md/rankings/.

Abbott, Carl. "Dimensions of Regional Change in Washington, DC." Letter to the editor. *American Historical Review* 95, no. 5 (1990): 1367–93.

"A Conversation with James Baldwin." American Archive of Public Broadcasting. June 24, 1963. http://americanarchive.org/catalog/cpb-aacip-15-0v89g5gf5r.

Acs, Gregory, Rolf Pendall, Mark Treskon, and Amy Khare. *The Cost of Segregation: National Trends and the Case of Chicago, 1990–2010.* Washington, DC: Urban Institute, 2017. www.metroplanning.org/uploads/cms/documents /cost-of-segregation-urban.pdf.

Action Committee for Transit. "The History of the Purple Line." Montgomery County's Advocates for Better Transportation. April 2023. http:// actfortransit.org/about_us.html.

Adkins, Lauren. "Building Consensus: Helping Wheaton, Maryland Design Its Future." *Main Street News* 182, no. 2 (December 2001): 2.

Aguilar, Louis, and Jackie Spinner. "Residents and Their Fears Fill Hearing on Silver Spring Mall." *Washington Post,* September 6, 1995.

Airgood-Obrycki, Whitney, Bernadette Hanlon, and Shannon Rieger. "Delineate the U.S. Suburb: An Examination of How Different Definitions of the Suburbs Matter." *Journal of Urban Affairs* 43, no. 9 (2021): 1263–84.

Ajayi, Shola, Lindolfo Carballo, and Zorayda Moreira-Smith. *The International Corridor: Portrait of a Threatened Small Business Community*. Hyattsville, MD: CASA de Maryland, 2011.

Alba, Richard D., John R. Logan, Brian J. Stults, Gilbert Marzan, and Wenquan Zhang. "Immigrant Groups in the Suburbs: A Reexamination of Suburbanization and Spatial Assimilation." *American Sociological Review* 64, no. 3 (1999): 446–60.

Allard, Scott W. *Places in Need: The Changing Geography of Poverty*. New York: Sage Foundation, 2017.

Allard, Scott W., and Benjamin Roth. *Strained Suburbs: The Social Service Challenges of Rising Suburban Poverty*. Metropolitan Opportunity Series. Washington, DC: Brookings Institution, 2010.

Alvarez, Nohely, Bi'Anncha Andrews, and Willow Lung-Amam. *Small Business Anti-displacement Toolkit: A Guide for Small Business Leaders*. College Park, MD: Small Business Anti-Displacement Network and National Center for Smart Growth, 2021. https://antidisplacement.org/wp-content/uploads/2021/09/Toolkit_FINAL.pdf.

Amin, Ash. 2002. "Ethnicity and the Multicultural City: Living with Diversity." *Environment and Planning A: Economy and Space* 34, no. 6 (2002): 959–80.

Anacker, Katrin B., ed. *The New American Suburb: Poverty, Race and the Economic Crisis*. Farnham: Ashgate, 2015.

&Access, Partners for Economic Solutions, and Ochoa Urban Collaborative. *Montgomery County: Retail in Diverse Communities Study*. Montgomery County Planning Department. April 2021. https://montgomeryplanning.org/wp-content/uploads/2021/05/Diverse-Community-Study_Final-Report_210412.pdf.

Anderson, J. W. "Largest Shopping Center in Washington Area Opens at Wheaton Plaza: Third Country Store." *Washington Post*, February 6, 1960.

Archer, John, Paul J. P. Sandul, and Katherine Solomonson, eds. *Making Suburbia: New Histories of Everyday America*. Minneapolis: University of Minnesota Press, 2015.

Armao, Jo-Ann. "Citizens Group Sees Tug of War: Montgomery Election Turns on Growth." *Washington Post*, May 26, 1988.

Arnett, Elsa C. "Arlington Losing Ethnic Flavor; Construction Displaces Vietnamese Businesses." *Washington Post*, September 4, 1989, A1.

Arocha, Zita. "Wheaton Is Waiting for Metro: Wheaton Is Gearing Up for Change Resulting from New Metro Station." *Washington Post*, August 8, 1987.

Asayesh, Gelareh. "Judge Delivers Setback for Mall in Silver Spring." *Baltimore Sun*, July 7, 1989.

Asch, Chris M., and George D. Musgrove. *Chocolate City: A History of Race and Democracy in the Nation's Capital*. Chapel Hill: University of North Carolina Press, 2017.

Asch, Chris M., and George D. Musgrove. "'We Are Headed for Some Bad Trouble': Gentrification and Displacement in Washington, DC, 1910–2014." In Hyra and Prince, *Capital Dilemma*, 107–35.

Atkinson, Rowland. "Measuring Gentrification and Displacement in Greater London." *Urban Studies* 37, no. 1 (January 2000): 149–65.

Ayres, B. Drummond, Jr. "Arlington Journal; Prosperity Threatens Refugee of Vietnam." *New York Times*, October 26, 1989, A18.

Bachman, Bob, and Sarah Hedlund. *The Suburban Boom: How Montgomery County Grew in the 1950s*. Montgomery History. 2018. https://sites.google.com/view/suburbanization/how-montgomery-county-grew?authuser=0.

Baker, Dwayne Marshall, and Bumsoo Lee. "How Does Light Rail Transit (LRT) Impact Gentrification? Evidence from Fourteen US Urbanized Areas." *Journal of Planning Education and Research* 39, no. 1 (2019): 35–49.

Barnes, William R. "A Battle for Washington: Ideology, Racism, and Self-Interest in the Controversy over Public Housing, 1943–1946." *Records of the Columbia Historical Society, Washington, DC* 50 (1980): 452–83.

Barr, Cameron W. "Worries for Silver Spring's Soul: As Chains Arrive, Some Fear 'Bethesdafication.'" *Washington Post*, June 15, 2005, B1.

Bates, Lisa K. "Gentrification and Displacement Study: Implementing an Equitable Inclusive Development Strategy in the Context of Gentrification." Working Paper. Portland, OR: City of Portland Bureau of Planning and Sustainability, 2013. https://doi.org/10.15760/report-01.

Bates, Lisa K., Sharita A. Towne, Christopher Paul Jordan, and Kitso Lyn Lelliot. "Race and Spatial Imaginary: Planning Otherwise." *Planning Theory and Practice* 19, no. 2 (2018): 254- 88.

Bauman, Gus. "The Silver Spring War and Rebirth: The Fall and Rise of an American Downtown." Lecture presented at Makeover Montgomery Conference, Silver Spring, MD, April 2011.

Bauman, John F. *Public Housing, Race and Renewal: Urban Planning in Philadelphia, 1920–1974*. Philadelphia: Temple University Press, 1987.

Baxamusa, Murtaza H. "Empowering Communities through Deliberation: The Model of Community Benefits Agreements." *Journal of Planning Education and Research* 27, no. 3 (2008): 261–76.

Beauregard, Robert A. *Cities in the Urban Age: A Dissent*. Chicago: University of Chicago Press, 2018.

Beauregard, Robert A. *Voices of Decline: The Postwar Fate of U.S. Cities*. New York: Routledge, 2003.

Bestebreurtje, Lindsey. "Built by the People Themselves: African American Community Development in Arlington, Virginia, from the Civil War through Civil Rights." PhD diss., George Mason University, 2017.

Borchert, James. *Alley Life in Washington: Family, Community, Religion, and Folklife in the City, 1850–1970.* Champaign: University of Illinois Press, 1980.

Boudreaux, Paul, Jr. "The New Silver Spring Isn't Golden to Me." *Washington Post,* October 5, 2003, B8.

Boyd, Michelle. "Defensive Development: The Role of Racial Conflict in Gentrification." *Urban Affairs Review* 43, no. 6 (2008): 751–76.

Boyd, Michelle. "The Downside of Racial Uplift: Meaning of Gentrification in an African American Neighborhood." *City and Society* 17, no. 2 (2005): 265–88.

Boyles, Andrea S. *Race, Place, and Suburban Policing: Too Close for Comfort.* Oakland: University of California Press, 2015.

Boyles, Andrea S. *You Can't Stop the Revolution: Community Disorder and Social Ties in Post-Ferguson America.* Oakland: University of California Press, 2019.

Brack, David. *Twenty Years of Civil Rights Progress: A History of the Human Relations Commission in Montgomery County, Maryland.* Maryland: Montgomery County Office of Human Rights, 1980. www .montgomerycountymd.gov/humanrights/Resources/Files/civil_right _progress.pdf.

Brenner, Neil, and Nik Theodore. "Cities and Geographies of Actually Existing Neoliberalism." *Antipode* 34, no. 3 (2002): 349–79.

Bridge, Gary, Tim Butler, and Loretta Lees, eds. *Mixed Communities: Gentrification by Stealth?* Bristol: Policy, 2012.

Brown-Saracino, Japonica. *A Neighborhood That Never Changes: Gentrification, Social Preservation, and the Search for Authenticity.* Chicago: University of Chicago Press, 2009.

Brown-Saracino, Japonica. "Social Preservationists and the Quest for Authentic Community." *City and Community* 3, no. 2 (2004): 135–56.

Building Bridges across the River. *11th Street Bridge Park Equitable Development Plan.* Accessed February 10, 2024. https://bbardc.org/wp-content /uploads/2018/10/Equitable-Development-Plan_09.04.18.pdf.

Bullard, Robert D., ed. *Growing Smarter: Achieving Livable Communities, Environmental Justice, and Regional Equity.* Urban and Industrial Environments. Cambridge: MIT Press, 2007.

Callcott, George H. *Maryland and America: 1940 to 1980.* Baltimore: Johns Hopkins University Press, 1985.

Calthorpe, Peter, and William B. Fulton. *The Regional City: Planning for the End of Sprawl.* Washington, DC: Island, 2001.

Cantwell, Thomas J. "Anacostia: Strength in Adversity." *Records of the Columbia Historical Society, Washington, DC* 49 (1973): 330–70.

Carpio, Genevieve, Clara Irazábal, and Laura Pulido. "Right to the Suburb? Rethinking Lefebvre and Immigrant Activism." *Journal of Urban Affairs* 33, no. 2 (2011): 185–208.

Carter, Philip D. "City's Shadows Reaches Wheaton Woods: Life in Wheaton Woods." *Washington Post,* December 1, 1969, B1.

Castaneda, Ruben. *S Street Rising: Crack, Murder, and Redemption in DC.* New York: Bloomsbury, 2014.

Castillo, Ricardo. "Langley Park Market Has the Flavor of Area's Many Cultures." *Washington Post,* September 1, 1992.

Caulfield, Jon. *City Form and Everyday Life: Toronto's Gentrification and Critical Social Practice.* Toronto: University of Toronto Press, 1994.

Center on Urban and Metropolitan Policy. *A Region Divided: The State of Growth in Greater Washington, DC.* Washington, DC: Brookings Institution, 1999.

Chacko, Elizabeth. "Ethiopian Ethos and the Making of Ethnic Places in the Washington Metropolitan Area." *Journal of Cultural Geography* 20, no. 2 (2003): 21–42.

Chacko, Elizabeth. "Washington, DC: From Biracial City to Multiethnic Gateway." In Price and Benton-Short, *Migrants to the Metropolis,* 203–25. Syracuse: Syracuse University Press, 2008.

Chang, Shenglin. "Asian and Latino Immigrants' Preferences for Walkable Sub-urban Neighborhoods." *Open House International* 34, no. 3 (2009): 16–25.

Chapple, Karen, Shannon Jackson, and Anne J. Martin. "Concentrating Creativity: The Planning of Formal and Informal Arts Districts." *City, Culture and Society* 1, no. 4 (2010): 225–34.

Chapple, Karen, and Rick Jacobus. "Retail Trade as a Route to Neighborhood Revitalization." In *Urban and Regional Policy and Its Effects,* edited by Nancy Pindus, Howard Wial, and Harold Wolman, 2:19–68. Washington, DC: Brookings Institution Press, 2009.

Chapple, Karen, and Anastasia Loukaitou-Sideris. *Transit-Oriented Displacement or Community Dividends? Understanding the Effects of Smarter Growth on Communities.* Cambridge: MIT Press, 2019.

Chapple, Karen, and Miriam Zuk. "Forewarned: The Use of Neighborhood Early Warning Systems for Gentrification and Displacement." *Cityscape* 18, no. 3 (2016): 109–30.

Charles, Suzanne Lanyi. "Understanding the Determinants of Single-Family Residential Redevelopment in the Inner-Ring Suburbs of Chicago." *Urban Studies* 50, no. 8 (2013): 1505–22.

Cho, Sarah Eunwon. "The People's Plan: A Model for Community-Led Community Planning and the Fight against Displacement amidst Transit-Oriented Development." *University of Pennsylvania Journal of Law and Social Change* 22, no. 3 (2019): 149–83.

Clark, William A. V. "Race, Class, and Place: Evaluating Mobility Outcomes for African Americans." *Urban Affairs Review* 42, no. 3 (2007): 295–314.

Clarke, Nina H., and Lillian B. Brown. *History of the Black Public Schools of Montgomery County, Maryland, 1872–1961.* New York: Vantage, 1978.

Clouse, Jerry. *Maryland Historical Trust Determination of Eligibility Form: Viers Mill Village Subdivision.* Silver Spring, MD: McCormick Taylor, 2015. https://mht.maryland.gov/secure/medusa/PDF/Montgomery/M;%2031-23.pdf.

Coalition for the Fair Redevelopment of Wheaton. "Petition to Tell B. F. Saul and Montgomery County to Do the Right Thing and Sign a Community Benefits Agreement for the Wheaton, Maryland Redevelopment Project." Change.org. 2012. www.change.org/p/tell-b-f-saul-and-montgomery-county-to-do-the-right-thing-and-sign-a-community-benefits-agreement-for-the-wheaton-maryland-redevelopment-project.

Coalition for the Fair Redevelopment of Wheaton. "Response to Draft Regulations for Small Business Assistance Program." Letter to Peter Bang. Montgomery County Department of Economic Development. Accessed February 12, 2024. https://astrongerwheaton.files.wordpress.com/2013/02/final-coalition-for-the-fair-redevelopment-of-wheaton-response-to-draft-small-business-assistance-program-regulations-1-31-13.pdf.

Cohn, D'Vera. "Inner Suburbs Fall through the Cracks." *Washington Post,* February 15, 2006, A7.

Cohn, D'Vera, and Richard Morin. "The Dispersion Decade." *Washington Post,* July 21, 1991.

Constable, Pamela. "On the Border." *Washington Post,* August 3, 1997, 1.

Conway, Sharon. "Lakeland Plan Upsets Residents." *Washington Post,* August 11, 1977.

Cooke, Thomas, and Sarah Marchant. "The Changing Intrametropolitan Location of High-Poverty Neighbourhoods in the US, 1990–2000." *Urban Studies* 43, no. 11 (2006): 1971–89.

Cottman, Michael H. "Some Minorities Feeling Left Out; Community Anxious about Its Role." *Washington Post,* April 3, 2003, B9.

"County Is Moving Forward." Letter to the editor. *Washington Post,* December 22, 2005, T4.

Covington, Kenya, Lance Freeman, and Michael Stoll. *The Suburbanization of Housing Choice Voucher Recipients.* Washington, DC: Brookings Institution, 2011.

Craig, Tim, and Cameron Barr. "Bill on House Heights Gets Trimmed." *Washington Post,* June 30, 2005, S2.

Crockett, Stephen A., Jr. "The Brixton: It's New, Happening and Another Example of African-American Historical 'Swagger-Jacking.'" *Washington Post,* August 3, 2012.

Curran, Winifred. "'From the Frying Pan to the Oven': Gentrification and the Experience of Industrial Displacement in Williamsburg, Brooklyn." *Urban Studies* 44, no. 8 (2007): 1427–40.

Curran, Winifred. "Gentrification and the Nature of Work: Exploring the Links in Williamsburg, Brooklyn." *Environment and Planning A: Economy and Space* 36, no. 7 (2004): 1243–58.

Davenport, Christian. "Wheaton's Challenge: Retain Soul in Revival Small, Ethnic Shops Worry about Surviving." *Washington Post*, April 30, 2006, C1.

Davis, Aaron, and Katherine Shaver. "Pr. George's Pushes for the Purple Line." *Washington Post*, November 27, 2008.

Dawkins, Casey, and Rolf Moeckel. "Transit-Induced Gentrification: Who Will Stay, and Who Will Go?" *Housing Policy Debate* 26, no. 4 (2016): 801–18.

Day, Kristen. "New Urbanism and the Challenges of Designing for Diversity." *Journal of Planning Education and Research* 23, no. 1 (2003): 83–95.

DC Fiscal Policy Institute. *DC's Two Economies: Many Residents Are Falling Behind.* Washington, DC: DC Fiscal Policy Institute, 2007. www.dcfpi.org /all/dcs-two-economies-many-residents-are-falling-behind/.

Debonis, Mike. "DC Public Housing Waiting List to Close: No New Applicants after April 12." *Washington Post*, April 3, 2013.

Denny, George, D. *Proud Past, Promising Future: Cities and Towns in Prince George's County, Maryland.* Brentwood, MD: Denny, 1997.

Dent, David J. "The New Black Suburbs." *New York Times*, June 14, 1992.

DeRenzis, Brooke, Audrey Singer, and Jill H. Wilson. *Prince William County Case Study: Immigrants, Politics, and Local Response in Suburban Washington.* Washington, DC: Brookings Institution, 2009.

De Vita, Carol J., Carlos A. Manjarrez, and Eric C. Twombly. *Poverty in the District of Columbia—Then and Now.* Washington, DC: Urban Institute, 2000.

Dreier, Peter, John H. Mollenkopf, and Todd Swanstrom. *Place Matters: Metropolitics for the Twenty-First Century.* 2nd ed. Lawrence: University Press of Kansas, 2004.

Drew, Emily M. "'Listening through White Ears': Cross-Racial Dialogues as a Strategy to Address the Racial Effects of Gentrification." *Journal of Urban Affairs* 34, no. 1 (2012): 99–115.

Duany, Andres, Elizabeth Plater-Zyberk, and Jeff Speck. *Suburban Nation: The Rise of Sprawl and the Decline of the American Dream.* New York: North Point, 2000.

Duany, Andres, Jeff Speck, and Mike Lydon. *The Smart Growth Manual.* New York: McGraw-Hill, 2010.

Duneier, Mitchell. *Ghetto: The Invention of a Place, the History of an Idea.* New York: Farrar, Straus and Giroux, 2016.

Duneier, Mitchell, and Ovie Carter. *Sidewalk.* New York: Farrar, Straus and Giroux, 1999.

Dunham-Jones, Ellen, and June Williamson. *Retrofitting Suburbia: Urban Design Solutions for Redesigning Suburbs.* Hoboken: Wiley and Sons, 2011.

Edmonds, Leiha, Peter A. Tatian, Mychal Cohen, and Jein Park. *Year 1 Evaluation of the PRO Neighborhoods Purple Line Collaborative.* Washington, DC: Urban Institute, 2009.

Ehrenhalt, Alan. *The Great Inversion and the Future of the American City.* New York: Knopf, 2012.

"Equitable Development Toolkit." PolicyLink. Last modified February 15, 2018. www.policylink.org/resources-tools/edtk.

Ewing, Reid H., and Shima Hamidi. *Costs of Sprawl.* New York: Routledge, 2017.

Fairlie, Robert W. *Immigrant Entrepreneurs and Small Business Owners, and Their Access to Financial Capital.* Report No. SBAHQ-10-R-0009. US Small Business Administration Office of Advocacy, 2012. www.sba.gov/sites /default/files/rs396tot.pdf.

Farrell, Chad R. "Immigrant Suburbanisation and the Shifting Geographic Structure of Metropolitan Segregation in the United States." *Urban Studies* 53, no. 1 (2016): 57–76.

Fauntroy, Michael K. *Home Rule or House Rule? Congress and the Erosion of Local Governance in the District of Columbia.* Lanham, MD: University Press of America, 2003.

Felland, Laurie E., Johanna R. Lauer, and Peter J. Cunningham. *Suburban Poverty and the Health Care Safety Net.* Washington, DC: Center for Studying Health System Change, 2009. www.issuelab.org/resources/11321 /11321.pdf.

Fenston, Jacob. "The 'Silver Spring War': Inside the Rebirth of a Downtown." WAMU 88.5, American University Radio. April 4, 2014. https://wamu.org /story/14/04/04/the_silver_spring_war_inside_the_rebirth_of_a_ downtown/.

Feola, Carolyn. "Langley Park: 'Maryland's International Corridor.'" *Washington Post,* July 6, 2002.

Finio, Nicholas, Willow Lung-Amam, Gerrit-Jan Knaap, Casey Dawkins, and Elijah Knaap. "Metropolitan Planning in a Vacuum: Lessons on Regional Equity Planning from Baltimore's Sustainable Communities Initiative." *Journal of Urban Affairs* 43, no. 3 (2021): 467–85.

Finio, Nicholas, Willow Lung-Amam, Gerrit-Jan Knaap, Casey Dawkins, and Brittany Wong. "Equity, Opportunity, and the Regional Planning Process: Data and Mapping in Five U.S. Metropolitan Areas." *Journal of Planning Education and Research* 44, no. 1 (2024): 16–27.

Fisher, Robert, Yuseph Katiya, Christopher Reid, and Eric Shragge. "We Are Radical: The Right to the City Alliance and the Future of Community Organizing." *Journal of Sociology and Social Welfare* 40, no. 1 (2013): 157–82.

Flanagan, Neil. "The Battle of Fort Reno." *Washington City Paper,* November 2, 2017.

Fleishman, Sandra. "Changing Lives, Changing Houses." *Washington Post,* August 25, 2001.

Florida, Richard. *Cities and the Creative Class.* New York: Routledge, 2005.

Florida, Richard. "Highest Levels of Overall Economic Segregation (All Metros)." University of Toronto. February 23, 2015. www-2.rotman.utoronto. ca/mpi/content/highest-level-of-overall-economic-segregation-all-metros/.

Fogelson, Robert M. *Downtown: Its Rise and Fall, 1880–1950.* New Haven: Yale University Press, 2001.

Foley, Douglas, and Angela Valenzuela. "Critical Ethnography: The Politics of Collaboration." In *The Sage Handbook of Qualitative Research,* edited by Norman K. Denzin and Yvonna S. Lincoln, 217–34. Thousand Oaks, CA: Sage, 2005.

Fong, Timothy. *The First Suburban Chinatown: The Remaking of Monterey Park, California.* Philadelphia: Temple University Press, 2010.

Forsyth, Ann. "Defining Suburbs." *Journal of Planning Literature* 27, no. 3 (2012): 270–81.

Franke-Ruta, Garance. "The Politics of the Urban Comeback: Gentrification and Culture in DC." *Atlantic,* August 10, 2012. www.theatlantic.com /politics/archive/2012/08/the-politics-of-the-urban-comeback-gentrification-and-culture-in-dc/260741/.

Freeman, Lance. *There Goes the "Hood": Views of Gentrification from the Ground Up.* Philadelphia: Temple University Press, 2006.

French, Esther. "Business Leaders Speak Out against Community Benefits Agreement Bill." *Patch,* November 2, 2011. https://patch.com/maryland /wheaton-md/business-leaders-speak-against-community-benefits-agr3ea523c744.

Frey, William H. *Diversity Explosion: How New Racial Demographics Are Remaking America.* Washington DC: Brookings Institution Press, 2018.

Friedman, Samantha, Audrey Singer, Marie Price, and Ivan Cheung. "Race, Immigrants, and Residence: A New Racial Geography of Washington, DC." *Geographical Review* 95, no. 2 (2005): 210–30.

Friends of the Silver Theatre. "Business Plan." Rockville, MD: Friends of the Silver Theatre, 1995.

Fullilove, Mindy T. *Root Shock: How Tearing Up City Neighborhoods Hurts America, and What We Can Do about It.* New York: New Village, 2016.

Fullilove, Mindy T., and Rodrick Wallace. "Serial Forced Displacement in American Cities, 1916–2010." *Journal of Urban Health* 88, no. 3 (2011): 381–89.

Gale, Dennis E. *Washington, DC: Inner-City Revitalization and Minority Suburbanization.* Philadelphia: Temple University Press, 1987.

Gallaher, Carolyn. *The Politics of Staying Put: Condo Conversion and Tenant Right-to-Buy in Washington, DC*. Philadelphia: Temple University Press, 2016.

Gallaher, Carolyn. "Why Langley Park Has Been Hit Hard by COVID-19." *Greater Greater Washington,* December 29, 2020. https://ggwash.org /view/79850/why-langley-park-has-been-hit-hard-by-covid-19-2.

Garreau, Joel. *Edge City: Life on the New Frontier.* New York: Doubleday, 1991.

Gearin, Elizabeth. "Smart Growth or Smart Growth Machine? The Smart Growth Movement and Its Implications." In *Up against Sprawl: Public Policy and the Making of Southern California,* edited by Jennifer R. Wolch, Manuel Pastor, and Peter Dreier, 279–308. Minneapolis: University of Minneapolis Press, 2004.

Getty, Mildred. "The Silver Spring Area." *Montgomery Count Story* 12, no. 2 (1969): 1–9. https://mchdr.montgomeryhistory.org/xmlui/bitstream /handle/20.500.12366/48/mcs_v012_n2_1969_getty.pdf?sequence= 1&isAllowed=y.

Ghafar Samar, Sara. "Connecting Crossroad: Designing an Equitable Future for Langley Park and the International Corridor." Master's thesis, University of Maryland, 2019.

Gillette, Howard, Jr. *Between Justice and Beauty: Race, Planning, and the Failure of Urban Policy in Washington.* Philadelphia: University of Pennsylvania Press, 2006.

Gilmore, Ruth Wilson. "Fatal Couplings of Power and Difference: Notes on Racism and Geographer." *Professional Geographer* 54, no. 1 (2002): 15–24.

Ginsberg, Steven. "In Virginia, Tiny Clarendon Is Thinking Big." *Washington Post,* October 5, 1996.

Giovanni, Nikki. *Gemini: An Extended Autobiographical Statement on My First Twenty-Five Years of Being a Black Poet.* New York: Viking, 1973.

Glass, Ruth. *London: Aspects of Change.* London: MacGibbon and Kee, 1964.

Golash-Boza, Tanya Maria. *Before Gentrification: The Creation of DC's Racial Wealth Gap.* Oakland: University of California Press, 2023.

Goldreich, Sonny. "Marchone's Italian Deli Changes Name to Filippo's (Not Felipe's)." *That's Silver Spring* (blog). October 9, 2014. http:// thatssilverspring.blogspot.com/2014/10/marchones-italian-deli-changes -name-to.html.

González, Jerry. *In Search of the Mexican Beverly Hills: Latino Suburbanization in Postwar Los Angeles.* New Brunswick: Rutgers University Press, 2017.

Gordon, Colin. *Citizen Brown: Race, Democracy, and Inequality in the St. Louis Suburbs.* Chicago: University of Chicago Press, 2020.

Gordon, Leslie, Mashael Majid, Tony Samara, Fernando Echeverria, and Seema Rupani. *Rooted in Home: Community Based Alternatives to the Bay Area*

Housing Crisis. San Francisco: Urban Habitat/East Bay Community Law Center, 2018. https://urbanhabitat.org/sites/default/files/Rooted%20in%20 Home.pdf.

Greason, Walter. *Suburban Erasure: How the Suburbs Ended the Civil Rights Movement in New Jersey.* Madison: Fairleigh Dickinson University Press, 2013.

Green, Constance M. *The Secret City: A History of Race Relations in the Nation's Capital.* Princeton, NJ: Princeton University Press, 1967.

Grier, Sonya A., and Vanessa G. Perry. "Dog Parks and Coffee Shops: Faux Diversity and Consumption in Gentrifying Neighborhoods." *Journal of Public Policy and Marketing* 37, no. 1 (2018): 23–38.

"Gudelsky, Lerner Built Center; Had a 'Feeling for Real Estate.'" *Washington Post,* March 30, 1960.

Hackworth, Jason, and Josephine Rekers. "Ethnic Packaging and Gentrification: The Case of Four Neighborhoods in Toronto." *Urban Affairs Review* 41, no. 2 (2005): 211–36.

Hackworth, Jason, and Neil Smith. "The Changing State of Gentrification." *Tijdschrift Voor Economische en Sociale Geografie* 92, no. 4 (2001): 464–77.

Hamnett, Chris. "Gentrification and the Middle-Class Remaking of Inner London, 1961–2001." *Urban Studies* 40, no. 12 (2003): 2401–26.

Hankin, Sam. "Higher Rents Squeeze Retailers in Wheaton." *Washington Post,* October 13, 1988.

Hanlon, Bernadette. "The Decline of Older, Inner Suburbs in Metropolitan America." *Housing Policy Debate* 19, no. 3 (2008) 423–56.

Hanlon, Bernadette. "Fixing Inner-Ring Suburbs in the US: A Policy Retrospective." *International Journal of Neighbourhood Renewal* 1, no. 3 (2008): 1–30.

Hanlon, Bernadette. *Once the American Dream: Inner-Ring Suburbs of the Metropolitan United States.* Philadelphia: Temple University Press, 2010.

Hanlon, Bernadette, and Whitney Airgood-Obrycki. "Suburban Revalorization: Residential Infill and Rehabilitation in Baltimore County's Older Suburbs." *Environment and Planning A* 50, no. 4 (2018): 895–921.

Hanlon, Bernadette, John Rennie Short, and Thomas J. Vicino. *Cities and Suburbs: New Metropolitan Realities in the US.* Oxford: Routledge, 2010.

Hanna, William J. "Mobility and the Children of Langley Park's Immigrant Families." *Journal of Negro Education* 72, no. 1 (2003): 63–78.

Hannah-Jones, Nikole. "It is Time for Reparations." *New York Times Magazine,* June 30, 2020.

Hanson, Royce. *Suburb: Planning Politics and the Public Interest.* Ithaca: Cornell University Press, 2017.

Harrell, Rodney. "Understanding Modern Segregation: Suburbanization and the Black Middle Class." PhD diss., University of Maryland, 2008.

Harris, Cheryl I. "Whiteness as Property." *Harvard Law Review* 106, no. 8 (1993): 1707–91.

Harris, Dianne S., ed. *Second Suburb: Levittown, Pennsylvania*. Pittsburgh: University of Pittsburgh Press, 2010.

Harris, Louis. "Races Agree on Ghetto Abolition and Need for WPA-Type Projects." *Washington Post*, August 14, 1967.

Harriston, Keith. "Drugs Erode Community's Closeness: Cultural, Economic Differences Turn Neighbors into Strangers." *Washington Post*, May 19, 1988, A1.

Hartman, Saidiya V. *Wayward Lives, Beautiful Experiments: Intimate Histories of Social Upheaval*. New York: Norton, 2019.

Harvey, David. *A Brief History of Neoliberalism*. Oxford: Oxford University Press, 2007.

Harvey, David. *Rebel Cities: From the Right to the City to the Urban Revolution*. London: Verso Books, 2012.

Hathaway, David, and Stephanie Ho. "Small but Resilient: Washington's Chinatown over the Years." *Washington History* 15, no. 1 (2003): 42–61.

Haynes, Bruce D. *Red Lines, Black Spaces: The Politics of Race and Space in a Black Middle-Class Suburb*. New Haven: Yale University Press, 2001.

Haynes, Emily C. "Currents of Change: An Urban and Environmental History of the Anacostia River and Near Southeast Waterfront in Washington, DC." PhD diss., Pitzer College, 2013.

Hedgpeth, Dana. "Redevelopment Carries a Price: Rent Increasing in Silver Spring." *Washington Post*, November 30, 2000.

Hedlund, Sarah, curator. "The Experience of Public School Desegregation in Montgomery County: The Integration Process and Experience, 1955–1961." Montgomery History. 2017. https://sites.google.com/view/school-desegregation/home?authuser=0.

Hendrix, Steve. "Prince George's Hispanics Turn to 'Don Jorge.'" *Washington Post*, December 29, 2009.

Hernandez, Arelis. "Deni Taveras Wins Prince George's Council Seat by Just Six Votes." *Washington Post*, July 7, 2014.

Hirsch, Arnold R. *Making the Second Ghetto: Race and Housing in Chicago, 1940–1960*. Cambridge: Cambridge University Press, 1983.

"Historic African American Communities." Heritage Montgomery. Last modified 2021. www.heritagemontgomery.org/moco-history/historic-african-american-communities/.

Hogle, Chase. "Exodus: Why DC's Jewish Community Left the Central Corridors, Then Came Back." *Greater Greater Washington*, May 22, 2020. https://ggwash.org/view/77533/exodus-why-dcs-jewish-community-left-the-center-city-then-came-back.

Holliday, Amy L., and Rachel E. Dwyer. "Suburban Neighborhood Poverty in US Metropolitan Areas in 2000." *City and Community* 8, no. 2 (2009): 155–76.

Holloway, Adrienne M. "From the City to the Suburbs: Characteristics of Suburban Neighborhoods Where Chicago Housing Choice Voucher Households Relocated." *Urban Studies Research* 2014, no. 2 (2014): 1–14.

Holloway, Adrienne M. "Suburban Safety Net Service Providers and the Latinx Community." *Latino Studies* 14, no. 3 (2016): 384–405.

Hooker, Meredith. "No Longer a 'Ghost Town,' Silver Spring's Downtown Is Changing." *Gazette*, November 5, 2003.

hooks, bell. "Choosing the Margin as a Space of Radical Openness." *Framework: The Journal of Cinema and Media*, no. 36 (1989): 15–23.

hooks, bell. *Teaching to Transgress: Education as the Practice of Freedom*. New York: Routledge, 1994.

Hopkinson, Natalie. *Go-Go Live: The Musical Life and Death of a Chocolate City*. Durham: Duke University Press, 2012.

Howell, Kathryn. "'It's Complicated . . .': Long-Term Residents and Their Relationships to Gentrification in Washington, DC." In Hyra and Prince, *Capital Dilemma*, 255–78.

Howell, Kathryn. "Planning for Empowerment: Upending the Traditional Approach to Planning for Affordable Housing in the Face of Gentrification." *Planning Theory and Practice* 17, no. 2 (2016): 210–26.

Howell, Kathryn. "Preservation from the Bottom-Up: Affordable Housing, Redevelopment, and Negotiation in Washington, DC." *Housing Studies* 31, no. 3 (2016): 305–23.

"How the Federal Housing Administration Shaped DC: Mapping Segregation in Washington DC." Story map. Prologue DC. Updated 2020. www.arcgis.com /apps/MapSeries/index.html?appid=34603bd48c9f496fa2750a770f655013.

Hsu, Evelyn. "Plan Would Reshape Clarendon with High-Rises, Old Facades; Proposal to Preserve Ethnic Shops, Restaurants Eases Merchants' Fear of Being Forced Out of 'Little Saigon.'" *Washington Post*, November 18, 1989.

Huron, Amanda. *Carving Out the Commons: Tenant Organizing and Housing Cooperatives in Washington, DC*. Minneapolis: University of Minnesota Press, 2018.

Hyra, Derek. "The Back-to-the-City Movement: Neighbourhood Redevelopment and Processes of Political and Cultural Displacement." *Urban Studies* 52, no. 10 (2015): 1753–73.

Hyra, Derek. *The New Urban Renewal: The Economic Transformation of Harlem and Bronzeville*. Chicago: University of Chicago Press, 2008.

Hyra, Derek. *Race, Class, and Politics in the Cappuccino City*. Chicago: University of Chicago Press, 2017.

Hyra, Derek, and Sabiyha Prince, eds. *Capital Dilemma: Growth and Inequality in Washington, DC*. New York: Routledge, 2015.

Ifill, Gwen. "Langley Park: Coping with Change." *Washington Post*, August 26, 1984.

Immergluck, Dan. *Red Hot City: Housing, Race, and Exclusion in Twenty-First-Century Atlanta*. Oakland: University of California Press, 2022.

"In Memoriam: Joseph Charles Jones." SNCC Legacy Project. Accessed February 1, 2024. https://sncclegacyproject.org/in-memoriam-joseph-charles -jones/.

Jackson, Kenneth T. *Crabgrass Frontier: The Suburbanization of the United States*. New York: Oxford University Press, 1985.

Jaffe, Harry. "The Insane Highway Plan That Would Have Bulldozed DC's Most Charming Neighborhoods." *Washingtonian*, October 21, 2015.

Jaffe, Harry. "So-Called 'Plan' for White Supremacy Lives On in D.C." *Washington Examiner*, August 30, 2010.

Jaffe, Harry S., and Tom Sherwood. *Dream City: Race, Power, and the Decline of Washington, DC*. New York: Simon and Schuster, 1994.

Jensen, Peter. "'Dream' Mall Comes with a Price." *Baltimore Sun*, October 9, 1996.

Johansen, Bruce R. "Imagined Pasts, Imagined Futures: Race, Politics, Memory, and the Revitalization of Downtown Silver Spring, Maryland." PhD diss., University of Maryland, 2005.

Johnson, Valerie C. *Black Power in the Suburbs: The Myth or Reality of African-American Suburban Political Incorporation*. SUNY Series in African American Studies. Albany: State University of New York Press, 2002.

Jones, William P. "What Is Owed." *Nation*, September 8, 2021.

Kaba, Mariame. *We Do This 'Til We Free Us: Abolitionist Organizing and Transforming Justice*. Edited by Tamara K. Nopper. Chicago: Haymarket Books, 2021.

Kathan, David, Amy Rispin, and L. Paige Whitley. "Tracing a Bethesda, Maryland, African American Community and Its Contested Cemetery." *Washington History* 29, no. 2 (2017): 24–41.

Katznelson, Ira. *When Affirmative Action Was White: An Untold History of Racial Inequality in Twentieth-Century America*. New York: Norton, 2005.

KCI Technologies. "Suburbanization Historic Context and Survey Methodology: I-495/I-95 Capital Beltway Corridor Transportation Study, Montgomery and Prince George's Counties, Maryland." Baltimore: Maryland Department of Transportation, State Highway Administration, 1999.

Keating, W. Dennis, and Thomas Bier. "Greater Cleveland's First Suburbs Consortium: Fighting Sprawl and Suburban Decline." *Housing Policy Debate* 19, no. 3 (2008): 457–77.

"Keeping the Mom-and-Pops." *Washington Times*, June 20, 2005. www .washingtontimes.com/news/2005/jun/20/20050620-100315-5233r/.

Keil, Roger. *Suburban Planet: Making the World Urban from the Outside In*. Urban Futures. Cambridge, UK: Polity, 2018.

Kelly, Barbara M. *Expanding the American Dream: Building and Rebuilding Levittown*. Albany: State University of New York Press, 1993.

Kelly, Clare Lise, and Maryland-National Capital Park and Planning Commission. *Places from the Past: The Tradition of Gardez Bien in Montgomery County, Maryland*. Silver Spring, MD: Maryland-National Capital Park and Planning Commission, 2001.

Kerner Commission. *Report of the National Advisory Commission on Civil Disorders*. Washington, DC: Government Printing Office, 1968.

Kijakazi, Kilolo, Rachel Marie B. Atkins, Mark Paul, Anne E. Price, Darrick Hamilton, and William A. Darity Jr. *The Color of Wealth in the Nation's Capital*. Durham, NC: Duke University; Washington, DC: Urban Institute; New York: New School; Oakland, CA: Insight Center for Community Economic Development, 2016.

Kneebone, Elizabeth, and Alan Berube. *Confronting Suburban Poverty in America*. Washington, DC: Brookings Institution Press, 2013.

Kneebone, Elizabeth, and Emily Garr, *The Suburbanization of Poverty: Trends in Metropolitan America, 2000 to 2008*. Washington DC: Brookings Institution, 2010.

Kneebone, Elizabeth, and Natalie Holmes. *U.S. Concentrated Poverty in the Wake of the Great Recession*. Washington, DC: Brookings Institution, 2016.

Kofie, Nelson F. *Race, Class, and the Struggle for Neighborhood in Washington, DC*. New York: Garland, 1999.

Kosmetatos, Sofia. "Making Sure Everyone Gains in Silver Spring Revitalization." *Daily Record*, May 3, 2004.

Kraut, Aaron. "Longtime Wheaton Triangle Businesses Face Uncertainty." *Southern Maryland News*, December 7, 2011. www.somdnews.com/archive/news/longtime-wheaton-triangle-businesses-face-uncertainty/article_2fd4594b-9803-5696-80c3-6ade9890c4e9.html.

Kraut, Aaron. "Montgomery County Executive Proposes $40 Million for Wheaton Redevelopment." *Gazette.Net*, January 18, 2012. www.gazette.netiapps/pbcs.dlllarticle?AID=/20120118INEWSI701189296&&tempL.1125/2012.

Kraut, Aaron. "Small Businesses Gear Up for Big Changes." *Gazette.Net*, November 23, 2011. www.gazette.netlapps/pbcs.dll/article?AID=/20111123INEWS171.

Kruse, Kevin M., and Thomas J. Sugrue, eds. *The New Suburban History*. Chicago: University of Chicago Press, 2006.

Kyriakos, Marianne. "In Veirs Mill Village: Room to Grow." *Washington Post*, April 24, 1993, E14.

Lacy, Karyn R. *Blue-Chip Black: Race, Class, and Status in the New Black Middle Class*. Berkeley: University of California Press, 2007.

Lacy, Karyn. "What Happens to the Suburbs When Black People Move In?" *Medium* (blog). December 2, 2020. https://krlacy.medium.com/what-happens-to-the-suburbs-when-black-people-move-in-30bf9fc5fb4a.

Lakeland Community Heritage Project. *Lakeland: African Americans in College Park.* Charleston, SC: Arcadia, 2009.

Lanari, Elisa. "Envisioning a New City Center: Time, Displacement, and Atlanta's Suburban Futures." *City and Society* 31, no. 3 (2019): 365–91.

Landry, Charles. *The Creative City: A Toolkit for Urban Innovators.* 2nd ed. New Stroud, UK: Comedia, 2008.

"Lawsuit Filed over Mall Planned in Silver Spring." *Washington Post*, December 15, 1988, 27.

Lazo, Luz. "Can Wheaton's Downtown Keep Family Feel?" *Washington Post*, November 24, 2011.

Lazo, Luz. "For Low-Income Communities, the Purple Line Is an Opportunity and a Threat." *Washington Post*, February 18, 2017.

Lazo, Luz. "In Langley Park, Fear of Losing the Spirit of the Neighborhood." *Washington Post*, October 1, 2011. www.washingtonpost.com/local/trafficandcommuting/for-low-income-communities-the-purple-line-is-an-opportunity-and-a-threat/2017/02/18/035666ce-f214-11e6-a9b0-ecee7ce475fc_story.html.

Lee, Barrett A., Daphne Spain, and Debra J. Umberson, "Neighborhood Revitalization and Racial Change: The Case of Washington, DC." *Demography* 22, no. 4 (1985): 581–602.

Lees, Loretta. "Gentrification and Social Mixing: Towards an Inclusive Urban Renaissance?" *Urban Studies* 45, no. 12 (2008): 2449–70.

Lees, Loretta. "A Reappraisal of Gentrification: Towards a 'Geography of Gentrification.'" *Progress in Human Geography* 24, no. 3 (2000): 389–408.

Lees, Loretta, Sandra Annunziata, and Clara Rivas-Alonso. "Resisting Planetary Gentrification: The Value of Survivability in the Fight to Stay Put." *Annals of the American Association of Geographers* 108, no. 2 (2018): 346–55.

Lees, Loretta, Tim Butler, and Gary Bridge, eds. "Introduction: Gentrification, Social Mix/ing and Mixed Communities." In Bridge, Butler, and Lees, *Mixed Communities*, 1–16.

Lees, Loretta, and Martin Phillips, eds. *Handbook on Gentrification Studies.* Cheltenham, UK: Elgar, 2018.

Lees, Loretta, Hyun Bang Shin, and Ernesto López-Morales. *Planetary Gentrification.* Urban Futures. Cambridge, UK: Polity, 2016.

Lees, Loretta, Tom Slater, and Elvin K Wyly. *Gentrification.* New York: Routledge, 2008.

Lefebvre, Henri. *Writings on Cities.* Translated and edited by Eleonore Kofman and Elizabeth Lebas. Cambridge: Blackwell, 1996.

"Leggett, StonebridgeCarras and Bozzuto Announce Agreement for Redevelopment of Downtown Wheaton; More Than One Million Square Feet of Mixed-Use Projects Will Reshape Wheaton Triangle and M-NCPPC Site in Silver Spring." Press release. Montgomery County. October 24, 2014. www2 .montgomerycountymd.gov/mcgportalapps/Press_Detail.aspx?Item_ID= 12262.

Leinberger, Christopher B. *The Option of Urbanism: Investing in a New American Dream*. Washington DC: Island, 2010.

Lesko, Kathleen M., Valerie Babb, and Carroll R. Gibbs. *Black Georgetown Remembered: A History of Its Black Community from the Founding of "the Town of George" in 1751 to the Present Day*. Washington, DC: Georgetown University Press, 2016.

Levey, Bob, and Jane F. Levey. "End of the Roads." *Washington Post,* November 26, 2000.

Levine, Harvey A. "The Resurrection of 'Scotland.'" *Montgomery County Story* 43, no. 2 (May 2000): 125–35. https://montgomeryhistory.org/pdf/43-2.pdf.

Levy, Anneli Moucka. "Washington, D.C. and the Growth of Its Early Suburbs: 1860–1920." Master's thesis, University of Maryland, 1980.

Lewis, Tom. *Washington: A History of Our National City*. New York: Basic Books, 2015.

Lewis-McCoy, R. L'Heureux. "The Changing Face of Suburban Inequality: How Racial and Ethnic Change Unfold in Suburban America." Presentation at Radcliff Seminar, November 21–22, 2019, Harvard University, Cambridge, MA.

Lewis-McCoy, R. L'Heureux. *Inequality in the Promised Land: Race, Resources, and Suburban Schooling*. Stanford: Stanford University Press, 2014.

Lewis-McCoy, R. L'Heureux, Natasha Warikoo, Stephen A. Matthews, and Nadirah Farah Foley. "Resisting Amnesia: Renewing and Expanding the Study of Suburban Inequality." *RSF: The Russell Sage Foundation Journal of the Social Sciences* 9, no. 1 (2023): 1–24.

Ley, David. "Artists, Aestheticisation and the Field of Gentrification." *Urban Studies* 40, no. 12 (2003): 2527–44.

Ley, David. "Gentrification and the Politics of the New Middle Class." *Environment and Planning D: Society and Space* 12, no. 10 (1994): 53–74.

Ley, David. *The New Middle Class and the Remaking of the Central City*. Oxford: Oxford University Press, 1996.

Li, Wei. *Ethnoburb: The New Ethnic Community in Urban America*. Honolulu: University of Hawai'i Press, 2009.

Li, Wei, ed. *From Urban Enclave to Ethnic Suburb: New Asian Communities in Pacific Rim Countries*. Honolulu: University of Hawai'i Press, 2006.

Libertz, John. *A Guide to the African American Heritage of Arlington County, Arlington County, Virginia*. 2nd ed. Arlington, VA: Department of

Community Planning, Housing, and Development Historic Preservation Program, 2016. https://projects.arlingtonva.us/wp-content/uploads/sites/31 /2016/09/A-Guide-to-the-African-American-Heritage-of-Arlington-County-Virginia.pdf.

Liebow, Elliot. *Tally's Corner: A Study of Negro Streetcorner Men*. Rev. ed. Lanham, MD: Rowman and Littlefield, 2003.

Lindner, Christoph, and Gerard Sandoval, eds. *Aesthetics of Gentrification: Seductive Spaces and Exclusive Communities in the Neoliberal City*. Amsterdam: Amsterdam University Press, 2021.

Lipsitz, George. "The Racialization of Space and the Spatialization of Race: Theorizing the Hidden Architecture of Landscape." *Landscape Journal* 26, no. 1 (2007): 10–23.

Lloyd, James M. "Fighting Redlining and Gentrification in Washington, DC: The Adams-Morgan Organization and Tenant Right to Purchase." *Journal of Urban History* 42, no. 6. (2016): 1091–109.

Lo, Lucia, Valerie Preston, Paul Anisef, Ranu Basu, and Shuguang Wang. *Social Infrastructure and Vulnerability in the Suburbs*. Toronto: University of Toronto Press, 2015.

Loewen, James W. *Sundown Towns: A Hidden Dimension of American Racism*. New York: New Press, 2005.

Logan, John R. "Separate and Unequal in Suburbia." Census Brief Prepared for US2010. Brown University. December 2014. www.s4.brown.edu /us2010.

Logan, John R., and Richard D. Alba. "Locational Returns to Human Capital: Minority Access to Suburban Community Resources." *Demography* 30, no. 2 (1993): 243–68.

Longstreth, Richard. *Housing Washington: Two Centuries of Residential Development and Planning in the National Capital Area*. Chicago: Center for American Places at Columbia College Chicago, 2010.

Longstreth, Richard. "Silver Spring, Georgia Avenue, Colesville Road, and the Creation of an Alternative 'Downtown' for Metropolitan Washington." In *Streets: Critical Perspectives on Public Space*, edited by Çelik, Zeynep, Diane Favro, and Richard Ingersoll, 247–57. Berkeley: University of California Press, 1994.

"A Look at the Past, Present and Future: Downtown Renaissance New Issues Arise on the Long Road to Revitalization." *Washington Post*, April 3, 2003, 1.

Lopez-Bernstein, Maria. "The Sky's the Limit." *Prince George's Suite Magazine and Media*, March 21, 2017. www.pgsuite.com/people/2017/3/21/deni-taveras.

Loukaitou-Sideris, Anastasia. "Regeneration of Urban Commercial Strips: Ethnicity and Space in Three Los Angeles Neighborhoods." *Journal of Architectural and Planning Research* 19, no. 4 (2002): 334–50.

Loukaitou-Sideris, Anastasia, and Konstantina Soureli. "Cultural Tourism as an Economic Development Strategy for Ethnic Neighborhoods." *Economic Development Quarterly* 26, no. 1 (2012): 50–72.

Lubar, Steven. "Trolley Lines, Land Speculation and Community-Building: The Early History of Woodside Park, Silver Spring, Maryland." *Maryland Historical Magazine* 81, no. 4 (1986): 316–29.

Lucy, William, and David L. Phillips. *Confronting Suburban Decline: Strategic Planning for Metropolitan Renewal.* Washington, DC: Island, 2000.

Lung-Amam, Willow. "Surviving Suburban Redevelopment: Resisting the Displacement of Immigrant-Owned Small Businesses in Wheaton, Maryland." *Journal of Urban Affairs* 43, no. 3 (2021): 449–66.

Lung-Amam, Willow. "That 'Monster House' Is My Home: The Social and Cultural Politics of Design Reviews and Regulations." *Journal of Urban Design* 18, no. 2 (2013): 220–41.

Lung-Amam, Willow. *Trespassers? Asian Americans and the Battle for Suburbia.* Oakland: University of California Press, 2017.

Lung-Amam, Willow, Nohely Alvarez, and Rodney Green. "Beyond Community Policing: Centering Community Development in Efforts to Improve Safety in Latinx Immigrant Communities." *Journal of Community Practice* 29, no. 4 (2021): 375–90.

Lung-Amam, Willow, Katrin B. Anacker, and Nicholas Finio. "Worlds Away in Suburbia: The Changing Geography of High-Poverty Neighborhoods in the Washington, DC Metro." In *Suburbia in the 21st Century: From Dreamscape to Nightmare?*, edited by Paul J. Maginn and Katrin Anacker, 179–201. New York: Routledge.

Lung-Amam, Willow, and Casey Dawkins. "The Power of Participatory Story Mapping: Advancing Equitable Development in Disadvantaged Neighborhoods." *Community Development Journal* 55, no. 3 (2020): 473–95.

Lung-Amam, Willow, Casey Dawkins, Zorayda Moreira, Gerrit-Jan Knaap, and Alonzo Washington. *Preparing for the Purple Line: Affordable Housing Strategies for Langley Park, Maryland.* Hyattsville, MD: National Center for Smart Growth Research and Education/CASA, 2017. https://purplelinecorridor.org/wp-content/uploads/2017/10/Langley-Park-Housing-Report-1.pdf.

Lung-Amam, Willow, and Katy June-Friesen. "Growing Together or Apart? Critical Tensions in Charting an Equitable Smart Growth Future." In *Handbook on Smart Growth: Promises, Principles, and Prospects for Planning*, edited by Gerrit-Jan Knaap, Rebecca Lewis, Arnab Chakraborty, and Katy June-Friesen, 259–75. Northampton, MA: Elgar, 2022.

Lung-Amam, Willow, Rolf Pendall, and Elijah Knaap. "Mi Casa No Es Su Casa: The Fight for Equitable Transit-Oriented Development in an Inner-Ring

Suburb." *Journal of Planning Education and Research* 39, no. 4 (2019): 442–55.

Lung-Amam, Willow, and Alex Schafran. "From Sanford to Ferguson: Race, Protest and Democracy in the American Suburbs." In *The Routledge Companion to the Suburbs,* edited by Bernadette Hanlon and Thomas Vicino, 220–29. London: Routledge, 2018.

Lung-Amam, Willow, Brittany Wong, Molly Carpenter, Alonzo Washington, and Julio Murillo. *Housing Matters: Ensuring Quality, Safe, and Healthy Housing in Langley Park, Maryland.* Hyattsville, MD: National Center for Smart Growth Research and Education/University of Maryland/CASA, 2019. https://wearecasa.org/wp-content/uploads/2019/10/HOUSING-MATTERS-REPORT__FINAL-1.pdf.

MacGillis, Alec. "Jared Kushner's Other Real Estate Empire in Baltimore." *New York Times Magazine,* May 23, 2017. www.nytimes.com/2017/05/23/magazine/jared-kushners-other-real-estate-empire.html.

Maher, Justin T. "The Capital of Diversity: Neoliberal Development and the Discourse of Difference in Washington, DC." *Antipode* 47, no. 4 (2015): 980–98.

Mahler, Sarah J. *Salvadorans in Suburbia: Symbiosis and Conflict.* Boston: Allyn and Bacon, 1995.

Mann, Jim. "Avowed Minuteman Spokesman Runs Town's All-White Teens Club." *Washington Post,* December 24, 1970.

Manning, Robert D. "Multicultural Washington, DC: The Changing Social and Economic Landscape of a Post-industrial Metropolis." *Ethnic and Racial Studies* 21, no. 2 (1998): 328–55.

"Mapping Segregation in Washington DC." Story map. Prologue DC. Updated 2023. https://mappingsegregationdc.org/.

Marcuse, Peter. "Abandonment, Gentrification, and Displacement: The Linkages in New York City." In *Gentrification of the City,* edited by Neil Smith and Peter Williams, 153–77. Boston: Allen and Unwin, 1986.

Markley, Scott N. "New Urbanism and Race: An Analysis of Neighborhood Racial Change in Suburban Atlanta." *Journal of Urban Affairs* 40, no. 8 (2018): 1115–31.

Markley, Scott. "Suburban Gentrification? Examining the Geographies of New Urbanism in Atlanta's Inner Suburbs." *Urban Geography* 39, no. 4 (2018): 606–30.

Markley, Scott, and Madhuri Sharma. "Gentrification in the Revanchist Suburb: The Politics of Removal in Roswell, Georgia." *Southeastern Geographer* 56, no. 1 (2016): 57–80.

Martin, Isaac, and Christopher Niedt. *Foreclosed America.* Stanford: Stanford University Press, 2020.

Massey, Douglas, and Nancy A. Denton. *American Apartheid: Segregation and the Making of the Underclass.* Cambridge: Harvard University Press, 1993.

May, Roger B. "Integrating Suburbs: 'Fair Housing' Groups Breach Racial Barriers in More Communities." *Wall Street Journal,* October 8, 1964.

McCann, Adam. "Most and Least Ethnically Diverse Cities in the U.S." WalletHub. February 22, 2023. https://wallethub.com/edu/cities-with-the-most -and-least-ethno-racial-and-linguistic-diversity/10264.

McCoy, Jerry A., and Silver Spring Historical Society. *Downtown Silver Spring.* Charleston: Arcadia, 2010.

McGovern, Stephen J. *The Politics of Downtown Development: Dynamic Political Cultures in San Francisco and Washington, DC.* Lexington: University Press of Kentucky, 2015.

Meltzer, Rachel. "Gentrification and Small Business: Threat or Opportunity?" *Cityscape* 18, no. 3 (2016): 57–85.

Meltzer, Rachel, and Jenny Schuetz. "Bodegas or Bagel Shops? Neighborhood Differences in Retail and Household Services." *Economic Development Quarterly* 26, no. 1 (2012): 73–94.

Mengestu, Dinaw. *The Beautiful Things That Heaven Bears.* New York: Riverhead Books, 2007.

Meyer, Eugene L. "Still Awaiting the Renaissance: Silver Spring Teeters on Brink of Progress; Silver Spring Awaits Downtown Revival." *Washington Post,* November 24, 1989, C1.

Meyers, Jessica. "Eden Center as a Representation of Vietnamese American Ethnic Identity in the Washington, DC Metropolitan Area, 1975–2005." *Journal of Asian American Studies* 9, no. 1 (2006): 55–85.

Milgram, Morris. *Good Neighborhood: The Challenge of Open Housing.* New York: Norton, 1977.

Miller, Justin. "The Subtle Force of Tom Perez." *American Prospect,* June 22, 2016.

Modan, Gabriella G. *Turf Wars: Discourse, Diversity, and the Politics of Place.* Malden, MA: Blackwell, 2007.

"Montgomery County Affordable Housing." PowerPoint presentation. Montgomery County Department of Housing and Community Affairs. January 2007. www.montgomerycountymd.gov/DHCA/Resources/Files/housing /multifamily/reports/affordable_housing_presentation.pdf.

Montgomery County Council. *Bill 6-12: Economic Development; Small Business Assistance.* Montgomery County. July 26, 2012. www .montgomerycountymd.gov/COUNCIL/Resources/Files/bill/2012/20120417 _6-12A.pdf.

Montgomery County Department of General Services. *Overview of 2012 Wheaton Small Business Survey.* Rockville, MD: Montgomery County, 2012.

www.wheatonmd.org/_files/docs/2012-business-survey-results-overview
.pdf.

"Montgomery County Economic Development Fund Annual Report." Montgomery County Department of Economic Development. March 15, 2011. www.montgomerycountymd.gov/COUNCIL/Resources/Files/agenda/cm /2011/110425/20110425_PHED4.pdf.

Montgomery County Planning Board. "Comprehensive Amendment to the Sector Plan for the Wheaton Central Business District and Vicinity." Maryland–National Capital Park and Planning Commission. September 1990. www.montgomeryplanning.org/community/plan_areas/georgia_ avenue/master_plans/wheaton/toc_wheaton.shtm.

Montgomery County Planning Department. *Approved and Adopted Silver Spring Central Business District and Vicinity Sector Plan*. Silver Spring, MD: Maryland-National Capital Park and Planning Commission, 2000.

Montgomery County Planning Department. *Long Branch Approved and Adopted Sector Plan*. Riverdale, MD: Maryland-National Capital Park and Planning Commission, 2013.

Montgomery County Planning Department. "Memorandum Re: Wheaton Central Business District (CBD) and Vicinity Sector Plan Amendment Preliminary Recommendations." Maryland-National Park and Planning Commission. November 6, 2009. www.montgomeryplanningboard.org /agenda/2009/documents/20091119_Wheaton_CBD_000.pdf.

Montgomery County Planning Department. *Takoma/Langley Crossroads Sector Plan*. Hyattsville, MD: Maryland–National Capital Parks and Planning Commission, 2012.

Montgomery County Planning Department. *Wheaton CBD and Vicinity Sector Plan: Approved and Adopted*. Silver Spring, MD: Maryland–National Capital Parks and Planning Commission, 2012.

Montgomery County Planning Department. *Wheaton CBD and Vicinity Sector Plan Design Guidelines: Approved and Adopted*. Silver Spring, MD: Maryland–National Capital Parks and Planning Commission, 2011.

Montgomery County's Housing Initiative Fund. *A Permanent Source of Funding for Affordable Housing and Neighborhoods*. Rockville, MD: Montgomery County, 2004. www.montgomerycountymd.gov/DHCA/resources/files /hif04.pdf.

"Montgomery County Small Business Assistance Program Surpasses $1 Million Distributed in Helping Wheaton Businesses during Construction of New Government Office Building." Press release. Montgomery County. February 11, 2020. www2.montgomerycountymd.gov/mcgportalapps/Press_Detail .aspx?Item_ID=23864.

Moore, Kesha S. "Gentrification in Black Face? The Return of the Black Middle Class to Urban Neighborhoods." *Urban Geography* 30, no. 2 (2009): 118–42.

Moriarty, Megan. *Real Stories from Rental Complexes in Silver Spring.* Silver Spring, MD: IMPACT Silver Spring, 2007.

Morgan, Perri. "Dream On." *Washington City Paper,* April 5, 1996.

Morgan, Thomas. "Wrecker's Ball Threatens Way of Life in Chinatown: Wrecker's Ball Swinging toward Chinatown." *Washington Post,* April 4, 1981.

Murphy, Alexandra K. "The Social Organization of Black Suburban Poverty: An Ethnographic Community Study." PhD diss., Princeton University, 2012.

Murphy, Alexandra K. "The Symbolic Dilemmas of Suburban Poverty: Challenges and Opportunities Posed by Variations in the Contours of Suburban Poverty." *Sociological Forum* 25, no. 3 (2010): 541–69.

Murphy, Alexandra K., and Danielle Wallace. "Opportunities for Making Ends Meet and Upward Mobility: Differences in Organizational Deprivation across Urban and Suburban Poor Neighborhoods." *Social Science Quarterly* 91, no. 5 (2010): 1164–86.

"NAACP Pickets New Store in Wheaton Plaza." *Washington Post,* February 6, 1960.

Naughton, Jim. "Hispanics Carve Niche in P.G." *Washington Post,* April 19, 1991.

Naveed, Minahil. *Income Inequality in DC Highest in the Country.* Washington, DC: DC Fiscal Policy Institute, 2017. www.dcfpi.org/wp-content/uploads/2017/12/12.15.17-Income-Inequality-in-DC.pdf.

Neibauer, Michael. "Nine Years to Recoup $4M for Costco, Wheaton Mall." *Washington Business Journal,* April 25, 2011. www.bizjournals.com/washington/blog/2011/04/nine-years-to-recoup-4m-for-wheaton.html.

Newman, Kathe, and Elvin K. Wyly. "The Right to Stay Put, Revisited: Gentrification and Resistance to Displacement in New York City." *Urban Studies* 43, no. 1 (2006): 23–57.

Nicolaides, Becky M. *My Blue Heaven : Life and Politics in the Working-Class Suburbs of Los Angeles, 1920–1965.* Historical Studies of Urban America. Chicago: University of Chicago Press, 2002.

Nicolaides, Becky M., and Andrew Wiese. *The Suburb Reader.* New York: Routledge, 2006.

Niedt, Christopher. "Gentrification and the Grassroots: Popular Support in the Revanchist Suburb." *Journal of Urban Affairs* 28, no. 2 (2006): 99–120.

Niedt, Christopher, ed. *Social Justice in Diverse Suburbs: History, Politics, and Prospects.* Philadelphia: Temple University Press, 2013.

Niedt, Christopher, and Brett Christophers. "Value at Risk in the Suburbs: Eminent Domain and the Geographical Politics of the US Foreclosure Crisis." *International Journal of Urban and Regional Research* 40, no. 6 (2016): 1094–111.

Nikhinson, Julia. "In Silver Spring, Hundreds Marched for Black Lives in a Protested Powered by UMD Alumni." *Diamondback*, June 29, 2020.

Ochoa, Manuel T. *Assessment Report for Silver Spring, Maryland's Fenton Street Commercial District*. Washington, DC: National Main Street Center, 1997.

O'Connell, Kim A. "Catching Fish with Two Hands: Preserving Vietnamese Heritage in Virginia's Little Saigon; A Cultural Heritage Assessment for the Vietnamese Community in the Clarendon Neighborhood of Arlington (1975–1980)." Goucher College. December 12, 2003. http://w.ncvaonline.org/archive/HP612_Final_Project_Part1.pdf.

O'Connell, Kim A. "Echoes of Little Saigon: Collecting and Preserving the Cultural History of the Vietnamese Community in Arlington." Virginia Tech Department of Urban Affairs and Planning. Accessed February 10, 2024. https://littlesaigonclarendon.com/the-history/.

Office of Planning and Capital Programming, Maryland Department of Transportation. *A Technical Assistance Panel Report: Wheaton Central Business District*. Bethesda, MD: Urban Land Institute, 2009.

Oliveri, Rigel C. "Setting the Stage for Ferguson: Housing Discrimination and Segregation in St. Louis." *Missouri Law Review* 80, no. 4 (2015): 1053–76.

Orfield, Myron. *American Metropolitics: The New Suburban Reality*. Washington, DC: Brookings Institution Press, 2002.

Orfield, Myron, and Thomas F. Luce. "America's Racially Diverse Suburbs: Opportunities and Challenges." *Housing Policy Debate* 23, no. 2 (2012): 395–430.

Oshel, Robert E. "Home Sites of Distinction: The History of Woodside Park." Woodside Park History Page. 1998. http://users.starpower.net/oshel/history.html.

"Our History and Government." Montgomery County Government, Maryland/ Montgomery County Historical Society. 1999. https://montgomerycountymd.gov/cct/Resources/Files/history.pdf.

Paden, Tina. "Disappearing Act: Affordable Housing in DC Is Vanishing amid Sharply Rising Housing Costs." *DC Fiscal Policy Institute* (blog). May 7, 2012. www.dcfpi.org/all/disappearing-act-affordable-housing-in-dc-is-vanishing-amid-sharply-rising-housing-costs-2/.

Pan, Philip. "Honorable Work or Illegal Activity? In Langley Park, It's 'Pupusa Ladies' vs. County Agencies, with Latino Officers Caught in Middle." *Washington Post*, August 24, 1997.

Park, Maki, and Margie McHugh. *Immigrant Parents and Early Childhood Programs: Addressing Barriers of Literacy, Culture, and Systems Knowledge*. Washington, DC: Migration Policy Institute, 2014.

Pastor, Manuel. *Regions That Work: How Cities and Suburbs Can Grow Together*. Globalization and Community. Minneapolis: University of Minnesota Press, 2000.

"Pathways to Opportunity: A Community Development Agreement for the Purple Line Corridor." Purple Line Corridor Coalition. Opened for signature October 2017. https://purplelinecorridor.org/wp-content/uploads/2017/10/PLCommunityDevelopmentAgreement.pdf.

Pattillo, Mary. *Black on the Block: The Politics of Race and Class in the City*. Chicago: University of Chicago Press, 2008.

Pattillo, Mary. *Black Picket Fences: Privilege and Peril among the Black Middle Class*. Chicago: University of Chicago Press, 2013.

Pearl, Susan G. *National Register of Historic Places Registration Form: McCormick-Goodhart Mansion, Langley Park, Prince Georges County, Maryland*. Bowie, MD: Prince George's County Historical Society, 2008.

Peck, Jamie. "Neoliberal Suburbanism: Frontier Space." *Urban Geography* 32, no. 6 (2011): 884–919.

Pendall, Rolf, Margaret Weir, and Chris Narducci. *Governance and the Geography of Poverty: Why Does Suburbanization Matter?* Chicago: MacArthur Foundation, 2013.

Perez-Rivas, Manuel. "Downtown Wheaton Ripe for Recovery." *Washington Post*, November 15, 1999, B1.

Perez-Rivas, Manuel. "Fresh Look at Future of Silver Spring." *Washington Post*, February 20, 1997.

Perez-Rivas, Manuel. "Huge Growth Spurt Bolsters Hispanic Population: Community Branches Out across Montgomery." *Washington Post*, March 29, 2001.

Perez-Rivas, Manuel. "Megamall Foes Deliver Petition." *Washington Post*, February 27, 1997.

Perez-Rivas, Manuel. "Silver Spring's Welcome Mat; Hardware Store Ushers in New Downtown." *Washington Post*, August 11, 2000.

Perez-Rivas, Manuel. "Wheaton Aims for a Face Lift." *Washington Post*, July 15, 1999, M1.

Pfeiffer, Deirdre. "Racial Equity in the Post–Civil Rights Suburbs? Evidence from US Regions, 2000–2012." *Urban Studies* 53, no. 4 (2016): 799–817.

Phelps, Nicholas, and Andrew Wood. "The New Post-suburban Politics?" *Urban Studies* 48, no. 1 (2011): 2591–610.

Phillips, Martin. "Other Geographies of Gentrification." *Progress in Human Geography* 28, no. 1 (2004): 5–30.

Phillips, Vanessa. "Mulling the Mall." *Gazette*, September 1995.

Pierre, Jon. "Comparative Urban Governance: Uncovering Complex Causalities." *Urban Affairs Review* 40, no. 4 (2005): 446–62.

Plath, David W. *Long Engagements: Maturity in Modern Japan.* Stanford: Stanford University Press, 1980.

Pollack, Stephanie, Barry Bluestone, and Chase Billingham. *Maintaining Diversity in America's Transit-Rich Neighborhoods: Tools for Equitable Neighborhood Change.* Boston: Northeastern University Dukakis Center for Urban and Regional Policy, 2010.

Pointer, Jack. "Prince George's County Launches Fund to Preserve Affordable Housing." *WTOP News,* November 29, 2021. https://wtop.com/prince -georges-county/2021/11/prince-georges-county-launches-fund-to -preserve-affordable-housing/.

powell, john a. "Addressing Regional Dilemmas for Minority Communities." In *Reflections on Regionalism,* edited by Bruce Katz, 218–46. Washington, DC: Brookings Institution Press, 2000.

powell, john a. "Race, Poverty, and Urban Sprawl: Access to Opportunities through Regional Strategies." *Forum for Social Economics* 28, no. 2 (1999): 1–20.

Price, Marie, and Lisa Benton-Short, eds. *Migrants to the Metropolis: The Rise of Immigrant Gateway Cities.* New York: Syracuse University Press, 2008.

Price, Marie, Ivan Cheung, Samantha Friedman, and Audrey Singer. "The World Settles In: Washington, DC as an Immigrant Gateway." *Urban Geography* 26, no. 1 (2005): 61–83.

Price, Marie, and Audrey Singer. "Edge Gateways: Immigrants, Suburbs, and the Politics of Reception." In *Twenty-First Century Gateways: Immigrant Incorporation in Suburban America,* edited by Audrey Singer, Susan W. Hardwick, and Caroline Brettell, 137–70. Washington, DC: Brookings Institution Press, 2008.

Prince, Sabiyha. *African Americans and Gentrification in Washington, DC: Race, Class and Social Justice in the Nation's Capital.* London: Routledge, 2014.

Prince George's County Planning Department. *Approved Takoma/Langley Crossroads Sector Plan.* Upper Marlboro, MD: Maryland-National Park and Planning Commission, 2009.

Puentes, Robert, and Myron Orfield. *Valuing America's First Suburbs: A Policy Agenda for Older Suburbs in the Midwest.* Washington, DC: Center on Urban and Metropolitan Policy, Brookings Institution, 2002.

Puentes, Robert, and David Warren. *One-Fifth of America: A Comprehensive Guide to America's First Suburbs.* Washington, DC: Brookings Institution, 2006.

Purple Line Corridor Coalition. *Housing Action Plan, 2019–2022.* Purple Line Corridor Coalition, 2019. https://purplelinecorridor.org/wp-content/uploads /2019/12/HAP-Full-Report-06-Dec-2019.pdf.

"Purple Line Transit Partner." Mass Transit. Last modified 2023. www
.masstransitmag.com/rail/infrastructure/company/21212863/purple-
line-transit-partners.

Queen, Michelle. "Dedication of Wheaton's 'Marian Fryer Plaza' and 'Night-
hawks' Concert Set for Friday." Montgomery Community Media. July 8,
2021. www.mymcmedia.org/dedication-of-wheatons-marian-fryer-plaza
-and-nighthawks-concert-set-for-friday/.

Rainey, Rebecca, Ellie Silverman, Helen Lyons, Naema Ahmed, Eliana Block,
Rosie Brown, Michelle Sloan, Changez Ali, and Amber Ebanks. "Pedestrian
Casualties Mount in Maryland Town as Officials Defer Action." Capital News
Service. May 17, 2017. https://cnsmaryland.org/2017/05/17/pedestrian-
casualties-mount-in-maryland-town-as-officials-defer-action/.

Ramírez, Margaret M. "Take the Houses Back/Take the Land Back: Black and
Indigenous Urban Futures in Oakland." *Urban Geography* 41, no. 5 (2020):
682–93.

Raphael, Steven, and Michael Stoll. *Job Sprawl and the Suburbanization of
Poverty*. Metropolitan Opportunity Series. Washington DC: Brookings
Institution, 2010.

Rapuano, Rina. "The Pupusa Queen." *Washingtonian*, June 20, 2008.

Rathner, Janet L. "Generations of Residents Settle Down in Scotland." *Washington Post*, June 18, 2005, G1.

Rayle, Lisa. "Investigating the Connection between Transit-Oriented Development and Displacement: Four Hypotheses." *Housing Policy Debate* 25, no. 3
(2015): 531–48.

Reale, Robin. "Race a Hidden Issue in Dream Plan." *Washington Journal*,
November 20, 1995.

"Real Property Data Search." Maryland Department of Assessments and Taxation.
Accessed October 2019. https://sdat.dat.maryland.gov/RealProperty/Pages
/default.aspx.

Reardon, Judy. "A Battle for the Soul of Silver Spring." *Washington Post*,
September 3, 1995, C8.

"Red Line Community Compact: Defining the Success of Baltimore's Red
Line Transit Project." Baltimore Red Line. September 12, 2008. https://
transportation.baltimorecity.gov/sites/default/files/Redline_community
_compact_11_4_09.pdf.

Reed, Dan. "Across Maryland and Virginia, Suburban Protestors Speak Out
against Police Brutality." *Just Up the Pike* (blog). June 2, 2020. www
.justupthepike.com/2020/06/across-maryland-and-virginia-suburban
.html.

Reed, Dan. "After 15 Years, Downtown Silver Spring Is Getting a Big Update."
Greater Greater Washington, October 9, 2019. https://ggwash.org/view
/74146/after-15-years-downtown-silver-spring-is-getting-a-big-update.

Reed, Dan. "County Council to Vote on Dueling Development Proposals in Wheaton (Updated)." *Just Up the Pike* (blog). April 5, 2012. www .justupthepike.com/2012/04/county-council-to-vote-on-dueling.html.

Reed, Dan. "DC's 'Little Ethiopia' Has Moved to Silver Spring and Alexandria." *Greater Greater Washington,* September 14, 2015. https://ggwash.org /view/39188/dcs-little-ethiopia-has-moved-to-silver-spring-and-alexandria.

Reed, Dan. "Do Costco and Safeway Proposals Signal Start of a Wheaton Revival?" *Just Up the Pike* (blog). January 18, 2010. www.justupthepike .com/2010/01/do-costco-and-safeway-proposals-signal.html.

Reed, Dan. "It Shouldn't Have Happened Again, but It Did." *Greater Greater Washington,* March 8, 2023. https://ggwash.org/view/88804/it-shouldnt -have-happened-again-but-it-did?emci=92f583bc-8ebe-ed11-a8e0- 00224832e811&emdi=367a607b-90be-ed11-a8e0- 00224832e811&ceid=21557113.

Reed, Dan. "Montgomery Picks Developers for Wheaton, Silver Spring." *Greater Greater Washington,* September 16, 2013. https://ggwash.org/view/32353 /montgomery-picks-developers-for-wheaton-silver-spring.

Reed, Dan. "Suburban Protestors Speak Out against Police Brutality." *Greater Greater Washington,* June 2, 2020. https://ggwash.org/view/77877/suburban -protestors-speak-out-against-police-brutality.

Reed, Dan. "Teens Need Things to Do, Not a Curfew." *Just Up the Pike* (blog). July 13, 2011. www.justupthepike.com/2011/07/teens-need-things-to-do -not-curfew.html.

Reed, Dan. "These 1970s Plans Show the Silver Spring That Could Have Been." *Greater Greater Washington,* June 5, 2019. https://ggwash.org/view/72300 /these-1970s-plans-show-the-silver-spring-that-could-have-been.

Reed, Dan. "They Used to Call It Georgian Towers (Part Two)." *Just Up the Pike* (blog). August 10, 2009. www.justupthepike.com/2009/08/they-used-to-call -it-georgian-towers_10.html.

Reed, Dan. "The Wonder Years Were Set in White Oak, Sort Of." *Just Up the Pike* (blog). March 10, 2009. www.justupthepike.com/2009/03/wonder-years -were-set-in-white-oak-sort.html.

Reese, Ashanté M. *Black Food Geographies: Race, Self-Reliance, and Food Access in Washington, DC.* Chapel Hill: University of North Carolina Press, 2019.

Reeves, Tracey A. "Langley Park School Bridges Cultures: Special Programs Reach Out to Community's Immigrants." *Washington Post,* September 22, 1988.

Repak, Terry A. *Waiting on Washington: Central American Workers in the Nation's Capital.* Philadelphia: Temple University Press, 1995.

Reynolds, Malvina. "Little Boxes." 1962. *Malvina Reynolds Sings the Truth.* New York: Columbia Records, 1967.

Richardson, Jason, Bruce Mitchell, and Juan Franco. *Shifting Neighborhoods: Gentrification and Cultural Displacement in American Cities.* Washington, DC: National Community Reinvestment Coalition, 2019. https://ncrc.org /gentrification/.

Richburg, Keith B. "Silver Spring: Home of Ethnic Diversity." *Washington Post,* November 14, 1981, B1.

Rios, Jodi. *Black Lives and Spatial Matters: Policing Blackness and Practicing Freedom in Suburban St. Louis.* Ithaca: Cornell University Press, 2020.

Rivas, Manuel P. "Fresh Look at Future of Silver Spring." *Washington Post,* February 20, 1997.

Roberts, Andrea. "Documenting and Preserving Texas Freedom Colonies." *Texas Heritage: A Publication of the Texas Historical Foundation* 2 (2017): 14–17.

Robinson, Jennifer. "Comparative Urbanism: New Geographies and Cultures of Theorizing the Urban." *International Journal of Urban and Regional Research* 40, no. 1 (2016): 187–99.

Ross, Benjamin. *Dead End: Suburban Sprawl and the Rebirth of American Urbanism.* Oxford: Oxford University Press, 2014.

Rotenstein, David S. "An Early History of Lyttonsville, Maryland." *History Sidebar* (blog). July 25, 2017. https://blog.historian4hire.net/2017/07/25 /early-history-of-lyttonsville/.

Rotenstein, David S. "Fairway: Silver Spring's Ghost Town." *History Sidebar* (blog). March 18, 2016. https://blog.historian4hire.net/2016/03/18 /fairway/.

Rotenstein, David S. "The Other Side of the Tracks: Contested Space, Commemoration, and Erasure." *Antipode Online* (blog). February 13, 2019. https://antipodeonline.org/2019/02/13/the-other-side-of-the-tracks/.

Rotenstein, David S. "Silver Spring, Maryland Has Whitewashed Its Past." *History News Network* (blog). October 15, 2016. https://historynewsnetwork .org/article/163914.

Roth, Benjamin J., and Scott W. Allard. "The Response of the Nonprofit Safety Net to Rising Suburban Poverty." In Anacker, *New American Suburb,* 247–84.

Roth, Benjamin J., Roberto Gonzales, and Jacob Lesniewski. "Building a Stronger Safety Net: Local Organizations and the Challenges of Serving Immigrants in the Suburbs." *Human Service Organizations: Management, Leadership and Governance* 39, no. 4 (2015): 348–61.

Rothstein, Richard. *The Color of Law: A Forgotten History of How Our Government Segregated America.* New York: Liveright, 2018.

Rowland, D. W. "The 1970s Tax Reform Initiative That Debilitated Prince George's County Libraries." *Greater Greater Washington,* December 15, 2020. https:// ggwash.org/view/79871/the-1970s-tax-reform-initiative-that-debilitated -prince-georges-county-libraries.

Roy, Ananya. "Dis/possessive Collectivism: Property and Personhood at City's End." *Geoforum* 80 (2017): A1–A11.

Ruble, Blair A. *Washington's U Street: A Biography.* Washington, DC: Woodrow Wilson Center Press; Baltimore: Johns Hopkins University Press, 2012.

Rucks-Ahidiana, Zawadi. "Theorizing Gentrification as a Process of Racial Capitalism." *City and Community* 21, no. 3 (2022): 173–92.

Rusk, David. *Cities without Suburbs.* Washington, DC: Woodrow Wilson Center Press, 1993.

Sandosharaj, Alice. "Ghetto Proclivities: Race and Class in Model Minority Memoir." PhD diss., University of Maryland, College Park, 2008.

Sandoval, Gerardo F. "Planning the Barrio: Ethnic Identity and Struggles over Transit-Oriented, Development-Induced Gentrification." *Journal of Planning Education and Research* 41, no. 4 (2018): 410–28.

"Saul Centers, Inc." *Washington Post,* 2005. www.washingtonpost.com/wp-srv /business/post200/2005/BFS.html.

Saunders, Doug. *Arrival City: How the Largest Migration in History Is Reshaping Our World.* London: Heinemann, 2010.

Scannell, Nancy. "Clarendon Easing toward Rebirth." *Washington Post,* December 12, 1985. www.washingtonpost.com/archive/local/1985/12/12/clarendon -easing-toward-rebirth/15c26d78-9dc3-4721-a134-6bdd49e713e5/.

Schaffer, Dana L. "The 1968 Washington Riots in History and Memory." *Washington History* 15, no. 2 (2003): 4–33.

Schafran, Alex. "Discourse and Dystopia, American Style: The Rise of 'Slumburbia' in a Time of Crisis." *City* 17, no. 2 (2013): 130–48.

Schafran, Alex. *The Road to Resegregation: Northern California and the Failure of Politics.* Oakland: University of California Press, 2018.

Schneider, Mark, and John R. Logan. "Suburban Racial Segregation and Black Access to Local Public Resource." *Social Science Quarterly* 63, no. 4 (1982): 762–70.

"Scholar's Guide, 2002." Lakeland History Project. Accessed October 1, 2019. https://lakeland.umd.edu/files/original/lakelandhistory_bfc9360816.pdf.

Schrag, Zachary M. "The Freeway Fight in Washington, DC: The Three Sisters Bridge in Three Administrations." *Journal of Urban History* 30, no. 5 (2004): 648–73.

Schuster, Hannah, and Gabe Bullard. "Tenant Activism in DC Has Surged during the Pandemic." *DCist* (blog). September 29, 2020. https://dcist.com /story/20/09/29/cancel-rent-strike-tenant-protest-dc-pandemic/.

Schweitzer, Ally. "Conditions Were Bad at This Langley Park Apartment. COVID Made Them Intolerable." WAMU. April 1, 2021. www.npr.org /local/305/2021/04/01/983405810/conditions-were-bad-at-this-langley -park-apartment-c-o-v-i-d-made-them-intolerable.

Schweitzer, Ally. "Langley Park Residents Say New Rezoning Plans Will Push Them Out." National Public Radio, WAMU 88.5. September 17, 2021. https://www.npr.org/local/305/2021/09/17/1038261007/langley-park-residents-say-new-rezoning-plans-will-push-them-out#

Scott, Molly, Graham MacDonald, Juan Collazos, Ben Levinger, Eliza Leighton, and Jamila Ball. *From Cradle to Career: The Multiple Challenges Facing Immigrant Families in Langley Park Promise Neighborhood.* Washington, DC: Urban Institute/CASA de Maryland/Prince George's County Public Schools, 2014.

Seaberry, Jane. "Sprucing Up Silver Spring: Bringing Business Back to Silver Spring's Scene." *Washington Post,* October 9, 1979.

Sesker, Jacob. *FY13-18 Capital Improvements Program: Wheaton Redevelopment Program.* Montgomery County Council. March 8, 2012. www .montgomerycountymd.gov/COUNCIL/Resources/Files/agenda/cm/2012 /120312/20120312_PHED1.pdf.

Shaver, Katherine. "Federal Officials Close Civil Rights Complaint about Baltimore Light-Rail Project." *Washington Post,* July 13, 2017.

Shaver, Katherine. "A Montgomery Bridge That Linked Black and White Neighborhoods during Segregation Soon Will Be Lost to History." *Washington Post,* September 24, 2016.

Shaver, Katherine. "Purple Line Will Open 4 1/2 Years Late and Cost $1.4 Billion More to Complete, State Says." *Washington Post,* January 12, 2022.

Shen, Fern. "Council Approves Funding for Silver Spring 'Town Center.'" *Washington Post,* May 14, 1998.

Shin, Annys. "A Big Boost for Small Businesses; County Plan Aimed at Silver Spring." *Washington Post,* May 6, 2004.

Shin, Annys. "Silver Spring Development Leaves Some Downtrodden; Rising Rents Squeezing Out Small Businesses Downtown." *Washington Post,* June 21, 2004, E10.

Shoenfeld, Sarah. "Race and Real Estate in Mid-Century DC." DC Policy Center. April 16, 2019. www.dcpolicycenter.org/publications/neighbors-inc/.

Shoenfeld, Sarah, and Mara Cherkasky, "'A Strictly White Residential Section': The Rise and Demise of Racially Restrictive Covenants in Bloomingdale." *Washington History* 29, no. 1 (2017): 24–41.

Silverman, Sherman E. "Arresting Suburban Blight in Silver Spring, Maryland." *Pennsylvania Geographer* 60, no. 1 (2002): 52–82.

Silverman, Steven A. "A Dream Come True for Silver Spring." *Washington Post,* January 28, 1996.

Silver Spring CBD: Approved and Adopted Plan for the Revival of Downtown Silver Spring. Silver Spring, MD: Maryland National Capital Park and Planning Commission, 1993.

"Silver Spring Shopping Center Open Today." *Washington Post,* October 27, 1938, S1.

Simms, Angela. "Fiscal Fragility in Black Middle-Class Suburbia and Consequences for K–12 Schools and Other Public Services." *Russell Sage Foundation Journal of the Social Sciences* 9, no. 2 (2023): 204–25.

Simpson, Bob. "My Old Neighborhood Is Now Multiracial—Why Is That a Problem for Some People?" *Z Blogs* (blog). February 22, 2013. https://zcomm.org/zblogs/my-old-neighborhood-is-now-multiracial-why-is-that-a-problem-for-some-people-by-bob-simpson/.

Sinclair, Molly. "County Tries to Turn Silver Spring into a Gold Mine: Montgomery Looks at Ways to Bring Flow of Affluence into Silver Spring." *Washington Post,* October 7, 1986, B1.

Sinclair, Molly. "Silver Spring Renaissance Spurs Debate: Downtown Area Changes Seen as Mixed Blessing." *Washington Post,* October 12, 1986.

Singer, Audrey. *At Home in the Nation's Capital: Immigrant Trends in Metropolitan Washington.* Washington, DC: Brookings Institution, 2003.

Singer, Audrey. "Latin American Immigrants in the Washington, DC Metropolitan Area." Paper presented at Woodrow Wilson International Center for Scholars, Washington, DC, November 2007.

Singer, Audrey. "Metropolitan Washington: A New Immigrant Gateway." In *Hispanic Migration and Urban Development: Studies from Washington DC,* edited by Enrique S. Pumar, 17:3–24. Bingley, UK: Emerald Group, 2012.

Singer, Audrey, Samantha Friedman, Ivan Cheung, and Marie Price. "The Nation's Capital Reveals the Nation's Future: The World in a Zip Code." *Brookings Review* 20, no. 1 (2002): 34–35.

Sinyangwe, Samuel. "Police Are Killing Fewer People in Big Cities, but More in Suburban and Rural America." *FiveThirtyEight,* June 1, 2020. https://fivethirtyeight.com/features/police-are-killing-fewer-people-in-big-cities-but-more-in-suburban-and-rural-america/.

Slater, Tom. "The Eviction of Critical Perspectives from Gentrification Research." *International Journal of Urban and Regional Research* 30, no. 4 (2006): 737–57.

Slater, Tom. "North American Gentrification? Revanchist and Emancipatory Perspectives Explored." *Environment and Planning A: Economy and Space* 36, no. 7 (2004): 1191–213.

Slocum, Karla. *Black Towns, Black Futures: The Enduring Allure of a Black Place in the American West.* Chapel Hill: University of North Carolina Press, 2019.

Smith, Neil. "Gentrification and Uneven Development." *Economic Geography* 58, no. 2 (1982): 139–55.

Smith, Neil. *The New Urban Frontier: Gentrification and the Revanchist City.* London: Routledge, 1996.

Smith, Neil. "Toward a Theory of Gentrification: A Back to the City Movement by Capital, Not People." *Journal of the American Planning Association* 45, no. 4 (1979): 538–48.

Squires, Gregory D. *Urban Sprawl: Causes, Consequences, and Policy Responses*. Washington, DC: Urban Institute Press, 2002.

Stack, Carol. *All Our Kin: Strategies for Survival in a Black Community*. New York: Basic Books, 2008.

Stack, Carol. *Call to Home: African Americans Reclaim the Rural South*. New York: Basic Books, 1996.

Stein, Perry. "DC's Poorer Residents Are Increasingly Concentrated East of the Anacostia." *Washington Post*, April 14, 2015.

Stein, Samuel. *Capital City: Gentrification and the Real Estate State*. London: Verso Books, 2019.

Stewart, Alexander Rupp. "Ethnic Entrepreneurship and Latino Placemaking in Suburban Washington: The Case of Langley Park, Maryland." PhD diss., George Washington University, 2011.

Straus, Emily E. *Death of a Suburban Dream: Race and Schools in Compton, California*. Politics and Culture in Modern America. Philadelphia: University of Pennsylvania Press, 2014.

Sugrue, Thomas J. *The Origins of the Urban Crisis: Race and Inequality in Postwar Detroit*. Princeton, NJ: Princeton University Press, 1996.

Summers, Brandi T. *Black in Place: The Spatial Aesthetics of Race in a Post-Chocolate City*. Chapel Hill: University of North Carolina Press, 2019.

Summers, Brandi T. "H Street, Main Street and the Neoliberal Aesthetics of Cool." In Hyra and Prince, *Capital Dilemma*, 306–21.

Suro, Roberto, Jill H. Wilson, and Audrey Singer. *Immigration and Poverty in America's Suburbs*. Metropolitan Opportunity Series. Washington, DC: Brookings Institution, 2011.

Sutton, Stacey A. "Rethinking Commercial Revitalization: A Neighborhood Small Business Perspective." *Economic Development Quarterly* 24, no. 4 (2010): 352–71.

Sweeney, Glennon, and Bernadette Hanlon. "From Old Suburb to Post-suburb: The Politics of Retrofit in the Inner Suburb of Upper Arlington, Ohio." *Journal of Urban Affairs* 39, no. 2 (2017): 241–59.

Swenson, Kyle, and Samantha Schmidt. "'It's Time to Unite': Prince George's County Neighbors Start Rent Strike against Living Conditions." *Washington Post*, October 24, 2020.

Tach, Laura M. "Diversity, Inequality, and Microsegregation: Dynamics of Inclusion and Exclusion in a Racially and Economically Diverse Community." *Cityscape* 16, no. 3 (2014): 13–46.

Tachieva, Galina. *Sprawl Repair Manual*. Washington, DC: Island, 2010.

Talen, Emily, ed. *Retrofitting Sprawl: Addressing Seventy Years of Failed Urban Form*. Athens: University of Georgia Press, 2015.

Tatian, Peter A. *Preserving and Expanding Inclusive Housing*. Washington, DC: Urban Institute, 2014. https://www.urban.org/sites/default/files /publication/33861/2000057-challenges-and-choices-for-the-new-mayor -preserving-and-expanding-inclusive-housing.pdf

Taylor, Keeanga-Yamahtta. *Race for Profit: How Banks and the Real Estate Industry Undermined Black Homeownership*. Chapel Hill: University of North Carolina Press, 2019.

Taylor, Monique M. *Harlem between Heaven and Hell*. Minneapolis: University of Minnesota Press, 2002.

Teaford, Jon. *Post-suburbia: Government and Politics in the Edge Cities*. Baltimore: Johns Hopkins University Press, 1997.

Thomas, June M. *Redevelopment and Race: Planning a Finer City in Postwar Detroit*. Baltimore: Johns Hopkins University Press, 1997.

Tolbert, Kathryn. "In Montgomery, Integration Is Moving Target." *Washington Post*, April 9, 1981.

"Top 101 Cities with the Most Residents Born in El Salvador." City-Data. Last updated 2023. www.city-data.com/top2/h144.html.

Tuan, Yi-Fu. *Space and Place: The Perspective of Experience*. Minneapolis: University of Minnesota Press, 1977.

Tuck, Eve. "Suspending Damage: A Letter to Communities." *Harvard Educational Review* 79, no. 3 (2009): 409–28.

Tuck, Eve, and K. Wayne Yang. "R-Words: Refusing Research." In *Humanizing Research: Decolonizing Qualitative Inquiry with Youth and Communities*, edited by Django Paris and Maisha T. Winn, 223–48. Thousand Oaks, CA: Sage, 2014.

Turner, Margery A., and Christopher Hayes. *Poor People and Poor Neighborhoods in the Washington Metropolitan Area*. Washington, DC: Urban Institute, 1997.

Turque, Bill. "Cracks in Silver Spring Transit Center Fracture Profitable Political and Corporate Marriage." *Washington Post*, April 13, 2013.

Urban Studies and Planning Program. *The Golden Mile: Outreach and Engagement to Immigrant and Minority-Owned Businesses*. Planning and Design in the Multicultural Metropolis. College Park: University of Maryland, 2014. www.umdsmartgrowth.org/wp-content/uploads/2019/06/Golden-Mile.pdf.

Urban Studies and Planning Program. *Minimizing Small Business Displacement in a Revitalization Zone: The Case of Silver Spring*. Economic Development Seminar, University of Maryland, College Park, 2005.

Urban Studies and Planning Program. "Strategies For Small, Independent, and Ethnic Businesses in Wheaton." Presentation, University of Maryland, College Park, 2013.

US Census Bureau. *2000 Census of Population and Housing.* Washington, DC: US Department of Commerce, 2001.

US Census Bureau. *2014 ACS 1-Year and 2010–2014 ACS 5-Year Data Releases.* Washington, DC: US Department of Commerce, 2015.

US Census Bureau. *2018 ACS 1-Year and 2014–2018 ACS 5-Year Data Releases.* Washington, DC: US Department of Commerce, 2019.

US Census Bureau. *2019 ACS 1-Year and 2015–2019 ACS 5-Year Data Releases.* Washington, DC: US Department of Commerce, 2019.

US Census Bureau. *American Community Survey, 2006–2010 Summary File.* Washington, DC: US Department of Commerce, 2011.

US Census Bureau. *American Community Survey, 2007–2011 Summary File.* Washington, DC: US Department of Commerce, 2012.

US Census Bureau. *Census 1970 on 2010 Geographies.* US Department of Commerce. Accessed February 15, 2024. www.socialexplorer.com/data /RC1970/documentation/9d85095f-bc6e-4a31-b42d-ea0848adc6d0.

US Census Bureau. *Census of Population and Housing, 1980.* Washington, DC: US Department of Commerce, 1982.

US Census Bureau. *Census of Population and Housing, 1990.* Washington, DC: US Department of Commerce, 1991.

US Census Bureau. *Longitudinal Employer Household Dynamics, 2011.* Department of Commerce. Accessed February 15, 2024. www.socialexplorer .com/data/LEHD2011/documentation/1e790ca1-2690-403c-bc2b-4438220d2fb2.

US Department of Labor. *The Negro Family: The Case for National Action.* Washington, DC: Government Printing Office, 1965.

Vallejo, Jody. *Barrios to Burbs.* Stanford: Stanford University Press, 2020.

Vicino, Thomas J. "The Quest to Confront Suburban Decline: Political Realities and Lessons." *Urban Affairs Review* 43, no. 4 (2008): 553–81.

Vicino, Thomas J. *Suburban Crossroads: The Fight for Local Control of Immigration Policy.* Lanham, MD: Lexington Books, 2012.

Vicino, Thomas J. *Transforming Race and Class in Suburbia: Decline in Metropolitan Baltimore.* New York: Palgrave MacMillan, 2008.

Villanueva, George. "Designing a Chinatown Anti-displacement Map and Walking Tour with Communication Asset Mapping." *Journal of Urban Design* 26, no. 1 (2021): 14–37.

Virta, Alan. "A County with Rich History: Prince George's County History." *Prince George's County History: Over 300 Years of History.* 1996. www .pghistory.org/PG/PG300/history.html.

Vitiello, Domenic. "The Politics of Immigration and Suburban Revitalization: Divergent Responses in Adjacent Pennsylvania Towns." *Journal of Urban Affairs* 36, no. 3 (2014): 519–33.

Wacquant, Loïc J. D. "Three Pernicious Premises in the Study of the American Ghetto." *International Journal of Urban and Regional Research* 21, no. 2 (2002): 341–53.

Walker, Peter, and Louise Fortmann. "Whose Landscape? A Political Ecology of the 'Exurban' Sierra." *Cultural Geographies* 10, no. 4 (2003): 469–91.

Walston, Mark. "The Commercial Rise and Fall of Silver Spring: A Study of the 20th Century Development of the Suburban Shopping Center in Montgomery County." *Maryland Historical Magazine* 81, no. 4 (1986): 330–39.

Wang, Ying. "From Urban Enclave to Ethnoburb: Changes in Residential Patterns of Chinese Immigrants." PhD diss., University of Maryland, College Park, 2012.

Ward, Kevin. "Toward a Comparative (Re)turn in Urban Studies? Some Reflections." *Urban Geography* 29, no. 5 (2008): 405–10.

Weir, Margaret, Harold Wolman, and Todd Swanstrom. "The Calculus of Coalitions: Cities, Suburbs, and the Metropolitan Agenda." *Urban Affairs Review* 40, no. 6 (2005): 730–60.

Weiss, Marc A. *The Rise of the Community Builders: The American Real Estate Industry and Urban Land Planning.* Washington, DC: Beard Books, 2002. First published 1987 by Columbia University Press (New York).

"Welcome to Local First Wheaton." Local First Wheaton. Accessed January 26, 2022. https://localfirstwheaton.wordpress.com/welcome-to-local-first-wheaton/.

Weller, Charles F. *Neglected Neighbors: Stories of Life in the Alleys, Tenements, and Shanties of the National Capital.* Philadelphia: Winston, 1909.

Wheaton and Kensington Chamber of Commerce. "History of Wheaton and Kensington." Accessed February 5, 2024. www.wkchamber.org/about/history-of-wheaton-kensington/.

Wiese, Andrew. *Places of Their Own: African American Suburbanization in the Twentieth Century.* Chicago: University of Chicago Press, 2004.

Williams, Rashad Akeem. "From Racial to Reparative Planning: Confronting the White Side of Planning." *Journal of Planning Education and Research* 44, no. 1 (2024): 64–74.

Williamson, June. "Protest on the Astroturf at Downtown Silver Spring: July 4, 2007." In Niedt, *Social Justice,* 54–70.

Williamson, June, and Ellen Dunham-Jones. *Case Studies in Retrofitting Suburbia: Urban Design Strategies for Urgent Challenges.* Hoboken: Wiley and Sons, 2021.

Wilson, Scott. "As Change Begins, Silver Spring Dreams of a Vibrant Future." *Washington Post,* April 17, 1999.

Wilson, William Julius. *The Truly Disadvantaged: The Inner City, the Underclass, and Public Policy.* Chicago: University of Chicago Press, 1987.

Wilson, William Julius. *When Work Disappears: The World of the New Urban Poor.* New York: Knopf, 1996.

Wong, Brittany, Willow Lung-Amam, and Gerrit Knaap. "Moderately Priced Dwelling Units: A Key Element of Montgomery County's Approach to Social Equity." Lincoln Institute of Land Policy Working Paper WP21BW1. May 2021. www.lincolninst.edu/publications/working-papers/moderately-priced-dwelling-units.

Woods, Clyde. "Les Misérables of New Orleans: Trap Economics and the Asset Stripping Blues, Part 1." *American Quarterly* 61, no. 3 (2009): 769–96.

"Woodside Park Is a Healthful Place." *Washington Post,* June 17, 1923.

Wrigley, Eric. "Fenton Village: How to Preserve and Revive a Struggling Small Business District in Already Developing Downtown Silver Spring." Master's thesis, University of Pennsylvania, 2007.

Wynter, Leon. "Lakeland: Urban Renewal Erases College Park Community." *Washington Post,* February 11, 1982.

Wysolmerski, Michael. "The Fight for a Neighborhood: Flood Control and Race on the Anacostia Tributaries." Senior project, University of Maryland, 2012. https://static.libnet.info/images/pdfs/pgcmls/Wysolmerski__Michael___The_Fight_for_a_Neighborhood___2012.pdf.

Yellin, Eric S. *Racism in the Nation's Service: Government Workers and the Color Line in Woodrow Wilson's America.* Chapel Hill: University of North Carolina Press, 2013.

Zheng, Shaobin. "The Rise and Fall of DC's Chinatown." *AHA Today* (blog). American Historical Association. December 29, 2017. www.historians.org/publications-and-directories/perspectives-on-history/december-2017/the-rise-and-fall-of-dcs-chinatown.

Zibart, Eve. "King of the Roadside Café." *Washington Post,* April 12, 2002.

"Zillow Home Value Index." Zillow. Accessed October 12, 2019. www.zillow.com/research/data/.

Zuk, Miriam, Ariel Bierbaum, Karen Chapple, Karolina Gorska, and Anastasia Loukaitou-Sideris. "Gentrification, Displacement, and the Role of Public Investment." *Journal of Planning Literature* 33, no. 1 (2018): 31–44.

Zukin, Sharon. *The Cultures of Cities.* Cambridge: Blackwell, 1995.

Zukin, Sharon. *Loft Living: Culture and Capital in Urban Change.* Baltimore: Johns Hopkins University Press, 1982.

Zukin, Sharon. *Naked City: The Death and Life of Authentic Urban Places.* Oxford: Oxford University Press, 2009.

Zukin, Sharon, Valerie Trujillo, Peter Frase, Danielle Jackson, Tim Recuber, and Abraham Walker. "New Retail Capital and Neighborhood Change: Boutiques and Gentrification in New York City." *City and Community* 8, no. 1 (2009): 47–64.

Index

Page numbers in *italics* denote photos, maps, and charts. Neighborhoods are listed as a group under each city or suburb of which they are a part. Interviewee names marked with "(pseud.)" indicate a pseudonym.

Founded in 1893,
UNIVERSITY OF CALIFORNIA PRESS
publishes bold, progressive books and journals
on topics in the arts, humanities, social sciences,
and natural sciences—with a focus on social
justice issues—that inspire thought and action
among readers worldwide.

The UC PRESS FOUNDATION
raises funds to uphold the press's vital role
as an independent, nonprofit publisher, and
receives philanthropic support from a wide
range of individuals and institutions—and from
committed readers like you. To learn more, visit
ucpress.edu/supportus.